# SAINT JOHN CHRYSOSTOM

## A Scripture Index

R.A. Krupp

UNIVERSITY PRESS OF AMERICA

LANHAM • NEW YORK • LONDON

University Press of America,™ Inc.

4720 Boston Way
Lanham, MD 20706

3 Henrietta Street
London WC2E 8LU England





Printed in the United States of America

**Library of Congress Cataloging in Publication Data**

Krupp, Robert Allen.
Saint John Chrysostom, a scripture index.

1. John Chrysostom, Saint, d. 407—Dictionaries, indexes, etc. 2. Bible—Use. I. Title.
BR65.C455K78 1985 270.2 84-21028
ISBN 0-8191-4380-4 (alk. paper)

To Collette

# Acknowledgements

The research for this work was carried out at the University of Portland, Western Conservative Baptist Seminary, The University of Michigan, the New York Public Library, the Library of Congress, and the Houston Public Library. The author wishes to thank the various librarians who came to his aid with expertise and suggestions at these institutions. He also wishes to single out the Inter Library Loan staffs at the University of Portland, the Houston Public Library, and Western Conservative Baptist Seminary for exceptional patience and professionalism. Mrs. Jane Railsback, who typed the final draft of the manuscript deserves special thanks.

## Table of Contents

## Preface

Saint John Chrysostom, the Patriarch of Constantinople who has been revered as the patron saint of Christian preachers, has stimulated much research and discussion in the Christian community. His idealistic stand for a life-encompassing Christian ethic in a culture that might be classified as Christianized but institutional and lukewarm has served as a model for many shepherds as they minister to their flocks. This work seeks to be an aid to research in the Chrysostom corpus based on a commitment to the appropriateness of historically considered theology.

This Scripture Index seeks to remedy a fundamental problem. There are worthy indices in many editions and translations of Chrysostom's works but the vast majority are keyed to the pagination of the particular volume. The problem is further compounded by the fact that as more critical editions of John's works are issued the indexing is becoming more fragmented making it more difficult to ascertain the complete pattern of his quotation of Scripture. To construct this index the most critical editions available of the various works were consulted. In this regard the Clavis Patrum Graecorum (Mauritii Geerard, ed. Brepols: Turnhout, 1974, II, 491f) was indispensable. Other editions and translations were consulted and the judgements of these editors and translators proved quite helpful.

Quotations from works cited as genuine in Clavis Patrum Graecorum have been incorporated into this index. In the index the works are cited in their usual fashion with the first roman numeral indicating the book or homily number and the second, arabic, numeral denoting the section or paragraph. In the case of quotation of the Old Testament in the New Testament and in quotations from synoptic gospels which are ambiguous in location the quotation is listed under all possible Scripture references. In quotations from some works where the paragraph numbers have not been carried into some of the major translations of the work, the chapter and verse of the book being commented upon is used as an additional location device for the quote. This is also done for the quotations from the first part of the Homilies on the Acts of the Apostles because of the confused state of the preserved text of the homilies. The Scripture notations are those of the King James Version; in the case of the Psalms the number of the exposition has not been changed even though the quotation references are the KJV. It has also been noted in the index if a verse is quoted more than once in a section.

Abbreviations:

| | |
|---|---|
| Ad Dem de comp | Ad Demetrium de compunctione libre 1 |
| Ad e q scan | Ad eos qui scandalizati sunt |
| Ad pop Anti | Ad populum Antiochenum homiliae 1-21 |
| Ad Stag a dae | Ad Stagirium a daemone uexatum libre 1-3 |
| Ad Stel de comp | Ad Stelechium de compunctione libre 2 |
| Ad Theo | Ad Theodorum lapsum libri 1-2 |
| Ad uid iun | Ad uiduam iuniorem |
| Adu cath | Aduersus catharos |
| Adu eos q n adf | Aduersus eos qui non adfuerant |
| Adu Iud | Aduersus Iudaeos orationes 1-8[1] |
| Adu op | Aduersus oppugnatores uitae monasticae libri 1-3 |
| C Iob | Commentarius in Iob |
| C Prou | Commentarius in Prouerbia |
| Cat ill | Catecheses ad illuminandos[2] |
| Con Anom | Contra Anomoeos homilia 11 |
| Con e q sub | Contra eos qui subintroductas habent uirgines |
| Con Iud et gen | Contra Iudaeos et gentiles quod Christus sit deus |
| Con l et t | Contra ludos et theatra |
| Cum Sat et Aur | Cum Saturninus et Aurelianus |
| De Anna | De Anna sermones 1-5 |
| De b Phil | De beato Philogonio |
| De bap Chris | De baptismo Christi |
| De Chris diuin | De Christi diuinitate |
| De Chris prec | De Christi precibus |
| De coem et de cru | De coemeterio et de cruce |
| De consub | De Consubstantiali |
| De cruce et lat | De cruce et latrone homiliae 1-2 |
| De D et S | De Dauide et Saule homiliae 1-3 |
| De dec mil | De decem millium talentorum debitore |
| De diab tent | De diabolo tentatore homiliae 1-3 |
| De Eleaz | De Eleazaro et septem pueris |
| De elee | De eleemosyna |
| De fato et pr | De fato et prouidentia orationes 1-6 |
| De fut uit | De futurae uitae deliciis |
| De glor in trib | De gloria in tribulationibus |
| De inani gloria | De inani gloria et de educandis liberis |
| De incomp dei | De incomprehensibili dei natura homiliae 1-5 |
| De laud s Paul | De laudibus sancti Pauli apostoli homiliae 1-7 |

| | |
|---|---|
| De Laz | De Lazaro conciones 1-7 |
| De lib rep | De libello repudii |
| De Mac | De Macabeis homiliae 1-3 |
| De mut nom | De mutatione nominum homiliae 1-4 |
| De n iter | De non iterando conuigio |
| De paen | De paenitentia homiliae 1-9 |
| De pet mat | De petitione matris feiliorum Zebedaei |
| De prod Iud | De proditione Iudae homiliae 1-2 |
| De prof eua | De profectu euangelii |
| De proph obscur | De prophetiarum obscuritate homiliae 1-2 |
| De rec Seur | De recipiendo Seueriano |
| De reg | De regressu |
| De res d n I C | De resurrectione d.n. Iesu Christi |
| De res mort | De resurrectione mortuorum |
| De s Bab c Iul | De s. Babyla contra Iulianum et gentiles |
| De s Dros | De s. Droside martyre |
| De s h Bab | De s. hieromartyre Babyla |
| De s h Phoc | De s. hieromartyre Phoca |
| De s Mel | De s. Meletio Antiocheno |
| De s Pel | De s. Pelagia uirgine et martyre |
| De sac | De sacerdotio libri 1-6 |
| De san pent | De sancta pentecoste homiliae 1-2 |
| De ss B et P | De ss. Bernice et Prosdoce |
| De ss mar A | De ss. martyribus (PG 50, 645-654) |
| De ss mar B | De ss. martyribus (PG 50, 705-712) |
| De stud p | De studio praesentium |
| De ter motu | De terrae motu |
| De uir | De uirginitate |
| E | Epistulae 1-242 |
| E ad e p d | Epistula ad episcopos, presbyteros, et diaconos |
| E ad I | Epistula ad Innocentium papam 1-2 |
| Ex in ps | Expositiones in psalmos 4-12, 41, 43-49, 103-106, 108-117, 119, 150 |
| F Ier | Fragmenta in Ieremian |
| F in epis cath | Fragmenta in epistulas catholicas |
| F Iob | Fragmenta in Iob |
| F Prou | Fragmenta in Prouerbia |
| F s d m Diod | Fragmenta sermonis de magistro Diodoro |
| H dicta in t s Anas | Homilia dicta in templo s. Anastasiae |
| H dicta p imp | Homilia dicta praesente imperatore |

| | |
|---|---|
| H dicta p r m | Homilia dicta postquam reliquiae martyrum ect. |
| H hab p p Gothus | Homilia habita postquam presbyter Gothus |
| H in il App | Homilia in illud: Apparuit gratia dei omnibus hominbus (Tit 2:11) |
| H in mar | Homilia in martyres |
| H in poen Nin | Homilia in poenitentiam Niniuitarum |
| H in san pascha | Homilia in sanctum pascha |
| In Acta | In Acta apostolorum homiliae 1-55 |
| In ascen d n I C | In ascensionem d. n. Iesu Christi |
| In Col | In Colossenses homiliae 1-12 |
| In 1 Cor | In epistulam i ad Corinthios argumentum et homiliae 1-44 |
| In 2 Cor | In epistulam ii ad Corinthios argumentum et homiliae 1-30 |
| In d P Nolo | In dictum Pauli: Nolo uos ignorare (1 Cor 10:1) |
| In d P Op | In dictum Pauli: Oportet haereses esse (I Cor 11:19) |
| In diem nat | In diem natalem |
| In Eph | In epistulam ad Ephesios argumentum |
| In Eut | In Eutropium |
| In Gal | In epistulam as Galatas Commentarius |
| H Gen | Homiliae 1-67 in Genesim |
| In Heb | In epistulam ad Hebraeos argumentum et homiliae 1-34 |
| In Hel | In Heliam et uiduam |
| In il Dil deum | In illud: Diligentibus deum omnia cooperantur in bonum (Rom 8:28) |
| In il Dom non est | In illud: Domine non est in homine (Ier 10:23) |
| In il Fil | In illud: Filius ex se nihil facit (Ioh 5:19) |
| In il Hab | In illud: Habentes eundem spiritum (2 Cor 4:13) |
| In il Hoc scit | In illud: Hoc scitote quod in nouissimis diebus (2 Tim 3:1) |
| In il In fac | In illud: In faciem ei restiti (Gal 2:11) |
| In il Is Ego | In illud Isaiae: Ego dominus deus feci lumen (Is 45:7) |
| In il Messis | In illud: Messis quidem multa (Mat 9:37, Luc 10:2) |
| In il Ne tim | In illud: Ne timueritis cum diues factus fuerit homo (Ps 48:17) homiliae 1-2 |
| In il Pater m | In illud: Pater meus usque modo operatur (Ioh 5:17) |

| | |
|---|---|
| In il Pater s p | In illud: Pater si possible est transeat (Mat 26:39) |
| In il Prop | In Illud: Propter fornicationes uxorem (1 Cor 7:2) |
| In il Sal P et A | In illud: Salutate Priscilliam et Aquilam (Rom 16:3) |
| In il Si esur | In illud: Si esurierit inimicus (Rom 21:20) |
| In il Ut sus | In illud: Utinam sustineretis modicum (2 Cor 11:1) |
| In il Uid elig | In illud: Uidua eligatur (1 Tim 5:9) |
| In il Uidi dom | In illud: Uidi dominum (Is 6:1) homiliae 1-6 |
| In Ioh | In Iohannem homiliae 1-88 |
| In Is | In Isaiam 1-8, 10 |
| In Iuu et Max | In Iuuentinum et Maximum martyres |
| In kal | In kalendas |
| In mar Aeg | In martyres Aegyptios |
| In Mat | In Matthaeum homiliae 1-89[3] |
| In para | In paralyticum demissum per tectum |
| In Phil | In epistulam ad Philippenses argumentum et homiliae 1-15 |
| In Philem | In epistulam ad Philemonem argumentum et homiliae 1-3 |
| In princ Act | In principium Actorum homiliae 1-4 |
| In Ps 145 | In psalmum 145 |
| In quat Laz A | In quatriduanum Lazarum (PG 48, 779-784) |
| In quat Laz B | In quatriduanum Lazarum (PG 50, 641-644) |
| In Rom | In epistulam ad Romanos homiliae 1-32 |
| In s Bar | In s. Barlaam martyrem |
| In s Eust | In s. Eustathium Antiochenum |
| In s Igna | In s. Ignatium martyrem |
| In s Iul | In s. Iulianum martyrem |
| In s Luc | In s. Lucianum martyrem |
| In s Rom | In s. Romanum |
| In 1 Thess | In epistulam i ad Thessalonicenses homiliae 1-11 |
| In 2 Thess | In epsitulam ii ad Thessalonicenses homiliae 1-5 |
| In 1 Tim | In epistulam i ad Timetheum argumentum et homiliae 1-18 |
| In 2 Tim | In epistulam ii ad Timotheum argumentum at homiliae 1-10 |
| In Tit | In epistulam ad Titum homiliae 1-6 |
| L Diod | Laus Diodori episcopi |
| Non esse ad grat | Non esse ad gratiam concionandum |

| | |
|---|---|
| Non esse desp | Non esse desperandum |
| Pec frat | Peccata fratrum non euuiganda |
| Q freq con | Quod frequenter conueniendum sit |
| Q nemo | Quod nemo laeditur nisi a se ipso |
| Q reg | Quod regulares feminae uiris cohabitare non debeant |
| Qual duc | Quales ducendae sint uxores |
| S ante iret | Sermo antequam iret in exsilium |
| S cum iret | Sermo cum iret in exsilium |
| S cum pres | Sermo cum presbyter fuit ordinatus |
| S Gen | Sermones 1-9 in Genesim |
| S post red | Sermo post reditum a priore exsilio |

[1] In Aduersus Iudaeos orationes the numbering system employed by Harkins in his translation (Discourses Against Judaizing Christians. Washington: Catholic University of America Press, 1979) has been adopted because the addition of a third numeral in the notation breaks the text into smaller units making location simpler.

[2] In Catecheses ad illuminandos the various homilies from the different series have been ordered as follows:

| | | |
|---|---|---|
| i | Stavronikita 1 | |
| ii | " 2 | |
| iii | " 3 | and Papadopoulos - Kerameus 4 |
| iv | " 4 | |
| v | " 5 | |
| vi | " 6 | |
| vii | " 7 | |
| viii | " 8 | |
| ix | Montfaucon 1 | and Papadopoulos - Kerameus 1 |
| x | | " 2 |
| xi | | " 3 |
| xii | Montfaucon 2 | |

This appears to be the best reconstruction of the homilies and agrees with Harkins english translation (Baptismal Instructions. New York: Newman Press, 1963). [3] In Matthaeum homiliae 1-89 the numbering of the Greek homilies is used; the Latin translation is numbered 1-90. The difference occurs when Homily 19 in the Greek text is divided at paragraph 6 into two homilies affecting the numbering of the remaining sermons.

## Genesis

| | |
|---|---|
| 1:1 | Ad pop Anti vii, 3; viii, 1; Ex in Ps viii, 8 (2x) ix, 4; In Gen iii, 1; In Ioh iv, 1; S Gen i, 1; i, 2; i, 3 (2x) |
| 1:2 | In Ioh iii, 2; S Gen i, 3 |
| 1:3 | In Gen iii, 2; In Heb ii, 2; In Mat lii, 3; S Gen ii, 1 |
| 1:4 | Ad e q scan iv; In Gen iii, 2; iii, 3 |
| 1:5 | In Gen iii, 1, iii, 2 |
| 1:6 | Con Anom xi, 2; In Gen iv, 1; iv, 2; In quat Laz A 1 S Gen ii, 1 |
| 1:7 | In Gen iv, 3 |
| 1:8 | In Gen iv, 4 |
| 1:9 | In Gen v, 1; In quat Laz A 1 |
| 1:10 | In Gen v, 3 |
| 1:11 | Adu Iud 6, 6, 3; Con Iud et gen 13; In elee 5, In Gen v, 4; In il Sal P et A i, 5; In quat Laz A 1; In 1 Thess vii, 3 (4:15); xv, 4 (5:20) |
| 1:12 | Ad pop Anti vii, 3; In Gen v, 4 |
| 1:13 | In Gen v, 5 |
| 1:14 | In Gen vi, 1; vi, 3 |
| 1:15 | In Gen vi, 3 |
| 1:16 | Adu Iud 7, 3, 1; In Gen vi, 3 |
| 1:17-<br>1:18 | In Gen vi, 4 |
| 1:19 | In Gen vi, 5 |
| 1:20 | De res d n I C 4; H in san pascha 5; In Gen vii, 1; vii, 3; In Ioh xxvi, 1; In quat Laz A 1 |
| 1:21 | In Gen vii, 4 |
| 1:22 | In Gen vii, 4; xxviii, 4 |
| 1:23-<br>1:25 | In Gen vii, 5 |
| 1:26 | Ad pop Anti iii, 18; vii, 3; Ad Stag a dae 1, 2; Con Anom xi, 2; De prop obscur ii, 5; De uir xlvi (2x); Ex in Ps iv, 2; viii, 7; viii, 8; xi, 3; xlviii, 1; cix, 1; F Iob 1:1; In Col v, 4 (2:5); vi, 4 (2:15); In Gen viii, 1; x, 1; In il Dom non est 3; In il ne tim i, 1; In Ioh xxxiii, 2; lxiv, 2; In Is i, 2; In quat Laz A 2; In Rom xxiii, 4 (13:10); I 1 Tim xvi, 2 (6:2) S Gen ii, 1 (2x); ii, 2; iii, 1; iv, 1 |
| 1:27 | Ex in Ps cxliii, 2; In Col xii, 5 (4:18); In Eph xx, 1 (5:24); In Gen x, 1; x, 3; In Tit iii, 4 (2:1) |
| 1:28 | De prod Iud i, 6; De uir xv; xvii; Ex in Ps cxlvii, 4; In Gen x, 3; xxiii, 5; xxvi, 5; xxvii, 4 (2x) In il Prop 3; In princ Act iii, 5 |

| | |
|---|---|
| 1:29-<br>1:30 | In Gen x, 5 |
| 1:31 | Ad e q scan iv (3x); Ex in Ps cxlviii, 1; In Eph xii, 1 (4:17); In Gen x, 5; xxiv, 5; xxix, 3; In 1 Thess xii, 1 (4:4) |
| 2:1 | In Gen x, 7 |
| 2:2 | De Chris diuin 4; In Col xii, 5 (4:18); In Gen x, 7; xxix, 3; In il Pater m 4 |
| 2:3 | In Gen x, 7 |
| 2:4 | In Gen xii, 1; In Mat ii, 5 |
| 2:5 | In 1 Cor vii, 8; In Gen xii, 1 |
| 2:6 | In Gen xii, 1 |
| 2:7 | In Col vi, 4 (2:15) In I Cor xli, 6; In Gen xii, 4; xiii, 1; In Ioh xxv, 2 |
| 2:8 | De mut nom ii, 3; In Gen vi, 5; xiii, 1; xiii, 3 |
| 2:9 | In Gen xiii, 4; S Gen vii, 1; vii, 2 |
| 2:10 | In Acta xxii, 3 (10:23) |
| 2:15 | In Gen xiv:1; xiv, 2 |
| 2:16 | Adu Iud 8, 2, 3; de paen v, 1; In 2 Cor ii, 9; In Gen i, 2; xiv, 3; S Gen viii, 1 |
| 2:17 | Ad pop Anti v, 13; Adu Iud 8, 2, 3; De coem et de cru 1; De paen v, 1; De res d n I C 4; Ex in Ps cxiv, 2; H in san pascha 1; In Col vi, 3 (2:15); vi, 4 (2:15); In Gen xiv, 3; xx, 4; xxvii, 4; In Ioh xxviii, 1; S Gen vi, 1; vii, 5 |
| 2:18 | De n iter 4; De uir xlvi (2x); Ex in Ps cxxii; In Col xii, 5 (4:18); In Gen xiv, 4; In Ioh xxv, 2; S Gen iv, 1 |
| 2:19 | De mut nom iii, 3; Ex in Ps iii, 1; H dicta p imp 1 (2x); In Gen ix, 4; xvii, 9; S Gen iii, 2; iv, 1 (2x) |
| 2:20 | Ad Stag a dae i, 2; In Gen xv, 1; S gen iv, 1 |
| 2:21 | Ex in Ps cxv, 3; In Gen xv, 2; xliv, 5; Qual duc 3 |
| 2:22 | In Gen xv, 2; xv, 3; xx, 2 |
| 2:23 | Cat ill 1, 13; iii, 18; In i Cor xxvi, 2; In Eph xx, 3 (5:29); In Gen xv, 3; xv, 4; xx, 2; S Gen vi, 2; vii, 2 |
| 2:24 | Cat ill i, 13; Con e q sub i; In Col xii, 5 (4:18); In i Cor xxxiii, 5; xxxiv, 5; In Eph xx, 3 (5:29); In Gen xv, 4; xx, 2; xxxviii, 5; xlv, 2; lvi, 1; In Rom iv, 2 (1:27); xxi, 2 (12:9); xxiii, 1 (13:1); In Tit iii, 4 (2:1); Qual duc 3 (2x); S anti iret 1; S Gen vi, 2 |
| 2:25 | Cat ill xi, 28; Ex in Ps v, 2; In Gen xv, 4; xvi, 1; lxvi, 2; In Mat xviii, 2 |
| 3(p) | Con e q sub 2; De paen ix, 1; Eiii, 3; Ex in Ps cxl, 7; In il uidi dom iii, 4; Q reg 9 |

3:1 De diad tent iii, 3; In Gen xvi, 1
3:2-
3:3 In Gen xvi, 3
3:4 De diad tent iii, 4; De prof eua 3; In 1 Cor vii, 9; In Gen xvi, 9
3:5 Ad pop Anti xi, 3; De mut nom ii, 4; iii, 1; H dicta p imp 1; H hab p p Gothus 3; In 2 Cor ii, 9; In Gen xvi, 3; xviii, 5; In ioh liv, 3; In Mat xiii, 4; In Rom x, 6 (6:4); In 2 Tim vii, 2 (3:4); S Gen vii, 2
3:6 Ad Stag a dae i, 5; In Acta liv, 3; In Gen xvi, 3; In 1 Tim ix, 1 (2:15)
3:7 In Gen xvi, 4; xviii, 6
3:8 Ad pop Anti viii, 2; In Gen xvii, 1
3:9 Ad pop Anti xii, 10; In Gen xvii, 3; xix, 2; In Heb xxxi, 5; In Ioh lxiv, 2; lxxvii, 3; In quat Laz A 1
3:10 Ad pop Anti xii, 10; In Gen xvii, 3; In Heb xxxi, 5; In quat Laz A 1
3:11 Ad pop Anti xii, 10; In Gen xvii, 3; xxx, 4; In Rom xxiii, 4 (13:10)
3:12 Ad pop Anti xii, 10; Ad Theo ii, 2; Ex in ps cxlii, 3; In Gen xvii, 4
3:13 In Gen xvii, 5; In Mat xlii, 3
3:14 Cat ill iii, 10; In Gen xvii, 5; xix, 3
3:15 In Gen xvii, 5
3:16 De paen vii, 6; De uir xli; lxv; E iii, 3; Ex in ps cxvi, 2; In 1 Cor xix, 2; xxvi, 2; xxxvii, 1; In Gen viii, 4; xvii, 7; xxix, 7; In Heb vi, 10; In il Prop 4; In Mat xxxi, 4; In princ Acta iii, 5; In 1 Tim ix, 1 (2:15); Q reg 6; 8; S Gen ii, 2; iv, 1 ; v, 1
3:17 Adu Iud 8, 2, 5; Ex in ps xliv, 4; In Gen xvii, 9; xix, 3
3:18 Adu Iud 8, 2, 5; In Gen xvii, 9; xxvii, 4; xxx, 4; In Heb vi, 10; In 1 Tim ix, 1 (2:15); S Gen vii, 5
3:19 Adu Iud 8, 2, 5; Cat ill ii, 5; De mut nom iii, 1; De paen v, 1; De proph obscur ii, 5; De san penti, 2; Ex in ps xlviii, 1; In Acta xvi, 3 (7:34); In ascen d I C, 3; In 1 Cor xlii, 2; In Gen ix, 5; xvii, 9; xx, 4; xxiv, 2; xxvi, 1; In Heb vi, 10; In il Sal P et A i, 5; In Mat xii, 4; xxxi, 4; In Rom xxxii, 1 (16:20); S Gen iii, x
3:20 In Gen xviii, 1
3:21 In Gen xviii, 1; Q reg 7
3:22 In Gen xviii, 1; xviii, 2; xxx, 4; In Mat xv, 3; xxx, 3
3:23 In Gen xviii, 1; xxx, 4

| | |
|---|---|
| 3:24 | In Colvi, 4 (2:15); In Gen xviii, 3; In quat Laz A 2 |
| 4 (p) | De inani gloria 39; In Col iii, 4 (1:20); In Gen xxiii, 2; xxix, 3; De laud s Paul i, 1 |
| 4:1 | De diab tent i, 3; In Gen xviii, 4; In Mat lix, 3 |
| 4:2 | In Gen xviii, 4 |
| 4:3 | Adu Iud 8, 8, 1; In Gen xviii, 4 |
| 4:4 | Adu Iud 8, 8, 1; De laud s Paul i, 1; In Gen xviii, 4; In Heb xxii, 3 |
| 4:5 | Adu Iud 1, 7, 3; 8, 8, 1 |
| 4:6 | Adu Iud 8, 8, 1; In Rom xxiii, 4 (13:10) |
| 4:7 | Ad Stag a dae i, 3; Adu Iud 8, 2, 6; 8, 8, 1; De diab tent iii, 2; De fato et pr iv; In Gen xxvi, 2; In Heb xxii, 3; In Rom vii, 6 (3:31); xxiii, 4 (13:10 (2x); S post red ii, 1 |
| 4:8 | Adu Iud 8, 2, 6; 8, 8, 1; In 2 Cor v, 4; In Gen xix, 1; lxi, 2; S Gen vii, 2 |
| 4:9 | Ad pop Anti xii, 11; Ad Stag a dae i, 3; Adu Iud 8, 2, 8; De paen ii, 1 (2x); Ex in ps cxv, 4; In Acta xv, 4 (7:5); In 1 Cor xliv, 5; In Heb xxxi, 5; In Rom viii, 9 (4:21); xx, 4 (12: 3); In 2 Tim vii, 1 (3:7); S Gen vii, 2 |
| 4:10 | Adu Iud 8, 2, 8; De paen ii, 1; De san pent ii, 3; Ex in ps cxv, 4; In Acta liv, 2; In Gen xix, 2; In Heb xxxii, 2; In Mat xix, 4; In Rom viii, 9 (4:21) (2x); xxiii, 4 (3:10) |
| 4:11 | In Gen xix, 3 |
| 4:12 | Ad Stag a dae i, 3; De paen ii, 1; In 1 Cor xxx, 8; In Gen xix, 3; xxvii, 4; In il Uidi dom iv, 6; In Mat xii, 4; S Gen vii, 2 |
| 4:13 | Ad pop Anti xii, 11; Adu Iud 8, 2, 8; De paen ii, 1; In Gen xix, 3 |
| 4:14 | Adu Iud 8, 2, 8; In 1 Cor vii, 9; In 1 Thess viii, 4 (4:18) |
| 4:15 | Adu Iud 8, 2, 9; In Gen xix, 4 |
| 4:16-21 | In Gen xx, 1 |
| 4:24 | In Mat lxxiv 2 |
| 4:25 | De diab Tent i, 3; In Gen xx, 4; xxi, 3 |
| 4:26 | Ex in ps xliv, 1; In Gen xx, 4; xxi, 3 |
| 5:1-2 | In Gen xxi, 1 |
| 5:3-5 | In Gen xxi, 2 |
| 5:9, 12, 15, 18, 21-23 | In Gen xxi, 4 |
| 5:24 | Ex in ps cxvii, 4; In Gen xxi, 4 |
| 5:25 | In Gen xxi, 5 |
| 5:28 | In Gen xxi, 5; S Gen ix, 6 |
| 5:29 | In Gen xxi, 5; xxiv, 3; li, 1; S Gen ix, 5 (2x) |

| | |
|---|---|
| 5:29cont | ix, 6 |
| 5:31 | In Gen xxii, 1; xxv, 1 |
| 5:32 | In Gen xxi, 5; xxiv, 1 |
| 6 (p) | Ad Stag a dae ii, 5 |
| 6:1 | De inani gloria 58; In Gen xxii, 1; xxii, 2 |
| 6:2 | De inani gloria 58; De uir xviii; Ex in ps iv, 5; xlix, 1; In Eph xviii, 3 (5:14); In Gen xxii, 2; xxxi, 1; In Heb xxix, 4; In il Uidi dom iii, 4; In Thess viii, 2 (4:18) |
| 6:3 | De inani gloria 58; F Ier 25:11; In Gen xxii, 3; xxiii, 4; xxv, 1 (2x); xxv, 5; In Rom xiii, 7 (8:8); In 1 Tim xiii, 4 (5:5) |
| 6:4 | De inani gloria 58; In Gen xxii, 4; xxxi, 1; In Is iii, 1; In 1 Thess viii, 3 (4:18) |
| 6:5 | In Gen xxii, 4; xxiv, 3; xxx, 4; In Heb v, 5 |
| 6:6 | In Gen xxii, 5 |
| 6:7 | In ascen d n I C 2; In Eut ii, 7; In Gen xxii, 5; xxx, 4 |
| 6:8 | In Gen xxii, 5; xxiii, 1 |
| 6:9 | De diab tent iii, 1; De laud s Paul i, 1; De uir lxxxiii; Ex in ps xi, 1; In Gen xxiii, 3; xxiii, 5; xxiv, 1; xxxiv, 3; In Heb xxix, 4; In 1 Thess i, 1 (1:7); S Gen is, 5 |
| 6:10 | In Gen xxiv, 1 |
| 6:11 | In Gen xxiii, 4; xxiv, 2; xxv, 6 |
| 6:12 | In Eph xxiv, 5 (6:24); In Gen xxiv, 2; xxv, 6 |
| 6:13 | In ascen d n I C 2; In Gen xxiv, 3 |
| 6:14-16 | In Gen xxiv, 3 |
| 6:17-18 | In Gen xxiv, 4 |
| 6:19-22 | In Gen xxiv, 5 |
| 7:1 | In Gen xxiv, 5; xxv, 1; xxvi, 3; In Ioh lxxi, 3 |
| 7:2-3 | In Gen xxiv, 5; xxv, 1 |
| 7:4 | In Gen xxiv, 6; xxv, 1; xxv, 6 |
| 7:5 | In Gen xxiv, 7; xxv, 1 |
| 7:6 | In Gen xxv, 1; xxv, 3 |
| 7:7 | In Col v, 4 (2:5); In Gen xxv, 3 |
| 7:8-16 | In Gen xxv, 3 |
| 7:17-19 | In Gen xxv, 5 |
| 7:21-23 | In Gen xxv, 6 |
| 7:24 | In Gen xxv, 6; xxvi, 2 |
| 8 (p) | De bap Chris 4; De laud s Paul i, 1; In Mat xii, 3; In s Luc i |
| 8:1 | In Gen xxvi, 1; xxvi, 2 |
| 8:2-3 | In Gen xxvi, 3 |
| 8:4-6 | In Gen xxvi, 4 |

| | |
|---|---|
| 8:7 | In Gen xxvi, 4; In Mat v, 5 |
| 8:8-13 | In Gen xxvi, 4 |
| 8:14-19 | In Gen xxvi, 5 |
| 8:20 | In Gen xxvi, 1; xxvii, 2 |
| 8:21 | Adu Iud 1, 7, 3; In Gen xxvii, 2; xxvii, 4; xxviii, 1; In Is i, 5; In Phil xv, 3 (4:18) |
| 8:22 | In Gen xxvii, 4 |
| 9:1 | Ex in ps cxiii, 5; In Gen xxvii, 4; xxix, 6 |
| 9:2 | Ad pop Anti viii, 1; De proph obscur ii, 5; Ex in ps viii, 7; In Gen xxvii, 4; In Mat lxiv, 1 |
| 9:3 | Ex in ps cix, 1; In Gen xxvii, 4 |
| 9:4 | In Gen xxvii, 4 |
| 9:5 | Ex in ps ix, 6; In Gen xxvii, 5; In Mat lxxiv, 2; Non esse ad grat 2 |
| 9:6-7 | In Gen xxvii, 5 |
| 9:8 | In Gen xxviii, 1 |
| 9:9 | De paen vi, 4; In Gen xxviii, 1 |
| 9:10 | De Laz iii, 9; De ss B et P 41; In Gen xxviii, 1 |
| 9:11 | In Gen xxviii, 1 |
| 9:12-15 | In Gen xxviii, 2 |
| 9:16-17 | In Gen xxviii, 3 |
| 9:18-19 | In Gen xxviii, 4 |
| 9:20 | In Acta xxvii, 3(13:3); In Gen xxix, 1; xxix, 2; S Gen iv, 2 |
| 9:21 | De san pent i, 1; In Gen xxix, 1; xxix, 2 |
| 9:22 | Ad e q scan xiii |
| 9:23 | In Gen xxix, 4 |
| 9:24 | In Gen xxix, 5 |
| 9:25 | De Laz vi, 7; Ex in ps cviii, 2; In Gen xxix, 6; In Mat vi, 8; viii, 5 |
| 9:26-27 | In Gen xxix, 7 |
| 9:28-29 | In Gen xxix, 8 |
| 10:6, 8-9 | In Gen xxix, 8 |
| 10:21, 25 | In Gen xxx, 1 |
| 11 (p) | De san pent ii, 2 |
| 11:1 | De proph obscur ii, 5; ii, 7; Ex in ps xlv, 2; In 1 Cor xxxiv, 7; In Gen xxx, 1 |
| 11:2 | In Gen xxx, 1 |
| 11:3 | In Gen xxx, 2 |
| 11:4 | In Gen xxx, 2; In Ioh lvii, 2 |
| 11:5 | In Gen xxx, 3 |

| | |
|---|---|
| 11:6 | De diab tent i, 4 (2x); In Gen xxx, 3 |
| 11:7 | Ex in ps viii, 2; cix, 1; In 2 Cor iii, 6; In Gen xxx, 4; In Mat xxxv, 1 |
| 11:8 | In Acta ix, 1 (3:11); In Gen xxx, 4; In Mat xxv, 1 |
| 11:9 | In Gen xxx, 4 |
| 11:31 | In Acta xv, 1 (7:1); In Gen xxxl, 1; xxxl, 3 |
| 11:32 | In Gen xxxi, 3 |
| 12 (p) | In 1 Cor xxxv, 10 |
| 12:1 | Ad Stag a dae ii, 6; Cat ill viii, 7; viii, 8 De laud s Paul i; De ss B et P 4; Ex in ps xliii, 5; cxiii, 6; In 2 Cor iii, 6; In Eph xxi, 4 (6:4); In Gen xxxi, 3; xxxvi, 1; xxxvii, 4; li, 2; In Heb xxv, 1; In Mat liii, 5; S Gen ix, 3; ix, 4 |
| 12:2 | In Gen xxxi, 3 |
| 12:3 | De D et S ii, 1; In Gen iii, 2 (3:6); In Rom xvi, 3 (9:6) |
| 12:4 | In Gal iii, 2 (3:8); In Gen xxxi, 5; xxxvii,3 |
| 12:5 | In Gen xxxi, 5 |
| 12:6 | In Gen xxxi, 6 |
| 12:7 | In Gen xxxii, 1; xxxvi, 2; In Heb xxiii, 2; xxv, 1; In Rom xvi, 2 (9:6); xvi, 3 (9:6); xxviii, 1 (15:8) |
| 12:8-10 | In Gen xxxii, 3 |
| 12:11 | De ss B et P 1; In Gen xxxii, 4; xxxvi, 2; In Mat lvi, 9 |
| 12:12 | Ad Stag a dae ii, 7; De ss B et P 1; 2; 3; E iii, 3; In Gen xxxii, 4 |
| 12:13 | Ad Stag a dae ii, 7; De ss B et P 1; E iii, 3 |
| 12:14-15 | In Gen xxxii, 6 |
| 12:16 | In Gen xxxii, 6; In Tim xii, 3 (4:10) |
| 12:17 | In Gen xxxii, 6 |
| 12:18 | In Gen xxxii, 7; S post red ii, 1 |
| 12:19 | In Gen xxxii, 7; lvii, 3; S post red ii, 1 |
| 13:1 | In Gen xxxii, 8 |
| 13:2-4 | In Gen xxxiii, 1 |
| 13:5 | In Gen xxxiii, 2 |
| 13:6 | In Gen xxxvi, 2 |
| 13:7 | In Gen xxxiii, 2 |
| 13:8 | In 1 Cor xxxv, 10; In Gen xxxiii, 2; xxxvi, 21; In Heb i, 5 |
| 13:9 | In 1 Cor xxv, 4 |
| 13:10 | Ad pop Anti xvii, 12; In Gen xxxiii, 4; In 1 Thess viii, 3 (4:18); x, 3 (5:18) |
| 13:11 | In Gen xxxiii, 4; In Thess x, 3 (5:18) |
| 13:12-13 | In Gen xxxiii, 4 |

| | |
|---|---|
| 13:14 | In Gen xxxiv, 1; xxxiv, 2; xxxvi 2 |
| 13:15 | Ex in ps xliii, 5; In Gen xxxiv, 1; xxxiv, 2; In Heb v, 3; xxiii, 2 |
| 13:17-18 | In Gen xxxiv, 4 |
| 14 (p) | In 1 Cor xxxv, 10; In Gen xxxv, 3 |
| 14:1-2 | In Gen xxxv, 1 |
| 14:14 | In Acta xlv, 4; In Eph xx, 6 (5:33); In Gen xxxv, 4; In Mat xxxv, 7 |
| 14:15 | In Gen xxxv, 4 |
| 14:16 | Ex in ps cxvii, 4; In Gen xxxv, 4 |
| 14:17 | In Gen xxxv, 4 |
| 14:18 | Adu Iud 7, 4, 5; In Gen xxxv, 4; xxxvi, 3 |
| 14:19-20 | Adu Iud 7, 4, 5; In Gen xxxv, 5 |
| 14:21-22 | H hab p p Gothus 2; In 1 Cor i, 5; In Eph xxi, 4 (6:4); In Gen xxxv, 5 |
| 14:23 | In 1 Cor i, 5; In Eph xxi, 4 (6:4); In Gen xxxv, 5 |
| 14:24 | In 1 Cor i, 5; In 2 Cor xxviii, 1; In Gen xxxv, 6 |
| 15:1 | In Gen xxxvi, 1; xxxvi, 3 |
| 15:2 | Ad Stag a dae ii, 8; De uir xvi; In Gen xxxvi, 4 |
| 15:3 | In Gen xxxvi, 4 |
| 15:4 | Ad Stag a dae ii, 8; In Gen xxxvi, 4 |
| 15:5 | Ad e q scan x (2x); In Gen xxxvi, 4; In Heb xxiii, 5 |
| 15:6 | Cat ill viii, 7; Ex in ps cx, 5; In 2 Cor iii, 6; In Gen xxxvi, 4; li, 2; In Heb xxiv, 7 |
| 15:7 | In Gen xxxvii, 1 |
| 15:8 | In Gen xxxvii, 1; xxxvii, 2 |
| 15:9-12 | In Gen xxxvii, 2 |
| 15:13 | Ad Stag a dae ii, 8; Adu Iud 5, 5, 2; De s Dros 5; Ex in ps viii, 5; In Gen xxxvii, 2 |
| 15:14 | Adu Iud 5, 5, 2; In Gen xxxvii, 2 |
| 15:15 | Adu Iud 5, 5, 2; In Gen xxxvii, 3; In Mat xxviii, 3 |
| 15:16 | Adu Iud 5, 5, 2; In Gal iv, 3 (4:22); In Gen xxxvii, 3 |
| 15:18-20 | In Gen xxxvii, 4 |
| 16:1-2 | In Gen xxxviii, 1 |
| 16:3 | In Gen xxxniii, 2 |
| 16:4 | In Gen xxxviii, 4 |
| 16:5 | In Eph xx, 6 (5:33); In Gen xxxviii, 4 |
| 16:6 | In Eph xx, 6 (5:33) |
| 16:7-9 | In Gen xxxviii, 5 |

| | |
|---|---|
| 18:21 | In quat Laz A 1; In 2 Tim ii, 3 (3:12) |
| 18:22 | In Gen xlii, 4; xliv, 1 |
| 18:23 | In Gen xlii, 4 |
| 18:24 | In Gen xlii, 4; xlv, 5 |
| 18:25 | In Gen xxv, 4; xlii, 4 |
| 18:26 | In Gen xlii, 4 |
| 18:27 | De incomp dei ii, 3; De proph obscur ii, 6; Ex in ps cxv, 4; cxl, 5; cxliii, 2; F Iob 42:6; In 1 Cor i, 4; In 2 Cor xxiii, 6; In Gen xxxi, 2; xlii, 4; In Is vi, 4; In Mat xxv, 5; lxv, 6; lxxii, 4; In Rom xxix, 4 (15:24) |
| 18:28-31 | In Gen xlii, 4 |
| 18:32 | In Gen xlii, 5 |
| 18:33 | In Gen xlii, 5; In Mat v, 7 |
| 19 (p) | De inani gloria 58; De paen ix, 1; De s Bab c Iul 21; In Hel 4 |
| 19:1 | In Acta xliii, 3; In Gen xliii, 1 |
| 19:2 | In Gen xliii, 2; In Mat xxvi, 1 |
| 19:3-5 | In Gen xliii, 3 |
| 19:6-7 | In Gen xliii, 4 |
| 19:8 | In Gen xliii, 4; In Mat iv, 5 |
| 19:9-12 | In Ger xliii, 5; In s Iul 3 |
| 19:13 | In Col iii, 3 (1:20); In Gen xliii, 5 |
| 19:14 | In Gen xliii, 6; In Mat iv, 5; In 1 Tim xii, 3 (4:10) |
| 19:15-16 | In Gen xliii, 6 |
| 19:17 | In 1 Cor xxv, 5; In Gen xliii, 6 |
| 19:18-23 | In Gen xliii, 6 |
| 19:24 | In Gen xliii, 6; In 2 Tim iii, 2 (1:18) |
| 19:25-26 | In Gen xliii, 6 |
| 19:27-29 | In Gen xliv, 1 |
| 19:30-33 | In Gen xliv, 4 |
| 19:34-38 | IN Gen xliv, 5 |
| 20:1 | In Gen xlv, 1 (2x) |
| 20:2 | In Gen xlv, 2 |
| 20:3 | In Gen xlv, 3; In Mat iv, 11 |
| 20:4-5 | In Gen xlv, 3 |
| 20:6 | In 2 Cor xxx, 4; In Gen xlv, 3 |
| 20:7-8 | In Gen xlv, 3 |
| 20:9-14 | In Gen xlv, 4 |
| 20:15-17 | In Gen xlv, 4 |

| | |
|---|---|
| 24:1-2 | In Gen xlviii, 2; Qual duc 5 |
| 24:3 | In Gen xlviii, 2; In il Ne tim i, 7; Qual duc 5 |
| 24:4 | In 2 Cor xxiii, 1; In Gen xlviii, 2; In il Ne tim i, 7; Qual duc 5 |
| 24:5-7 | In Gen xlviii, 3; Qual duc 5 |
| 24:8-11 | In Gen xlviii, 3 |
| 24:12 | In Gen xlviii, 3; Qual duc 5; 6 |
| 24:13-14 | In Gen xlviii, 3; Qual duc 6 |
| 24:15 | Qual duc 6 (2x) |
| 24:16 | Qual duc 6; 7 |
| 24:17-19 | Qual duc 7 |
| 24:20 | In Gen xlviii, 4; Qual duc 7 |
| 24:21 | In Gen xlviii, 4; Qual duc 8 |
| 24:22 | In Gen xlviii, 4; In 1 Tim xii, 3 (4:10) |
| 24:23-25 | In Gen slviii, 4; Qual duc 8 |
| 24:26-32 | In Gen xlviii, 4 |
| 24:33-35 | In Gen xlviii, 5; Qual duc 8 |
| 24:36-49 | In Gen xlviii, 5 |
| 24:50-51 | In Gen xlviii, 5; Qual duc 8 |
| 24:52-64 | In Gen xlviii, 6 |
| 24:65 | In Col xii, 4 (4:18); In Gen xlviii, 6; Qual duc 9 |
| 24:66 | In Gen xlviii, 6 |
| 24:67 | In Gen xlviii, 6; Qual duc 9 |
| 25:19 | In Gen xlix, 1 |
| 25:20 | In Gen xlix, 1; Pec frat 9 |
| 25:21 | In Eph xxi, 4 (6:4); xxiv, 4 (6:22); In Gen xlix, 3; 1, 1; Pec frat 6; 9 |
| 25:22 | Ad Stag a dae ii, 10; In Gen xlix, 3; 1, 1 |
| 25:23 | In Gen xlix, 3; 1, 1; In Rom xvi, 5 (9:13) |
| 25:24 | In Gen xlix, 3; 1, 1 |
| 25:25-26 | In Gen xlix, 3; 1, 1; Pec frat 9 |
| 25:27 | De inani gloria 43; In 1 Cor xxxiii, 8; In Gen 1, 1; In Ioh lxi, 3 |
| 25:28-32 | In Gen 1 |
| 25:33 | In Acta xxvii, 3 (13:3); In Gen 1, 1 |
| 26 (p) | De laud s Paul 1 |
| 26:1-3 | In Gen li, 1 |
| 26:4 | In Gal iii, 4; In Gen li, 2 |

| | |
|---|---|
| 26:6-11 | In Gen li, 3 |
| 26:12-16 | In Gen lii, 1 |
| 26:17-20 | In Gen lii, 2 |
| 26:21 | In Gen lii, 2; S Gen vii, 3 |
| 26:22 | In Gen lii, 2 |
| 26:23 | In Gen lii, 3 |
| 26:24 | In Gen lii, 3; lv, 1 |
| 26:25-29 | In Gen lii, 3 |
| 26:30-33 | In Gen lii, 4 |
| 26:34 | In Gen liii, 1; liv, 3 |
| 26:35 | Ad Stag a dae ii, 10; In Gen liii, 1; liv, 3 |
| 27 (p) | Ex in ps cxv, 4 |
| 27:1-10 | In Gen liii, 1 |
| 27:11-12 | In Gen kiii, 2 |
| 27:13 | In Gen liii, 2; In il Uidi dom vi, 4 |
| 27:14-18 | In Gen liii, 2 |
| 27:19 | De sac i, 8; In Gen liii, 2 |
| 27:20-26 | In Gen liii, 3 |
| 27:27 | In Acta xviii, 5 (8:25) |
| 27:28 | Ex in ps cviii, 2; In Gen liii, 3 |
| 27:29 | In Gen liii, 3; In Mat viii, 5 |
| 27:30 | In Gen liii, 3 |
| 27:31-35 | In Gen liii, 4 |
| 27:36 | Ex in ps xlviii, 3; In Gen li, 1; liii, 4 |
| 27:37-40 | In Gen liii, 4 |
| 27:41 | De inani gloria 46; In Gen liii, 5; In Heb xxxi, 3; In Mat xl, 4 |
| 27:42 | Ad Stag a dae ii, 10; In Gen liv, 1; liv, 2 |
| 27:43-44 | In Gen liv, 2 |
| 27:45 | In Gen liv, 2; In Rom xxiii, 5 (13:10) |
| 27:46 | Ad Stag a dae ii, 10; In Col viii, 6 (3:15); In Gen liv 2 |
| 28 (p) | De Laz i, 8 |
| 28:1 | In Col viii, 6 (3:15); In Gen liv, 3 |
| 28:2-11 | In Gen liv, 3 |
| 28:12 | In Gen liv, 4 |
| 28:13 | De ss mar B 2; In Col v, 4 (2:5); In Gen liv, 4 |

| | |
|---|---|
| 31:19-23 | In Gen lvii, 4 |
| 31:24 | In Gen lvii, 4; lviii, 2 |
| 31:25 | In Gen lvii, 4 |
| 31:26 | In Gen lvii, 4; lvii, 5 |
| 31:27-28 | In Gen lvii, 5 |
| 31:29 | In Gen lvii, 5; In Mat xlii, 2 |
| 31:30-35 | In Gen lvii, 5 |
| 31:36 | In 1 Cor xxxiii, 8; In Gen lvii, 6 |
| 31:37-38 | In Gen lvii, 6 |
| 31:39 | Ad Stag a dae ii, 11; iii, 1; In Gen lvii, 6 |
| 31:40 | Ad Stag a dae ii, 11; iii, 1; In Acta iii, 5 (1:26); In Gen lvii, 6 |
| 31:41 | Ad Stag a dae ii, 11 (2x); In Gen lvii, 7 |
| 31:42 | In Gen lvii, 7; In 1 Thess, 4 (1:7) |
| 31:43-44 | In Gen lvii, 7 |
| 31:45 | In Gen lvii, 8; In 1 Tim xvi, 1 (5:23) |
| 31:46-55 | In Gen lvii, 8 |
| 32:1 | In Gen lviii, 1 |
| 32:2 | De ss mar B 1; In ascen d n I C 1; In Gen lviii, 1; S Gen vii, 3 |
| 32:3-9 | In Gen lviii, 1 |
| 32:10 | In Acta xxxviii, 4; In Gen lviii, 1; lxvi, 3 |
| 32:11 | Ad Stag a dae ii, 11; De ss B et P 2; 3; In Gen lviii, 1 |
| 32:12 | In Gen lviii, 1 |
| 32:13-27 | In Gen lviii, 2 |
| 32:28 | In Gen lviii, 2; In Rom xvi, 4 (9:10) |
| 32:29 | In Gen lviii, 3; In Rom xxvi, 4 (14:23) |
| 32:30 | In Gen lviii, 3; S Gen vii, 3 |
| 32:31-32 | In Gen lviii, 3 |
| 33:1-2 | In Gen lviii, 4 |
| 33:3 | In Gen lviii, 41; In Mat viii, 5 |
| 33:4-12 | In Gen lviii, 4 |
| 33:13-14 | Ad Stag a dae ii, 11; In Gen lviii, 4 |
| 33:15-17 | In Gen lviii, 4 |
| 33:18-20 | In Gen lix, 1 |
| 34:1-12 | In Gen lix, 2 |

| | |
|---|---|
| 34:13-29 | In Gen lix, 3 |
| 34:30 | Ad Stag a dae ii, 11; In Gen lix, 3; lxv, 3 |
| 34:31 | In Gen lix, 3 |
| 35:5 | Ad Stag a dae ii, 11 |
| 35:7-13 | In Gen lx, 1 |
| 35:14-17 | In Gen lx, 2 |
| 35:18 | Ad Stag a dae ii, 11; In Gen lx, 2; In Philem ii, 2 (v12) |
| 35:19 | In Gen lx, 2; In Mat ix, 4 |
| 36:6-8 | In Gen lx, 2 |
| 37 (p) | E vii, 2; Ex in ps cxxvii, 1; In 2 Cor v, 4 |
| 37:1 | In Gen lx, 2; lxiii, 3 |
| 37:2 | Ad Stag a dae ii, 12; In Gen lxi, 1; lxvii, 3 |
| 37:3 | E iii, 10; In Gen lxi, 1 |
| 37:4 | Ad Stag a dae ii, 12; In Gen lxi, 1 |
| 37:5-6 | In Gen lxi, 2 |
| 37:7 | De Laz iv, 5; In Gen lxi, 2 |
| 37:8 | In Gen lxi, 2 |
| 37:9 | In Eph iv, 2 (2:6) |
| 37:10 | In Gen lxi, 2; lxv, 1 |
| 37:11-13 | In Gen lxi, 2 |
| 37:14 | In 1 Cor xxiv, 4; In Gen lxi, 2 |
| 37:15-18 | In Gen lxi, 3 |
| 37:19 | Ad Stag a dae i, 6; In Gen lxi, 3 |
| 37:20 | Ad Stag a dae i, 6; De Laz iv, 5; In Gen lxi, 3; In 1 Thess iv, 5 (3:13) |
| 37:21-27 | In Gen lxi, 3 |
| 37:28-32 | In Gen lxi, 4 |
| 37:33 | Ad Stag a dae ii, 11; De Laz iv, 6; In Gen lxi, 4 |
| 37:34 | Ad Stag a dae ii, 11; In Gen lxi, 4 |
| 37:35 | In Gen lxi, 4; lxv, 1 |
| 38 (p) | Ex in ps cxxvii, 1 |
| 38:2-3 | In Gen lxii, 1 |
| 38:7,10 14 | In Gen lxii, 2 |
| 38:15 | De ss B et P 2 |
| 38:16-18, 24,25 | In Gen lxii, 2 |
| 39 (p) | Ad e q scan xxii; De paen iii, 3; E iii, 10 |
| 39:1-2 | In Gen lxii, 3 |

| | |
|---|---|
| 39:3 | Ad Stag a dae ii, 12; In Gen lxii, 3 |
| 39:4-5 | In Gen lxii, 3 |
| 39:6 | In 2 Cor vii, 7; In Gen lxii, 3; In 1 Tim iv,3 (1:17); Qual duc 6 |
| 39:7 | In 2 Cor vi, 4; Ex in ps xlviii, 9; In Gen lxii, 4; S cum iret i |
| 39:8 | In Gen lxii, 4 |
| 39:9 | Ad Stag a dae ii, 12; In 2 Cor vi, 4; In Gen lxii, 4 |
| 39:10 | In Gen lxii, 4 |
| 39:11 | In Iuu et Max 3 |
| 39:12 | In Mat xviii, 2; xxxvii, 9 |
| 39:17 | In Gen lxii, 5; In Mat lxxxiv, 4 |
| 39:19-22 | In Gen lxii, 5 |
| 39:23 | In Gen lxii, 5; lxiii, 1 |
| 40:1-6 | In Gen lxiii, 1 |
| 40:7 | In Gen lxiii, 1; In Tit iv, 5 (2:10) |
| 40:8 | In Acta xxx, 2 (14:15); In Gen lxiii, 1; In Mat lix, 3; In Phil v, 2 (2:4) |
| 40:9-13 | Cat ill ix, 2; In Gen lxiii, 1 |
| 40:14 | Ad Stag a dae ii, 12; Cat ill ix, 2; xi, 30; In Gen lxiii, 1; In Tit vi, 4 (3:15) |
| 40:15 | Ad Stag a dae ii, 12; Cat ill xi, 30; E iii, 13; In 2 Cor v, 5; In Gen lxiii, 1; In Tit vi, 4 (3:15) |
| 40:19 | In Gen lxiii, 2 |
| 41 (p) | In Gen lxiii, 2 |
| 41:1, 8,9 14-16 24-25 | In Gen lxiii, 3 |
| 41:32 | In Gen lxiii, 3; In Mat lxxxiii, 1 |
| 41:37-45 | In Gen lxiii, 3 |
| 41:46-52 54-57 | In Gen lxiv, 1 |
| 42:1-7 | In Gen lxiv, 1 |
| 42:9 | De Laz iv, 6; In Gen lxiv, 2 |
| 42:10-20 | In Gen lxiv, 2 |
| 42:21 | De Laz iv, 6; E vii, 2; In Acta xii, 4 (5:16); In Gen lxiv, 2; lxiv, 7 |

| | |
|---|---|
| 42:22 | De Laz iv, 6; In Gen lxiv, 3; lxiv, 7 |
| 42:23-37 | In Gen lxiv, 3 |
| 42:38 | Ad Stag a dae ii, 11; De coem et de cru 1; De ss B et P 3; H in san pascha 1; In Gen lxiv, 4 |
| 43 (p) | In Gen lxiv, 4 |
| 43:6, 13 | Ad Stag a dae ii, 11 |
| 43:14 | Ad Stag a dae ii, 11; In Col ix, 2 (3:17) |
| 43:21 | Ad pop Anti iii, 20 |
| 43:23-29 | In Gen lxiv, 5 |
| 43:30 | In Gen lxiv, 5; In 1 Thess iv, 5 (3:13) |
| 43:31-33 | In Gen lxiv, 5 |
| 44:1-2 | In Gen lxiv, 5 |
| 4-5, 7, 9-10, 12-17 | |
| 44:18-27 | In Gen lxiv, 6 |
| 44:28 | In Gen lxiv, 6; In 1 Thess iv, 5 (3:13) |
| 44:29-31, 33 | In Gen lxiv, 6 |
| 45:1-2 | In Gen lxiv, 6 |
| 45:3 | In Gen lxiv, 6; lxvii, 3 |
| 45:4 | In Gen lxiv, 6 |
| 45:5 | In Acta vi, 1 (2:23); ix, 1 (3:17); In Gen lxiv, 6; lxv, 3; In Philem ii, 2 (v16) |
| 45:6 | In Gen lxiv, 6 |
| 45:7 | In Gen lxiv, 6; lxv, 3 |
| 45:8 | In Gen lxiv, 6 |
| 45:9-12, 14-24 | In Gen lxiv, 7 |
| 45:25-28 | In Gen lxv, 1 |
| 46:1 | In Gen lxv, 1 |
| 46:2-7 | In Gen lxv, 2 |
| 46:27 | In Gen lxv, 2 (2x) |
| 46:28-33 | In Gen lxv, 2 |
| 47:2-8 | In Gen lxv, 3 |
| 47:9 | Ad Stag a dae ii, 1 (2x); iii, 9; De Laz iii, 9; In Gen lxv, 3; In Heb xxvi, 1; xxix, 4 |
| 47:10-13 | In Gen lxv, 3 |
| 47:14-19 | In Gen lxv, 4 |
| 47:20 | In Gen lxv, 5 |

| | |
|---|---|
| 47:21-25 | In Gen lxv, 4 |
| 47:27 | In Gen lxv, 5 |
| 47:29-31 | In Gen lxvi, 1 |
| 48:1-6 | In Gen lxv, 2 |
| 48:7 | In Gen lxv, 2; In Mat ix, 4 |
| 48:8-9 | In Gen lxv, 2 |
| 48:10 | In Gen lxvi, 2; lxvi, 3 |
| 48:11-12 | In Gen lxvi, 2 |
| 48:15 | In Col iii, 3 (1:20); In Gen lxvi, 3 |
| 48:16 | De laud s Paul vii; In Acta xxxviii, 4; In ascen d n I C 1; In Col iii, 3 (1:20); In Gen lxvi, 3 |
| 48:17-20 | In Gen lxvi, 3 |
| 48:21-22 | In Gen lxvii, 1 |
| 49 (p) | In Is ii, 1 |
| 49:1 | Ex in ps cviii, 2; In Gen lxvii, 1 |
| 49:2 | In Gen lxvii, 1 |
| 49:3 | Ad Stag a dae ii, 11; Ex in ps cviii, 2; In Gen lxvii, 1 |
| 49:4 | Ad Stag a dae ii, 11; In Gen lxvii, 1 |
| 49:6 | In Gen lxvii, 2 |
| 49:7 | In Acta xxix, 4 (13:41); In Gen lxvii, 2; In Is ii, 1; In Mat viii, 5 |
| 49:8 | In Gen lxvii, 2 |
| 49:9 | Ex in ps xliv, 2; In Gen lxvii, 2; In il Pater s p i, 3; In Ioh lxviii, 1; In 2 Tim viii, 1 (3:5) |
| 49:10 | Con Iud et gen 3; In Gen lxvii, 2; In il Uidi dom ii, 3; In Mat ii, 7; vi, 5 |
| 49:11 | Con Iud et gen 3; In Gen lxvii, 2; In Is ii, 3 |
| 49:12 | Con Iud et gen 3; Ex in ps xliv, 4; In Gen lxvii, 3 |
| 49:13-29 | In Gen lxvii, 3 |
| 49:33 | In Gen lxviii, 4 |
| 50:1-3, 5,7-10 | In Gen lxvii, 4 |
| 50:11 | In Gen lxvii, 4; In Mat xlix, 2 |
| 50:14-16, 18 | In Gen lxvii, 4 |
| 50:19 | In Gen lxvii, 5 |

| | |
|---|---|
| 50:20 | In Gen lxvii, 5; In Mat xlix, 2 |
| 50:21-23 | In Gen lxvii, 5 |
| 50:24 | Cat ill ix, 14; De s Dros 5; In Gen lxvi, 1; lxvii, 5 |
| 50:25 | In Gen lxvii, 5 |

Exodus

| | |
|---|---|
| 1 (p) | In Gen xxviii, 4 |
| 1:2 | In 1 Cor i, 4 |
| 1:7 | Ex in ps viii, 3 |
| 1:20 | Ex in ps cxxxiv, 4 (2x) |
| 1:21 | In Acta liv, 2 |
| 2 (p) | Ad pop Anti i, 29 |
| 2:11 | In Acta iv, 2 (2:13) |
| 2:13 | In Rom xxi, 2 (12:10) |
| 2:14 | Ad Stag a dae iii, 1; In Acta xvii, 1 (7:35); liv, 21; In 2 Cor xv, 4; In Heb xxvi, 4; xxvi, 5; In 1 Tim x, 1 (3:4) |
| 2:22 | In Acta xvii, 4 (7:53) |
| 2:24 | In Mat xxvi, 9 |
| 3 (p) | De imcomp dei i, 3; Ex in ps cxvii, 3; In s Bar 3 |
| 3:1 | In Rom xxx, 4 (16:5) |
| 3:2 | Ex in ps viii, 3; cix, 1; In Acta iv, 2 (2:13); In 1 Cor xxxviii, 4; In Is vi, 5 |
| 3:5 | De ter motu |
| 3:6 | De Anna iv, 4; Ex in ps vii, 3; cxiii, 3; cxxxv, 1; cxliv, 1; In Acta xvii, 1 (7:35); In 1 Cor xxix, 7; In 2 Cor viii, 2; In Gen xxxix, 2; xlviii, 3; xlix, 1; In Heb xxiv, 7; Pec frat 6 |
| 3:7 | Ex in ps cxvii, 2; cxix, 1; cxxxv, 3 |
| 3:8 | Ex in ps cxix, 1; In Eph i, 1 (1:3); In Is v, 2; L Diod 4 |
| 3:13 | F Ier 1:6 |
| 3:14 | De imcomp dei iv, 4; In Ioh xv, 2; In Phil vi, 3 (2:8) |
| 3:22 | Adu Iud 5, 5, 2 |
| 4:2 | In Mat xxxi, 3 |
| 4:3-4 | In Mat xxviii, 1 |
| 4:5 | De mut nom i, 1 |
| 4:10 | In Acta iv, 2 (2:13); In Is i, 1; vi, 4; vi, 5 (2x); In Mat xxxii, 6; lvi, 3; xc, 2; In 2 Tim x, 2 (4:18) |
| 4:11 | Ex in ps viii, 2; In Mat xxxii, 6 |
| 4:12 | In Mat xxxii, 6; xc, 2 |
| 4:13 | In Is vi, 5; In Mat xxxii, 6 |

| | |
|---|---|
| 15:11 | Adu Iud 5, 3, 3 |
| 15:14 | Ex in ps vii, 13 |
| 15:15 | F Ier 45:45 |
| 15:16 | In 2 Tim i, 2 (1:7) |
| 15:20 | H dicta p r m 3 |
| 16:3 | In Col iv, 3 (1:24); iv, 4 (1:24); In Mat viii, 6 |
| 16:14 | Ex in ps xlvi, 2 |
| 16:18 | In Eph xxiii, 3 (6:14) |
| 16:29 | In Mat lxxxix, 1 |
| 16:33 | Ad pop Anti xvii, 11 |
| 17 (p) | In Gen xlvi, 1; In kal 1 |
| 17:4 | Ex in ps xliv, 6; In Col i, 3 (1:7); In 1 Cor v, 9 |
| 17:6 | De D et S iii, 7 |
| 17:12 | In Ioh xiv, 4 |
| 18 (p) | De mut nom iii, 2 |
| 18:14 | De mut nom iii, 2; In 2 Cor xviii, 3 |
| 18:21 | De mut nom iii, 2; In Acta xliv, 1 |
| 18:22 | De mut nom iii, 2 |
| 18:24 | In 1 Cor i, 4 |
| 19:6 | In Phil i, 1 (1:2) |
| 19:8 | In Mat lxvii, 2 |
| 19:10 | In L Cor ix, 1 |
| 19:12 | Ex in ps cxlii, 1 |
| 19:13 | In Eph iii, 5 (1:22) |
| 19:14 | Ex in ps cxlii, 1 |
| 19:15 | De uir xxx, Ex in ps cxlii, 1 |
| 19:16 | In Heb iii, 6 (2x) |
| 19:18 | In Gen xxxvii, 2; In Heb xxxii, 3; In Mat lvi 5 |
| 19:19 | In Heb iii, 6; xxxii, 3; In Ioh xl, 3 |
| 19:20 | In 1 Cor ix, 1; In Heb iii, 6 |
| 20:2 | De incomp dei v, 2 |
| 20:4 | De paen vii, 5 |
| 20:5 | F Ier 3:13; In Mat lxxiv, 2; In Rom xxiii, 3 (13:10); Q reg 5 |
| 20:9 | In Heb xxxiii, 3 |
| 20:10 | Ad pop Anti xii, 9; De fato et pr iii |
| 20:12 | In Gen xxix, 5; S Gen iv, 3 |
| 20:13 | Ad pop Anti xii, 9; Ex in ps iii, 1; iv, 7; In Eph ii, 3 (1:14); xvii, 1 (5:3); In il Uidi dom iv, 6; In Ioh lxvi, 1 |
| 20:14 | De paen vi, 2; vi, 4; vii, 5; Ex in ps iii, 1; cx, 6; In Eph xvii, 1 (5:3) |
| 20:16 | F Ier 31:2 |
| 20:19 | In Heb xxxii, 1 |
| 20:21 | In Heb xxxii, 1; In Mat lvi, 5 |
| 21:2 | F Ier 34:8; 34:17 |
| 21:16 | De b Phil 1 |

| | |
|---|---|
| 21:17 | De fate et pr ii; In Gen xxix, 5; In il Sal P et A ii, 5; In il Uid elig 7; In Mat li, 2; S Gen iv, 3 |
| 21:21 | In Rom xxv, 3 (14:9) |
| 21:24 | De cruce et lat i, 5; ii, 5; De D et S i, 1; i, 4 |
| 21:25 | De cruce et lat i, 5; ii, 5 |
| 22:1 | In Mat lii, 6; lxxxv, 3 |
| 22:24 | In il Prop 2 |
| 22:25 | In Mat lvi, 9 |
| 22:28 | Ex in ps xlix, 1 (2x); cxxxvii, 1 |
| 23:1 | De dec mil 4; De proph obscur ii, 9; In Gen xv, 5; xlii, 3; xlii, 4 |
| 23:2 | In Acta xxxvii, 3 (17:15); In Gen xxii, 1 |
| 23:3 | In Ioh xlix, 3 |
| 23:4 | In 1 Cor xliv, 5 |
| 23:5 | In 1 Cor xliv, 5; In Gen xliii, 4; In il Uidi dom vi, 4; In Mat xv, 14 |
| 23:8 | In Acta xxix, 4 (13:41) |
| 23:11 | De sac iv, 1 |
| 23:15 | Ad Stag a dae iii, 4; In il Si esur 4; In 2 Tim i, 4 (1:7) |
| 23:17 | De san pent i, 1 |
| 23:20 | In Col iii, 2 (1:20) |
| 23:22 | In Col iv, 4 (1:24) |
| 23:26 | F Iob 1:2 |
| 24:3 | In Col vi, 3 (2:15) |
| 24:7 | Ex in ps cxxxi, 3; In Col iv, 3 (1:24) |
| 24:18 | In Gen i, 3 |
| 28 (p) | Adu Iud 6, 4, 1; In dien nat 3 |
| 28:4 | De sac iii, 4 |
| 29:39 | In Rom xx, 1 (12:1) |
| 31:13 | De fato et pr iii |
| 31:18 | In Gen i, 3 |
| 32 (p) | Ex in ps viii, 5; In mar Aeg 1; In mat v, 7 |
| 32:1 | Adu Iud 5, 4, 4; De paen vii, 5; De prod Iud i, 4; ii, 4; Ex in ps iv, 3; In 2 Tim x, 3 (4:20) |
| 32:3 | De reg 5 |
| 32:4 | Cat ill v, 17; De paen vii, 5 (2x) |
| 32:5 | In Acta xvii, 2 |
| 32:6 | Ad Stag a dae i, 3; Ex in ps cxl, 5; In Acta xvii, 2 (7:50); xxvii, 3 (13:3); In Gen i, 2; In d P Nolo i, 6; In Mat vi, 9; lvii, 5 |
| 32:10 | Ad pop Anti xxi, 6; De sac iv, 1; F Ier 7:16; In Gen xxix, 2; In Mat xxxv, 6; In Rom xiv, 8 (8:27); xxvii, 4 (15:7); Non esse ad grat 5 |
| 32:11 | De sac iv, 1 |
| 32:13 | Ex in ps cxiii, 6 |

## Leviticus

| | |
|---|---|
| 15 (p) | Adu Iud 7, 1, 5 |
| 15:4 | In Tit iii, 4 (2:1) |
| 15:5, 13 | De bap Chris 2 |
| 15:19 | In Tit iii, 4 (2:1) |
| 15:25 | In Mat xxxi, 2 |
| 16:1 | In diem nat 4 |
| 16:17 | In diem nat 4; 5 |
| 16:20, 25 | In diem nat 4 |
| 16:29 | In diem nat 4; 5 |
| 17:4 | Ex in ps cxxxiv, 1 |
| 17:10 | Ex in ps vi, 6 |
| 17:11 | In Gen xiii, 3 |
| 18:5 | De uir lxxxiii; In Rom xvii, 1 (10:5) |
| 18:6 | In 1 Cor xxxiv, 6 |
| 18:8 | In Gen lxvii, 2 |
| 18:18 | In Gen lx, 2 |
| 19:18 | In Gal v, 4 (5:14) |
| 19:23-24 | In ascen d n I C 3 |
| 20:9 | De b Phil 1 |
| 21:9 | De sac vi, 11 |
| 22:22 | In Rom xx, 1 (12:1) |
| 22:23 | In Gen lx, 4; In Rom xx, 1 (12:1) |
| 24:10 | In Eph xvi, 3 (4:32) |
| 24:15 | Ex in ps xlix, 1 (2x) |
| 24:16 | Ex in ps xlix, 1 |
| 24:20 | In Col iv, 4 (1:24) |
| 25:35-36 | In Mat lvi, 9 |
| 26:12 | Cat ill 1, 45; De ss mar A 1; In 2 Cor ii, 8; In doem nat 6 |

<u>Numbers</u>

| | |
|---|---|
| 3 (p) | De uir xxiv |
| 3:11-13 41-45 | In Mat 1 |
| 3:46-51 | In Mat lviii, 1 |
| 5:12-14 | Adu Iud 7, 1, 6 |
| 5:15-20 | Adu Iud 7, 1, 7 |
| 6 (p) | In Eph i, 1 (1:3) |
| 9:7-8 | Adu Iud 3, 5, 5; 4, 4, 6 |
| 9:9 | Adu Iud 4, 4, 6 |
| 9:10-11 | Adu Iud 3, 5, 5; 4, 4, 6 |
| 9:12 | In Ioh lxxxv, 3 |
| 10:2, 10 | Adu Iud 4, 7, 5 |

| | |
|---|---|
| 10:29 | In Rom xxx, 4 (16:5) |
| 11:4 | In Col iv, 4 (1:24) |
| 11:5 | Ad pop Anti vi, 8; Ad Stag a dae iii, 4; In Col iv, 4 (1:24) |
| 11:6 | Ex in ps cxi, 1 |
| 11:12 | In Heb iii, 9; In Mat xxv, 6 |
| 11:14 | In Acta xiv, 3 (6:7) |
| 11:15 | De Laz iii, 9; De sac iv, 1 |
| 11:16 | Adu Iud 6, 4, 5; In Acta xiv, 3 (6:7) |
| 11:18 | De paen viii, 1 |
| 11:21 | Con e q sub 8 |
| 11:22 | Con e q sub 8; F Ier 33:3 |
| 11:24-26 | Adu Iud 6, 4, 5 |
| 11:29 | Ex in ps xliv, 6; In 1 Tim iii, 4 (1:14) |
| 12 (p) | In Acta xiv, 3 (6:7); In Col iii, 4 (1:20); In Mat v, 7 |
| 12:1 | De uir xxi |
| 12:3 | Adu Iud 6, 6, 1; Cat ill iii, 26; De inani gloria 69; De mut nom iii, 2; De sac iv, 1; Ex in ps xliv, 6; cxxxi, 1; In Acta xvii, 4 (7:53); In 1 Cor i, 4; In Gen xxxiv, 1; In Mat lxxviii, 4 |
| 12:8 | In Mat lxxviii, 4 |
| 12:10 | De paen vii, 2; In il Sal P et A ii, 6 |
| 12:13 | Ex in ps xliv, 6; In Acta x, 5 (4:22); In Mat xxvi, 9 |
| 12:14 | Ad pop Anti xx, 11; In Acta xxxiii, 4 (16:12); In Mat v, 7; xxvi, 9 |
| 13:23 | In Eph xxiii, 2 (6:14) |
| 14:3 | In Heb vi, 12 |
| 14:4 | Ad pop Anti vi, 8 |
| 14:10 | In 1 Cor v, 9 |
| 14:23 | Ex in ps xliii, 3 |
| 15:32 | De Chris diuin 4; De Eleaz 5; Ex in ps vi, 2; In Acta xviii, 2 (8:19); In 2 Cor vi, 2; In Gal i, 6 (1:7); In Mat xxxix, 3; In Rom xxv, 4 (14:15); In 1 Thess viii, 4 (4:18) |
| 15:33-34 | De Chris diuin 4; In 2 Cor vi, 2; In Mat xxxix, 3 |
| 15:35 | De Chris diuin 4; In Acta xi, 4 (4:34); xii, 2 (5:16); In 2 Cor vi, 2; In Mat xxxix, 3 |
| 15:36 | De Chris diuin 4; De Eleaz 5; In 2 Cor vi, 2; In Gal i, 6 (1:7); In Mat xxxix, 3 |
| 15:38-39 | In Mat lxxii, 2 |
| 16 (p) | Adu Iud 6, 6, 4; De uir xxiv; Ex in ps iii, 1 In Col iv, 4 (1:24); In Eph xi, 5 (4:16); In il Uidi dom iv, 5; v, 2; v, 3; In Mat xl, 3; |

| | |
|---|---|
| 16 (p) cont | In 2 Tim ii, 3 (1:12) |
| 16:5 | In Ioh lx, 11; In 2 Tim v, 3 (2:18) |
| 16:15 | Ex in ps xliv, 6 |
| 16:32 | Ex in ps cx, 2; cxbii, 1 |
| 17 (p) | In s Rom 4 |
| 17:12 | In Heb xxiii, 8 |
| 17:16-17 | Adu Iud 6, 6, 1 |
| 18:16 | In Mat lviii, 1 |
| 20 (p) | In Gen xlvi, 1 |
| 20:12 | Con e q sub 8; De sac iv, 1 |
| 22 (p) | In Col iii, 3 (1:20); In 2 Tim ii, 3 (1:12) |
| 22:4 | Ex in ps cxxxiv, 1 |
| 23 (p) | In Tit iii, 2 (1:14); S Gen ix, 5 |
| 24 (p) | In Gen xxi, 5 |
| 24:9 | Ex in ps cxl, 6; In Rom xvi, 8 (9:20) |
| 24:14 | F Ier, Introduction |
| 25 (p) | De uir xlvi; Ex in ps viii, 3; cix, 1; In Acta xvii, 4 (7:53); In kal 6; Q reg 2 |
| 25:1 | Adu Iud 6, 2, 6; F Ier 2:23 |
| 25:2 | Adu Iud 6, 2, 6 |
| 25:3 | Adu Iud 6, 2, 6; Ex in ps viii, 5 |
| 25:4 | Adu Iud 6, 2, 6 |
| 25:5 | Ad Stag a dae iii, 4; Adu Iud 6, 2, 6 |
| 25:6 | Adu Iud 4, 2, 6; 6, 3, 1 |
| 25:7 | Ad Theo ii, 3; Adu Iud 6, 3, 1; De sac i, 8; In Mat xxv, 2 |
| 25:8 | Ad Theo ii, 3; Adu Iud 6, 3, 1; In Mat xvii, 5; xxxv, 2 |
| 25:9-11 | Ad Theo ii, 3; Adu Iud 6, 3, 1; In Mat xxxv, 2 |
| 25:12 | Adu Iud 6, 3, 1; Ex in ps viii, 3 |
| 25:13 | Adu Iud 6, 3, 1; 6, 3, 2; Ex in ps viii, 3 |
| 28:9-10 | In Mat xxxix, 3 |
| 29:7 | In Mat xxx, 4 |
| 30:2 | In Mat xvii, 5 |
| 31:8,11 15-16 | In 1 Cor xxiii, 4 |
| 31:47 | In Gal vi, 2 (6:6) |
| 35:1-8 | In Gal vi, 2 (6:6) |

Deuteronomy

| | |
|---|---|
| 1:13-15 | In il Hab iii, 8 |
| 3:26 | Ex in ps vii, 4; In Acta xliv, 4; In Rom xiv, |

| | |
|---|---|
| 4:2 | In Mat li, 1 |
| 4:7 | Ex in ps cxiii, 5; cxlvii, 2 |
| 4:21-22 | Ad Stag a dae iii, 4 |
| 4:24 | In Rom xvi, (9:20) |
| 4:26 | In Acta xliv, 1; In 1 Tim xvi, 1 (5:23) |
| 4:32 | In Rom vi, 4 (3:1) |
| 4:33 | In Ioh xl, 3; In Rom vi, 4 (3:1) |
| 4:39 | De paen vii, 5 |
| 5:9 | In Ioh lvi, 1 |
| 5:17-18 | De fato et pr iii |
| 5:26 | In Rom vi, 4 (3:1) |
| 5:29 | Ad Theo i, 15; In Ioh lxiv, 2; In Rom xviii, 5 (11:6) |
| 6:3 | De incomp dei v, 2 |
| 6:4 | De paen vii, 5; De s h Phoc 3; Ex in ps cic, 1; In Acta i, 2 (1:2); In Gal iii, 5 (3:20); In il Hal ii, 6; In Ioh xv, 3; In Mat xvii, 1; xxxvi, 3; lxxii, 1 |
| 6:5 | Ex in ps cx, 1 |
| 6:7 | Ad pop Anti vi, 18; F Prou 6:21; In Acta xix, 3 (9:4); In Heb viii, 9 |
| 6:8 | In Mat lxxii, 2 |
| 6:11 | Ad pop Anti xvii, 2; In Acta xvi, 3 (7:34); In Mat lx, 6; In Rom xxxii, 1 (16:18) |
| 6:12 | Ad pop Anti xvii, 2; De paen iv, 2; In Acta xvi, 3 (7:34); xxvii, 3 (13:3); In Mat lx, 6; In Rom xxxii, 1 (16:18) |
| 7:6 | In Eph i, 2 (1:4); In Phil i, 1 (1:2) |
| 7:7 | In Ioh xiv, 2 |
| 7:13 | In Eph i, 1 (1:3) |
| 8:3 | Con Anom xi, 3; In Mat lv, 7 |
| 8:10-11 | De Laz i, 8 |
| 8:15 | In Eph xxiii, 2 (6:14) |
| 9:4-5 | Ex in ps cx, 5 |
| 9:28 | In Rom xvi, 2 (9:6) |
| 10:6 | In Rom vi, 2 (2:25) |
| 10:12 | Ad Theo i, 15; In 2 Cor xxx, 4 |
| 10:18 | De fato et pr iii |
| 11:10 | F Ier 2:18 |
| 12:31 | Ad pop Anti xiv, 7 |
| 13:2-3 | Adu Iud 1, 7, 7; 8, 5, 7 |
| 13:4 | Adu Iud 1, 7, 7; 1, 7, 8; 8, 5, 7 |
| 14:2 | In Eph i, 2 (1:4) |
| 16:5 | Adu Iud 3, 3, 6; 4, 4, 3 |
| 16:6 | Adu Iud 3, 3, 6 |
| 16:10, 13-15 | Adu Iud 4, 4, 3 |
| 16:16 | In 2 Tim i, 4 (1:7) |
| 16:19 | In Acta xxix, 4 (13:41) |
| 17:6 | In Acta ii, 3 (1:11); xxxiii, 1 (15:15) |

| | |
|---|---|
| 17:7 | In 1 Cor xvi, 3 |
| 17:15-19 | In 2 Cor vii, 3 |
| 18:15 | De Chris diuin 1; In Acta ix, 2 (3:21); xvii, 1 (7:35); xvll, 3 (7:53); In Gal ii, 7 (2:19); In Ioh xvi, 2; xxxiii, 2 |
| 19:15 | In 1 Tim xv, 3 (5:20) |
| 19:20 | In Eph xvi, 3 (4:32) |
| 19:21 | Ex in ps vii, 4; In il Si esur 6 |
| 21:18 | Ad pop Anti xii, 9 |
| 21:23 | Con Iud et gen 9; In Phil vii, 3 (2:11) |
| 22:1 | De mut nom iii, 1 |
| 22:4 | In Mat xv, 14 |
| 22:5 | In 1 Cor xxvi, 4 |
| 22:10 | Ex in ps vi, 6 |
| 22:27 | In Mat v, 4 |
| 22:32 | F Ier 2:21 |
| 23:13 | In Col iv, 4 (1:24) |
| 23:19 | In Gen xli, 2; In Mat lvi, 9 |
| 23:24 | In Mat xvii, 5 |
| 24 (p) | Ex in ps cix, 1 |
| 24:1 | De lib rep 2; De uir xli; In Mat xvii, 4 |
| 24:2-3 | De lib rep 2; In Mat xvii, 4 |
| 24:4 | De lib rep 2 (3x); In mat xvii, 4 |
| 24:13 | Ex in ps vi, 6 |
| 24:16 | In Gen xxix, 6; In Ioh lvi, 1 |
| 25:4 | In Mat xxx, 3; In 2 Thess v, 1 (3:11); In i Tim xv, 1 (5:18) |
| 25:5 | In Gen lxii, 1; In Mat xlviii, 4 |
| 27 (p) | F Ier 2:2 |
| 27:26 | Ex in ps xliv, 4; In Gal iii, 3 (3:8) (2x); In Ioh xiv, 4 |
| 28 (p) | De uir xlix |
| 28:4 | In Eph i, 1 (1:3) |
| 28:8, 11 12,14 | In il Hab iii, 8 |
| 28:16 | Ex in ps cviii, 2 |
| 28:23 | In 1 Cor xxxix, 13 |
| 28:49-50 | Adu Iud 5, 6, 1 |
| 28:56-57 | Adu Iud 5, 6, 2 |
| 28:65 | E iii, 4 |
| 29:5 | In Phil ix, 6 (2:30) |
| 29:18 | In Heb xxxi, 1 |
| 30:6 | In Rom vi, 2 (2:25) |
| 30:19 | Adu Iud 1, 8, 1 |
| 32:1 | De paen viii, 3 |
| 32:6 | In Is v, 1 |

| | |
|---|---|
| 32:8 | Ex in ps cxiii, 6; In Col iii, 3 (1:20); In Eph vii, 1 (3:16); In Mat lix, 4 |
| 32:9 | In Heb i, 2 |
| 32:11 | Ex in ps cxxxiv, 3 |
| 32:15 | Ad Stag a dae i, 3; Adu Iud 1, 11, 5; Cat ill v, 16; De Laz i, 8; De paen iv, 2; In Acta xvi, 3 (7:34); xxvii, 3 (13:3); In Col iv, 3 (1:24); In 1 Cor xxxix, 17; In Gen i, 2; In hen xxxiii, 8; In Mat lv, 6; In Phil xv, 2 (4:14); In Rom xiv, 3 (8:15); xxxii, 1 (16:18); In 1 Tim xii, 2 (4:10) |
| 32:18 | Adu Iud 3, 3, 8 |
| 32:21 | Con Iud et gen 71; In 1 Cor xxiv, 6; In Rom xvii, 2 (10:18) |
| 32:35 | In Gen lvii, 3; In Rom xxii, 2 (12:19) |
| 32:49-50 | Ex in ps cxv, 4 |
| 33:2 | In Heb xxxii, 1 |
| 33:9 | In Mat xxxv, 3 |
| 34:10 | De mut nom iii, 2 |

Joshua

| | |
|---|---|
| 1:2 | Ex in ps cxv, 5; In Rom i, 1 (1:2) |
| 1:5 | Ad pop Anti vi, 3 |
| 1:7 | In Rom xxv, 4 (14:15) |
| 2:3-4 | De paen vii, 5 |
| 2:9 | De paen vii, 5; Ex in ps iv, 6 |
| 2:10 | Ex in ps xlvii, 3 |
| 6 (p) | Ex in ps xliii, 3 |
| 6:3, 5 | De paen vii, 4 |
| 6:15 | In Mat xxxix, 1 |
| 6:17 | De paen vii, 5; In il Uidi dom 5 |
| 6:18 | In il Uidi dom 5 |
| 6:20 | Ex in ps cx, 5 |
| 7 (p) | De uir xxiv; In Eph vi, 4 (3:7); In il Uidi dom 5 |
| 7:1 | In il Uidi dom 5 |
| 7:2 | In Acta xii, 2 (5:16); In il Uidi dom 5 |
| 7:4,5 | In il Uidi dom 5 |
| 7:6 | Ad Stag a dae iii, 5; In Rom xiv, 8 (8:27) |
| 7:7-9 | Ad Stad a dae iii, 5 |
| 7:10, 12 | In il Uidi dom 6 |
| 7:20,24 25 | In il Uidi dom 6 |
| 9 (p) | In Acta xiii, 4 (5:33) |
| 9:27 | In Mat viii, 5 |
| 10:12 | De D et S iii, 6; In Heb xxvii, 6 |

| | |
|---|---|
| 10:13 | Ex in ps xi, 3; cxlii, 5 |
| 24:2 | In Mat viii, 7; In Rom xxvi, 4 (14:23) (2x) |
| 24:25 | In Rom xxv, 4 (15:15) |

## Judges

| | |
|---|---|
| 2:1 | Ex in ps xi, 3; In Heb iii, 6 |
| 4 (p) | Ex in ps cx, 5 |
| 5 (p) | In Is v, 1 |
| 7 (p) | Ex in ps xliii, 4; cxvii, 3 |
| 11:31, 39-40 | Ad pop Anti xiv, 7 |
| 13:3 | In Heb iii, 6 |
| 14:14 | Ex in ps xlviii, 2 |
| 14:18 | In Rom xxvi, 4 (14:23) |
| 19-20 (p) | Ex in ps iii, 1 |
| 21:5-10 | In Acta xiii, 4 (5:33) |

## I Samuel

| | |
|---|---|
| 1 (p) | Ex in ps cxii, 3 |
| 1:1 | In Ioh iii, 2 |
| 1:5 | De Anna i, 5; Ex in ps cxv, 5; In Eph xxiv, 3 (6:22) |
| 1:6 | De Anna i, 4; In Eph xxiv, 3 (6:22) |
| 1:7 | De Anna i, 4; ii, 1 |
| 1:8 | De Anna i, 5; In Eph xxiv, 3 (6:22) |
| 1:9 | De Anna i, 5; ii, 5; In Eph xxiv, 3 (6:22) |
| 1:10 | De Anna i, 5; Ex in ps cxxix, 1; In Acta x, 5 (4:22); In Eph xxiv, 3 (6:22) |
| 1:11 | De Anna i, 5; ii, 2; Ex in ps cxxix, 1; In Eph xxiv, 3 (6:22) |
| 1:12 | De Anna ii, 2 (2x); In Eph xxiv, 3 (6:22) |
| 1:13 | De Anna ii, 2; iv, 5; Ex in ps iv, 2; v, 3; In Eph xxiv, 3 (6:22); In Mat vi, 8; xix, 4 |
| 1:14 | De Anna ii, 3; ii, 4; In Acta xv, 4 (7:5) |
| 1:15 | De Anna ii, 4; ii, 6; iii, 3 |
| 1:16 | De Anna ii, 6; In Eph xxiv, 3 (6:22) |
| 1:17 | De Anna ii, 6; iii, 4 |
| 1:18 | De Anna ii, 6 |
| 1:19 | De Anna iv, 5 |
| 1:20 | Ex in ps cxv, 4 |
| 1:20-23 | De Anna iii, 2 |
| 1:24 | De Anna iii, 3; In Eph xxi, 2 (6:4) |
| 1:26-27 | De Anna iii, 3 |

| | |
|---|---|
| 1:28 | De Anna iii, 3; Ex in ps xlix, 5 |
| 2 (p) | In Eph xxi, 2 (6:4) |
| 2:1 | De Anna iv, 3; v, 2 |
| 2:2 | De Anna v, 3 |
| 2:5 | De Anna ii, 2; In Gen xix, 5; In Mat lxi, 1 |
| 2:6 | Ad pop Anti xi, 1 |
| 2:10 | De Anna iv, 3 |
| 2:11 | In il Uid elig 8 |
| 2:12 | In Ioh 1, 2 |
| 2:16 | Adu op iii, 3 |
| 2:20 | De Anna iii, 4 |
| 2:24 | Ad op iii, 8; Ex in ps xliii, 9; In Acta viii, 3 (3:12); In il Uid elig 8 |
| 2:25 | De prod Iud i, 1; ii, 1; Ex in ps xlix, 7; In Eph xi, 6 (4:16); In Mat lxxv, 5 |
| 2:27 | In 2 Tim ii, 2 (1:12) |
| 2:28 | De fato et pr v |
| 2:30 | Ex in ps cxlviii, 1; In Eph ii, 2 (1:14); In Gen vii, 2; In Ioh iii, 6; In kal 6; In Mat xxix, 3; In Phil v, 2 (2:4); In Rom viii, 6 (4:21) |
| 3:1 | Ad Stag a dae iii, 6; Adu op iii, 20; De san pent i, 3; In il Uidi dom iv, 6; In 1 Thess i, 4 (1:7) |
| 3:3 | In Acta iv, 2 (2:13) |
| 3:13 | Ex in ps lviii, 2; In Acta viii, 3 (3:12); In Mat xvii, 6 |
| 3:14 | Adu op iii, 3 |
| 3:18 | Ad Stag a dae iii, 6; Adu op iii, 3; In Philem ii, 3 (v16) |
| 4:18 | In Gen lix, 5 |
| 4:21 | In Philem ii, 2 (v13) |
| 5:2 | De s Bab c Iul 21 |
| 6:6 | Ex in ps cxxxv, 2; In Mat viii, 2 |
| 6:7 | In il Sal P et A ii, 6 |
| 6:9 | In Mat vi, 4; xxii, 5; In Tit iii, 2 (1:12) |
| 8:7 | Ad Stag a dae iii, 6; De cruce et lat i, 5; ii, 5; In 2 Thess ii, 2 (1:12) |
| 8:11-18 | In 2 Cor xxiv, 3 |
| 9:21 | De sac iv, 1 |
| 10:3 | In Mat lxxxi, 1 |
| 10:21 | In Eph vii, 2 (3:19) |
| 10:22 | In 1 Tim v, 1 (1:19) |
| 10:23 | De sac ii, 2 |
| 12:1-2 | In il Ut sus 8 |
| 12:3 | An Acta xliv, 1; In 2 Cor xxiv, 3; In il ut sus 8; 9 |
| 12:4 | In il ut sus 9 |
| 12:5 | An Acta xliv, 1; In 2 Cor xxiv, 3; In il ut sus 9 |

| | |
|---|---|
| 12:11 | In il ut sus 9 |
| 12:14 | In 2 Cor xxiv, 3 |
| 12:21 | De cruce et lat i, 5 |
| 12:23 | De cruce et lat i, 5; ii, 5 (2x); In 2 Cor xv, 4; In Rom xxix, 4 (15:24); In 1 Thess i, 3 (1:7) |
| 13:12 | In Mat lxxxvi, 3 |
| 13:14 | Ad Stel de comp ii, 4; De D et S i, 1; In Mat iii, 9 |
| 14:12 | De D et S ii, 4 (2x) |
| 14:24 | In Acta xiii, 4 (5:33) |
| 14:26 | Ad pop Anti xiv, 6 |
| 14:27 | Ad pop Anti xiv, 7 |
| 14:28 | Ad pop Anti xiv, 8 |
| 14:36 | Ad pop Anti xiv, 9; xiv, 11 |
| 14:37-38 | Ad pop Anti xiv, 11 |
| 14:42-44 | Ad pop Anti xiv, 12 |
| 14:45 | Ad pop Anti xiv, 12; Ex in ps cxxxiv, 5 |
| 15 (p) | Ad Theo ii, 3 |
| 15:22 | Ex in ps xliii, 4 |
| 15:35 | Ex in ps xlviii, 4; In Acta xxxiii, 4 (16:12); In Rom xiv, 8 (8:27) |
| 16:1 | Ad Stag a dae iii, 6; De paen vii, 4; In Mat v, 7 |
| 16:7 | De paen vii, 3; In Mat xxix, 2; In 1 Thess iv, 1 (3:8) |
| 16:12 | In 2 Cor vii, 7 |
| 16:13 | In Acta iv, 2 (2:13) |
| 16:23 | Ex in ps viii, 2 |
| 17 (p) | Con Anom xi, 1; De s Dros 3; Ex in ps xliv, 6; cxvii, 3; In Gen xlvi, 2; In il Sal P et A i, 3; In il Ut sus 7 |
| 17:13 | De D et S ii, 4 |
| 17:18 | In Is vii, 2 |
| 17:26 | In Gen xlvi, 3; In Rom xxix, 4 (15:24) |
| 17:28 | In Gen xlvi, 3 |
| 17:29 | Ex in ps xliv, 6; In Gen xlvi, 3 |
| 17:32 | De D et S i, 2; In il Ut sus 7 |
| 17:33 | De D et S i, 2; ii, 4; In il Ut sus 7 |
| 17:34 | De laud s Paul v; Ex in ps iv, 2; In Acta ix, 1 (3:12); xliv, 1; In il Ut sus 7 |
| 17:35 | In Acta xliv, 1; In il Ut sus 7 |
| 17:36 | In il Ut sus 7 |
| 17:42 | In 2 Cor vii, 1 |
| 17:45 | De D et S iii, 6 |
| 17:49 | Ex in ps cx, 5 |
| 17:51 | Con Anom xi, 1 |

| | |
|---|---|
| 26:16 | In Mat lxii, 6 |
| 26:19 | In Acta xvi, 3 (7:34) |
| 28 (p) | In Mat vi, 4 |
| 28:8 | In Tit iii, 2 (1:14) |
| 28:15 | Ex in ps cxl, 7; In Mat lxii, 6; lxxxvi, 3 |
| 29:4 | Ad Stag a dae iii, 7 |

## 2 Samuel

| | |
|---|---|
| 1:19-20 | Adu Iud 8, 4, 10 |
| 1:21 | De D et S ii, 5; In Rom xxiii, 5 (13:10) |
| 1:23 | In Iuu et Max 3 |
| 1:24 | De D et S ii, 5 |
| 1:25 | In 2 Tim vii, 3 (3:17); (2x) |
| 1:26 | Ad Stag a dae iii, 7; In Eph xx, 1 (5:24); In 2 Tim vii, 3 (3:7) |
| 2 (p) | In 2 Tim ix, 1 (3:17) |
| 2:11 | Ex in ps xlvi, 4 |
| 3:1 | De sant pent 1, 3 |
| 3:23-30 | In Mat xlii, 2 |
| 3:32-34 | Ad Stag a dae iii, 8 |
| 5:6 | Ad Stag a dae iii, 8 |
| 6 (p) | Ad Stag a dae iii, 8 |
| 6:6 | In Gal i, 6 (1:7) |
| 6:7 | An Acta xii, 2 (5:16); In Gal i, 6 (1:7) |
| 7:18-20 | Ad Stel de comp ii, 7 |
| 9 (p) | De D et S iii, 9 |
| 11:2 | De paen ii, 2 |
| 12:1-4, 5(2x),6 | De paen ii, 2; Ex in ps iii, 3 |
| 12:7 | De paen ii, 2; In Mat lxxv, 5 |
| 12:8 | De fato et pr v; Ex in ps ii, 1; In Heb xx, 9; In Mat lxxv, 5 |
| 12:9 | Ex in ps iii, 1; In Mat lxxv, 5 |
| 12:10-11 | Ex in ps iii, 1 |
| 12:12 | Ex in ps iii, 1; In Heb xxxi, 7 |
| 12:13 | De paen ii, 2; vii, 4 (2x); Ex in ps xlviii, 4; cxl, 7; In il Uidi dom v, 2 |
| 12:17 | In 2 Cor iv, 6 |
| 12:20 | In Mat xx, 1 |
| 12:23 | De cruce et lat i, 5; In Col viii, 6 (3:15) |
| 13 (p) | In Col viii, 6 (3:15) |

| | |
|---|---|
| 14:21 | Ex in ps vii, 5 |
| 15 (p) | Ex in ps vii, 1 |
| 15:6 | In Eph xv, 3 (4:31) |
| 15:26 | In Acta xvi, 3 (7:34); In Philem ii, 3 (v16) |
| 16 (p) | De Anna ii, 3; Ex in ps iii, 1; xliv, 6 |
| 16:1-3 | In Phil v, 3 (2:4) |
| 16:5 | De s Bab c Iul 7; In 2 Cor iv, 6 |
| 16:7 | Ad Stag a dae iii, 9; Ex in ps vii, 7; F Iob 2:10; In Phil v, 3 (2:4) |
| 16:8 | Ad Stag a dae iii, 9 |
| 16:9 | In 2 Cor iv, 6 |
| 16:11 | Ad Stag a dae iii, 8; iii, 9; Ex in ps cxli, 1; In 2 Cor xxiii, 7; In Heb xxvii, 10; In Mat ix, 2; xv, 9; In Phil vii, 5 (2:11) |
| 16:12 | Ad Stag a dae ii, 9; De Anna ii, 3; Ex in ps cxli, 1; In 2 Cor xxiii, 7; In Heb xxvii, 10; In Mat ix, 2; xv, 9 |
| 16:17-19 | Ex in ps vii, 2 |
| 17 (p) | Ex in ps vii, 2 |
| 17:1-4 | In Phil v, 3 (2:4) |
| 18:5 | Ad Stag a dae iii, 9; De s Bab c Iul 10; Ex in ps vii, 12; xliv, 6 |
| 18:14 | Ex in ps iii, 1 |
| 18:16, 22,28 | De D et S ii, 3 |
| 18:33 | Ex in ps vii, 12; In Rom xxix, 4 (15:24) |
| 19 (p) | In Eph xiii, 2 (4:22) |
| 19:1 | De D et S ii, 3 |
| 19:34-35 | Ad Stag a dae ii, 3 |
| 20:9-10 | In Mat xlii, 2 |
| 21:1 | Ad Stag a dae iii, 9 |
| 21:17 | In 2 Thess iv, 3 (3:2) |
| 22:3 | In Heb iv, 5 |
| 24:15 | In Rom xxv, 4 (14:15) |
| 24:16 | In Col iii, 2 (1:20) |
| 24:17 | Ad Stag a dae iii, 9; De cruce et lat i, 5 (2x); ii, 5 (2x); Ex in ps cxl, 7; In 1 Cor xxv, 4; In 2 Cor xi, 6; In Heb xix, 4; In Is Rom v, 6 (2:16); xxix, 4 (15:24) |

## 1 Kings

| | |
|---|---|
| 2:5-6 | In Mat xlii, 2 |
| 2:30 | Cat ill vi, 10 |
| 3:1 | In Is iii, 2 |
| 3:10 | In Mat xxiii, 5 |

| | |
|---|---|
| 3:11 | Ex in ps vii, 4; xliii, 5; In Mat xxiii, 5 |
| 3:12-14 | In Mat xxiii, 5 |
| 4:29 | Ad pop Anti xvii, 10 |
| 5:4 | In 2 Cor xxvi, 2 |
| 8:39 | In Ioh xxiv, 1; In Is vii, 5; In para 6 |
| 11:3-4 | Ad Theo ii, 2 |
| 11:11 | Ad Theo i, 14 |
| 11:12-13 | Ad Theo 11, 2 |
| 13 (p) | In Is vii, 1 |
| 13:1 | In Is i, 2 |
| 13:2 | De paen viii, 3; De s h Phoc; In Is i, 2 |
| 13:4 | De s h Phoc 2; In Is iii, 7 |
| 13:21 | In s Igna 5 |
| 13:24 | Ex in ps iii, 1 |
| 15:23 | In Ioh xxxviii, 1 |
| 16:24 | In Ioh xxxi, 2 |
| 17 (p) | De paen iii, 2; Ex in ps cxvii, 3; In Col i, 6 (1:7); In il Uid elig 11; 12; 13; In Hel 1 |
| 17:1 | In Hel 2; In il Is Ego 5 |
| 17:3 | In Hel 4 |
| 17:6 | In Hel 2 |
| 17:9 | In Gen xlii, 6 (2x); In Hel 2; 4 |
| 17:10 | In elee 3; In Gen xlii,6; In Hel 7 |
| 17:11 | In Gen xlii, 6; In Hel 7;8 |
| 17:12 | In 2 Cor xix, 4; In Gen xlii, 4; In Hel 8; In Phil i, 5 (1:7); Q nemo 6 |
| 17:14 | In Gen xlii, 6; In Phil i, 5 (1:7) |
| 17:16 | In Mat xlix, 3 |
| 17:19-22 | Ex in ps cxxix, 1 |
| 18:17 | Ad pop Anti viii, 3 |
| 18:18 | Ad pop Anti viii, 3; In Heb xviii, 4; In Mat lviii, 6; In Phil v, 3 (2:4) |
| 18:21 | Adu Iud 4, 4, 1; F Ier 14:10; In Acta xvii, 4 (7:53); In Mat xxix, 4; In Phil v, 3 (2:4); In Rom xvii, 5 (10:13); In 2 Thess viii, 4 (3:14) |
| 18:34 | De sac i, 8 |
| 18:36 | De sac iii, 4; Ex in ps cxxix, 1 |
| 18:37 | Ex in ps cxxix, 1 |
| 18:38 | De san pent i, 2; Ex in ps cxxix, 1 |
| 18:42 | Ex in ps cxxix, 1 |
| 19 (p) | E iii, 3 |
| 19:2 | De ss B et P 2; Q freg 4 |
| 19:3 | De ss B et P 2; E iii, 4; Q freg 4 |
| 19:4 | Ad Stag a dae iii, 11; De Laz iii, 9; E iii, 4 |
| 19:6 | De uir lxxix |
| 19:8 | De uir lxxix; In Gen i, 3 |
| 19:10 | De proph obscur i, 3; Ex in ps xlix, 4; In |

| | |
|---|---|
| 19:10 | Acta xvii, 2 (7:53); xxxi, 3 (14:20); In 1 |
| cont | Cor v, 91; In il Fil 3; In 1 Thess iv, 1 (3:8) |
| 19:13 | Q freg con 4 |
| 19:14 | In Rom xviii, 4 (11:5); Q freg con 4 |
| 19:18 | In Mat xxi, 5; In Rom xviii, 4 (11:5) (3x); In 1 Thess iv, 1 (3:8); Q freg con 4 |
| 19:19 | H dicta p r m 1 |
| 19:20 | In Mat xiv, 3; lxviii, 5 |
| 19:21 | In Acta iv, 2 (2:13); In Mat xiv, 3 |
| 20:27 | Ad pop Anti vii, 6 |
| 20:35-36 | In Rom ii, 6 (1:17) |
| 20:39-41 | Adu Iud 4, 2, 4 |
| 20:42 | Adu Iud 4, 2, 4; 4, 2, 5 |
| 21 (p) | De paen ii, 3; In il Uid elig 12; In Mat xxxv, 1 |
| 21:4 | Ex in ps vii, 13 |
| 21:11 | De uir xlvi |
| 21:19 | In Acta xii, 4 (5:16); In Mat xxiv, 4 |
| 21:20 | In 2 Cor xxviii, 3 |
| 21:23 | In Rom xxv, 3-4 (14:13) |
| 21:25 | De uir xlvi; In Rom xxv, 3-4 (14:13) |
| 21:27 | In Ioh lxxxviii, 3 |
| 21:29 | Ad Theo i, 6; De Laz vi, 9; De paen ii, 3; iii, 1; In 2 Cor iv, 7; In Rom xxv, 3-4 (14:13) |
| 22:8 | In 1 Cor vii, 6 |
| 22:11 | F Ier 14:14 |
| 22:17 | In Is i, 1 |
| 22:19 | Con Anom xi, 3; De incomp dei iv, 3 |
| 22:22 | F Ier 4:11 |
| 22:23 | F Ier 4:11; In 1 Cor xxix, 1 |

2 Kings

| | |
|---|---|
| 1:8 | In Heb xxviii, 1; In Mat x, 3 |
| 1:9 | De sac i, 8; De uir xxii |
| 1:10-12 | De sac i, 8 |
| 2 (p) | Ad Stag a dae iii, 11; In ascen d n I C 5 |
| 2:10 | In Acta i, 6 (1:5) |
| 2:11 | Ex in ps cxvii, 4; In Acta ii, 2; In Col v, 4 (2:5); In Mat ii, 6 |
| 2:12 | An Acta ii, 3 (1:11); In Mat ii, 6 |
| 2:13 | In Mat ii, 6 |
| 2:23 | De uir xxii |
| 2:24 | De uir xxii; In Rom xxv, 4 (14:15) |
| 2:25 | De uir xxii |
| 4:10 | In Acta xlv, 4 |

| | |
|---|---|
| 4:12-13 | De laud s Paul iii |
| 4:16 | Ex in ps cxiii, 5 |
| 4:27 | Ex in ps cxix, 1; In 1 Thess iv, 1 (3:8) |
| 4:35 | Ex in ps viii, 2 |
| 4:40 | De fato et pr iii |
| 4:42 | In Mat xlix, 1 |
| 4:43 | In Ioh xliii, 2 |
| 5 (p) | De s h Phoc 2 |
| 5:11 | Ex in ps xliii, 4; In Iohlvi, 2; In Mat xxxi, 1 |
| 5:15 | Ex in ps viii, 2 |
| 5:19-21 | In Mat xlix, 1 |
| 5:26 | In 1 Cor xv, 3 |
| 6:5-6 | In 1 Cor iv, 5 |
| 6:8-12, 13,16 | In Eph ix, 1 (4:3) |
| 6:17 | In Eph ix, 1; In Ioh xii, 1 |
| 6:18 | F Ier 36:26 |
| 6:28 | In 1 Thess viii, 3 (4:18) |
| 6:31 | In Hel 7 |
| 7 (p) | Ex in ps cxvii, 3 |
| 8:13 | In 1 Cor ix, 9 |
| 9:31 | In Phil v, 3 (2:4) |
| 9:34 | In 1 Thess i, 4 (1:7) |
| 10:15 | F Ier 35:6 |
| 13 (p) | In Acta iv, 2 (2:13) |
| 13:21 | H dicta p r m 1; In Mat lvii, 3; lxxxviii |
| 14:6 | In Ioh lvi, 1 |
| 15 (p) | In il Uidi dom iii, 1; In Is vi, 1 |
| 15:17, 22 | F Ier 41:9 |
| 15:29 | In Ioh xxxi, 2 |
| 16:3 | Adu Iud 6, 2, 6 |
| 16;7 | F Ier 2:36 |
| 17:3-4 | In Ioh xxxi, 2 |
| 18 (p) | Ex in ps xliii, 4 |
| 19 (p) | Ex in ps xlvii, 2 |
| 19:20 | In Acta xvi, 3 (7:34) |
| 19:34 | Ad Theo i, 14; Adu op iii, 20; In Gen xlii, 5; lxxxv, 6; In Mat ii, 6 |
| 19:35 | Ex in ps vii, 11; xlv, 2; In Mat lxxxiv, 1 |
| 20 (p) | De Anna iv, 6 |
| 20:3 | In Mat liii, 7 |
| 20:6 | In Phil iii, 4 (1:24); Non esse ad grat 5 |
| 20:11 | Ex in ps xi, 3; cxvii, 2 |
| 20:17 | Ex in ps cxvii, 2 |
| 21 (p) | In Mat xxii, 6 |
| 22:8 | In Mat ix, 6 |
| 25:1-3 | Ad pop Anti xix, 9 |

| | |
|---|---|
| 25:4 | Ad pop Anti xix, 9; xix, 11 |
| 25:5-7 | Ad pop Anti xix, 11 |
| 25:9, 13-20 | Ad pop Anti xix, 10 |

## 2 Chronicles

| | |
|---|---|
| 3:3 | Ad pop Anti xvii, 11 |
| 6:30 | In Mat xxix, 2 |
| 8:7-8 | In Mat viii, 5 |
| 9:29 | In Mat ix, 6 |
| 16:9 | Ex in ps x, 2 |
| 18:19 | In Ioh lxiv, 2 |
| 24:21 | In Mat lxxiv, 2 |
| 26 (p) | De laud s Paul vii; In Is vi, 1 |
| 26:4 | In il Uidi dom iii, 1 |
| 26:16 | In il Uidi dom iii, 1; iii, 3; iii, 5; iv, 4; v, 1 |
| 26:18 | In il Uidi dom iv, 5 |
| 26:19 | In il Uidi dom iv, 5; v, 3 |
| 33 (p) | In Mat xxii, 6 |
| 33:10-19 | Ad Theo i, 6 |
| 34:14 | In 1 Cor vii, 6 |

## Ezra

| | |
|---|---|
| 6:15 | In Ioh xxiii, 2 |

## Nehemiah

| | |
|---|---|
| 2-3 (p) | Adu Iud 5, 10, 3 |
| 9:33 | Ad pop Anti xvii, 15 |

## Esther

| | |
|---|---|
| 6:2-12 | In Acta xxxviii, 4 |

## Job

| | |
|---|---|
| 1 (p) | E ii, 8; In Col iii, 4 (1:20) |
| 1:1 | Cat ill xii, 5; Ex in ps v, 6; cxlii, 2; In Mat iv, 7; xvi, 6; In 1 Thess i, 4 (1:7) |
| 1:2 | In 1 Thess xiii, 4 (5:5) |
| 1:5 | Adu op iii, 20; In il uid elid 9; In Mat |

| | |
|---|---|
| 3:15 | F Iob 4:6 |
| 3:23 | De coem et de cru 1; E iii, 7; Ex in ps cx, 1; I in san pascha 1; In Gen xxi, 5; xxxiv, 3; S Gen ix, 5; ix, 6 |
| 3:25 | Cum Sat et Aur 5; Ex in ps ix, 10; In Mat xxxiii, 7 |
| 3:26 | Cum Sat et Aur 5; Ex in ps ix, 10 |
| 4:2-6 | De Laz i, 10 |
| 4:19 | De incomp dei ii, 5 |
| 5:13 | In 1 Cor x, 3; In s Bar 2 |
| 6:7 | Adu Iud 8, 6, 2; De diab tent iii, 5; E ii, 8; In Phil viii, 3 (2:16) |
| 6:8-10 | E iii, 7 |
| 7:1 | Ad Stag a dae ii, 4; In 2 Tim viii, 3 (3:12) |
| 7:4 | Ad eos q n adf 2; Cum Sat et Aur 5; De diab tent iii, 6; In Phil viii, 3 (2:16) |
| 7:5 | E iii, 7; F Iob 2:8; In Eph xxiv, 5 (6:24); In Phil viii, 3 (2:16) |
| 7:14 | Ad eos q n adf 2; De diab tent iii, 6; F Iob 7:4; In Phil viii, 3 (2:16) |
| 7:16 | In Mat xxxiii, 7 |
| 7:17 | S Gen ix, 1 |
| 9:6 | De incomp dei ii, 3 |
| 9:8 | In Ioh xliii, 2 |
| 9:25 | Ad Theo ii, 3 |
| 9:31 | De diab tent iii, 6 |
| 9:33 | Ex in ps cxlii, 2 (2x) |
| 9:34 | Ex in ps cxlii, 2 |
| 10:8 | In Gen xiii, 1 |
| 10:9 | In Eut ii, 11 |
| 11:6 | In Mat xxxiii, 7; In Phil viii, 3 (2:16) |
| 11:12 | In Eph xix, 4 (5:21) |
| 12:3 | F Iob 15:1 |
| 13:2 | F Iob 15:1 |
| 13;23 | F Iob 15:11 |
| 14:3 | Ex in ps xlviii, 7 |
| 14:4 | De paen viii, 4 |
| 16:2 | In Phil viii, 3 (2:16) |
| 17:16 | De coem et de cru 1 |
| 18:17 | In il Prop 3 |
| 19:5,9 10 | De diab tent iii, 6 |
| 19:14 | De diab tent iii, 6 (2x) |
| 19:16-17 | De diab tent iii, 6 |
| 20:15 | In 1 Cor xxxiv, 10 |
| 21:7 | Ad Stag a dae i, 7 |
| 21:10 | F Ier 12:2 |
| 23:3 | F Iob 25:2 |
| 26:7 | Ad pop Anti ix, 8 |

| | |
|---|---|
| 26:8 | Ex in ps cxxxiv, 2 |
| 26:14 | Ad Stag a dae i, 7 |
| 29:2 | In Is iii, 10 |
| 29:14 | Ad e q scan xiii |
| 29:15 | Adueos q n adf 4; E iii, 6; In Gen lxvi, 4; In il Ne tim i, 3; In 2 Tim vii, 4 (3:7) |
| 29:16 | Adueos q n adf 4; E iii, 6; In il Ne tim i, 3 |
| 29:17 | Adueos q n adf 4; Ad e q scan xiii, E iii, 6 (2x); F Iob 1:1; In Gen lxvi, 4 |
| 30:1 | E ii, 8; In Phil viii, 3 (2:16) |
| 30:10 | Cum Sat et Aur 5; E ii, 8 |
| 30:24 | F Iob 2:9 |
| 30:25 | Ad e q Scan xiii; In Mat xxxiii, 7 |
| 31:1 | Adu eos q n adf 5; Con e q sub 4; F Iob 1:1; In Mat xvii, 2; xxxiii, 7; In Rom xii, 6-7 (7:13) |
| 31:5 | Adu eos q n adf 5; Ex in ps cxl, 7 |
| 31:6 | F Iob 2:3 |
| 31:13 | Ad e q scan xiii, Adu eos q n adf 4; De inani gloris 72; F Iob 1:1 (2x) |
| 31:14-15 | Ad e q scan xiii; Adu eos q n adf 4; De inani gloria 72 |
| 31:16 | E iii, 6; In Gen lxvi, 4 |
| 31:22 | F Iob 1:1 |
| 31:24 | Cum Sat et Aur 5; In Mat xxxiii, 7 |
| 31:25 | Ad e q scan v; Cum Sat et Aur 5; In Mat xxi, 2; xxxiii, 7 |
| 31:26 | Ad e q scan v; Cum Sat et Aur 5 |
| 31:31 | Ad e q scan xiii; De inani gloria 72; E iii, 6; F Iob 1:1; In 1 Cor xxiv, 7; In Ioh xlvi, 3 |
| 31:32 | Ad pop Anti xv, 10; Adu eos q n adf 5; De Laz ii, 5; E iii, 6; In il Is Ego 4; In il Ne tim i, 3 |
| 31:33 | Ad e q scan xiii; In Eph x, 3 (4:4) |
| 31:34 | Ad e q scan xiii; E iii, 6; In Eph x, 3 (4:4) |
| 33:6 | In Acta xlv, 4 |
| 33:27 | Ex in ps vii, 7 |
| 34:3 | In Heb viii, 7 |
| 34:34 | Non esse ad grat 4 |
| 34:36 | F Iob 1:20 |
| 37:15 | Ad pop Anti xi, 1 |
| 38 (p) | In Rom xvi, 7-8 (9:20) |
| 38:3 | Ex in ps cxlii, 2; In Eph xxiii, 2 (6:14) |
| 38:4 | Ad pop Anti ix, 7 |
| 38:7 | Ad e q scan vii; In Mat lxxvi, 3; In Phil iv, 1 (1:26); In Rom xviii, 5-6 (11:6) |

| | |
|---|---|
| 39:9 | De diab tent iii, 6 |
| 40:2 | Ex in ps cxlii, 2 (2x) |
| 40:4 | De diab tent iii, 5; Ex in ps cxlii, 2; In Mat xxxiii, 8 |
| 40:5 | De diab tent iii, 5 |
| 40:8 | Ad e q scan xii; Adu Iud 1, 7, 11; De diab tent iii, 5; De Laz vi, 9; In Ioh xxxviii, 1; In Mat xxxiii, 8; In 2 Tim viii, 3 (3:14); S post red ii, 2 |
| 40:11 | Ex in ps cxlv, 3 |
| 42 (p) | In 1 Thess iii, 5 (3:4) |
| 42:2 | Ex in ps x, 1 |
| 42:4 | Ex in ps cxlii, 2 |
| 42:5-6 | De diab tent iii, 5; Ex in ps cxlii, 2; In Mat xxxiii, 8 |
| 42:8 | In 1 Thess i, 4 (1:7) |
| 42:10 | Ex in ps xi, 3 |

Psalms

| | |
|---|---|
| 1:1 | Ad pop Anti xviii, 10; De Anna iii, 3; Ex in ps cxl, 7; In Col ix, 2 (3:17); In il Prop 1; In princ Act iii, 2 |
| 1:2 | De Anna iii, 3; In Gen x, 8; In Heb viii, 9; In il Prop 1; In princ Act iii, 2 |
| 1:3 | De Anna iii, 3; F Ier 12:1; 17:7; In Ioh xvii, 4; In princ Act iii, 2 |
| 1:4 | In Rom x, 5 (6:4) |
| 2:1 | Con Iud et gen 4; De coem et de cr 2; Ex in ps xliv, 3; H hab p p Gothus 5; In Acta xi, 1 (4:25); In il Pater s p 2; In Mat xxxvi, 3 |
| 2:2 | In il Pater s p 2; In Mat xxxvi, 3 |
| 2:3 | Con Iud et gen 4; Ex in ps viii, 5 |
| 2:4 | F Prou 1:28; In Heb iii, 4 |
| 2:5 | Ex in ps viii, 5; In Heb iii, 4; In Ioh liii, 2 |
| 2:7 | Cat ill ix, 23; In Mat xxv, 5 |
| 2:8 | Cat ill ix, 23; Con Iud et gen 6; De proph obscur ii, 2; In 1 Cor xxxix, 11; In Heb i, 2; In princ Act iv, 9 |
| 2:9 | Cat ill ix, 23; Ex in ps cix, 3; In Eut ii, 11 |
| 2:10 | De paen vii, 3 |
| 2:11 | De s Bab c Iul 12; H in mar 1; In Col xii, 6 (4:18); In Eph xvii, 2 (5:4); In Heb x, 1; In il Uidi dom i, 2; In Phil viii, 1 (2:16); In Rom xxiv, 3 (13:14) |
| 2:12 | Ad pop Anti xviii, 10 |
| 3:1 | Ex in ps iii, 1 (2x) |

| | |
|---|---|
| 7:10 | Ex in ps vii, 9 |
| 7:11 | Ex in ps vii, 10; In Col ix, 2 (3:17); In 2 Cor ix, 4; In Ioh xxxix, 4; In 2 Tim iii, 3 (1:18) |
| 7:12 | Ex in ps vii, 10; xliv, 5; In Heb vii, 2 |
| 7:13 | Ex in ps vii, 10 |
| 7:14 | Ex in ps vii, 12 |
| 7:15 | Ex in ps vii, 12; vii, 14 |
| 7:16 | Ex in ps vii, 14 |
| 7:17 | Ex in ps vii, 15; viii, 1 |
| 8:1 | De incomp dei i, 3; Ex in ps viii, 1; In s Rom 4 |
| 8:2 | In Mat vii, 2; In s Rom 4 |
| 8:3 | De paen ii, 3 |
| 8:4 | Ad Stel de comp ii, 5; ii, 7; De incomp dei v, 3; Ex in ps viii, 6; xlviii, 7; cxv, 4 (2x); In Phil iv, 5 (1:30); In 1 Thess xiv, 4 (5:10) |
| 8:5 | Ad Stel decomp ii, 7; De incomp dei v, 3; De s mar B 1; Ex in ps viii, 7; xlviii, 7; In Acta xxxii, 3 (15:11); In Gen xvi, 1; In Rom xxviii, 2 (15:13) |
| 8:6 | Ex in ps viii, 7; In 2 Cor iii, 5; In Rom xxviii, 2 (15:13) |
| 8:7 | Ex in ps viii, 7; xlviii, 7 |
| 8:8 | Ex in ps viii, 7; xlviii, 7; In Ioh xlv, 1 |
| 8:9 | Ex in ps viii, 7 |
| 9:1 | Ex in ps ix, 1 |
| 9:2 | Ex in ps ix, 2 |
| 9:3 | Ex in ps vii, 6; ix, 3; In Ioh vi, 2 |
| 9:4 | Ex in ps ix, 3 |
| 9:5-6 | Ex in ps xii, 2 |
| 9:7-9 | Ex in ps ix, 4 |
| 9:10 | Ex in ps ix, 5 |
| 9:11-14 | Ex in ps ix, 6 |
| 9:15 | Ex in ps ix, 7; In Ioh lxv, 1 |
| 9:16 | Ex in ps ix, 7; In Acta xii, 2 (5:16); In Heb xxxiii, 8 |
| 9:17 | Ex in ps ix, 8 |
| 9:18 | De paen vii, 7; Ex in ps ix, 8 |
| 9:19-20 | Ex in ps ix, 8 |
| 10:1-3 | Ex in ps ix, 9; x, 1 |
| 10:4 | Ex in ps ix, 9; x, 1; In Acta xxxix, 3 |
| 10:5 | Ex in ps ix, 9; x, 2; In Col ii, 6 (1:15); |

| | |
|---|---|
| 10:6 | Ex in ps ix, 10; x, 2 |
| 10:7 | Ex in ps ix, 10; x, 2; F Iob 4:1; In Acta vii 3 (2:47) |
| 10:8 | Ex in ps ix, 10; x, 2 |
| 10:9-10 | Ex in ps ix, 10 |
| 10:11 | Ex in ps ix, 11-18 |
| 10:13 | In Heb vi, 4 |
| 10:16 | De ss B et P 1 |
| 10:17 | In Eph xxiv, 1 (6:17) |
| 11:5 | In Heb xxv, 5; In Ioh xlix, 3 |
| 11:7 | In Ioh xlix, 3 |
| 12:1 | Ex in ps xi, 1; cxix, 3 |
| 12:2 | De proph obscur ii, 7; Ex in ps xi, 1; In Eph xiv, 1 (4:27) |
| 12:3 | Ex in ps xi, 1; In Eph xiv, 3 (4:29) |
| 12:4 | Ex in ps xi, 1; In Heb vi, 4 |
| 12:6 | Adu Iud 5, 1, 1; Ex in ps xi, 2; In il Prop 1; In il Uidi dom ii, 2 |
| 12:7 | Ex in ps xi, 9 |
| 12:8 | Ex in ps xi, 9; cxxxvii, 1 |
| 13:1 | De incomp dei v, 5; Ex in ps xii, 1; In Acta xxxix, 3 |
| 13:2 | Ex in ps viii, 4 |
| 13:3 | Ad Stel de comp ii, 7; In Acta xxxvii, 3 (17:15) |
| 13:4 | Ex in ps xii, 1 |
| 14:1 | In Col ix, 1 (3:17); In Eph xiii, 1 (4:19); In Heb vi, 4; In il Dom non est 2; In Rom xx, 4 (12:3) |
| 14:2 | In 2 Cor iii, 6; In Heb v, 5; In il Fil 3 |
| 14:6 | Ad pop Anti iv, 11 |
| 15:3 | Ex in ps iv, 5; F Iob 30:1; In kal 4 |
| 15:4 | In Col ix, 2 (3:17); In 1 Cor xxix, 9 |
| 15:5 | F Ier 12:1 |
| 16:2 | Ad pop Anti x, 8; In Eph xix, 3 (5:21); In Heb xxix, 3; In 1 Tim xvi, 2 (6:2); In 2 Tim ii, 2 (1:18) |
| 16:4 | In Heb xiv, 8 |
| 16:10 | Con Iud et gen 5; In 1 Cor xxxviii, 4; In il Pater s p 2 |
| 17:3-4 | In Heb xiv, 8 |
| 17:8 | De pet mat 1; In Is vi, 3 |
| 17:10 | In princ Act iv, 4 |
| 18:1 | In Eph iii, 1 (1:22) |
| 18:5 | In Acta v, 4 (2:20) |
| 18:6 | In Ioh xxvi, 1 |

| | |
|---|---|
| 18:7 | In Acta xi, 2 (4:32) |
| 18:9 | In Heb xxxii, 3 |
| 18:11 | De ss mar A 1 |
| 18:13 | In Ioh xlv, 1 |
| 18:22 | In 2 Thess ii, 3 (1:8) |
| 18:24 | In Eph i, 2 (1:4); In Heb xxxiv, 6 |
| 18:42 | Ad pop Anti ii, 26 |
| 18:43-44 | In Ioh ix, 1 |
| 18:45 | Con Iud et gen 8; In 1 Cor xv, 10; In Ioh ix, 1; In Is ii, 3 |
| 18:46 | F Ier 2:21 |
| 18:47 | Con Iud et gen 11 |
| 19:1 | Ad pop Anti ix, 4; x, 8; xii, 4; Ex in ps xlix 6; cx, 6; cxliv, 1; cxlv, 3; cxlviii, 1; In 1 Cor ii, 9; In 2 Cor xxi, 4; In il Is Ego 1:2; In Mat xxii, 1; In Rom iii, 2 (1:20) xviii, 5-6 (11:6); xxviii, 2 (15:13); In s Iul 2 |
| 19:2 | Ex in ps cxliv, 1; In 2 Cor xxi, 4; In il Is Ego 1 |
| 19:3 | Ad e q scan v; Ad pop Anti ix, 5; H hab p p Gothus 1; In il Is Ego 1; In Rom xxviii, 2 (15:13) |
| 19:4 | Con Iud et gen 6; F Prou 9:3; H hab p p Gothus 1; In Mat xxv, 3; In princ Act iii, 1; In Rom xviii, 2 (10:18); In 1 Tim xi, 2 (3:16) |
| 19:5 | Ad e q scan vii; In 1 Cor xxiv, 7; In Eph viii 8 (4:2); In Gen vi, 3; In Hen xiv, 6 |
| 19:6 | Ad e q scan vii; Ad pop Anti x, 8; In Gen vi, 3; Ex in ps cx, 6 |
| 19:8 | Ex in ps cx, 6; In Is ii, 5 |
| 19:9 | In Gen xxii, 6 |
| 19:10 | De inani gloria 28; In Gen xiv, 1; In Ioh i, 5; In Phil x, 5 (3:7) |
| 21:18 | In 1 Cor xxxviii, 3 |
| 22 (p) | In Gen xxxiv, 6 |
| 22:1 | De Anna iv, 4; In il Pater s p 2; In Mat lxxxviii; S anti iret 1 |
| 22:5 | Ad Stel de comp ii, 7 |
| 22:6 | In Mat lxxii, 4 |
| 22:13 | In 2 Tim viii, 1 (3:4) |
| 22:16 | De consub 5; In Gen x, 4; In il Pater s p 1; In Ioh xii, 3; In Mat xxxvi, 3 |
| 22:17 | Con Iud et gen 4; In il Pater s p 1 |
| 22:18 | Con Iud et gen 4; In Gen x, 4; In il Pater s p1; In Ioh xiii, 3; In Mat xxxvi, 3 |
| 22;22 | In d P Nolo 3; In Heb iv, 5 |
| 22:30 | In Ioh xxvi, 2 |
| 23:1 | In Heb x, 7 |
| 23:2 | In Phil vi, 6 (2:8) |

23:4 Ex in ps cix, 3; In Heb iv, 7; In Mat liv, 8
In Phil iii, 4 (1:24); In 1 Tim xiv, 4 (5:10)
23:5 De res d n I C 21; In Mat lxx, 2
24:1 De paen ii, 3; v, 3; E xxv; In Col vi, 2 (2:
10); In Eut ii, 2; In Hen xxvi, 2; S cum iret
1
24:2 Ad pop Anti ix, 7; ix, 8; In Rom xxviii, 2
(15:13)
24:6 In Mat lxxvii, 1
24:7 Con Iud et gen 5; De san pent i, 5
24:8 F Prou 20:9; In Mat xix, 12
25:7 In Heb vii, 8
25:8 In Ioh xiv, 2
25:14 In Phil xiv, 3 (4:9)
25:17 Ad Stag a dae iii, 14; In Mat ix, 2
25:18 In 2 Cor xxiii, 7; In Heb v, 6; In Mat ix, 2
25:19 In 2 Cor xxiii, 7; In Heb v, 6
26:4 Ex in ps iv, 13; cxl, 7; In Col ix, 2 (3:17)
26:6 De sac iv, 5; F Iob 9:31
26:10 Ad pop Anti iv, 11
27:1 In 1 Cor xli, 9; In 2 Cor i, 3
27:2 In Rom viii, 8 (4:21)
30:5 Ex in ps cxl, 1
30:6 In Acta xvi, 3 (7:34)
30:12 In Rom xix, 1 (11:8)
31:22 F Ier 12:1
32:1 In Ioh xxvi, 2; In Rom xi, 5 (6:18)
32:4 In Heb x, 2
32:5 De diab tent ii, 6; In Heb ix, 8; xxi, 8; In
Ioh vii, 2
32:7 In Heb iv, 7
32:10 In Rom xxviii, 3 (15:13)
33:6 Ex in ps cxiii, 6; In princ Act ii, 1
33:9 In Rom xxviii, 2 (15:13); S Gen i, 2
33:12 Ad pop Anti xviii, 10
33:15 Ad Stag a dae i, 9; De pane iv, 4; F Iob 1:8
In Col ii, 5 (1:15); In Gen xvii, 2; In Ioh
xxiv, 1; In Rom xxvi, 3 (14:23)
33:16 Ex in ps vii, 2; cxliii, 1; In Is ii, 7; In
Rom xxviii, 3 (15:13)
33:17 Ex in ps cxliii, 1
33:19 In 2 Cor iv, 7
33:22 In Phil iii, 1 (1:20)
34:3 In 2 Cor ii, 6
34:6 F Iob 35:10
34:7 In Eph ix, 2 (4:3)
34:8 In Eph xviii, 2 (5:14); In Rom xxiii, 5 (13:
10)
34:10 De bap Chris 1

34:11 In Heb viii, 10; In Ioh lviii, 5; In Is i, 6
34:12 In Heb viii, 10
34:13 In Heb i, 4; viii, 10; In Mat x, 7
34:14 Ex in ps iv, 8; In Heb viii, 10; In Mat x, 7
34:18 In il Uidi dom vi, 2; In Mat xlvii, 4
34:19 In Rom xxviii, 3 (15:13)
34:21 Ad pop Anti v, 7; De coem et de cr 1; De s Dros 6; Ex in ps cx, 2; H in san pascha 1; In Gen lxvi, 1; In il Is Ego 4; In Rom xxviii, 3 (15:13)
35:13 F Peou 16:33
35:15 In Ioh li, 2
36:1 In Eph xiii, 1 (4:19); In Heb vi, 4
36:2 In Heb vi, 4
36:6 Ad Stag a dae i, 7 (2x); Ex in ps cxlvi, 1; In 1 Cor xxix, 7; In 2 Tim iii, 2 (1:18)
36:7 In Phil iv, 5 (1:30)
36:8 In Gen xxix, 4
36:9 F Prou 7:18; In Rom xv, 3 (8:34)
37:1 Ex in ps cxl, 5; In Col ix, 2 (3:17); In 1 Cor xv, 12; In 2 Tim viii, 3 (3:14)
37:2 In 1 Cor xv, 12; In Eut i, 4
37:4 In Ioh xxii, 3; In Rom xxiii, 5 (13:10)
37:5 De diab tent i, 1; In Heb xxx, 6
37:10 In Acta iii, 5 (1:26)
37:20 In 1 Cor xxxix, 3
37:25 In Acta xxiii, 4 (10:43)
37:27 Cat ill i, 26; F Ier 4:3; In Gen ix, 6; In Ioh lxxiii, 3
37:35 Ex in ps iii, 1; F Ier 12:2; In Col ix, 2 (3:17)
37:36 Ex in ps cxl, 8
38:3 In Ioh xli, 2
38:4 Cat ill vi, 22; x, 17; De paen v, 3; De proph obscur ii, 9; Ex in ps cxl, 3; H in il App 8
38:5 Cat ill vi, 22; x, 17; In Acta x, 5 (4:22); In Col ix, 1 (3:17); In 1 Cor xliv, 5; In Eph xxiv, 5 (6:24); In Ioh lii, 4; lxxiii, 3; In 1 Tim ii, 3 (1:11)
38:6 Ex in ps cxl, 3; H in il App 8
38:7 In Col ix, 2 (3:17); In heb v, 8
38:11 In Mat xv, 5
38:12 E ccxxxiii; In Gen xxix, 1
38:13-16 In Gen xxix, 1
39:1-3 E iii, 5
39:4 E iii, 5; In Ioh l, 3
39:5 In 1 Thess vii, 3 (4:15)
39:6 Ad pop Anti ii, 13; Ex in ps cxv, 4; In x Cor

| | |
|---|---|
| 39:6 cont | xxix, 6; In Eph xii, 1 (4:17) |
| 39:7 | In 1 Cor x, 6 |
| 39:9 | In 2 Tim viii, 1 (3:5) |
| 39:10 | F Ier 8:22 |
| 39:11 | In Ioh lxv, 3 |
| 39:12 | In Heb xxiv, 4; xxiv, 6; In Mat lxiv, 5 |
| 39:13 | Ad Stag a dae iii, 14 |
| 40:1 | In Heb xi, 7 |
| 40:2 | In 2 Tim ix, 3 (4:8) |
| 40:5 | Adu Iud 7, 2, 4; 7, 2, 6; 7, 2, 7 |
| 40:6 | Adu Iud 7, 2, 4; 7, 2, 6; 7, 2, 7; 7, 4, 1; Con Iud et gen 8 (2x); Ex in ps xliii, 4; In Heb xv, 5 |
| 40:7 | Adu Iud 7, 2, 0; 7, 3, 1; Con Iud et gen 8; In Heb xi, 5 |
| 40:8-9 | Adu Iud 7, 3, 1 |
| 40:10 | In Ioh li, 1 |
| 40:17 | Ex in ps ix, 4 |
| 41:1 | Ex in ps xlviii, 3 |
| 41:9 | Con Iud et gen 4; Ex in ps xlviii, 3; In il Pater s p 2; In Ioh xiii, 3 |
| 42:1 | Ad Stel de comp ii, 3; Ex in ps cxlix, 1; In Gal v, 5 (5:17) |
| 42:2 | Ex in ps cxxi, 1; cxlix, 1 (3x); In Gen xxx, 6 |
| 42:4 | Ex in ps cxxi, 1 |
| 42:5 | In Gen xxix, 1; In Rom xxviii, 3 (15:13) |
| 42:6 | Ex in ps cxxi, 1; In Gen xxix, 1; In Heb xxvi, 6 |
| 42:10 | In Heb xxi, 1 |
| 43:4 | In 1 Cor ii, 2 |
| 43:5 | Ad Stag a dae iii, 14 |
| 44:1 | Ex in ps xliii, 1 |
| 44:2 | Ex in ps xliii, 3 |
| 44:3 | Ex in ps xliii, 1 |
| 44:4 | Ex in ps xliii, 5 |
| 44:5-10 | Ex in ps xliii, 6 |
| 44:11-13 | Ex in ps xliii, 7 |
| 44:14 | Ex in ps xliii, 2; xliii, 7 |
| 44:15-16 | Ex in ps xliii, 7 |
| 44:17 | Ex in ps xliii, 7; F Iob 13:5; In Rom xviii, 3 (15:13) |
| 44:18-20 | Ex in ps xliii, 8 |

| | |
|---|---|
| 44:21 | Ex in ps xliii, 8; F Prou 9:2; In Gen xvii, 2; In Rom xv, 4 (8:36) |
| 44:22 | De res mort 4; Ex in ps xliii, 8; In Acta xxvi, 2 (12:17); In Ioh lxxxii, 1; In Rom xxviii, 2 (15;13); In 1 Thess xiv, 4 (5:10) |
| 44:23 | De pet mat 1; Ex in ps xliii, 8; F Ier 1:12; In Eut ii, 7 |
| 44:26-36 | Ex in ps xliii, 9 |
| 45:1 | Ad pop Anti iv, 11 (2x); Cat ill iii, 20; Ex in ps xliv, 1; cxlv, 2; In il Prop 1; In Is i, 1 |
| 45:2 | Con Iud et gen 4; Ex in ps xliv, 2; In Mat xxvii, 3 |
| 45:3 | Ex in ps xli, 4; xliv, 4 |
| 45:4 | Ex in ps xli, 4; xliv, 4; xliv, 5 |
| 45:5 | Ex in ps xliv, 4 |
| 45:6 | De incomp dei v, 3; Ex in ps vii, 6; xliv, 7; cix, 3 |
| 45:7 | Ex in ps xliv, 7; cix, 1 |
| 45:8 | Ex in ps xliv, 4; xliv, 9; In 1 Cor xx, 6 |
| 45:9 | Cat ill xi, 7 (2x); Ex in ps v, 2; xliv, 10 |
| 45:10 | Cat ill i, 6; i, 8; i, 10; De Chris diuin 5; Ex in ps xliv, 10; In 2 Cor xxiii, 1; In Eph xx, 5 (5:33); In Eut ii, 9; ii, 14; In Heb xiv, 8; In il Ut sus 1; In Mat xxx, 6; lii, 1; Q reg 9 |
| 45:11 | Cat ill i, 6; i, 8; i, 10; Ex in ps xliv, 10; In 2 Cor xxiii, 1; In Eph i, 3 (1:6); xx, 5 (5:33); In Heb xiv, 8 (2x); xxviii, 15; In Mat iii, 5 |
| 45:12 | Ad Theo i, 13; Ex in ps xliv, 10; In Mat iii, 5; xxxiv, 5 |
| 45:13 | Cat ill xi, 8; De uir vi, Ex in ps xliv, 12; H in il App 26; In Heb xxviii, 12 (2x); In il Sal P et A i, 3; In princ Act iii, 5; S cum pres 3 |
| 45:14 | Con Iud et gen 7; Ex in ps xliv, 12 |
| 45:15 | Ex in ps xliv, 12 |
| 45:16 | Con Iud et gen 6; Ex in ps xliv, 12; In Acta v, 2 (2:20) |
| 45:17 | Con Iud et gen 6; Ex in ps xliv, 13 |
| 46:1 | Ex in ps xlv, 1 |
| 46:2 | De paen vii, 4 |
| 46:3 | Ex in ps xlv, 1 |
| 46:4 | De ter motu; Ex in ps xlv, 1 |
| 46:5 | Ex in ps xlv, 1 |
| 46:6-9 | Ex in ps xlv, 2 |

| | |
|---|---|
| 46:10 | De bap Chris 1; Ex in ps xlv, 3 |
| 46:11 | Ex in ps xlv, 3 |
| 47:1 | Ex in ps xlvi, 1; xlvii, 1 |
| 47:3 | Ex in ps xlvii, 1 |
| 47:4 | Ex in ps xlvi, 4 |
| 47:5 | De proph obscur ii, 2; Ex in ps xlvi, 2; xlvi, 4; In il Pater s p 2 |
| 47:6, 9 | Ex in ps xlvi, 5 |
| 48:1 | In Phil vi, 2 (2:8) |
| 48:4-6 | Ex in ps xlvii, 2 |
| 48:7 | De incomp dei v, 5; Ex in ps xlvii, 2 |
| 48:9 | Ex in ps xlvii, 2 |
| 48:10 | Ex in ps xlvii, 2; In 2 Tim iii, 2 (1:18) |
| 48:10 | Ex in ps xlvii, 2 |
| 48:11-14 | Ex in ps xlvii, 3 |
| 49:1 | Ex in ps xlviii, 1 |
| 49:3-4 | Ad pop Anti Ad pop Anti iv, 11; Ex in ps xlviii, 2 |
| 49:5 | Ex in ps xlviii, 3 |
| 49:6 | Ad pop Anti ii, 13; Ad Theo ii, 3; Ex in ps xlviii, 2; In Is ii, 7; In Rom xxviii, 3 (15:13) |
| 49:7 | De Laz iii, 9; vi, 1; Ex in ps xlviii, 4; In Gen xliii, 1; In Heb i, 4; xxi, 6; In Ioh xii 3; xxi, 3; In Mat v, 7 |
| 49:8 | Ex in ps xlviii, 4; In Heb xxxi, 8; In Rom v, 6 (2:16) |
| 49:9-10 | Ex in ps xlviii, 5 |
| 49:11 | De paen iii, 1; Ex in ps xlviii, 5 |
| 49:12 | Ad Stel de comp ii, 5; E vii, 3; Ex in ps xlviii, 6; In Gen xii, 3 |
| 49:13 | Ex in ps xlviii, 8 |
| 49:14 | Ex in ps xlviii, 9 |
| 49:15 | De coem et de cr 1; Ex in ps xlviii, 10; In Rom xxviii, 2 (15:13); In 1 Tim xiv, 4 (5:10) |
| 49:16 | De fate et pr iv; Ex in ps xlviii, 10; In 1 Cor xxix, 9; In Gen xxiii, 1; xxix, 1; In il Ne tim i, 1; i, 2; ii, 1; In 1 Tim xiv, 4 (5:10) |
| 49:17 | De fate et pr iv (2x); Ex in ps xlvii, 1; In Col ix, 2 (3:17); In Gen xxix, 1; In Rom xxvii, 3 (15:13); In 1 Tim ii, 2 (1:11); xviii, 2 (6:21) |
| 49:18-19 | Ex in ps xlviii, 11 |

49:20 De fate et pr 1; Ex in ps xlviii, 11; In ascen d n I C 3; In 1 Cor ix, 10; xvi, 8
50:1-2 Ex in ps xlix, 1
50:3 Con Iud et gen 8 (2x); Ex in ps xlix, 1; In Heb xxiii, 8; In 1 Thess ix, 5 (5:11)
50:4 Con Iud et gen 8; In Is i, 4
50:5 Con Iud et gen 8 (2x); Ex in ps xlix, 3
50:6 Con Iud et gen 8 (2x); In Eph xiii, 2 (4:22)
50:7 Ex in ps xlix, 4
50:8 Ex in ps xlix, 4; In Is i, 4; In Mat xxx, 3
50:9 Adu Iud 7, 3, 4; 7, 3, 6; Ex in ps xlix, 4; In Is i, 4; In Mat xxx, 3
50:10-11 Ex in ps xlix, 4; In Mat xxx, 3
50:12 Ex in ps vii, 15; xlix, 4; In Mat xxx, 3 (2x)
50:13 F Iob 1:1; In Mat xxx, 3; In Phil xv, 3 (4:18) In Rom xx, 1 (12:1)
50:14 Ex in ps xlix, 5; In Heb xi, 5; In Mat xvi, 12; xxx, 3; In Rom xx, 1 (12:1)
50:15 In Mat xxx, 3
50:16 In Acta xxx, 3 (14:15); In il Sal P et A ii, 5; In il Si esur 4; In Ioh lxxxiii, 5; In Is i, 5; In Rom vi, 6 (3:8)
50:17 Ex in ps xlix, 6; In il Si esur 4
50:18 Adu Iud 1, 4, 10; De fato et pr iii; Ex in ps xlix, 7; In Is i, 5
50:19 Ex in ps xlix, 7
50:20 De uir xxi; Ex in ps xlix, 7; In 1 Cor xliv, 7 (2x); In Gen xv, 5; In Heb xxi, 7; In il Sal P et A ii, 5; In Ioh lxxxiii, 5; In Is i, 5
50:21 In Ioh lxxiii, 3; In Is i, 6
50:22 Ex in ps xlix, 11; In Is i, 6
50:23 Ex in ps xlix, 11; cxii, 1; In Heb xi, 5; In Mat xvi, 12; In Rom xx, 1 (12:1)
51:1 De paen vii, 4; In Eph iv, 1 (2:4); In Heb xxxii, 7; In Ioh lx, 4
51:4 De paen iii, 4; In Ioh lvi, 1; In Mat xxxvii, 5; In Rom vi, 5 (3:4)
51:6 De incomp dei i, 4; In 1 Cor xliv, 5
51:9 De san pent i, 5
51:10 In Heb xii, 7
51:11 De Chris pec 4; In 2 Cor vii, 5; In Heb ii, 2; xii, 7; In 2 Tim vi, 4 (2:26); In Tit iii, 2 (2:1)
51:16 Ex in ps xliii, 4; In Heb xviii, 1; In Phil v, 2 (2:4)
51:17 De mut nom iv, 6; De paen iv, 4; Ex in ps cxlvi, 1; In 1 Cor i, 4; In 2 Cor iv, 7; In Gen ix, 5; In Heb ix, 8; xi, 5; In il Uidi

51:17 cont dom i, 3; In Mat xv, 2; xlvii, 4; lxv, 6; In Phil v, 2 (2:4); In Rom xx, 1 (12:1); xxxii, 3 (16:24); In 2 Thess i, 2
52:8 De Mac i, 3; In Eph xxiv, 5 (6:24); In Heb xxxii, 8
53:1 In Mat lxxi, 1
53:5 In Eph xii, 3 (4:17); In Ioh xxvi, 2
53:6 In Col x, 2 (4:1)
55:11 In Acta vii, 3 (2:47)
55:12 In Heb xxi, 1; In il Hab iii, 5; S post red ii, 5
55:13 In il Hab iii, 5
55:15 In Eph xx, 6 (5:33)
55:17 Ex in ps cxl, 1
55:23 Ad uid iun 6; In 1 Cor xvi, 11; In Gen xxix,1
57:1 In il Uidi dom iii, 2
57:4 Ad pop Anti iv, 11; De proph obscur ii, 7; In Mat lxxxi, 3
58:3 In ascen d n I C 3
58:4 Ad pop Anti iv, 11; Ex in ps xlviii, 8
58:5 F Ier 9:17; In Gen xxiii, 4
58:6 In Mat lvi, 8
58:10 In Philem iii, 2 (v25)
60:12 In Ioh v, 3
60:14 F Prou 5:5
62:1 In 1 Cor ii, 2
62:3 In Phil vi, 3 (2:8); In 2 Tim ix, 3 (4:8)
62:10 In Col ix, 2 (3:17); S anti iret 5
62:12 In Col ix, 2 (3:17); In Ioh xxviii, 1
63:1 De Anna iv, 4; Ex in ps vii, 3; xli, 3; cxl, 1; cxlv, 2; cxlix, 1; In Gal ii, 7 (2:20)
63:2 Ex in ps cxl, 1
63:6 In Heb xiv, 9
63:7 In Acta xxvi, 4 (12:17)
63:8 Ad Stel de comp ii, 3
64:5 In 1 Tim i, 1 (1:2)
64:7-8 De s Bab 2; E cxciv
65:9 De ter mort; In Heb x, 2
66:1 In il Uidi dom i, 3
68:1 Ex in ps xliv, 5; In Is ii, 8
68:5 Ad uid iun 1; Cat ill vi, 12; De paen vii, 3; In 1 Cor xli, 9; In 1 Tim xv, 1 (5:15)
68:6 In 1 Tim xiv, 4 (5:10)
68:8 In Acta xi, 2 (4:32)
68:11 Ex in ps cxlvii, 4; S cum pres 1
68:12 In Rom i, 1 (1:2)
68:13 In Heb xxxii, 7
68:17 De ss mar A 1
68:18 Cat ill x, 14; Ex in ps xlvi, 2; In Eph xi, 2

| | |
|---|---|
| 68:18 cont | (4:8); In Mat xix, 12 |
| 69:1 | In 2 Tim ix, 3 (4:8) |
| 69:2 | F Prou 1:5 |
| 69:5 | De paen vii, 7 |
| 69:9 | Con Iud et gen 4; Ex in ps cxii, 2; In ascen d n I C 2; In Ioh xv, 3; xxiii, 2; In Rom xiv, 8 (8:27); xxvii, 2 (15:3) |
| 69:11 | In il Pater s p 1 |
| 69:13 | F in epis cath James 2:13 |
| 69:14 | F Prou 1:5 |
| 69:16 | In Eph iv, 1 (2:4) |
| 69:20 | E viii; In Phil viii, 3 (2:16) |
| 69:21 | In Ioh xiii, 3; In Mat xxxvi, 3; lxxxvii, 1 |
| 69:25 | Ex in ps cviii, 2; In Acta iii, 2 (1:20) |
| 69:28 | De san pent i, 5 |
| 69:30-31 | Ex in ps xlix, 5; cxii, 1; cxxxiv, 1; In Rom xx, 1 (12:1); S cum pres 1 |
| 71:7 | In 1 Cor xxxvi, 2 |
| 72:5 | Ex in ps cix, 7; In Is ii, 1 |
| 72:6 | Con Iud et gen 3; Ex in ps xliv, 5; xlix, 2; In il Pater s p 3; In Mat liii, 3 |
| 72:7 | In Mat v, 5 |
| 72:17 | Ex in ps cix, 7; In Is ii, 1 |
| 72:18 | Cat ill iii, 5; iii, 6 |
| 73:2 | Ad Stag a dae i, 7; Ex in ps vii, 9; cxv, 3 |
| 73:3 | Ad Stag a dae i, 7; Ex in ps cxv, 3 |
| 73:4 | Ad Stag a dae i, 7 |
| 73:5 | Ad Stag a dae i, 7; De uir xxiv |
| 73:6 | An Acta xvi, 3 (7:34); In Col ix, 2 (3:17) |
| 73:7 | In Col ix, 2 (3:17) |
| 73:12-13,15 | Ex in ps cxv, 3 |
| 73:16 | Ad Stag a dae i, 7; Ex in ps cxv, 3 |
| 73:17 | Ex in ps cxv, 3 |
| 73:18 | Ad pop Anti xvii, 1 |
| 73:23 | In Rom ix, 4 (5:11) |
| 73:25 | Ad Stag a dae iii, 14; In Rom v, 7 (2:16) |
| 73:27 | Ad Stag a dae i, 6; Ex in ps iii, 1; In Col ix, 2 (3:17); In 1 Cor vii, 7; In Ioh lxviii, 2; In Phil xi, 5 (3:12) |
| 74:12 | Ex in ps cxxxiv, 5 |
| 74:13-14 | In Phil vi, 5 (2:8) |
| 74:16 | Ex in ps cxl, 1 |
| 74:17 | In 1 Tim xv, 4 (5:20) |
| 75:10 | De Anna iv, 3 |
| 76;9 | In Mat xlvii, 4 |
| 76:10 | De dec mil 5 |

77:2 In Heb xxii, 6
77:8 Ex in ps cxlii, 4
77:10 De paen vii, 2; H in poen Nin
77:13 In Mat xxxvii, 3
78:2 Con Iud et gen 4; Ex in ps xlviii, 3; In Mat xlvii, 1
78:12 F Iob 21:7
78:15 Ad pop Anti viii, 3
78:20 In Mat xlix, 2
78:24 Ad pop Anti x, 8; Adu Iud 6, 2, 7; In 1 Cor xxxiv, 10
78:25 Adu Iud 6, 2, 7
78:30 Ad Stag a dae iii, 4; In Col ix, 2 (3:17)
78:33 In Acta xxix, 4 (13:41); In 2 Cor xxii, 4; In kal 3
78:34 Ad pop Anti xvii, 2; Ad Stag a dae i, 3; Cat ill v, 17; De diab tent i, 5; De paen iv, 2; Ex in ps ix, 3; ix, 7; In Acta xli, 3; In Gen ix, 6; In Heb xxxiii, 8
78:49 In 2 Cor ii, 10
78:50 In Acta xliii, 3
79:3 In Mat xvii, 4
80:8 In Mat xliv, 4
80:12 In Eph v, 2 (2:15); In Mat iii, 4; In Phil vi, 4 (2:8)
80:13 In Phil vi, 4 (2:8)
80:16 Ad pop Anti ii, 22
81:5 In Ioh xl, 3
81:7, 10 In Col vi, 1 (2:8)
81:16 Ad pop Anti ii, 22; Q nemo 8
82 (p) De consub 2
82:1 Ex in ps xlix, 1
82:6 De consub 2; Ex in ps iv, 5; xi, 3; xlix, 1 (2x); In Acta xxxii, 3 (15:11); In Eut ii, 8; In Gen xxii, 2; In Ioh iii, 2; xiv, 2; In Rom xiv, 2 (8:14)
82:7 Ex in ps iv, 5
82:8 In Heb vii, 6; In Is ii, 8
83:2 Ex in ps cxliii, 1
83:4 F Ier 12:2
83:10 In Gen xxxiii, 2
83:18 De incomp dei v, 2 (2x); De s h Phoc 3
84:2 In Gal v, 5 (5:17)
84:7 De paen vii, 2
84:10 De mut nom iv, 1; In Mat iv, 18
86:8 In Ioh lxiv, 2; In Mat xxxvii, 3
86:10 In Phil vi, 2 (2:8)
86:13 H in sanc pascha 1

| | |
|---|---|
| 86:17 | In 1 Cor xxxvi, 2 |
| 87:5 | S cum iret 1 |
| 88:5 | Con Iud et gen 5; In il Pater 2 |
| 88:11 | In Acta xix, 5 (9:9) |
| 89:7 | De paen vii, 2 |
| 90:2 | Ex in ps cix, 7; In Col v, 1 (1:28); In 1 Cor xxxix, 8; In Heb ii, 2; In Ioh iv, 3; In Mat v, 5 |
| 90:10 | Ad Stag a dae iii, 9; De Laz iii, 9; In Acta vii, 3 (2:47); In Heb xxi, 6 |
| 91:2 | De Anna iv, 4; In Eph ix, 2 (4:3) |
| 91:5-6 | In 1 Tim xiv, 4 (5:10) |
| 91:13 | Ex in ps vii, 3 |
| 92:4 | Ex in ps xli, 2 |
| 92:5 | De Anna i, 2; Ex in ps xlvi, 3 |
| 92:15 | F Ier 6:28 |
| 94:7 | In Heb vi, 4 |
| 94:11 | In quat Laz A 1 |
| 94:12 | Ad pop Anti xviii, 10; H in il App 19; In Ioh lviii, 5; In Phil xv, 5 (4:23) |
| 94:19 | Ad pop Anti xiv, 1 |
| 95:2 | De paen vii, 5; vii, 6; In Acta xxxvi, 3 (16:39); In 1 Cor xxiii, 7; In 2 Cor ix, 4; In Heb xxi, 6; In Mat xiv, 6 |
| 95:4 | Ad pop Anti ix, 8; Ex in ps vii, 11; ix, 6; In il Pater s p 3; In Ioh vi, 1 |
| 95:5 | De paen ii, 3 |
| 95:7 | In Mat lxxxvi, 4; In Rom xxviii, 3 (15:13) |
| 95:8 | Cat ill xii, 3; De paen i, 4; Ex in ps cxlii, 5; In Rom xxviii, 5 (15:13) |
| 95:9 | Ad Theo i, 6; Ex in ps cxlii, 5 |
| 95:10 | Adu Iud 6, 2, 7 |
| 96:5 | In princ Act i, 4 |
| 96:10 | In Ioh xxxix, 4 |
| 97:2 | Ex in ps xliv, 8; In Acta ii, 3 (1:11); In Mat lvi, 5 |
| 97:3 | In Heb xxiii, 8 |
| 97:7 | Ex in ps cxl, iii, 1 |
| 98:9 | Ex in ps xlvi, 1 |
| 101:1 | In Is i, 6 |
| 101:5 | Ad pop Anti iii, 14; De proph obscur ii, 9; In Col ix, 2 (3:17); In 1 Cor xliv, 7; In Gen xv, 5; xlii, 3; In quat Laz A 1 |
| 101:6 | In Col ix, 2 (3:17) (2x); In Mat xlvii, 4; In 1 Tim xi, 3 (3:16) |
| 101:7 | In Col ix, 2 (3:17) |
| 102:3 | In Mat ii, 9 |
| 102:4 | In Eut i, 4 |
| 102:6 | In 1 Tim xi, 1 (3:16) |
| 102:9 | In Heb ix, 8; In 1 Tim xiv, 4 (5:10) |

| | |
|---|---|
| 102:11 | In 2 Cor xxix, 6 |
| 102:14 | Ex in ps cxxi, 1 |
| 102:24 | F Prou 10:27 |
| 102:25 | Ad pop Anti x, 8; Ex in ps viii, 8; F Ier 10:11; In 1 Cor iv, 4; In Ioh v, 2; In Rom xiv, 5 (8:20) |
| 102:26 | Ad pop Anti x, 8; In Rom xiv, 5 (8:20); xxviii, 2 (15:13) |
| 102:27 | In 1 Cor xxxix, 8; In Ioh iv, 4; xi, 2; xxxviii, 4 |
| 103:1 | Ex in ps cxii, 5; cxlv, 2 |
| 103:2 | In 2 Cor iii, 5 |
| 103:4 | Ex in ps v, 6; In 2 Cor iii, 5; xx, 3 |
| 103:5 | In Heb ix, 5 |
| 103:6-7 | Ex in ps cxlvii, 2; In Eph v, 2 (2:15); In Ioh xiv, 2 |
| 103:8-9 | De ter motu |
| 103:11 | Ad e q scan vi; Ad Stag a dae i, 5; Ex in ps vii, 2; xli, 4; cxxix, 3; In Rom xxviii, 2 (15:13) |
| 103:12 | Ad e q scan vi; Ex in ps vii, 2; cxxix, 3; In Rom xxviii, 2 (15:13) |
| 103:13 | Ex in ps xli, 4; In Col x, 1 (4:1); In Rom xxviii, 2 (15:13) |
| 103:14 | De laud s Paul iii; In Rom xxviii, 2 (15:13) |
| 103:15 | Ad pop Anti i, 11; In il Uidi dom iv, 4; In Rom xxviii, 3 (15:13) |
| 103:20 | De laud s Paul i; Ex in ps xlv, 2; cxii, 2; cxlviii, 1; In Ioh iv, 1; xxxvi, 2; In Mat xix, 7; In Rom ix, 3 (5:11) |
| 103:22 | In Mat xix, 12 |
| 104:2 | Ex in ps ix, 3; H dicta p r m 1; In Eph xiii, 3 (4:24); In Heb xxvi, 8; In Rom xxviii, 2 (15:13) |
| 104:3 | In Acta ii, 2 (1:9); In Is vi, 3; In Mat lvi, 5; In Rom xxviii, 2 (15:13) |
| 104:4 | In Gen xxii, 2; xliii, 6; In Is vi, 2 |
| 104:2 | In princ Act ii, 1 |
| 104:12, 14 | In Rom xxviii, 2 (15:13) |
| 104:15 | In Eph xix, 1 (5:18); In Mat lvii, 5; In Rom xxviii, 2 (15:13) |
| 104:17-18 | In Rom xxviii, 2 (15:13) |
| 104:19 | Ex in ps cx, 2; In Rom xxviii, 2 (15:13) |
| 104:20 | De consub 7; Ex in ps cx, 2; cxlviii, 4; In Rom xxviii, 2 (15:13) |
| 104:21 | De consub 7; Ex in ps cxliv, 4 |
| 104:22 | De consub 7 |

104:23 In Gen xi, 1
104:24 Ad e q scan vii, Ad pop Anti x, 5; De diab tent ii, 3; Ex in ps cxlv, 3; cxxxv, 2; In Gen iv, 5; In il Is Ego 1
104:26 Ex in ps cxlviii, 2; In Phil vi, 4 (2:8); In 1 Tim xv, 4 (5:20) (2x)
104:27 Ex in ps cxlii, 2; In Rom xxviii, 2 (15:13)
104:28 Ex in ps cxlii, 2
104:29 Ex in ps cxlii, 2; In Rom xxviii, 2 (15:13)
104:30-31 Ex in ps cxlii, 2
104:32 De incomp dei ii, 3; Ex in ps vii, 11; xliv, 5; cxlii, 5 (2x); In Gen xxiii, 6; xxxvii, 2; In il Pater s p 31; In Is ii, 8; In Rom xxviii 2 (15:13); S anti iret 1
104:34 In Gen xxx, 5
105:15 Ex in ps xliv, 9; In Rom i, 1 (1:2)
105:17 In Rom xxv, 4 (14:15)
105:18 In Eph ix, 2 (4:3)
105:24 Ex in ps iii, 1
105:37 Adu Iud 5, 5, 2; Q nemo 13
106 (p) Ad pop Anti iii, 18
106:1 Non esse ad grat 4
106:2 Ad e q scan viii; De coem et de cr 2; Ex in ps xli, 4; H in san pascha 2; In Gen xiii, 2; In Mat lxxv, 3; lxxxii, 5; In Phil iv, 1 (1:26); In 1 Thess viii, 1 (4:18); In Tit v, 4 (3:6)
106:13 H in sn pascha 1
106:17-18 In il Uidi dom iv, 5; v, 2
106:24 In Eph xxiii, 2 (6:14)
106:30 Adu Iud 6, 3, 1; In Gen liii, 2
106:31 In Mat xvii, 5
106:32 In Eph vii, 4 (3:19)
106:36 In kal 6
106:37 Adu Iud 3, 3, 8; 6, 2, 6; De lib rep 2; De ss B et P 5; Ex in ps viii, 3; viii, 4; H hab p p Gothus 3; In il Fil 3; In Tit v, 4 (3:6)
106:38 Ex in ps viii, 3
107:16 Ad pop Anti vii, 1
107:25 In Mat xxviii, 1
107:27 In 1 Cor xliv, 5
107:37-38 In il Fil 3
108:1 In Eph xxiii, 2 (6:14)
109:1 Con Iud et gen 4; In Acta iii, 3 (1:26); vi, 3 (2:34)
109:4 In Gen xxix, 1; In 1 Tim vii, 1 (2:4)
109:5 F Iob 19:19

109:8-10 Con Iud et gen 4
109:18 In Eph xiii, 3 (4:24)
109:19 In Eph xxiv, 2 (6:22)
109:21 In Eph ii, 2 (1:14)
109:31 De paen vii, 7
110:1 Adu Iud 7, 4, 6; 7, 5, 1; Con Iud et gen 5; De proph obscur ii, 2; Ex in ps vii, 6; cix, 8; cxlv, 2; In Acta v, 2 (2:20); In ascen d n I C 3; In 1 Cor xx, 6; In Heb vii, 6; In il Pater s p 2; In Mat vii, 2; xxvi, 9; In 2 Tim iii, 2 (1:18)
110:2 Ex in ps cxxxiv, 4; In Acta xii, 3 (5:16); In 1 Cor iv, 10
110:3 Adu Iud 7, 5, 2; 7, 5, 9; Ex in ps cix, 8; In 2 Cor vii, 3
110:6 Ex in ps lix, 8
110:7 Ex in ps lix, 8; In Mat lxx, 2
112:1 Ad pop Anti xviii, 10
112:5 In Col ix, 2 (3:17)
112:8 In 1 Cor xxi, 10
112:9 Ad pop Anti xvi, 14; De paen vii, 7; De ss mar B; In Col ix, 2 (3:17); In Eph xii, 1 (4:17); In Eutii, 3; In Gen xxx, 2; lv, 5; In Heb xviii, 6; In s Luc 1
112:10 Ex in ps cxi, 6; In Acta xxix, 4 (13:41)
113:7-8 Ad Theo i, 1
113:9 Ad Theo i, 1; Ex in ps cxlii, 5
114:1 De glor in trib 2; Ex in ps cxlviii, 1
114:2 De glor in trib 2
114:3 De glor in trib 2; De incomp dei ii, 3; F Ier 14:21
114:4 De glor in trib 2; De incomp dei ii, 3; Ex in ps xlvi, 1; cxlviii, 1; In Phil iv, 2 (1:26)
115:3 In Col v, 3 (2:5)
115:11 Ex in ps cxvii, 4
115:14 S cum red i, 2
115:16 Ex in ps cxlvii, 1
116:7 De ss B et P 3; In Heb iv, 7; In Mat xxxi, 4; In Rom xxviii, 2 (15:13)
116:10 In 2 Cor ix, 2; In il Hab i, 1; i, 2; ii, 1; ii, 2; iii, 8; In Is vii, 4
116:11 F Ier 12:1
116:12 Ex in ps xli, 4
116:15 De coem et de cr 1; De s Dros 6; Ex in ps cx, 2; In Gen lxvi, 7; In il Is Ego 4; In Rom xxviii, 3 (15:13)
118 (p) In Gen xxxiv, 6
118:9 F Ier 44:29

118:15 In Heb xxxii, 6; In 1 Tim xiv, 4 (5:10)
118:22 Ex in ps cxvii, 1; In Acta x, 2 (4:11)
118:24 Ex in ps cxvii, 1
119:1 Ad pop Anti xvii, 10
119:11 De san pent i, 2
119:18 In Ioh xv, 1
119:30 Ad Stel de comp ii, 4
119:46 E cxxv; In Acta xvii, 3 (7:53); In Rom xxxii, 3 (16:24)
119:62 Ex in ps cxlv, 6; In Acta xxvi, 4 (12:71); In Gen xxx, 6; In 1 Tim xiv, 4 (5:10)
119:71 Ad pop Anti i, 15; Ad Stag a dae i, 3; Ex in ps ix, 7; cxiv, 2; cxxii, 1; cxli, 1; In Acta xvi, 3 (7:34); In Heb xxxiii, 8; In il Uidi dom iii, 5; In Mat x, 8; In Phil xv, 5 (4:19)
119:85 In Acta ii, 5 (1:11)
119:89 In 1 Cor xxxix, 8
119:91 In Rom i, 1 (1:2)
119:103 De inani gloria 28; Ex in ps cxi, 1; In Heb viii, 9; In il Prop 1; In Ioh i, 5; S Gen vii, 5; viii, 2
119:105 In Acta xxvi, 4 (12:17); In Is ii, 5; S Gen viii, 1
119:116 In Col ix, 2 (3:17)
119:120 In Ioh liv, 1; In 2 Tim ix, 3 (4:8)
119:125 In Tit i, 2 (1:5)
119:164 De Anna iv, 5; In 1 Tim xiv, 4 (5:10)
119:165 Ex in ps iv, 11
120:1 De incomp dei v, 6
120:5 In 1 Cor xxxiii, 5
120:6 In 1 Tim vii, 1 (2:4)
120:7 Con Iud et gen 4; In Phil xiv, 1 (4:9); In 1 Tim vii, 1 (2:4)
121:3-4 In Heb xii, 5
123:2 Ad Theo i, 1
123:3 Ad Theo i, 1; In Rom xvii, 4 (10:13)
124:1 Ad pop Anti viii, 4
125:1 In Is ii, 2
125:2 In Is v, 2
125:5 Ad pop Anti iv, 2
126:5-6 De Anna ii, 1; In Gen xxxii, 8; S post red ii, 3
127:1 De uir xxvii (2x); Ex in ps cxlii, 5; In 2 Cor ii, 9; In Gen xxx, 2; In Heb xxxi, 4; In il Dom non est 2; In 2 Tim iii, 1 (1:18)
127:5 Ex in ps cxxvii, 1
128:1 In Heb xx, 9
128:3 In Eph iii, 5 (1:22)
130:1 De incomp dei v, 7
130:3 Ad pop Anti xx, 3; Ad Stel de comp ii, 5; De

| | |
|---|---|
| 130:3 cont | diab tent i, 7; Ex in ps vi, 1; xli, 5; cx, 6; In Phil iv, 5 (1:30) |
| 130:6 | F Prou 4:23 |
| 131:1 | In Col ix, 2 (3:17); In il Uidi dom iii, 5; In Mat xix, 4 |
| 132:1 | Ex in ps xliv, 6; In Gen xxxiv, 1; In il Si esur 6 |
| 132:12 | In Heb xxvii, 4 |
| 133:1 | H dicta p r m 2; In Ioh xix, 1; In princ Act ii, 4 |
| 133:2 | H dicta p r m 2 |
| 134:3 | In 1 Tim xiv, 4 (5:10) |
| 135:4 | Ex in ps cxiii, 6 |
| 135:5 | Ex in ps cxxxv, 1 |
| 135:6 | De incomp dei ii, 4 |
| 136:6 | In Gen xii, 2 |
| 137:1 | Con Iud et gen 17; De prod Iud i, 5; ii, 5; In 1 Cor xxiii, 5 |
| 137:2 | Con Iud et gen 17; De prod Iud i, 5; ii, 5; In il Is Ego 6; In Rom vi, 6 (3:8) |
| 137:3 | Adu Iud 4, 5, 1; Con Iud et gen 17 |
| 137:4 | Adu Iud 4, 4, 9; 4, 5, 1; Con Iud et gen 17; In il Is Ego 6; In Rom vi, 6 (3:8) |
| 139:5 | De incomp dei i, 5; Ex in ps xliii, 3 |
| 139:6 | De incomp dei i, 5; Ex in ps cxlvi, 1 |
| 139:7 | Ad pop Anti v, 17; De paen v, 3; In Phil xi, 5 (3:12) |
| 139:8, 10 | De paen v, 3 |
| 139:12 | In 1 Cor xi, 6 |
| 139:13 | In Gen lvi, 3 |
| 139:14 | Adu Iud 1, 1, 1; De incomp dei i, 4; In 1 Cor x, 6 |
| 139:16 | Adu Iud 1, 1; De san pent i, 5 |
| 139:17 | In kal 4 |
| 139:19 | Ex in ps cxxxix, 2 |
| 139:21-22 | In 1 Cor xxxiii, 5 |
| 140:3 | Ad pop Anti xii, 6; De proph obscur ii, 7; Ex in ps xlviii, 8; In Gen xii, 3; xxiii, 4; xxx, 1; In Mat lxviii, 5 |
| 140:11 | In Acta xxix, 4 (13:41) |
| 141:2 | Ad pop Anti iv, 11; Cat ill ix, 32; In Heb xxii, 7; In Mat xvi, 12; lxxiii, 3 |
| 141:3 | Cat ill ix, 32; F Prou 13;3; In Gen xv, 5 |
| 141:10 | In Is ii, 7 |
| 142:1 | De s h Phoc 2 (3x); 3 |
| 143 (p) | In Gen xxxiv, 6 |
| 143:2 | Ad Stel de comp ii, 4; Ex in ps vi, 1; vii, 7; |

| | |
|---|---|
| 143:2 cont | cx, 6; In Phil iv, 5 (1:30); In Rom xxviii, 3 (15;13) |
| 143:6 | Ad Stel de comp ii, 3 |
| 143:7 | In Eph xi, 2 (4:10) |
| 144:4 | Ex in ps cxv, 3; In 1 Cor xii, 9; In il Uidi dom iv, 4; In 1 Tim xiv, 4 (5:10); In 2 Tim i, 3 (1:7) |
| 144:5 | In 1 Thess vii, 3 (4:15) |
| 144:11-14 | Ad pop Anti i, 22 |
| 144:15 | Ad pop Anti i, 22; Ex in ps cxl, 5; In Col ix, 2 (3:17) |
| 145:2 | Ex in ps cxlv, 1 |
| 145:3 | De incomp dei i, 4; Ex in ps cxlvi, 1; In Ioh iv, 1; In Phil vi, 2 (2:8) |
| 145:8 | In Heb xxxii, 7 |
| 145:9 | De paen vii, 2; In Heb xxxii, 7 |
| 145:13 | De paen vii, 7; Ex in ps xliv, 9 |
| 145:15 | De paen vii, 7; Ex in ps cxliv, 1 |
| 145:16 | De paen vii, 7; In Mat xxi, 5 |
| 145:18 | De b Phil 4; Ex in ps cxlii, 1 |
| 146:2 | Ex in ps cxlv, 2 |
| 146:4 | In Eph xiii, 2 (4:22) |
| 146:9 | Ad uid iun 1; In Heb xxxii, 7 |
| 147:3 | F Ier 10:19 |
| 147:5 | De incomp dei v, 2; De mut nom ii, 4; In Ioh iv, 1 |
| 147:9 | Ex in ps cxiii, 5; cxliv, 4; In Mat xxi, 5 |
| 147:12-14 | S Gen viii, 1 |
| 147:17 | Ex in ps vii, 11 |
| 147:19 | S Gen viii, 1 |
| 147:20 | In Eph vi, 2 (3:4); In Rom vi, 4 (3:1); S Gen viii, 1; viii, 2 |
| 148:1 | Ex in ps cxii, 1; In 1 Tim xiv, 4 (5:10); S cum pres 2; S Gen i, 2 |
| 148:2 | Ex in ps cxii, 1; cl, 1; In Ioh xv, 1 |
| 148:4 | Ad pop Anti ix, 8; In Gen iv, 3 |
| 148:5 | Con Iud et gen 15; S Gen i, 2 |
| 148:8 | Ex in ps cx, 2 |
| 148:9 | In Mat xxii, 1 |
| 148:10 | S cum pres 2 |
| 148:12 | In Mat v, 4 |
| 150 (p) | In Ps 145 ii |

Proverbs

| | |
|---|---|
| 1:6 | Ex in ps xlviii, 2; S Gen i, 1 |
| 1:7 | De inani gloria 85; In Ioh xli, 2 |

| | |
|---|---|
| 1:9 | In 2 Cor iii, 5; In Gen xlii, 1 |
| 2:4 | In Ioh xv, 1 (2x) |
| 2:6 | Ex in ps cxliii, 2 |
| 2:14 | Ex in ps cxxxix, 3 |
| 3:3 | In Eph xxiv, 5 (6:24); In Phil Introduction, 3 |
| 3:11 | Ad Stag a dae i, 6; In Phil xv, 5 (4:23) |
| 3:12 | Adu Iud 8, 7, 13; Ex in ps cx, 3 |
| 3:13 | In Ioh xv, 1 |
| 3:21 | In Heb iii, 5 |
| 3:27 | In Heb xxxii, 8 |
| 3:34 | In Col ix, 2 (3:17); In il Uidi dom iii, 4 |
| 4:9 | Ex in ps v, 6 |
| 4:18 | Ex in ps x, 3; In Ioh xiii, 4 |
| 4:27 | In 1 Thess ix, 4 (5:11) |
| 5:2 | In Mat lxxiii, 4 |
| 5:3 | Ad pop Anti xiv, 10; De inani gloria 2; In il Prop 5; In Mat lxxiii, 4; In princ Act iv, 1; In 1 Thess v, 3 (4:18) (2x) |
| 5:4 | Ad pop Anti xiv, 10; In il Prop 5; In Mat lxxiii, 4; In princ Act iv, 1; In 1 Thess v, 3 (4:8) |
| 5:8 | In Rom xii, 6 (7:13); xxi, 8 (7:13) |
| 5:15 | Ad pop Anti xiv, 10; In il Prop 5 |
| 5:17-18 | Ex in ps ix, 4 |
| 5:19 | Ad pop Anti xiv, 10; Ex in ps ix, 4; In il Prop 5; In Is v, 3 |
| 5:22 | Ex in ps cxv, 5 |
| 6:2 | Ad pop Anti xv, 13 |
| 6:6 | Ad pop Anti xii, 5; Ex in ps xlviii, 9; cx, 3; In ascen d n I C 3; In il Fil 4; In Is i, 3; In Mat vii, 7; xvii, 6; xxi, 4 |
| 6:7 | Ex in ps xlviii, 8; cx, 3; In Mat xvii, 6; xxi, 4 |
| 6:8 | Ex in ps xlvii, 8 (2x); cx, 3; In Mat xvii, 6; xxi, 4 |
| 6:9 | Ex in ps xlvii, 8 |
| 6:23 | De ss mar A 4; In Is ii, 5; S Gen viii, 1 |
| 6:27 | Con l et t 2; De uir xxxiv; E iii, 12 |
| 6:28 | Con l et t 2; De uir xxvii; xxxiv; E iii, 12; In s Bar 1 |
| 6:29 | Con l et t 2; E iii, 12; In s Bar 1 |
| 6:30 | Ad pop Anti x, 11; Ex in ps xlix, 8; In il Uidi dom iii, 3; In Mat lxxv, 5 |
| 6:31 | In il Uidi dom iii, 3 |
| 6:32 | Ad pop Anti x, 11; In il Uidi dom iii, 3 (2x) |
| 6:34 | Ad Stag a dae ii, 7; De ss B et P 1; De uir lii; In Gen xxxii, 4; xlv, 2; In Mat iv, 7; |

| | |
|---|---|
| 6:35 | Ad Stag a dae ii, 7; De ss B et P 1; De uir lii; In Gen xxxii, 4; xlv, 2; In Tit iv, 4 (2:10) |
| 7:17-18 | Q reg 1 |
| 8:22 | In Heb iii, 1 |
| 9:9 | De Anna v, 5; Ex in ps viii, 6; H hab p p Gothus 4; In Gen xi, 2; xxiii, 2; In il Is Ego 4; In Ioh xiv, 2; In Mat vi, 4 |
| 9:10 | In Rom xx, 4 (12:3) |
| 9:12 | De diab tent iii, 1; Ex in ps vii, 13; cxxxix, 1; In Acta vii, 3 (2:47); In Mat lxii, 5 |
| 9:18 | De fato et pr ii |
| 10:3 | In 1 Cor xvi, 11 |
| 10:4 | E ccxxxviii; In Heb xviii, 4 |
| 10:7 | De b Phil 1; De incomp dei iii, 2 |
| 10:8 | In Ioh xvii, 4 |
| 10:9 | In Acta vii, 3 (2:47); In Eph xv, 2 (4:31) |
| 10:19 | Cat ill xii, 37; Ex in ps cxl, 6 |
| 11:25 | In Acta vii, 3 (2:47); xxix, 4 (13:41); In Gen xxviii, 6; In Ioh xlviii, 3 |
| 11:26 | In 1 Cor xxxix, 13; In kal 6 |
| 12:1 | De mut nom iii, 1 |
| 12:28 | Adu op iii, 5; In Heb xxvii, 9; In Mat lxxix, 5 |
| 13:8 | In Acta xxv, 3 (11:30) |
| 14:12 | In 2 Thess v, 3 (3:15) |
| 14:16 | Cum Sat et Aur 4 |
| 14:23 | In Ioh xx, 1 |
| 14:29 | In Heb xix, 5; xxii, 8 |
| 14:31 | In 2 Thess v, 3 (3:15) |
| 15:1 | De D et S iii, 7; De sac iii, 14 |
| 15:13 | In Gen i, 1; lxiii, 1 |
| 15:17 | In Col i, 3 (1:7); In Gen xlv, 1 |
| 15:27 | De san pent i, 5 |
| 16:1 | In Acta xxxi, 3 (14:20) |
| 16:5 | In Acta xxix, 4 (13:41); In 2 Cor xxviii, 2; In Ioh ix, 2; In Mat lxv, 6 |
| 16:6 | In Heb ix, 8 |
| 17:2 | Ex in ps xlviii, 10 |
| 17:17 | In Heb xix, 3 |
| 18:3 | Ad Theo i, 1; F Prou 14:2; In Acta xvii, 4 (7:53); In 1 Cor viii, 8; In Gen xxii, 4; In Heb vi, 4; In il Uidi dom iii, 2; In Phil viii, 2 (2:16) |
| 18:17 | Ad Theo i, 18; Adu Iud 8, 3, 3; De paen viii, 2; De proph obscur ii, 8; Ex in ps xlix, 7; In Gen xix, 4; xx, 2; In Mat ix, 8 |
| 18:19 | Adu Iud 3, 1, 3; De pro evan 5; De sac i, 7; Ex in ps cxxxii; In Acta iii, 5 (1:26); In |

| | |
|---|---|
| 18:19 cont | Eph ix, 3 (4:3); In Heb xix, 3; xxx, 6; In princ Act ii, 4 |
| 18:21 | Cat ill ix, 33; In Mat li, 5 |
| 19:10 | De sac iii, 9 |
| 19:12 | Ad pop Anti iii, 5; In il Uidi dom v, 2 |
| 19:14 | In Rom xxiii, 1 (13:1) |
| 19:17 | De paen vii, 6; vii, 7 (2x); In 1 Cor xv, 15; In Gen iii, 6; In Mat xv, 13; lxvi, 5 |
| 20:6 | De paen iii, 1; Ex in ps iii, 2; In 2 Cor xvi, 5; In Mat lii, 6; In Phil iv, 5 (1:30); In 1 Thess xiii, 4 (5:5) |
| 20:9 | De fato et pr iv; De Laz iii, 4; vi, 9; Ex in ps vi, 1; xlix, 7; cxxix, 2; In 1 Cor viii, 8; Non esse ad grat 1; Q freg con 2 |
| 20:17 | F Prou 9:18 (2x) |
| 21:3 | In Mat xxx, 3 |
| 21:8 | In Ioh xli, 2 |
| 21:13 | In Heb xi, 7 |
| 22:1 | In Acta xl, 3; In Rom iii, 1 (1:18) |
| 22:28 | In il Uidi vi, 1 |
| 23:13-14 | In Mat lv, 3 |
| 23:27 | In Ioh lxxxvii, 4 |
| 23:19-30 | In Acta xxvii, 2 (13;3) |
| 24:11 | Ad Stel de comp ii, 7; In Heb x, 9; In Phil i, 5 (1:7) |
| 24:17 | Ad pop Anti xx, 7; In Mat xl, 4 |
| 24:18 | In Mat xl, 4 |
| 24:27 | De Laz ii, 3; De s Dros 1 |
| 24:30-31 | Adu eos q n adf 1 |
| 25:15 | De D et S iii, 7 |
| 25:20 | Ad Stag a dae iii, 13 |
| 25:21 | In il Si esur 6 |
| 25:22 | De uir xlix; In il Si esur 6 |
| 25:27 | In il Prop 1 |
| 26:11 | Ad Theo i, 18; In Gen vi, 1; In 1 Thess v, 3 (1:20) |
| 26:12 | De mut nom iii, 1; In Gal i, 9 (1:17); In Is v, 7; In Phil vii, 5 (2:11) |
| 26:27 | Ex in ps vii, 14; In Ioh li, 3; In Phil xiv, 3 (4:9) |
| 27:1 | Ad pop Anti xx, 22; In 2 Cor xxii, 4 |
| 27:6 | De mut nom iii, 1; Ex in ps cxl, 8; In Acta iii, 5 (1:26); In Eut i, 1; In princ Act i, 2; S Gen iv, 3 |
| 27:7 | Ad pop Anti ii, 22; De fato et pr vi; De mut nom i, 2; Q nemo 8 (2x) |

| | |
|---|---|
| 27:8 | Ad Stag a dae iii, 1 |
| 28:1 | Ad pop Anti viii, 3; De s h Phoc 2; In Acta liii, 5; In Eph xxiv, 2 96:22) (2x); In Mat xxiv, 4; In Phil xi, 5 (3:12) |
| 28:14 | In Gen xxx, 5 |
| 28:24 | In Gen lv, 5 |
| 30:4 | Ex in ps cxxxiv, 2 |
| 30:8 | In Heb xviii, 4; In 1 Thess iii, 4 (3:4) |
| 31:6 | De Laz vi, 7; In Eph xix, 1 (5:18); In Gen xxix, 2 |

Ecclesiastes

| | |
|---|---|
| 1:2 | Ad pop Anti xiii, 4; xv, 5; xix, 3; Ad Stag a dae ii, 12; In 1 Cor xi, 2; In Eph xii, 1 (4:17); In Eut i, 1; In Heb xv, 9; In Mt lxxvi,5 |
| 1:9 | Ad pop Anti vi, 8 |
| 2:1 | Ad Stag a dae i, 6; Adu Iud 8, 6, 6; In il Hab iii, 7 |
| 2:2 | Ad Stag a dae i, 6 (2x); Adu Iud 8, 6, 6 |
| 2:4 | In Eph xii, 1 (4:17); In Heb xv, 9; In 1 Tim xv, 4 (5:20) |
| 2:5 | Adu Iud 8, 6, 6; In Eph xii, 1 (4:17); In il Hab iii, 7; In 1 Tim xv, 4 (5:20) |
| 2:6-7 | In Eph xii, 1 (4:17); In Heb xv, 9 |
| 2:8 | In Eph xii, 1 (4:17) |
| 2:10 | Ad iud iun 6 |
| 2:11 | F Ier 17:7 |
| 2:13 | In Mat lxxxiii, 3 |
| 3:7 | Ex in ps cxl, 4; In il Uidi dom ii, 3 |
| 4:1 | De Laz ii, 4 |
| 4:3 | De Laz ii, 6 |
| 5:2 | F Iob 7:14 |
| 5:3 | Ex in ps cxlii, 1 |
| 6:5 | In Acta xl, 3 |
| 7:2 | In Acta xvi, 3 (7:34); In Ioh lx, 5; In Mat xl, 5; In 1 Tim xiv, 3 (5:10) |
| 7:3 | Ad pop Anti xv, 6 |
| 7:24 | In Acta xix, 5 (9:9) |
| 8:1 | In il Ne tim i, 6 |
| 9:8 | Ad pop Anti xiv, 10 |
| 9:13 | Ex in ps cxli, 2 |
| 9:20 | De laz iii, 1 |
| 11:3 | In Is i, 3 |
| 12:8 | In Eph xii, 1 (4:17); In Heb xv, 9; In 1 Tim xv, 4 (5:20) |
| 12:13 | F Iob 1:1; In 1 Cor xxix, 9 |
| 12:14 | In Rom xxxi, 5 (16:16) |

| | |
|---|---|
| 1-8 (p) | De ss B et Pl |
| 1:3 | In Col ix, 2 (3:17); In Eph xiv, 3 (4:29) |
| 2:10 | In 1 Thess vi, 4 (4:13) |
| 4:7 | Ex in ps v, 2 |
| 5:2 | De paen i, 1 |
| 8:5 | In 1 Cor xxxiii, 9 |
| 8:6 | Ad Stag a dae ii, 7; De uir lii; In Gen xxxii, 4; In Mat iv, 7 |

## Isaiah

| | |
|---|---|
| 1:1 | De paen viii, 3; Ex in ps cxlii, 2; In 1 Thess viii, 1 (4:17) |
| 1:2 | De fato et pr iv; De paen viii, 3; viii, 4; Ex in ps xlviii, 7; In Col vi, 1 (2:8); In Gen xxii, 2; In Heb v, 5; xxiii, 8; In Is v, 1; In Rom v, 6 (2:16); xiv, 2 (8:14) |
| 1:3 | Ad pop Anti xii, 6; Ex in ps xlviii, 7; In ascen d n I C 3; In il Fil 3; In Ioh 1, 2; lxxx, 1; In Is v, 1; In Mat xliii, 4 |
| 1:4 | De paen viii, 4 (2x); In Is ii, 6 |
| 1:5 | De paen viii, 4; Ex in ps cxix, 3; In Is vii, 9 |
| 1:6 | De paen viii, 4; In Is vii, 9 |
| 1:7 | De paen viii, 4; In Ioh lxx, 3 |
| 1:9 | Adu Iud 4, 6, 2; In Rom xvi, 10 (9:29) |
| 1:10 | Afu Iud 4, 6, 2; De paen viii, 4; In 1 Cor viii, 8; In Ioh lii, 1; In Mat xi, 2; lvii, 1 |
| 1:11 | Adu Iud 4, 6, 3; 7, 3, 4; Ex in ps xlix, 4; In Mat xxx, 3 |
| 1:12 | Adu Iud 4, 6, 3; 7, 3, 4; Ex in ps xliii, 4; xlix, 4; In Heb xviii, 2; In Mat xxx, 3; In Rom xx, 1 (12:1) |
| 1:13 | Adu Iud 4, 6, 3; 5, 12, 6; 7, 3, 4; De paen viii, 4; Ex in ps xliii, 4; In Gen xxvii, 3; In Mat xxx, 3 |
| 1:14 | De paen viii, 4; Ex in ps xliii, 4; In Eut ii, 7; In Mat xxx, 3 |
| 1:15 | Adu Iud 7, 3, 5; De lib rep 2; De paen viii, 4; De proph obscur i, 3; Ex in ps iv, 1; vii, 3; xii, 1; cxl, 1; cxlii, 6; F Prou 1:28; In il Uid elig 2; In Ioh lxvi, 1; In Mat xxx, 3; li, 5; lxviii, 1; In 2 Tim i, 4 (1:7) |
| 1:16 | De paen vii, 3; viii, 4 (2x); In Heb viii, 10; xii, 7; In Ioh lxx, 2; In 1 Thess iv, 4 (3: 13); In 2 Tim vi, 4 (2:26); In Tit iii, 4 (2: 1); S Gen i, 1 |
| 1:17 | Cat ill vi, 12; De paen viii, 4; F Ier 29:12; |

| | |
|---|---|
| 1:17 cont | In 1 Cor xxiii, 6; In 2 Cor iv, 7; In Heb xii, 7 (2x); In il Uid elig 2; In Rom xxv, 6 (14:13); In 1 Tim xiv, 6 (5:10); In 2 Tim i, 4 (1:7) |
| 1:18 | Cat ill vi, 12; De mut nom iv, 1; De paen vii, 2; viii, 4 (2x); F in epis cath James 4:9; F Iob 22:4; In 2 Cor iv, 7; In heb xii, 7; In il Uid elig 2; In Ioh lxix, 3; In Mat lii, 5; In Rom xviii, 6 (11:6); xxv, 6 (14:13); S Gen i,1 |
| 1:19 | De fato et pr ii; In 1 Cor xiv, 5; In Eph i, 1 (1:3); In il Dom non est 5; In Mat i, 5; In Rom iii, 1 (1:18); In 1 Thess v, 4 (4:8) |
| 1:20 | De fato et pr ii; In il Dom non est 5; In Rom iii, 1 (1:18); In 1 Thess v, 4 (4:8) |
| 1:21 | In Iss vii, 6 |
| 1:22 | In 2 Cor v, 3 |
| 1:23 | In Ioh lii, 1 |
| 1:24 | In Is ii, 7 |
| 1:26 | In 1 Cor xli, 6; In Is vii, 6; In Mat v, 3 |
| 1:27 | In Mat v, 3 |
| 1:30 | Ad pop Anti ii, 3 |
| 2:2 | Con Iud et gen 6; De mut nom i, 1 |
| 2:3 | Ex in ps xlix, 1 |
| 2:4 | Con Iud et gen 6; Ex in ps xlv, 3; xlix, 1; In Mat xix, 12 |
| 2:6 | In Eph vi, 4 (3:7) |
| 3:3 | In il Fil 1 |
| 3:7 | In Rom xviii, 1 (10:15) |
| 3:12 | De mut nom iii, 1 |
| 3:15 | In Rom xxix, 3 (15:21) |
| 3:16 | E ii, 6 |
| 3:17-18 | E ii, 6; ii, 9; Ex in ps xliv, 10; In Mat xvii 3; lxxxix, 3; In 1 Tim viii, 3 (2:10) |
| 3:24 | E ii, 6; In 1 Tim viii, 2 (2:10) |
| 4:6 | In Heb xxviii, 3 |
| 5:1 | F Ier 2:21; In Mat xl, 2; xliv, 4; In Phil vi, 4 (2:8) |
| 5:2 | F Ier 2:21; In Eph v, 2 (2:15); In Mat iii, 4; In Phil vi, 4 (2:8) |
| 5:3 | In Phil vi, 4 (2:8) |
| 5:4 | In Heb ii, 9; In Mat xii, 2; xxxvii, 5; xliv, 4; lxviii, 2; In Phil vi, 4 (2:8) |
| 5:5 | Ex in ps viii, 5; In Eph v, 2 (2:15); In Mat xix, 4; In Phil vi, 4 (2:8) |
| 5:6 | Ex in ps viii, 5; In Heb x, 2; In Phil vi, 4 (2:8) |
| 5:7 | Ex in ps viii, 5 |
| 5:8 | In Gen xxii, 6; xlviii, 1; In Ioh lxiv, 4; lxxii, 5 |

| | |
|---|---|
| 5:9 | In Ioh lxiv, 4 |
| 5:11-12 | In Mat xiii, 2 |
| 5:14 | H in san pascha 1 |
| 5:15 | H hab p p Gothus 4 |
| 5:18 | In Col ii, 4 (1:15) |
| 5:19 | In Col ii, 4 (1:15); In Mat xi, 4; In 1 Thess ix, 2 (5:3) |
| 5:21 | In Gal 1, 9 (1:17) |
| 5:22 | In Rom xxii, 2 (12:6) |
| 6 (p) | De paen ix, 1 |
| 6:1 | Con Anom xi, 3; De incomp dei iii, 3; iv, 3; Ex in ps xliv, 8; In Gen xxxii, 2; In il Uidi dom i, 1; ii, 1; iv, 1; iv, 2; v, 1 (2x); v, 3; vi, 1; In Ioh xv, 1; lxviii, 2; In Is ii, 1 S Gen ii, 2 |
| 6:2 | De incomp dei iii, 3; Ex in ps xli, 4; In Gen viii, 2; In il Uidi dom i, 3; ii, 2; vi, 2 (2x); S Gen ii, 2 |
| 6:3 | Ad pop Anti vii, 9; Adu Iud 1, 1, 2; De incomp dei i, 6; De s h Bab 2; Ex in ps xli, 4; In il Uidi dom i, 3; ii, 2; vi, 2; In Mat xix, 7 |
| 6:4 | In Heb xxxii, 3 |
| 6:5 | De diab tent i, 1; De proph obscur ii, 9; Ex in ps ii, 1; In Ioh xiv, 2 |
| 6:6 | In il Uidi dom vi, 3 |
| 6:8 | In Ioh lxviii, 2 |
| 6:9 | In Acta lv, 1; In Mat xlv, 2 |
| 6:10 | In Ioh lxviii, 2; In Mat xlv, 2 |
| 6:11 | In Rom xiv, 8 (8:27) |
| 7:3 | In il Uidi dom iv, 2 |
| 7:4 | In Is i, 9 |
| 7:8 | Con Iud et gen 2 |
| 7:9 | In Ioh xxxi, 2 |
| 7:14 | Con Iud et gen 2; De consub 6; De incomp dei v, 2; Ex in ps xliv, 8; xlix, 3; cxvii, 5; In 1 Cor xli, 6; In il Pater s p 3; In Ioh xiii, 1; In Mat v, 4 |
| 7:16 | Con Iud et gen 2 |
| 7:18 | In Is ii, 2 |
| 8:2 | Adu Iud 5, 4, 6 |
| 8:3 | In Ioh xix, 2; In Mat v, 3 |
| 8:6 | In Is ii, 2 |
| 8:7 | In Is ii, 2; v, 3 |
| 8:18 | Cat ill xii, 14; De ss B et P 6; In Eph xx, 6 (5:33); In Heb iv, 5; In Is vii, 3 |
| 8:20 | In Eph v, 2 (2:15); S Gen viii, 1 |
| 9:1 | Con Iud et gen 3; In Mat xiv, 1 |
| 9:2 | H in il App 10; In Mat xiv, 1 |

| | |
|---|---|
| 9:5 | Con Anom xi, 2; Con Iud et gen 2; In Mat vi, 6 |
| 9:6 | Con Iud et gen 2; De consub 6; De incomp dei v, 2; Ex in ps xliv, 5; xliv, 8; xlvi, 2; cix, 5; In Acta xvi, 3 (7:33); In Gen viii, 3; xiv, 4; In il Pater s p 3; In Ioh lxxxi, 1; In Mat vi, 6; In Phil vi, 2 (2:8); S Gen ii, 2 |
| 9:7 | Con Iud et gen 2; Ex in ps xliv, 7 |
| 10:14 | F Ier 50:18; In Rom xx, 4 (12:3) |
| 10:22 | Ad pop Anti xvii, 13; F Ier 31:34; In 2 Cor ii, 5; In Rom xvi, 5 (9:15); xvi, 9 (9:27) |
| 11:1 | Con Iud et gen 2; Ex in ps cix, 2; In il Pater s p 3 |
| 11:2 | Con Iud et gen 2; Ex in ps xliv, 2; F Prou 9:21 |
| 11:3 | Con Iud et gen 2; Ex in ps xliv, 2; L Diod 1 |
| 11:4 | De proph obscur ii, 6; Ex in ps xliv, 4 |
| 11:5 | De proph obscur ii, 6 |
| 11:6 | Ad pop Anti iii, 5; De res d n I C 3; Ex in ps xlvi, 1; In Is ii, 2; In Mat x, 3 |
| 11:7 | Ad pop Anti iii, 5 |
| 11:9 | Con Iud et gen 6 (2x); De proph obscur ii, 2; Ex in ps ii, 2; In Heb xiv, 6 |
| 11:10 | Con Iud et gen 8; De proph obscur ii, 2; In Mat vii, 2; x, 3; xxxvi, 3 |
| 13:3 | In Gen xxii, 4 |
| 13:9 | Ad Theo i, 12; In Mat xliii, 5 |
| 13:10 | Cat ill iii, 2 |
| 13:13 | Ad Theo i, 12 |
| 13:21-22 | In Is vii, 9; In Mat lix, 7 |
| 14:10 | In 1 Tim x, 3 (3:7) |
| 14:11 | Ad pop Anti xi, 4 |
| 14:12 | F Iob 1:6; H hab p p Gothus 4; Q reg 2 |
| 14:13 | Ad pop Anti xi, 4; De proph obscur ii, 6; Ex in ps cxl, 5; In Mat xxv, 5 |
| 14:14 | Ad pop Anti xi, 4; In il Uidi dom iii, 3; In Rom xx, 4 (12:3) |
| 14:27 | Adu Iud 5, 11, 6 |
| 15:1 | F Ier 48:11 |
| 19:1 | In Acta ii, 2; In ascen d n I C 5; In Mat lvi, 5 |
| 19:12 | F Ier 9:17 |
| 20:1 | In Is ii, 1 |
| 20:2 | In Mat xviii, 2 |
| 20:3 | Cat ill x, 14; In Mat xviii, 2 |
| 22:4 | Ad pop Anti xviii, 8; Ad Stag a dae iii, 10; Ad Theo i, 3; In Col xii, 3 (14:8); In Gen xxix, 2; In Is Introduction; In Rom xiv, 5 (8:27) |

| | |
|---|---|
| 22:12 | In Is iii, 9 |
| 22:13 | De fato et pr vi; In 1 Cor xl, 4 |
| 22:14 | In 1 Cor xl, 4 |
| 22:31 | In Ioh lxxii, 5 |
| 24 (p) | De gloria in trib 2 |
| 24:7 | Ex in ps xlix, 8; cxiii, 2 |
| 24:19-22 | Ad Theo i, 12 |
| 26:9 | In 1 Tim xiv, 4 (5:10) |
| 26:10 | In Ioh xii, 3 |
| 26:12 | Ad pop Anti vi, 14; De Laz iii, 5; In 2 Cor xxiii, 7; In Heb v, 6; In para 6 |
| 26:18 | Ex in ps vii, 14 |
| 26:19 | Con Iud et gen 8 |
| 27:1 | In Eph xxiv, 3 (6:22); In Phil vi, 5 (2:8) |
| 27:8 | De incomp dei v, 5 |
| 27:9 | Ex in ps cviii, 2 |
| 28:1 | De res d n I C 1 |
| 28:5 | Ex in ps v, 6 |
| 28:11 | Con Iud et gen 7 |
| 28:16 | In Rom xvi, 3 |
| 29:9 | Adu Iud 8, 1, 1; Cat ill v, 4 |
| 29:13 | In Mat xi, 9; li, 2; In Rom xviii, 5 (11:6) |
| 30:1 | Ad pop Anti iii, 5 |
| 30:8 | Adu Iud 5, 4, 6 |
| 30:10 | In Acta xix, 3 (9:4) |
| 30:26 | In mar Aeg 2 |
| 32:6 | In Acta ii, 4 (1:11); In Rom xx, 4 (12:3) |
| 32:8 | F Iob 1:1 |
| 32:20 | In Is vii, 9 |
| 33:11 | F Ier 11:21 |
| 33:17 | F Prou 30:31 |
| 34:4 | Ad Theo i, 12; Cat ill iii, 2 |
| 35:1 | In Rom xxxii, 2 (16:24) |
| 35:6 | Con Iud et gen 3; Ex in ps viii, 2; In Acta xix, 5 (9:9) |
| 35:10 | Ad Theo i, 11; In Heb vi, 10; In Mat xxxi, 4; liv, 9 |
| 36:12 | In Mat xxxvii, 7 |
| 37:35 | In Mat xxvi, 9; xxxii, 1 |
| 38 (p) | Ex in ps cxlii, 5 |
| 38:18 | In Rom xviii, 6 (11:6) |
| 39:2 | Ex in ps ix, 5 |
| 40:1 | De Laz iii, 5; Ex in ps cxli, 1; In 2 Cor xxiii, 7; In para 6 |
| 40:2 | De Laz iii, 5; F Ier 16:18; In 2 Cor xxiii, 7; In Heb v, 6; In para 6 |
| 40:3 | In Ioh xvi, 3 |
| 40:4 | In il Messis 3 |

40:5 Ad uid iun 4
40:6 Ad uid iun 4; De Anna iv, 3 (2x); De fato et pr iv; De Laz ii, 3; De proph obscur ii, 6; E i, 1; Ex in ps cxv, 3; cxliii, 2; In 2 Cor xxiv, 4; In Eut i, 4; In Gen xxviii, 3; In il Ne tim i, 1; In il Uidi dom v, 1; In Phil xii, 4 (3:17); In s Luc 1
40:7 De Anna iv, 3 (2x); De uir xlvii; In 1 Cor xxix, 9; In Eut i, 4
40:8 De Laz ii, 3; In Eut ii, 2 (2x); In il Uidi dom iv, 4
40:12 Ex in ps viii, 8; cxii, 2; In Eut ii, 9
40:13 De incomp dei v, 3; Ex in ps xlix, 8
40:15 De incomp dei ii, 4; Ex in ps vii, 11; In Eph iii, 2 (1:22); In il Uidi dom vi, 4; In Phil iv, 5 (1:30); vi, 5 (2:8)
40:16 Adu Iud 4, 6, 4
40:22 Ad pop Anti x, 8; De incomp dei ii, 3; ii, 4; Ex in ps vii, 11; cxii, 2
40:23 De incomp dei ii, 3; In 1 Cor iv, 4
40:26 In Ioh lxvi, 2
40:28 Ex in ps vi, 1
40:31 In Rom xvi, 4 (9:9)
41:8 In Rom xxx, 3-4 (16;5)
41:9 Ex in ps cxlvi, 1
41:22-23 In 1 Cor xxxii, 3
42:1 In Mat xl, 2
42:2 In Ioh xxiv, 2; In Mat xl, 2; liii, 3
42:3 Con Iud et gen 3; Ex in ps cxvii, 1; In Ioh xxiv, 2; In Mat xl, 2
42:4 In Mat xl, 2
42:6-7 Ad pop Anti xiii, 4
42:19 Adu Iud 3, 3, 9
43 (p) Non esse ad grat 4
43:10 In Ioh iv, 2 (2x); xv, 3
43:12 In Ioh xix, 2
43:22-24 Adu Iud 7, 3, 4
43:25 De paen vii, 4; viii, 2 (2x); Ex in ps cxxix, 3; cxliv, 3; In Heb xiv, 9; In il uti sus 6; Non esse ad grat 3; 4; Non esse desp 3
43:26 Ad Theo i, 15; Adu Iud 8, 3, 1; De cruce et lat i, 3; ii, 3; De diab tent ii, 6; De Laz iv, 4; vi, 2; De paen ii, 1; ii, 2; vii, 4; viii, 2 (2x); De proph obscur ii, 8; Ex in ps cxlii, 2; In 1 Cor xi, 4; In 2 Cor iv, 7; v, 4; In Eph x, 3 (4:4); In Gen xx, 3; In Heb ix, 8; xiv, 9; In il Uidi dom iii, 1; In Ioh vii, 2; In Mat xli, 6; In Rom xxv, 6 (14:13); Non esse

54:4 In 2 Cor ii, 7
54:13 In 2 Cor ii, 7; In Ioh xlvi, 1; In Mat i, 1; In Phil xii, 3 (3:17); In 1 Thess vi, 1 (4:10); In 2 Tim ii, 4 (1:12)
54:15 In Is ii, 3
55:1 De paen vii, 6
55:7 Ad e q scan vi
55:8 Ad e q scan vi; Ad Theo i, 15
55:9 Ad e q scan vi; Ad Stag a dae i, 5; Ad Theo i, 15; In Acta 1, 4
55:12 Ex in ps xlvi, 1
56:1 In Gen xxiii, 4
56:7 In Mat lxvii, 1
56:10 Adu Iud 4, 6, 3; E vii, 3; In Gen xii, 3; In il Fil 3
57:15 Ex in ps cxlvi, 1
57:17 Ad pop Anti v, 13; Ad Theo i, 6; De ss mar A 3; In 1 Cor viii, 8; xxiii, 6; In 2 Cor iv, 7; In Heb ix, 9
57:18 Ad Theo i, 6; De Laz vi, 2; De ss mar A 3; In 1 Cor vii, 8; In 2 Cor iv, 7; In Heb ix, 9
58:1 De dec mil 5
58:2 Ex in ps iv, 7; vii, 8; xliii, 5; cxlii, 2
58:3 In Mat xxx, 4
58:4 Ad pop Anti ii, 14; Adu Iud 1, 11, 6; F Ier 14:12
58:5 Ad pop Anti ii, 14; Adu Iud 1, 11, 6; Ex in ps xlii, 4; In Gen viii, 5
58:6 Cat ill i, 41; Ex in ps cxxxvii, 1; In Gen viii, 5; In Mat liv, 9
58:7 In Gen viii, 5; In Mat xlv, 3; liv, 9; lvi, 3; In Phil vi, 6 (2:8) (2x); In 1 Tim xiv, 1 (5:8)
58:8 In Gen viii, 5; In Mat liv, 9; In Phil iv, 5 (1:30)
58:9 Ex in ps iv, 1; ix, 5; cxxix, 3; cxl, 2; cxlii, 1; In Gen xxvii, 6; xliv, 2; In il Dil deum 3; In Mat liv, 8; liv, 9; Qual duc 6
59:1 Ex in ps cxlii, 5
59:2 Ad Theo i, 8; (attributed to Jeremiah ); In Eph v, 2 (2:15); In Ioh lxviii, 2; In Phil xi, 5 (3:12)
59:5 Ex in ps vii, 14; xliv, 11; xlviii, 8
59:7 In Eph x, 1 (4:4)
59:17 In Eph xxiv, 2 (6:22)
59:20 De laud s Paul iii; Ex in ps cxiii, 2
60:1 In Ioh xxvi, 2
60:17 Con Iud et gen 7
61:1 Cat ill x, 14; Con Iud et gen 4; Ex in ps xliv, 5; cxxv, 1; In Mat xix, 12

| | |
|---|---|
| 61:10 | In Eph xiii, 3 (4:24) |
| 62:5 | Ad e q scan vi |
| 63 (p) | In Ioh xv, 1 |
| 63:1-3 | Ex in ps xliv, 7 |
| 63:9 | De gloria in trib 3 |
| 64:1-2 | De paen vii, 4 |
| 64:4 | Ad pop Anti v, 5; Ad Theo i, 13; In 1 Cor vii, 6 |
| 65:1 | Con Iud et gen 7 (2x); De proph obscur i, 6; In Is Introduction; In Rom xviii, 2 (10:20) |
| 65:5 | De fato et pr vi |
| 65:8 | Ad pop Anti xix, 8 |
| 65:16 | In Ioh lxxxi, 1 |
| 65:17 | In Acta xix, 5 (9:9); In Heb xiv, 6 |
| 65:24 | In Gen xxxiv, 2; In Mat liv, 8 |
| 65:25 | H hab p p Gothus 1; In Is ii, 2 |
| 66:1 | Ex in ps ix, 6; cxiii, 6; F Irt 7:2; In Acta xvii, 1 (7:50); In Gen xvii, 1 |
| 66:2 | De Chris prec 4; Ex in ps ix, 6; cxxxi, 2; cxlii, 5; F Prou 22:12; In Gen ix, 6; lv, 5; In il Uidi dom i, 6; In Ioh vii, 2; In Mat xv, 2; xlvii, 4; lxv, 6 |
| 66:24 | De sac iv, 2 |

Jeremiah

| | |
|---|---|
| 1:1 | In Is i:1; In 1 Thess viii, 1 (4:7) |
| 1:5 | In Rom i, 1 (1:2) |
| 1:6 | In Acta iv, 2 (2:13); In 1 Cor xxix, 2; In Is vi, 4; In Mat xxxii, 6; xc, 2 |
| 1:8 | In Mat xc, 2 |
| 1:9 | In Acta iv, 2 (2:13); In Ioh lxix, 2 |
| 1:13-14 | Ex in ps xlvii, 1 |
| 1:16 | In Is vi, 5 |
| 1:18 | F Ier 1:1; In Is i, 1; In Mat liv, 3 |
| 2:5 | Con 1 et t 1; De fato et pr iv; De paen iv, 5; Ex in Ps cxlii, 2; In Mat lxviii, 2 |
| 2:6 | In Eph xxiii, 2 (6:14) |
| 2:8 | Ex in ps xlix, 6 |
| 2:9 | Ex in ps xlix, 1 |
| 2:10 | Adu Iud 4, 3, 7; In Is i, 2; In Mat xvii, 6 |
| 2:11 | Adu Iud 4, 3, 7; In Is i, 2; In Mat xvii, 6; In Tit iii, 2 (1:14) |
| 2:12 | Adu op ii, 1; Ex in ps xlix, 8; In Mat lxi, 3; In Rom v, 6 (2:16) |
| 2:13 | De incomp dei v, 5; In Rom iii, 2 (1:21); S Gen vii, 2 |

| | |
|---|---|
| 2:19 | De paen i, 4; Ex in ps xii, 1 |
| 2:20 | Adu Iud 1, 11, 4 |
| 2:21 | F Ier 12:13 |
| 2:22 | In Rom xiv, 8 (8:27) |
| 2:23 | F Ier 1:1 |
| 2:27 | Ex in ps cxx, 1 |
| 2:31 | Ex in ps cxiii, 1 |
| 2:32 | In Mat xliii, 4 |
| 3 (p) | In Mat iii, 5 |
| 3:1 | De uir xxxv |
| 3:2 | Ad Theo i, 3; E vii, 3; Ex in ps xlviii, 8 |
| 3:3 | Adu Iud 1, 3, 1; De sac ii, 4; Ex in ps viii, 4; In Heb xv, 7; In il Fil 3; In Ioh lxxiv, 1 |
| 3:6 | De Anna iv, 1 |
| 3:7 | Ad Theo i, 15; In Gen xliv, 2; In Mat lxvii, 4; lxiv, 3 |
| 3:9-11 | F Prou 30 |
| 3:12 | F Prou 30; In Rom v, 6 (2:16) |
| 3:18 | F Ier 4:10 |
| 4:2 | Ad pop Anti iv, 2; In Mat xvii, 5 |
| 4:4 | In Phil x, 2 (3:3) |
| 4:14 | In Heb xii, 7; In Ioh lxxiii, 3; In 1 Thess iv, 4 (3:13); In 2 Thess vi, 4 (2:26) |
| 4:19 | In Rom viii, 8 (4:21) |
| 4:22 | Ex in ps cx, 7; F Iob 1:1 |
| 5:1 | In Gen xxiii, 4; Non esse ad grat 5 |
| 5:4 | De paen vii, 3 |
| 5:5 | De sac ii, 4; In Is ii, 3 |
| 5:8 | Adu Iud 1, 6, 8; 4, 6, 3; Ex in ps viii, 4; xlviii, 7; In Gen xii, 3; xxiii, 4; In il Fil 3; In Mat xiii, 7 |
| 5:22 | Ad pop Anti ix, 9 |
| 5:24 | In Acta xxxi, 1 (14:16) |
| 5:30 | Adu op ii, 1 |
| 6:8 | Ad Stag a dae i, 3 |
| 6:10 | De mut nom i, 1; In 1 Cor xxiii, 6; S Gen ix, 1 |
| 6:14 | In il Is Ego 6 |
| 6:20 | Adu Iud 7, 3, 4; Ex in ps xliii, 4; xlix, 4; In Heb xi, 5 |
| 6:29 | In il Fil 3 |
| 7:4 | Adu Iud 1, 7, 4; In Heb xvii, 1 |
| 7:11 | Adu Iud 8, 6, 11; De Laz iii, 10; Ex in ps vii, 4; cxlii, 6; In il Dom non est 4; In Mat xliii, 3; In 1 Thess i, 3 (1:7) |
| 7:17 | Ex in ps vii, 4; In 1 Cor viii, 8; In Gen xliv, 2; In Mat xliii, 3; In 1 Thess i, 4 (1:7) |
| 7:18 | In 1 Cor viii, 8 |
| 7:19 | Ex in ps vi, 1 (2x) |

| | |
|---|---|
| 7:21 | Adu Iud 7, 3, 4 |
| 7:22 | In Is i, 4 |
| 8:4 | Ad Theo i, 7; ii, 4; De Laz vii, 2; De paen i, 4; iii, 4; vii, 2; De prod Iud ii, 2; Ex in ps cxlii, 5; In 1 Cor xxiii, 6; In Gen xxix, 1; xliv, 3; In Heb ix, 8; In Mat xxvi, 7; lxvii, 4; lxxxvi, 4 |
| 8:5 | De paen vii, 2 |
| 8:7 | Ad pop Anti xii, 6; Ex in ps xlix, 6; In ascen d n I C 3; In Is i, 3; In Mat xxi, 4 |
| 8:8 | Ex in ps xlix, 6 |
| 9:1 | Ad Stag a dae iii, 10; Ad Theo i, 1; In Col iii 3 (4:18); In Gen xxix, 2; In Heb xxiii, 9; In Rom vii, 7 (4:21) |
| 9:2 | Ad Stag a dae iii, 10 |
| 9:4 | Cum Sat et Aur 1 |
| 9:17 | Ad pop Anti ii, 7; F Ier 9:20; In Ioh lxiv, 4 |
| 9:18 | Ad pop Anti ii, 7 |
| 9:23-24 | Ex in ps cxxx, 1 |
| 10:5 | Adu Iud 1, 7, 6 |
| 10:11 | Ex in ps xlix, 1; In 1 Cor xx, 5; In Gen xxxv, 5; In Ioh iv, 3 |
| 10:19-22 | In il Dom non est 4 |
| 10:23 | De laud s Paul iii; F Ier 11:28; In il Dom non est 1 |
| 10:24 | In ascen d n I C 4; In il Dom non est 4 (2x) |
| 11:5 | In Rom xiv, 8 (8:27) |
| 11:14 | F Ier 11:19; In Mat v, 7; lx, 2; In Rom xiv, 8 (8:27) |
| 11:15 | Ex in ps xliii, 4 |
| 12:1 | Ad Stag a dae i, 7; Ex in ps vii, 9 |
| 12:2 | F Ier 1:1; F Prou 13:25 |
| 12:7 | Adu Iud 1, 3, 1; In il Fil 3 |
| 13:1-9 | In Gal iii, 4 (3:15) |
| 13:10-12 | In Mat xxx, 5 |
| 13:23 | F Ier 2:22; In il Fil 3; In Ioh lxviii, 2; Q reg 6 |
| 14:5 | Ad pop Anti iii, 9 |
| 14:7 | Ad pop Anti xvii, 15; De laud s Paul iii; Ex in ps xlviii, 4 |
| 14:9 | De per mat 1; Ex in ps vi, 1 |
| 14:11 | Adu Iud 5, 5, 5; Ex in ps xlviii, 4 |
| 14:12 | Adu Iud 5, 5, 5 |
| 15 (p) | E iv, 2 |
| 15:1 | Ad pop Anti xii, 14; xx, 6; Ex in ps xlviii, 4; In Mat v, 7; In Rom xiv, 6 (8:26); In 1 Thess |

| | |
|---|---|
| 15:1 cont | i, 4 (1:7) |
| 15:10 | Ad Stag a dae iii, 10 |
| 15:19 | Ad pop Anti xvi, 17; Adu Iud 8, 4, 3; Cat ill vi, 19; Con e q sub 13; In Acta xviii, 5; 8:25; In 1 Cor iii, 9; In Gen iii, 4; In Mat lxxviii, 2 |
| 16:7 | In Gen xliv, 2 |
| 16:19 | Ex in ps viii, 1 |
| 17:5 | Ex in ps x, 3; cxvii, 2; F Ier 2:26; 7:9; In Gen lvi, 6 |
| 17:9 | In Mat xxix, 2 |
| 17:12 | In Col ii, 4 (1:15) |
| 17:17 | In Mat xi, 4 |
| 17:21 | Adu Iud 6, 3, 3 |
| 18:1-5 | In Gal iii, 4 (3:15) |
| 18:6 | Cat ill ix, 26; In Gal iii, 4 (3:15) |
| 18:7 | Ad pop Anti v, 6; Ex in ps cxliv, 4; F Ier 22:26; In Gen xxv, 2; In Mat lxiv, 1 |
| 18:8 | Ad pop Anti v, 16; Ex in ps cxliv, 4; In Gen xxv, 2; In Mat lxiv, 1 |
| 18:9-10 | Ex in ps cxliv, 4; In Gen xxv, 2; In Mat lxiv, 1 |
| 18:20 | Ad Stag a dae iii, 7 |
| 19:10 | F Ier 1:1 |
| 19:11 | Cat ill ix, 25 |
| 20:3 | F Ier 1:1 |
| 20:7 | In Col vi, 1 (2:8) |
| 20:8 | De Laz i, 1 |
| 20:9 | Ad Stag a dae ii, 5; De Laz i, 1; In 2 Cor xii, 3 |
| 20:14 | d Stag a dae iii, 10 |
| 21:4 | F Ier 1:1 |
| 21:7 | F Ier 12:2 |
| 21:11 | In Col ii, 4 (1:15) |
| 22:13 | In Ioh lxiv, 4 (as Nahum) |
| 22:17 | In Mat lxxiii, 3 |
| 22:29-30 | In Is i, 2 |
| 23:23 | Ad pop Anti x, 8; Ad Theo i, 8; De Anna iii, 1; De b Phil 4; Ex in ps iv, 2; ix, 5; In il Dil deum 3; In Mat liv, 8 |
| 23:24 | Ad pop Anti x, 8 (as Isaiah); Ex in ps cxiii, 6 |
| 25:9 | In Rom i, 1 (1:2) |
| 25:11 | F Ier 1:1 |
| 27:6 | In Heb xxvi, 8 |

| | |
|---|---|
| 28:13 | F Ier 1:1 |
| 29:9 | Ad pop Anti xii, 16 |
| 29:10 | Ex in ps viii, 5 |
| 30:9 | In Mat ii, 6; lvii, 1 |
| 31:15 | Con Iud et gen 3; In Ioh xiii, 1; In Mat ix, 4 |
| 31:18 | Adu Iud 1, 11, 5 |
| 31:29 | In Gen xxix, 6 |
| 31:31 | Con Iud et gen 10; De Eleaz 3 (3x); De paen vi 4; Ex in ps xlvi, 6; cxlix, 1; In Acta xix, 5 (9:9); In il Hab ii, 4; In Is ii, 3; In Mat i, 1; xvi, 9 |
| 31:32 | Con Iud et gen 10; De Eleaz 3 (3x); De paen vi, 4; Ex in ps xlvi, 6; In Is ii, 3 (2x); In Mat i, 1; xvi, 9 |
| 31:33 | Con Iud et gen 10; De Eleaz 3; In Mat i, 1 |
| 31:34 | Con Iud et gen 6; 10 (2x); De Eleaz 3; 4; De Laz iii, 3; In Is ii, 3; In Phil xii, 3 (3:17) In Rom xxvi, 3 (14:23); In 2 Tim ii, 4 (1:12) |
| 32:3 | Ex in ps xlix, 4 |
| 32:5 | Ad pop Anti xix, 11 |
| 35:2 | In Mat xliii, 4 |
| 35:3 | In Acta xiv, 3 (6:7) |
| 35:6 | F Ier 1:1 |
| 36:1-3 | De proph obscur i, 4 |
| 36:4 | De proph obscur i, 5 |
| 36:5-6 | De proph obscur i, 5; F Ier 36:26 |
| 36:7,14 15,21, 22 | De proph obscur i, 5 |
| 36:23 | De proph obscur i, 5; In Is vii, 6; In Mat ix, 6 |
| 36:26 | De proph obscur i, 5 |
| 37:14 | F Ier i, 1 |
| 38:4 | De proph obscur i, 3; In Eph xviii, 1 (5:6) |
| 38:6 | F Ier 1:1 |
| 38:17-23 | Ad pop Anti xix, 9 |
| 39:2 | Ad pop Anti xix, 9 |
| 39:8-9 | Ad pop Anti xix, 10 |
| 43:12 | In Heb xxvi, 5 |
| 44:8 | In Rom xiv, 8 (8:27) |
| 44:16-18 | Adu Iud 5, 4, 4 |
| 48:10 | Ex in ps xliv, 4; In diem nat 7 |
| 50:37 | In Mat iv, 2 |
| 52:6 | Ad pop Anti xix, 9 |

## Lamentations

| | |
|---|---|
| 1:1 | F Ier 1:1 |
| 3:27 | Ad Stag a dae i, 3; Adu op iii, 17; Ex in ps iv, 13; In Phil xv, 5 (4:23) |
| 3:28 | Ex in ps iv, 13 |
| 4;2 | De glor in trib 2 |
| 4:10 | Adu Iud 5, 6, 2; In s Luc 2; In 1 Thess viii, 3 (4:18) |
| 4:18 | De glor in trib 2 |
| 4:20 | De incomp dei v, 5 |

## Ezekiel

| | |
|---|---|
| 1 (p) | In Ioh xv, 1 |
| 1:3-4 | De incomp dei iii, 5 |
| 1:27 | In Mat xi, 6 |
| 2-3 (p) | In Mat xc, 2 |
| 2:1 | De incomp dei iii, 5; iv, 1 |
| 2:5 | In Ioh xiii, 1; In Mat lxviii, 1; lxxvii, 3 |
| 2;6 | In Is i, 1 |
| 2:9 | De san pent i, 5 |
| 2;10 | In Acta iv, 2 (2:13) |
| 3:1 | In Ioh lxix, 2 |
| 3:2 | In Acta iv, 1 (2:4) |
| 3:3 | Ex in ps xliv, 1; In Acta iv, 2 (2:13) |
| 3;11 | In Ioh lxiv, 2 |
| 3:12 | Adu Iud 1, 1, 2; De incomp dei i, 6; In Acta xix, 2 (8:40) |
| 3:15 | In 1 Cor xxix, 2 |
| 3:17 | De Laz vi, 2; In Is vi, 5; Non esse ad grat 2 |
| 3:18 | In Ioh xiii, 1; In Is vi, 5 |
| 3:19 | In Eph xi, 6 (4:16); In Heb iv, 2 |
| 3:20 | Ex in ps cxl, 5; In il Uidi dom iii, 3 |
| 3:21 | In Eph xi, 6 (4:16) |
| 4 (p) | In Mat xxxvii, 5 |
| 4:12 | Ad Stag a dae iii, 10 |
| 5:7 | Ex in ps viii, 4; In Mat lxxv, 5 |
| 7:7-8 | Ad pop Anti xix, 9 |
| 8:5 | In Mat xliii, 3 |
| 8:6 | In Rom xiv, 8 (8:27) |
| 8:14 | In Is i, 1 |
| 9:4 | Ad pop Anti xviii, 9; E cxxi; Ex in ps cxl, 5; In Rom xxxi, 5 (16:16); Q reg 2 |
| 9:8 | Ad Stag a dae ii, 5; In Acta xliii, 3; In ascen d n I C 4; In 1 Cor xxxiii, 5; In Gen xxv, 4; xxix, 2; In Rom xiv, 8 (8:27); In 1 Thess i, 4 (1:7) |
| 9:11 | In Eph xxiii, 2 (6:14) |

| | |
|---|---|
| 10 (p) | In Ioh xv, 1 |
| 10:12 | In Rom xxxii, 3 (16:24) |
| 11:2 | Ad uid iun 7 |
| 12:9 | In Mat xlvii, 1 |
| 12:13 | Ad pop Anti xix, 11 |
| 12:22, 27 | In Mat xi, 4 |
| 13:10 | In Mat lxviii, 2 |
| 13:19 | In Eph xviii, 1 (5:6) |
| 14:1, 4 | De uir lxxxiv |
| 14:14 | Ex in ps xlviii, 4; cxlii, 6; In Ioh lxxxiv, 3; In Mat v, 7; xx, 6; In 1 Thess i, 4 (1:7) (2x) |
| 14:16 | Ex in ps cxlii, 6; In Ioh xii, 3; In Mat v, 7 In 1 Thess i, 4 (1:7) (2x) |
| 14:18 | Ex in ps xlviii, 4 |
| 14:20 | C Iob; Ex in ps xlviii, 10; In Gen xliii, 1 |
| 16 (p) | Ex in ps v, 2 |
| 16:3 | Ex in ps xliv, 11; In Gen xxix, 7 |
| 16;4 | In 1 Cor xxxix, 17 |
| 16:6,9, 14 | In Mat xliii, 5 |
| 16:20 | F Ier 2:34; In Mat lxxv, 5 |
| 16:21 | In 1 Cor xxvi, 6; In Mat lxxv, 5 |
| 16:22 | In 1 Cor xxvi, 6 |
| 16:23 | In Mat xliii, 1 |
| 16:26 | In Mat xliii, 5 |
| 16:33 | Ad Theo i, 13 |
| 16:37-42 | In Rom xxiii, 5 (13:10) |
| 16:49 | In Gen i, 2; In Heb xxix, 4; In Mat vi, 9; xiii, 2; lvii, 5 |
| 16:51 | In Mat xxxvii, 6; lxxv, 5 |
| 17:1 | Ex in ps xlviii, 2 |
| 17:2 | Ad pop Anti xix, 9; Ex in ps xlviii, 2 |
| 17:3 | Ad pop Anti xix, 9; Ex in ps xlviii, 2; In Is v, 3 |
| 17:5-6, 9,12, 14,16-20 | Ad pop Anti xix, 9 |
| 18:2-3 | In Ioh lvi, 1 |
| 18:4 | In Eph xviii, 2 (5:14); In 1 Thess x, 2 (5:18) |
| 18:15 | F Iob 1:1 |
| 18:20 | De coem et de cr 1; Ex in ps xlviii, 9; In Gen xxix, 6 |
| 18:21 | In il Uidi·dom iii, 2 |
| 18;23 | Ad Stag a dae i, 4; De paen iii, 4; F Ier 7:22; In Gen xxx, 4; vi, 2; xviii, 6; xxi, 6; |

| | |
|---|---|
| 18:23 cont | xxix, 1; xxix, 5; xliv, 2; xlv, 2; In Mat lxxxvi, 4; Q reg 2 |
| 18:24 | De paen vii, 2; In 2 Tim iii, 2 (1:18) |
| 18:26 | Ad uid iun 7 |
| 18:32 | Ad pop Anti xviii, 9; In Ioh lxviii, 2; In Rom xxxi, 5 (16:16) |
| 20:9 | Con e q sub 8; Ex in ps cxiii, 3 |
| 20:10 | Ex in ps xliii, 4 |
| 20:12 | In Mat xxxix, 3 |
| 20:25 | Ex in ps xliii, 4; In Acta xvii, 1 (7:50) |
| 22:27 | Ex in ps viii, 4 |
| 23:4 | In Mat iii, 5 |
| 23:5 | Adu Iud 6, 2, 5; In Mat iii, 5 |
| 23:6-9 | Adu Iud 6, 2, 5 |
| 23:11 | In Mat iii, 5 |
| 24:18 | In 1 Thess i, 4 (1:7) |
| 24:19 | In Mat xlvii, 1 |
| 25:8 | In Ioh lv, 2 |
| 28:2 | H hab p p Gothus 4; In Rom xx, 4 (L2:3) |
| 28:3 | In Heb xxvi, 8; In Phil v, 2 (2:4) |
| 28:9 | Ad pop Anti xi, 4 |
| 32:2 | In Phil vi, 5 (2:8) |
| 32:10 | In Ioh xiii, 1 |
| 33:6 | De sac vi, 1 |
| 33:8 | In Mat lxxxii, 6 |
| 33:9 | In Ioh xiii, 1 |
| 33:11 | De Laz vi; De paen vii, 2; In Heb xviii, 2; In 2 Tim iii, 2 (1:18) |
| 33:13 | In Ioh xv, 1 |
| 33:17 | Ex in ps cxlii, 2 |
| 33:19 | Ex in ps cxxxvii, 2 |
| 33:32 | Ex in ps xlix, 4 |
| 34:2 | In Acta iii, 5 (1:26); In Ioh lx, 1; In Rom xxix, 4 (15:24); In 2 Thess iv, 3 (3:2) |
| 34:3 | In Gen lvii, 6; In Rom xxix, 4 (15:24) |
| 34:4 | In Gen lvii, 6; In Ioh lx, 1 |
| 34:5-6 | In Gen lvii, 6 |
| 34:17 | De sac vi, 11 |
| 34:23-24 | In Mat ii, 6; lvii, 1 |
| 36:20 | Cat ill vi, 10; In Rom vi, 2 (2:24) |
| 36:22 | Con e q sub 8; Ex in ps viii, 5; cxxix, 3; In Mat iii, 6 |
| 36:23 | In Rom vi, 2 (2:24) |
| 36:26 | F Ier 3:16 |
| 37 (p) | De s h Bab 2 |
| 37:3 | Ex in ps vii, 13 |

| | |
|---|---|
| 37:11 | Ex in ps xlvii, 3 |
| 37:13 | Ex in ps cxv, 1 |
| 37:18 | In Mat xlvii, 1 |
| 37:24 | In Mat ii, 6; lvii, 1 |
| 37:25 | In Mat ii, 6 |
| 39:3 | In Phil vi, 5 (2:8) |
| 39:10 | Ex in ps xlv, 3 |
| 44:19 | In Rom xx, 2 (12:7) |

Daniel

| | |
|---|---|
| 1-6 (p) | Adu Iud 5, 1, 4 |
| 1:6-7 | De mut nom iii, 3 |
| 1:8 | In s Luc 2 |
| 1:10 | Q nemo 15 |
| 2 (p) | Ad Theo i, 5; In Col iii, 4 (1:20) |
| 2:4 | In Phil v, 3 (2:4) |
| 2:13 | In 2 Cor v, 5 |
| 2:17 | In Mat iv, 18 |
| 2:18 | In 2 Cor v, 5; In Mat iv, 18 |
| 2:24 | In Mat v, 7 |
| 2:27-28 | S Gen v, 2 |
| 2:30 | In Acta ix, 1 (3:12); xxx, 2 (14:15); In Heb xxvi, 9; In Phil v, 2 (2:4) |
| 2:46 | In Heb xxvi, 7; In Phil v, 2 (2:4) |
| 2:47 | In 1 Cor xxxvi, 3; In Eph viii, 9 (4:2) |
| 3 (p) | Ad pop Anti vii, 1; De Anna iv, 4; De D et S ii, 2; iii, 6; De laud s Paul vi; De Mac ii, 2; De sac iii, 14; E i, 2; cxxv; Ex in ps ix, 5; x, 1; cxiii, 2; cxlviii, 1; In Acta liv, 3; In Eph viii, 8 (4:2); In Gen xii, 3; xxxii, 7; xliv, 6; lvii, 5; lxii, 4; In il Si esur 2; In Mat xxiv, 2; In quat Laz A 1; In 1 Thess i, 3 (1:7) |
| 3:2,4 6,12 | Ad pop Anti iv, 8 |
| 3:14 | S Gen v, 2 |
| 3:15 | Ad pop Anti vi, 11; In Rom xx, 4 (12:3) |
| 3:16 | Q nemo 17; S Gen v, 2 |
| 3:17 | Ad pop Anti i, 30; Adu Iud 4, 5, 8; In 1 Cor xviii, 6; xx, 12; In Mat iv, 18; In 1 Thess ix, 2 (5:2); In Tit iv, 4 (3:15); Q nemo 17; S Gen v, 2 |
| 3:18 | Ad pop Anti i, 30; iv, 8; Ex in ps vii, 16; In 1 Cor xx, 12; In Mat iv, 18 (2x); xxxiii, 8; In Tit vi, 4 (3:15); Q nemo 17 |
| 3:21 | In 2 Cor i, 3 |
| 3:22 | In Mat xliii, 5 |

| | |
|---|---|
| 8:8-9 | Adu Iud 5, 7, 4 |
| 8:10 | Ad pop Anti vi, 11 |
| 8:11-12 | Adu Iud 5, 7, 4 |
| 8:14 | In Rom xix, 1, 2 (11:10) |
| 8:17 | In Acta i, 5 (1:4) |
| 8:27 | Adu Iud 5, 5, 4 |
| 9 (p) | In Gen xix, 2 |
| 8:2-3 | Adu Iud 5, 5, 4 |
| 9:4 | Adu Iud 5, 5, 7 |
| 9:5-6 | Adu Iud 5, 5, 8 |
| 9:8 | Ad Stag a dae iii, 10 |
| 9:11 | Adu Iud 5, 6, 1 |
| 9:12 | Adu Iud 5, 6, 2 |
| 9:15 | Adu Iud 5, 6, 3 |
| 9:17 | Adu Iud 5, 6, 4; 5, 9, 3 |
| 9:18 | Adu Iud 5, 6, 4; Ex in ps xliii, 6 |
| 9:23 | Ex in ps viii, 5 |
| 9:24 | Adu Iud 5, 9, 4; 5, 9, 5; 5, 9, 6 |
| 9:25 | Adu Iud 5, 10, 3 |
| 9:26 | Adu Iud 5, 10, 4 |
| 9:27 | Adu Iud 5, 10, 5; In Is ii, 7; In princ Act iv, 9 |
| 10:2 | Adu Iud 4, 5, 3; In Rom xiv, 8 (8:27) |
| 10:3 | Adu Iud 4, 5, 3; De incomp dei iii, 4; In Gen i, 3; In Mat xx, 1 |
| 10:4 | Adu Iud 4, 5, 3 |
| 10:5 | De incomp dei iii, 4 |
| 10:6 | Ad Theo i, 14 |
| 10:7 | In Gen xxii, 2 |
| 10:8 | De incomp dei iii, 4; In Gen xxii, 2 |
| 10:9-10 | In Gen xxii, 2 |
| 10:11 | De incomp dei iii, 4; In Gen xxii, 2 |
| 10:12 | De incomp dei iii, 4 |
| 10:13 | In Eph vii, 1 (3:11) |
| 10:16-17 | De incomp dei iii, 4 |
| 11:20-34 | Adu Iud 5, 7, 5 |
| 11:35 | Adu Iud 5, 7, 5; 5, 7, 6 |
| 11:36 | Adu Iud 5, 7, 6 |
| 12:1 | Adu Iud 5, 7, 7 |
| 12:2 | In Rom xiii, 8 (8:11) |
| 12:8-10 | Adu Iud 5, 8, 2 |
| 12:11 | Adu Iud 5, 8, 3; 5, 8, 4 |
| 12:12 | Adu Iud 5, 8, 4 |

## Hosea

| | |
|---|---|
| 1:2 | In Mat iii, 5 |
| 1:4,6 | In Ioh xix, 2 |
| 1:9 | H in il App 16 |
| 2:1 | H in il App 16 |
| 2:5 | In Gal iii, 4 (3:15) |
| 2:23 | In Rom xvi, 9 (9:25) |
| 3:5 | In Mat ii, 6; lvii, 1 |
| 4:2 | Ad Stag a dae iii, 10; De lib rep 2; Ex in ps viii, 4 (2x); In Heb xxiii, 7; In il Fil 3; In Mat lxviii, 1; lxxiv, 2 |
| 4:6 | In Ioh lxviii, 2 |
| 4:8 | In 1 Tim xiv, 2 (5:10) |
| 4:14 | Adu Iud 7, 1, 6; 7, 1, 7 |
| 4:16 | Adu Iud 1, 11, 5 |
| 5:9 | In Is iii, 4 |
| 6:2 | Ad uid iun 1 |
| 6:3-4 | In Mat xxii, 8 |
| 6:5 | Ex in ps xliv, 9; In Eph vii, 1 (3:13) |
| 6:6 | Ad Stag a dae i, 5; De elee 5; In 1 Cor xxxii 9; In Eur 5; In Heb xi, 5; In Ioh xiii, 4; In Mat xxx, 3; xxxix, 2; l, 6; lxxix, 1; In 2 Tim vi, 3 (2:26) |
| 8:4 | Ad pop Anti iii, 5 |
| 9:4 | In Rom xx, 1 (12:1) |
| 9:7 | In Mat xliii, 4 |
| 9:10 | Ad pop Anti xix, 8; F Ier 24:2; In Is v, 1 |
| 10:2 | Ex in ps iv, 7 |
| 11:1 | Con Iud et gen 3; In Ioh xiii, 1; In Mat viii, 5 |
| 11:3 | Ex in ps cxxxiv, 3 |
| 11:4 | In Is ii, 8 |
| 11:8 | Ad e q scan vi; De paen viii, 4 |
| 11:9 | Ex in ps vi, 1 |
| 12:10 | De incomp dei iv, 3; De laud s Paul v; In Gen xxxii, 2; lviii, 3; In Heb i, 1; In Ioh xv, 1; In Is vi, 1 |
| 12:12 | In Ioh xxi, 3 |
| 13:2 | In 1 Tim xviii, 2 (6:21) |
| 13:8 | In Rom xvi, 8 (9:20) |
| 13:14 | Ad pop Anti vii, 1; De coem et de c ru 2; H in san pascha 1; In 1 Cor xlii, 4; In Mat xix, 12 |
| 14:3 | S cum pres 1 |
| 14:4 | Ex in ps cxvii, 2 |

## Joel

| | |
|---|---|
| 1:3 | Ad pop Anti xxi, 20 |

| | |
|---|---|
| 1:6 | In Mat iv, 17 |
| 1:14 | Adu Iud 1, 11, 7 |
| 1:17 | Ad pop Anti iii, 9 |
| 2:11 | De Chris diuin 3 |
| 2:13 | Ad pop Anti iv, 2; In 2 Cor iv, 7; In Mat xix 4 |
| 2:15 | De uir xxx |
| 2:16 | Ad pop Anti iii, 9; De uir xxx |
| 2:25 | In 2 Cor viii, 3; In Rom ii, 6 (1:16) |
| 2:28 | Con Iud et gen 5; Ex in ps xliv, 2; xliv, 3; xliv, 9; In Acta iv, 1 (2:3); v, 1 (2:17); In 1 Cor xxvi, 4; I Eph ii, 2 (1:14) |
| 2:31 | De bap Chris 2 |
| 2:32 | Con Iud et gen 5; In Rom xvii, 3 (10:13) |

Amos

| | |
|---|---|
| 2:7 | Ex in ps viii, 4 |
| 2:11 | De fato et pr v; De sac vi, 11; In Tit ii, 3 (1:11) |
| 2:12 | De uir xxi |
| 3:2 | De sac vi, 11 |
| 3:6 | De diab tent i, 4; i, 5; In il Is Ego 3; 6 |
| 3:7 | F Ier Introduction |
| 4:5 | Adu Iud 7, 1, 5; Con Iud et gen 17 |
| 4:9,11 | Ex in ps cx, 3 |
| 4:13 | In 1 Tim xv, 4 (5:20) |
| 5:2 | Con Iud et gen 17 |
| 5:8 | AD pop Anti xi, 11; Ex in ps cxlvii, 2; In 1 Tim xv, 4 (5:20) |
| 5:9 | Ex in ps cxii, 3 |
| 5:18 | In Is v, 6; In Mat xi, 4; In 1 Thess ix, 2 (5:3) |
| 5:19 | Ad Stag a dae ii, 11 |
| 5:20 | In Is v, 6 |
| 5:21 | Adu Iud 1, 7, 1; Ex in ps xliii, 4; In il Fil 3 |
| 5:22 | Ex in ps xliii, 4 |
| 5:23 | Adu Iud 1, 7, 2; 7, 3, 4; Ex in ps xliii, 4; In Heb xi, 5 |
| 5:25 | Ex in ps xliii, 4; In Acta xvii, 1 (7:44); In Is i, 4 |
| 6:3 | De Laz i, 7; De uir 1; In Gen i, 4 |
| 6:4 | De fato et pr vi; De Laz i, 7; Ex in ps xliv, 10; In Col i, 6 (1:7); In Gen i, 4; In s Bar 4 |
| 6:5 | Cat ill viii, 14; De res mort 5; In Col i, 6 (1:7); In Gen i, 4; In Is v, 5; In s Bar 4; S Gen ix, 4 |

| | |
|---|---|
| 6:6 | Ad pop Anti xviii, 9; De fato et pr vi; De Laz i, 7; De uir 1; In Col i, 6 (1:7); In Heb x, 9; In Is v, 5; In Mat xlviii, 8; lxxix, 4; In s Bar 4; Q reg 2 |
| 7:2 | Ad Stag a dae iii, 10 |
| 7:3 | In Gen xxix, 2 |
| 7:6 | Ad Stag a dae iii, 10 |
| 7:13 | Ex in ps xlix, 4 |
| 7:14 | Ad pop Anti v, 15; In 2 Cor xxiv, 3; In Is i, 1; In Mat xlviii, 1 |
| 7:15 | In 2 Cor xxiv, 3; In Mat xlviii, 1 |
| 8:9 | Ad pop Anti ii, 6; E iii, 2 |
| 8:11 | Con Anom xi, 3; E ii, 11; Ex in ps cxxi, 1; cxliii, 1; In Gen liv, 1; In Heb viii, 6; x, 2; In Mat ii, 10 |
| 9:1 | De incomp dei iv, 3 |
| 9:7 | Ex in ps xliv, 11; In Mat viii, 5; xi, 2; lvii, 1 |
| 9:11 | In Ioh xi, 2 |

Jonah

| | |
|---|---|
| 1 (p) | E cxxv |
| 1:2 | De paen ii, 3; In para 3 |
| 1:3 | De paen ii, 3; In 1 Cor xxix, 2 |
| 1:5 | Ad pop Anti xx, 21 |
| 1:7 | In Acta iii, 4 (1:26) |
| 2:4 | Ad pop Anti xx, 21 |
| 3 (p) | Ad pop Anti v, 15; Cum Sat et Aur 4; De b Phil 4; De laud s Paul iv; Ex in ps cxl, 6 |
| 3:4 | Ad Theo i, 15; De paen ii, 3; In Eph x, 3 (4:4); In Gen xxiv, 6; In 1 Tim xv, 3 (5:20) |
| 3:7 | Ad pop Anti iii, 9; In Gen xxiv, 6 |
| 3:9 | Ad pop Anti v, 17; Ad Theo i, 15; In Gen xxiv 6 |
| 3:10 | Ad pop Anti iii, 8; iii, 10; xx, 21; Ad Theo i, 15; In 2 Cor ii, 5; iv, 6; In Eph x, 3 (4:4) |
| 4:2 | De paen ii, 3 |
| 4:11 | In Acta xxxvii, 3 (17:15); In 2 Cor ii, 5 (2x) |

Micah

| | |
|---|---|
| 1:4 | Ad pop Anti xviii, 9 |
| 1:11 | In Acta xliii, 3; In Mat lxxix, 4; Q reg 2 |
| 1:16 | In Is iii, 9 |

| | |
|---|---|
| 3:1 | In Ioh lii, 1 |
| 3:8 | In 2 Cor xxiv, 3; In Is i, 1 (3x) |
| 3:10 | De lib rep 2; In Mat lxviii, 1 |
| 4:2 | Ex in ps xlvii, 1 |
| 4:3 | In Mat xix, 12 |
| 5:2 | Con Iud et gen 3; Ex in ps xliv, 8 (2x); In diem natal 2; In Ioh xx, 1; xx, 2; In Mat vi, 5; vii, 2 |
| 6:1 | In Rom v, 6 (2:16) |
| 6:2 | Ex in ps xlix, 1; cxlii, 2 (2x); In ascen d n I C 3; In Heb v, 5; In Is i, 2; In 1 Tim xvi, 1 (5:23) |
| 6:3 | Con 1 et t 1; De fut iud 5; De mut nom iii, 4; De paen iv, 5; In Col vi, 1 (2:8); In 2 Cor iv, 4; In Mat xxix, 3; lxviii, 2 |
| 6:4 | Ex in ps cx, 3 |
| 6:6 | In Mat xxx, 3 |
| 6:7 | Adu Iud 7, 3, 4 (2x); In Is i, 6; In Mat xxx, 3 |
| 6:8 | Adu Iud 7, 3, 4; In Heb xi, 5; In Is i, 6; In Mat xxx, 3; S Gen vii, 2 |
| 7:1 | Ad Stag a dae iii, 10; Ex in ps cxix, 3; In Heb xxiii, 8 |
| 7:2 | Ad Stag a dae ii, 5; Ex in ps cxix, 3; In Heb xxiii, 8; In il Fil 3 |
| 7:5 | Cum Sat et Aur 1; In Mat xxxv, 2 |
| 7:6 | Cum Sat et Aur 1 |
| 7:18 | De Chris pres 3; In para 6 |

Nahum

| | |
|---|---|
| 1:1 | In Is i, 1 |
| 1:4 | In 1 Cor xxxiv, 10 |

Habakkuk

| | |
|---|---|
| 1:3 | Ad Stag a dae ii, 5; F Ier 20:14; In Gen xxix 2 |
| 1:5 | In Heb xv, 8 |
| 1:13 | Ex in ps cxl, 5; cxlii, 5; S Gen iv, 2 |
| 1:14 | Ad Stag a dae ii, 5; In Gen xxv, 4; xxix, 2; S Gen iv, 2 |
| 2:4 | In Gal iii, 3 (3:4); In Rom ii, 6 (1:17) |
| 2:14 | In princ Act iv, 9 |
| 2:15 | De uir xxi |
| 2:16 | F Prou 21:30; In Rom xiii, 8 (8:11) |

## Zephaniah

| | |
|---|---|
| 2:11 | Adu Iud 5, 12, 8; Ex in ps cxii, 1; In princ Act iv, 9 |
| 3:3 | Ex in ps viii, 4; xlviii, 8 |
| 3:9 | Con Iud et gen 6 |
| 3:10 | Con Iud et gen 17 |

## Haggai

| | |
|---|---|
| 1:4 | De Anna iii, 4; Ex in ps cxxxi, 2 |
| 1:9 | De bap Chris 1 |
| 2:8 | In 1 Cor xxxiv, 9 |
| 2:9 | In il Dom non est 3 |
| 2:10 | Ad Theo i, 3; Ex in ps xlvii, 3; In il Dom non est 3 |

## Zechariah

| | |
|---|---|
| 1 (p) | In Gen xxxii, 2 |
| 1:3 | De paen vii, 2 |
| 1:12 | F Ier 25:11 |
| 1:14 | Q reg 5 |
| 1:15 | In 2 Cor xxiii, 8 |
| 5:1 | Ad pop Anti xv, 13; xix, 6; In Mat xi, 4 |
| 5:2 | Ad pop Anti xix, 6; In Acta xii, 3 (5:16) |
| 5:4 | Ad pop Anti xv, 13 |
| 5:7-8 | In Mat xxxviii, 3 |
| 7:3 | Ex in ps cxiii, 1 |
| 7:5 | Adu Iud 4, 5, 2; Con Iud et gen 17; In Gen iv, 7 |
| 7:6,9 | In Gen iv, 7 |
| 7:10 | Ad pop Anti xx, 6; In Gen iv, 7; In Is i, 8 |
| 7:11 | Ex in ps xlix, 4 |
| 8:16 | De prod Iud ii, 6 |
| 8:17 | Ad pop Anti xx, 6; Cat ill i, 41; De prod Iud ii, 6 |
| 9:9 | Con Iud et gen 4; In Ioh xxvi, 2; xlii, 3; lxvi, 1; In Mat xix, 12; lxvi, 2 |
| 12:10 | De cruce et lat i, 4; ii, 4; In 1 Cor xxxviii, 3; In il Pater s p 1; In Ioh lxxxv, 3 |
| 13:7 | In Mat lxxxii, 2; In 1 Tim i, 1 (1:2) |

## Malachi

| | |
|---|---|
| 1:1 | In Rom xvi, 5 (9:13) |
| 1:2 | In Gen li, 1; In Rom xvi, 5 (9:13); In 2 Tim vii, 1 (3:7) |
| 1:3 | In Gen li, 1; In 2 Tim vii, 1 (3:7) |
| 1:6 | De incomp dei ii, 5; Ex in ps cxliv, 1 |
| 1:9 | Adu Iud 5, 12, 3 |
| 1:10 | Con Iud et gen 7 (2x); 17; Ex in ps cxii, 1; In princ act iv, 9 |
| 1:11 | Adu Iud 5, 12, 3; Con Iud et gen 17; Ex in ps viii, 1; cxii, 1 |
| 1:12 | Adu Iud 5, 12, 3; Con e q scan 8; Ex in ps viii, 1 |
| 2:7 | Ex in ps cxxxvii, 1; In Gal i, 7 (1:8-9) |
| 2;10 | In Ioh xlix, 2; In Rom xiv, 3 (8:15) |
| 2:13 | De lib rep 2; In Mat lxxxv, 3 |
| 2:14 | De lib rep 2 (2x) |
| 2:15 | Ex in ps cxiii, 5; In Col xii, 5 (4:18) |
| 2:17 | De san pent i, 5; Ex in ps cxl, 5 (2x); cxlii, 2; In Is iii, 4 |
| 3:1 | In Acta xxxii, 3 (15:11); In Ioh vi, 1; In Mat xix, 12; xxxvii, 2; xxxvii, 4 |
| 3:2 | Ad Theo i, 12; Con Iud et gen 11; In Mat xix, 12 |
| 3:3 | Ad Theo i, 12; Con Iud et gen 8 |
| 3:10 | De Laz ii, 4 |
| 3;14 | Adu Iud 5, 5, 9; De san pent i, 5 |
| 3:15 | Adu Iud 5, 5, 9; De san pent i, 5; Ex in ps cxl, 5; cxlii, 2 |
| 3:16 | De san pent i, 5; Ex in ps cxxxviii, 4 |
| 4:1 | In Heb xxiii, 8 |
| 4:2 | In il Fil 4; In Is ii, 4 |
| 4:5 | De proph obscur ii, 5; In Mat xxxvii, 4; lvii 1; In 2 Thess iv, 2 (2:12) |
| 4:6 | De proph obscur ii, 5; In Acta v, 2 (2:20); In Mat xxxvii, 4; lvii, 1 |

## Torbit

| | |
|---|---|
| 4:16 | Ad pop Anti xiii, 7; Ex in ps v, 1 |
| 12:9 | In Acta xxi, 2 (9:35); In Phil iv, 5 (1:30) |

## Baruch

| | |
|---|---|
| 1:1 | F Ier 1:1 |
| 1:15-16 | Ad Stag a dae iii, 10 |

I Maccabees



II Maccabees



Wisdom of Solomon

| | |
|---|---|
| 9:10 | F Ier 9:23 |
| 9:14 | Con Anom xi, 1; De uir xii; In Gen ii, 2; In il Hoc scit 2; In Ioh iv, 2; S Gen i, 3 |
| 11:23 | In Phil iv, 4 (1:30) |
| 13:5 | Ad pop Anti ix, 4; De diab tent ii, 3; In Gen iv, 5 |
| 13:6 | Ex in ps cxliii, 2 |
| 14:3 | In Gen xi, 1 |
| 14;16 | In Eph xviii, 3 (5:14) |
| 16:28 | Ex in ps v, 3; cix, 7 |
| 16:29 | In Mat xxv, 5 |
| 18:15 | In Mat ii, 1 |
| 19:20 | In Heb xxvii, 2 |

Song of the Three Children

| | |
|---|---|
| (p) | Ad pop Anti iv, 6 |
| 2-3 | Ex in ps cxl, 5 |
| 4 | E iii, 13; Ex in ps cxl, 5; In Mat iii, 7 |
| 5 | De proph obscur ii, 9; Ex in ps xliii, 7; cxlii, 2 |
| 6 | In Heb xxvi, 8; In Mat iii, 7; In Philem ii, 3 (v16) |
| 8 | Adu Iud 5, 6, 1; Ex in ps xliii, 7; In Mat iii, 7 |
| 9 | De incomp dei v, 3 |
| 11 | Ex in ps cxiii, 6 |
| 13 | Ex in ps cxiii, 5; cxxii, 1 |
| 14 | Adu Iud 4, 5, 1; Con Iud et gen 17; De san pent i, 3; Ex in ps xliii, 7; In Is vi, 4; In Iuu et Max 2; Q nemo 15 |
| 15 | In Iuu et Max 2; In Mat xv, 2; In Rom xiv, 8 (8:27); xx, 1 (12:1) |
| 16 | In Mat iv, 18; xv, 2; In Rom xiv, 8 (8:27); xx, 1 (12:1) |
| 26 | In Mat iv, 19 |
| 32 | De ss mar A 1 |
| 34 | E cxxv |

Susanna

| | |
|---|---|
| 22 | De mut nom ii, 1 |
| 42 | De decmil 5; Ex in ps cxxxviii, 1; In quat Laz A 1 |
| 45 | De paen ii, 2 |
| 56 | In Gen xxix, 7 |

## Bel and the Dragon

| | |
|---|---|
| (p) | De D et S ii, 2; In 1 Cor xxiv, 7; In Gen xxxii, 7 |
| 23-25 | H in il App 18 |
| 36 | In Acta xix, 2 (8:4) |
| 38 | In Heb xxvi, 8 |
| 39 | Ex in ps cxvii, 3 |

## Ecclesiasticus

| | |
|---|---|
| 1:1 | In para 2 |
| 1:2 | Ex in ps iv, 6; In para 2 |
| 1:22 | Cat ill v, 5; In Acta xxix, 4 (13:41); In Heb ii, 2; v, 8; In Ioh iv, 4; xlviii, 3; In Mat lxxxvii, 4 |
| 2:1 | Ad pop Anti i, 30; De Laz i, 12; F in epis cath James 1:2; In il Dom non est 5 |
| 2:2 | In il Dom non est 5; In Mat x, 8; In 2 Tim i, 2 (1:7) |
| 2:3 | Ad pop Anti i, 23 |
| 2:4 | Ad pop Anti xviii, 7; In Eph xix, 2 (5:21); In s Eust 1 |
| 2:5 | Ad pop Anti xviii, 7; In s Eust 1 |
| 2:6-8 | In s Eust 1 |
| 2:10 | Ad uid iun 6; Ex in ps cxvii, 2; In Phil iii, 1 (1:20) |
| 2:11 | Ex in ps ix, 5; x, 3; cxlii, 4; In il Dom non est 5; In Phil ii, 5 (1:19) |
| 2:12 | Ex in ps ix, 5; In Heb xix, 3; In il Dom non est 5; In para 2 |
| 2:14 | Ex in ps cxx, 1 |
| 2:18 | In Heb xx, 4 |
| 3:4 | In il Is Ego 4 |
| 3:8 | S Gen iv, 3 |
| 3:10 | In 2 Tim ii, 4 (1:12) |
| 3:11 | In Phil ix, 4 (2:30); In 2 Tim ii, 4 (1:12) |
| 3:12 | In Gen xxix, 4; In 2 Tim ii, 4 (1:12); S Gen iv, 2 |
| 3:15 | In il Sal P et A ii, 6 |
| 3:20 | De mut nom iv, 6 |
| 3:21 | Ad pop Anti xii, 7 |
| 3:22 | Ad e q scan iii; Ad pop Anti xii, 7 |
| 3:25 | Ad e q scan iii |
| 3:30 | In Heb ix, 8; In Ioh vii, 2; lxxiii, 3 |
| 4:1 | E vii, 4 |
| 4:3 | Ad pop Anti vi, 10 |

De Chris prec 4
De sac iii, 16; In Gen xxxiv, 3; In Mat xxxv, 5; li, 5; In princ Act ii, 5

Ex inps cxxxii
In Gen x, 1; xxiii, 2; In s Iul 5
De s Bab c Iul 7
Ex in ps cxl, 4; cxl, 6
Ex in ps xlix, 5
In Eph iv, 3 (2:10); In Heb xx, 4; In Ioh xxviii, 1
In 2 Cor xxii, 4; In Mat lxviii, 5
Ad Theo ii, 4; Adu op iii, 17; De diab tent ii, 5; In il Hoc scit 6
In il Hoc scit 6
De uir lxx
Ex in ps cxl, 4

In 1 Thess ii, 3 (2:8)
In Phil x, 5 (3:7)
In Gen xxxv, 2
Ad e q scan iv; Ad pop Anti xv, 5
In il Uidi dom iii, 1
In Tit ii, 2 (1:11)
Ex inps cxlii, 1
In il Uidi elig 7
S Gen iv, 3
In 2 Tim ii, 2 (1:12)
Non esse ad grat 1
Cat ill ii, 15
In il Uidi dom iii, 4; In Mat xvii, 3 (as Scripture)
In Acta xxix, 4 (13:41); In il Uidi dom iii, 4
Ad pop Anti xv, 1; xv, 6; In 1 Thess iii, 4 (3:4)
In 1 Cor xv, 10; In Heb viii, 9; In Mat li, 5; In Phil x, 5 (3:7)
Ex in ps xlviii, 2; In Heb xviii, 4
In Phil xiv, 3 (4:9)
De paen ix, 1; De proph obscur ii, 6; Ex in ps xlviii, 1; cxv, 4; In 2 Cor xxiii, 6; In Ioh xlviii, 3; In Mat lxxx, 3; In Phil v, 2 (2:4)
De proph obscur ii, 6
In 2 Thess Argumentum, 2
In Ioh ix, 2; In 2 Thess Argumentum, 2
In Acta xxix, 4 (13:41); In il Uididom iii, 4
Ex in ps cxl, 4; In Heb xxv, 5
In Phil xv, 5 (4:23)

| | |
|---|---|
| 19:11 | Ex in ps cxl, 4; In Heb xxi, 7 |
| 19:14-15 | In 2 Thess iv, 4 (3:2) |
| 19:16 | In quat Laz A 1 |
| 19:26 | De Bab c Iul 6 |
| 19:27 | Cat ill iv 26; E ii, 9; H in mar 1; In Is iii 8; In kal 5 |
| 20:4 | In Mat lxxxiii, 3 |
| 20:5,8 | Ex in ps cxl, 4 |
| 20:20 | Cat ill ix, 31; In 2 Thess ii, 4 (1:8) |
| 20:29 | In Heb xviii, 6; In Ioh lxiv, 4 |
| 20:33 | Ex in ps cxl, 4 |
| 21:1 | Ad Theo i, 18; De duab tent iii, 2; F Ier 5:7 |
| 21:2 | In Rom viii, 6 (4:21); In Tit iii, 4 (2:1) |
| 22:10 | De Laz v, 3 |
| 22:21-22 | In Eph ix, 4 (4:3) |
| 22:27 | In Acta xl, 3 |
| 23:2 | Ex in ps cxl, 6; cxl, 7 |
| 23:10 | Ad pop Anti xiv, 16; In Acta x, 4 (4:22) |
| 23:17 | In 1 Thess ix, 2 (3:1); In 2 Thess Argumentum 2 |
| 23:26 | De Anna ii, 4; In il Prop 5 |
| 24:22 | In Heb xxv, 6 |
| 25:1 | In Eph xx, 1 (5:24); In Tit iv, 2 (2:5) |
| 25:2 | Ex in ps cxxxii, 1; In Acta xlix, 4 |
| 25:11 | In Phil iii, 4 (1:24) |
| 25:12 | In Gen iv, 1; xli, 2; In il Hoc scit 1; In il Ne tim i, 1; In il Uidi dom iv, 1; Non esse desp 1 |
| 25:14 | In 1 Cor xxix, 9 |
| 25:26 | De Anna iv, 3 |
| 26:27 | In Tit vi, 4 (3:15) |
| 26:28 | Ad Theo i, 18 |
| 27:5 | In 1 Cor xxii, 7 |
| 27:28 | De incomp dei iii, 1 |
| 28:3 | Ad Dem de comp i, 5; In Heb ix, 8; In Mat lxxix, 5 |
| 28:5 | Ad Dem de comp i, 5 |
| 28:6 | In 2 Thess ii, 3 (1:8) |
| 28:14 | De D et S iii, 7 |
| 28:22 | Cat ill i, 32; ix, 30; Ex in ps cxl, 4 |
| 28:25 | Cat ill ix, 31; In Heb xxi, 8 |
| 29:27 | De proph obscur ii, 6 |
| 29:28 | In Gen xxix, 3 |
| 30:7 | In il Uid elig 10; In Mat lv, 3 |
| 30:20 | In Mat lxxxiii, 3 |
| 31:1 | In Phil ii, 4 (1:19) |
| 31:20 | In Acta xvi, 4 (7:34) |

| | |
|---|---|
| 31:24 | Adu op ii, 10 |
| 32:10 | De Eleaz 1; Ex in ps cxl, 4; In Mat xlvii, 4 |
| 32:11 | De Eleaz 1; Ex in ps cxl, 4 |
| 32:14 | De Eleaz 1; In Eph xvii, 3 (5:4) |
| 32:15 | De Eleaz 1 |
| 34:11 | De res mort 4 |
| 34:20 | In Mat lii, 6 |
| 34:23 | Ad Theo i, 18 |
| 34:24 | Ad Theo i, 18; In Ioh xiii, 4 |
| 34:25 | Ad Theo i, 18 |
| 34:28 | De Laz vii, 1; De paen vi, 2 |
| 39:2 | Ex in ps cxlviii, 3 |
| 39:21 | Ad e q scan iii |
| 40:23 | In Eph xx, 1 (5:24) |
| 42:1-4 | F Iob 3:21 |
| 42:9 | De sac iii, 17 |
| 44:17 | AD pop Anti vi, 13 |
| 51:11 | In Acta ii, 1 (1:6) |

Matthew

| | |
|---|---|
| 1:1 | Ex in ps xliv, 8; In Rom vii, 2 (3:21) |
| 1:3 | In Gen lxii, 2; In Mat iii, 3 |
| 1:7 | In Mat iii, 8 |
| 1:18 | Cat ill xi, 17; In Ioh liii, 3; In Mat iv, 4; iv, 5 |
| 1:19 | In Mat iv, 7 |
| 1:20 | In Acta ii, 4 (1:11); In Heb xv, 4; In Ioh v, 3; In Mat iv, 10 |
| 1:21 | H in il App 14; 16; In Col i, 2 (1:4); In Eph vii, 1 (3:11); In Gal i, 3 (1:3); In Heb v, 3; In Mat iv, 12; vii, 2 |
| 1:22 | In Ioh xiii, 1; In Mat xvi, 3 |
| 1:23 | De incomp dei v, 2; Ex in ps xliv, 8; cxvii, 5; F Ier 2:21; In Mat xvi, 3 |
| 1:24 | Cat ill xii, 12; In Acta xli, 3; In 1 Cor xxix, 3 |
| 2 (p) | In Col iii, 4 (1:20); In Tit iii, 2 (1:14) |
| 2:1 | Ex in ps xlix, 3; cx, 4; In diem nat 3 |
| 2:2 | H hab p p Gothus 4; 6; In diem nat 3 |
| 2:3 | Con Iud et gen 2 |
| 2:4 | In il Pater s p 1; In Ioh 1, 1 |
| 2:5 | De diab tent iii, 3; In Ioh xx, 2 |
| 2:6 | In diem nat 2; In Ioh xx, 1 |
| 2:7 | In Acta xxxii, 3 (15:11); In Mat vii, 3 |
| 2:8 | In Mat vii, 3 |
| 2:9 | De Chris prec 3; In Mat vii, 4 |
| 2:11 | Ex in ps xlix, 3 |

| | |
|---|---|
| 2:12 | In Mat viii, 1 |
| 2:13 | In Mat viii, 2 |
| 2:15 | In Ioh xiii, 1 |
| 2:17 | In Mat ix, 4 |
| 2:18 | In Ioh xiii, 1; In Mat ix, 4 |
| 2:19 | In il Pater s p 1; In Mat ix, 5 |
| 2:20 | In Mat ix, 5 |
| 2:23 | In Mat ix, 6 |
| 3 (p) | De laud s Paul 1 |
| 3:3 | In Eph xxiv, 2 (6:22) |
| 3:4 | In Mat x, 4 |
| 3:5 | In Ioh xxix, 1; In Mat x, 5 |
| 3:6 | In Mat x, 5; xi, 1; xxx, 1; xl, 2 |
| 3:7 | Ex in ps xlviii, 8; In Eph xxiii, 2 (6:14); In Gen xiii, 3; xxiii, 4; xxxi, 4; In Is i, 3; In Mat xxiv, 2; xxiv, 4; In Rom xvii, 5 (10:13) |
| 3:8 | De bap Chris 3 (2x); In Gen xxxi, 4; In Is i, 3; In Mat x, 2; x, 3; x, 7 |
| 3:9 | In Gen xxxi, 4; In Ioh liv, 1; In Mat ix, 7; xi, 3; xxvi, 5; xxvi, 6; xliv, 2; In Rom xix, 4 (11:17) |
| 3:10 | De sac iii, 17; In Mat xi, 4 (2x); xi, 7 |
| 3:11 | Cat ill iii, 4; De bap Chris 3; In Acta iv, 1 (2:4); vi, 2 (2:34); xxiv, 2 (11:16); In Eut ii, 11; In Ioh xvi, 1; xxxii, 1; In Mat xi, 5; xii, 2; xxxvi, 1; xxxvi, 3; xxxvii, 3 |
| 3:12 | Ex in ps vii, 11; In Mat xi, 7; xxxii, 4; xliii, 1; lxvii, 2 |
| 3:14 | De bap Chris 3 (2x); In Ioh xvii, 2; In Mat xii, 1; xxxvi, 1; In 2 Tim ii, 4 (1:12) |
| 3:15 | De bap Chris 3; 4; De prod Iud i, 4; ii, 4; Ex in ps xlix, 2; In 1 Cor xxxviii, 3 (2x); In Ioh v, 1; xvii, 1; In Mat x, 1; xii, 1; xii, 2; xvi, 3; liv, 6 |
| 3:16 | Cat ill xi, 13; In Ioh xl, 3; In Mat xii, 3 |
| 3:17 | Cat ill xi, 13; De mut nom iii, 5; Ex in ps xliv, 4; In Gen xlvii, 3 |
| 4:2 | In Gen i, 3; In Mat xiii, 2; xix, 12 |
| 4:3 | Ex in ps xlix, 2; In Mat xiii, 2 |
| 4:4 | Con Anom xi, 3; De mut nom i, 2; Ex in ps cx, 5; In Gen ii, 1; xxi, 6; In Mat xiii, 3; xxi, 3; lv, 7; In s Luc 2 |
| 4:5 | In Mat xxxvi, 2 |
| 4:6 | Adu Iud 6, 6, 8; Ex in ps xlix, 2; In Heb xxvi, 5; In Mat xiii, 4 |
| 4:7 | In Mat xiii, 4 |
| 4:8 | In Mat xiii, 5 |
| 4:9-10 | In Mat xiii, 5; xx, 2 |
| 4:11 | In Ioh xiii, 5; xxi, 1 |

4:12 In Mat xlix, 1

4:14-16 In Mat xiv, 1

4:17 S Gen vii, 5

4:18 Ex in ps xliv, 2; In Gal i, 2 (1:3); In Mat xiv, 3

4:19 De cruce et lat i, 2; ii, 2; De res d n I C 4; De san pent i, 2; H in san pascha 5; In Eut ii, 17; In Ioh xviii, 3; In Mat xiv, 3; In princ Act iv, 4

4:21-22 Ex in ps xliv, 3

4:23 In Eph vii, 4 (3:19)

4:24 De ss mar A 1; In Ioh xii, 2; xx, 1; xxi, 2; In Mat lvii, 3

5 (p) De uir xxxiii; xxxvi

5:1 De Chris prec 4

5:3 Ad e q scan xiii; Ad pop Anti xviii, 10; Adu op iii, 14; Cat ill viii, 3; De Chris prec 4; De mut nom iv, 6; Ex in ps ix, 6; In Acta xliv 1; In 2 Cor xxx, 4; In Eph i, 1 (1:3); ix, 2 (4:3); In Heb xviii, 4; In il Pater s p 4; In Ioh lix, 4; In Mat xi, 2; xxxviii, 3; In Rom xx, 3 (12:3); In 2 Thess i, 2 (Introduction)

5:4 Ad e q scan xiii; Ad pop Anti xviii, 10; Ad Stel de comp i, 1; Adu op iii, 14; Cat ill viii, 3; De Chris prec 4; De Laz iii, 3; In Acta xiii, 4 (5:33); In Col xii, 3 (4:18); In 2 Cor xxx, 4; In Ioh lxii, 4; In Mat xv, 4; xl, 5; In Phil xiv, 1 (4:7)

5:5 Ad e q scan xiii; Ad pop Anti xviii, 10; Adu op iii, 10; Cat ill viii, 3; De paen vii, 6; De ss mar B 3; Ex in ps vi, 4; cxix, 1; cxl, 5; In 2 Cor xxx, 4; Non esse ad grat 3

5:6 Ad e q scan xiii; Ad pop Anti xviii, 10; Adu op iii, 14; Cat ill viii, 3; De mut nom ii, 1; In Acta xiii, 4 (5:33); In 2 Cor xxx, 4; In Eph xxiv, 1 (6:17); In Gen iv, 1; xxiv, 1; In il Ne tim i, 1; In il Uidi dom iv, 1; In Ioh li, 1; In Mat xv, 6

5:7 Ad e q scan xiii; Ad pop Anti xviii, 10; Adu op iii, 14; Cat ill viii, 3; In Acta xxv, 4 (11:30); In 2 Cor xxx, 4; In Ioh lix, 4; In Mat xx, 6; In Philem iii, 2 (v25)

5:8 Ad e q scan xiii; Ad pop Anti xviii, 10; Adu op iii, 14; Cat ill viii, 3; De Chris prec 4; In Acta xiii, 4 (5:33); In 2 Cor xxx, 4; In Eph i, 1 (1:3); In Gen xxxvi, 6; lx, 3; In Heb xii, 7; In Ioh xv, 2; lix, 4; lxxiii, 2;

5:8 cont In Mat xv, 6; xlvii, 4; In Rom xxxii, 3 (16:24); In 1 Thess iv, 3 (3:13); In 2 Tim vi, 4 (2:26)

5:9 Ad pop Anti xviii, 10; Adu op iii, 14; Cat ill viii, 3; De prod Iud i, 6; F Prou 6:14; In Acta xxxvii, 3 (17:15); In Col iii, 3 (1:20); In 2 Cor xxx, 4; In Mat xv, 6; In Phil xiv, 1 (4:9); xiv, 3 (4:9)

5:10 Ad e q scan xiii; Ad pop Anti xviii, 10; Adu op iii, 14; Cat ill viii, 3; De prod Iud i, 1; ii, 1 (2x); In Acta xiii, 4 (5:33); In Eph v, 1 (2:12); In Gen ii, 5; In Mat xv, 7

5:11 Ad e q scan xiii; Ad pop Anti i, 19; xviii, 7; Adu op iii, 14; Cat ill viii, 3; De sac iii, 11; De D et S ii, 4; De fut iut 4; E vii, 4; E ad e p d (2x); In 2 Cor xii, 3; In Eph i, 1 (1:3); v, 1 (2:12); viii, 2 (4:2); In Heb xxxiii, 9; In Ioh lxxvii, 3; In Mat xv, 6; In para 8; In Rom x, 6 (6:4); xxii, 1 (12:12)

5:12 Ad e q scan xiii; Ad pop Anti i, 19; xviii, 7; Adu op iii, 14; De D et S ii, 4; De fut iut 4; E vii, 4; E ad e p d (2x); In 2 Cor xii, 3; In Eph i, 1 (1:3); v, 1 (2:12); In Eut ii, 12; In Heb xxxiii, 9; In Ioh lxxvii, 3; In Mat xv, 6; In para 8; In Phil vi, 1 (2:8); In Rom x, 6 (6:4)

5:13 Con e q sub 7; De sac vi, 4; Ex in ps ix, 7; In il Si esur 2; In Mat xv, 10 (2x)

5:14 In il Si esur 2; In Mat xv, 11 (2x)

5:15 In Acta viii, 3 (3:12); In Mat xv, 11 (2x); xliii, 7

5:16 Ad pop Anti ix, 10; Cat ill iv, 19-21; vi, 11; Ex in ps xlix, 5; cxii, 1; cxiii, 3; cxxxiii; cxlv, 1; cxlv, 4; cxlviii, 1; In Acta xlvi, 3; In 1 Cor vi, 8; In Gen vii, 2 (2x); xxvi, 6; In IOh xiii, 4; In Mat xv, 11; xix, 7; xlvi, 3; In princ Act i, 5; ii, 4; ii, 6; In Rom viii, 5 (4:21); xxii, 2 (12:18); xxvi, 4 (14:23); In 1 Tim x, 2 (3:7); Pec frat 11; S cum pres 2; S Gen i, 3

5:17 De Chris prec 4 (2x); Ex in ps cx, 6; In Ioh xlix, 2; lxiv, 3

5:18 In Mat xvi, 4

5:19 Ad Dem de comp i, 10; De paen v, 5; De sac iv, 8; Ex in ps xlix, 6; In Eph iv, 3 (2:10); In Gen viii, 5; In il Pater s p 4; In Ioh lxxi, 2; In Mat xvi, 5

5:20 Adu eos q 'n adf 3; De diab tent i, 7; De Laz v, 5; De lib rep 2; De paen vi, 5; De uir lxxxiii; E iv, 3; Ex in ps vii, 4; cxxxvi, 2;

5:20 cont In Eph xiii, 2 (4:24); In Gen xxiv, 8; In Heb viii, 6; xix, 4; In il Ne tim i, 5; In Ioh li, 3; In Mat xvi, 5; xvi, 6; xvii, 6; lvi, 3; In Rom xi, 3 (6:14); xii, 5 (7:6)

5:21 Ad Dem de comp i, 2; De Chris prec 3; 4; 5; In il Fil 5; In il Hab ii, 3; In Ioh iii, 4; xxiv 2; In Mat xvi, 7; In Rom xii, 4 (7:6)

5:22 De Chris prec 4; De diab tent i, 7; De laud s Paul vi; De paen vii, 2; De sac iii, 13; De uir i; xxi; Ex in ps iv, 7; cxl, 5; cxl, 6; In Acta xvii, 4 (7:53); xxix, 4 (13:41); In 1 Cor xlii, 5; In 2 Cor ccii, 8; In Eph iv, 2 (2:10) iv, 3 (2:10); v, 2 (2:15); xiv, 4 (4:30); In Gal iii, 1 (3:1); In Gen xxviii, 6; In Heb i, 4; ii, 2; xxvii, 9; In il Fil 5; In il Hab ii, 3; In Ioh iii, 4; xxiv, 2; xlviii, 3; In Mat xv, 5; xvi, 7; lxi, 2; lxiv, 4; lxxxvi, 4; In Tit i, 2 (1:5); iii, 4 (2:1)

5:23 Ad Dem de comp i, 3; Ad pop Anti xx, 12; Adu Iud 2, 3, 1; 3, 6, 2; Cat ill xi, 22; De prod Iud i, 6; ii, 6; In 2 Cor xxx, 4; In il Si esur 6; In Is iii, 6; In Tit i, 2 (1:5)

5:24 Ad Dem de com i, 3; Ad pop Anti xx, 12; xx, 18 Adu Iud 2, 3, 1; 3, 6, 2; Cat ill xi, 22; De prod Iud i, 6; ii, 6; In 1 Cor xix, 4; In il Si esur 6; In Is iii, 6; In Mat lx, 1; In Tit i, 2 (1:5)

5:25 In 1 Cor vii, 16; xvi, 9; In Mat xv, 5 (2x); xvi, 13

5:27 De Chris prec 4; De paen vi, 2; In Rom xii, 4 (7:6)

5:28 Ad pop Anti xv, 12; Cat ill i, 32; xii, 58; Con 1 et t 2; De Chris prec 4; De diab tent i, 7; De D et S iii, 1; De paen vi, 2 (2x); vi, 4; vi, 5 (2x); Ex in ps iv, 13; vi, 6 xliii, 9; F Ier 31:1; H in il App 2; In 1 Cor vii, 16; xlii, 5; In Gen vi, 2; xv, 5; xxii, 3; xxvii, 3; In il Fil 5; In Mat vii, 7; lxi, 2; lxxxvi, 4; In Rom xii, 6-7 (3:15)

5:29 De dec mil 5; Ex in ps iv, 13; vi, 5; In Col viii, 4 (3:15); In Ioh lvii, 2; In kal 4; In Mat xvii, 3; xlvi, 4; In Phil ii, 1 (1:9)

5:30 Ex in ps vi, 5

5:31 In Rom xiii, 4 (7:25)

5:32 Adu Iud 2, 3, 2; De dec mil 3; De lib rep 1; 2; 3; De uir xxviii; In 1 Cor xix, 4; In Gen xxvi, 2; In Ioh lxiii, 3; In Is iii, 6; In 1 Thess v, 2 (4:8); Non esse ad grat 7; Qual duc 1; 2

5:33 Cat ill i, 42; In Gen xv, 5; In Mat xvii, 5; In Rom xii, 5 (7:6)
5:34 Ad pop Anti xv, 14; Adu op iii, 14; Cat ill i. 42; Ex in ps xlvi, 2; In Gen xv, 5; In Mat xvii, 5; xxii, 2; xxii, 5
5:35 Ex in ps xlvi, 2; In Mat xxii, 2
5:36 Ad pop Anti vii, 10; In Mat xvii, 5; In Rom xx, 4 (12:3)
5:37 Ad Dem de comp i, 4; Cat ill ix, 40; De diab tent i, 7; De uir lxxxiii; Ex in ps v, 2; In Acta viii, 3 (3:12); x, 5 (4:22); In Mat xvii, 5
5:38 In Rom xiii, 4 (7:25)
5:39 De fut uit 4; 5; De prod Iud i, 3; ii, 3; Ex in ps vii, 14; In Eph xvi, 3 (4:32); xxii, 1 (6:8); In il Sal p et A ii, 3; In Ioh lxxxiii, 5; In Mat xvi, 9; lx, 1; In Rom xii, 8 (7:13); xxii, 3 (12:21); S post red ii, 2
5:40 In Acta i, 3 (1:2); In 1 Cor xvi, 9; In Gen xxiv, 8; In Mat xviii, 2
5:41 De Chris prec 3; In Mat xviii, 3; In princ Act iv, 7
5:42 In Heb xi, 9; In Mat xviii, 3
5:43 In Mat xviii, 4
5:44 Ad e q scan xiii; De fut uit 4 (3x); De laud s Paul ii, De uir l; Ex in ps iv, 5; vii, 4; cxxvii, 3; cxl, 6; In Gen xxvii, 8; lii, 4; lxiv, 7; In Heb xix, 5; In il Pater s p 4; In il Si esur 6; In Ioh lxxi, 3; In Mat xviii, 4; lx, 2; In Rom xix, 8 (11:35); In 1 Tim iii, 4 (1:14); Non esse desp 1; Pec frat 11
5:45 Ad pop Anti xii, 5; De cruce et lat i, 5; ii, 5; De fut uit 4; De Laz ii, 5; De uir xlix; Ex in ps xi, 3; cx, 5; cxxvii, 3; cxl, 6; cxliv, 4; F Ier 12;3; In Acta 1, 4; In Col iii, 3 (1:20); In 2 Cor xx, 3; In Eph vii, 4 (3:19); xvii, 1 (5:2); In Gen iv, 7; ix, 3; x, 7; liv, 5; In il Hab i, 7; ii, 7; In Ioh xxxviii, 2; lx, 5; lxxxi, 3; In Mat xviii, 4; xviii, 5; xix, 1; xix, 11; xxii, 2; lxi, 5; In Phil Introduction, 3; vi, 3 (2:8); In Philem iii, 2 (v25); In Rom xi, 4 (5:11); x, 6 (6:4); S Gen iii, 1
5:46 De cruce et lat i, 5; ii, 5; In 1 Cor xlii, 5; In 2 Cor xxvii, 3; In Eph vii, 3 (3:19); In Gen iv, 8; xi, 3; xxiv, 8; lii, 5; lviii, 5; In Mat xviii, 7; xl, 4; lx, 2; In Rom xxvii, 3 (15:7)
5:47 In Acta xiv, 3 (6:7); In 1 Cor xlii, 5; In Mat xviii, 9

5:48 In Mat xviii, 9; In Rom xix, 8 (11:35)
6:1 In Acta v, 4 (2:20); In 2 Cor xx, 3; In Mat xix, 2; lxxi
6:2 De fato et pr iv; De paen ix, 1; In Mat xix, 2
6:3 De fato et pr iv; In Mat xix, 2; lxxi; In 1 Tim viii, 1 (2:10); xiv, 6 (5:10); (2x)
6:4 In 2 Cor xx, 3; In Mat xix, 2; xxii, 4
6:5 In Mat xix, 3; In 1 Tim viii, 1 (2:10); In 2 Tim viii, 4 (3:14); In Tit ii, 4 (1:11)
6:6 De paen iv, 4; In Mat xix, 3; xix, 4; In 1 Tim viii, 1 (2:10)
6:7 De Anna ii, 2; In Eph xxiv, 1 (6:20); In Mat xix, 5
6:8 Cat ill viii, 19; Ex in ps cx, 3; In Heb xxix, 5; In Mat xix, 5
6:9 Ex in ps cxii, 1 (2x); cxliv, 1; cxlix, 1; In il Fil 4; In Mat xix, 6
6:10 Ex in ps cxii, 2; cxiv, 3; cxix, 2; In Col iii 3 (1:20); In Mat xix, 7; S ante iret 2
6:11 Ex in ps cxii, 1; cxxvii, 4; cxl, 4; In Gen liv, 5; In Mat xix, 8; In Phil xv, 4 (4:19)
6:12 Ad Dem de comp i, 5; Ad pop Anti iii, 2; xx, 15; xxi, 17; De dec mil 7; De Laz vi, 9; Ex in ps iv, 4; cxii, 1; In Eut i, 5; In il Si esur 6; In Ioh xxxix, 4; In Mat xix, 9; lx, 1
6:13 Ex in ps cxii, 1; cxxxix, 1; cxlix, 1; In Mat xix, 10; xxiii, 7; xxxviii, 3; In Philem i, 3 (v3)
6:14 Ad pop Anti xx, 17; Adu op iii, 7; De D et S iii, 9; De dec mil 7; De diab tent ii, 6; E cxvii; Ex in ps cxv, 4; In 1 Cor xxiii, 6; In Gen xxvii, 7; In il Si esur 6; In Ioh xxxiv, 3; In Mat xix, 9; xix, 11; xxiii, 7; xxxviii, 1; In Rom xxv, 6 (14:13)
6:15 In Eph xvii, 1 (5:2); In Mat xix, 11; xxxviii, 1; In 1 Tim vi, 2 (2:4)
6:16 In Mat xxxviii, 1
6:17 Ex in ps xlvi, 1; In Gen xxxi, 1; In Mat. xxx, 4; xxxviii, 1
6:18 In Gen xxxi, 1; In Heb xviii, 4; In Mat xxxviii, 1; lviii, 6; S anti iret 4
6:19 Ad pop Anti xvi, 14; F Prou 10:2; In Eph xxiii, 3 (6:14); In Mat xx, 2; xxxviii, 1; lxxiv, 5
6:21 Cat ill vii, 15; De Anna iii, 4; Ex in ps ix, 1; cxi, 5 (2x); In Mat xx, 3
6:22 In Mat xx, 3 (2x)
6:23 Ex in ps iv, 5 (In 1 Cor xxiii, 8; In Eph vi, 3 (3:7); In Gal iii, 1 (3:5); In Mat xx, 5;

6:23 cont In Tit ii, 1 (1:6)

6:24 Adu op iii, 6; Con e q sub 6; In Acta xxix, 4 (13:41); In 1 Cor i, 2; In Eph xviii, 2 (5:14) In Heb xv, 7; In Ioh viii, 2; lix, 4; In Mat xxviii, 5; lix, 6; lxxiv, 5; In Phil vi, 5 (2:8); In Rom xiii, 3-4 (7:23); In 1 Thess xi, 4 (5:28); In 1 Tim xi, 1 (3:16) (2x)

6:25 In Col ix, 1 (3:17); In 1 Cor xlii, 5; In 2 Cor xix, 3; In Mat xxi, 3; In 1 Thess vi, 3 (4:13)

6:26 Ad pop Anti xii, 6; Cat ill viii, 23; Ex in ps cx, 3; In Acta xiii, 4 (5:33); In Mat xxi, 3; xxxii, 7; lxxiv, 5; In Phil ii, 5 (1:19); vii, 6 (2:11)

6:27 In Mat xx, 3; xxi, 5

6:29 Ex in ps cx, 3

6:30 In Ioh xxxviii, 2; In Mat xxii, 1; xxii, 2

6:31 In Mat xxii, 3

6:32 Cat ill viii, 19; In Mat xxii, 3

6:33 Adu op iii, 21; Cat ill vii, 16; De paen iv, 4; Ex in ps cxi, 2; cxl, 2; In Acta xxiii, 4 (10:43); Ex in ps cxi, 2; cxl, 2; In Acta xxiii, 4 (10:43); In Eph xx, 9 (5:33); In Gen xxiv, 8; liv, 5; In Heb viii, 10; In Ioh iii, 6; In Mat xv, 5; xxii, 4; xxvi, 5; lv, 8; lxviii, 3; lxviii, 5; In Rom vii, 8 (3:31); In 1 Tim xi, 2 (3:16) (2x); Q reg 9; Qual duc 6; S Gen vi, 2

6:34 Ad Dem de comp i, 5; De diab tent i, 5; In Eph xix, 1 (5:17); xxiii, 3 (6:14) (2x); In d P Nolo 5; In il Is Ego 6; In Ioh xliv; In Mat xix, 8

7:1 Ad Dem de comp i, 5; Ad pop Anti iii, 16; De cruce et lat i, 3; ii, 3; In 1 Cor xi, 1; xliv 1; In Eph xviii, 1 (5:13); In Gen xlii, 3; In Heb xxi, 7; In Mat x, 7: In Phil ix, 4 (2:30)

7:2 Ad Dem de comp i, 5; De Laz ii, 6; vi, 8; In Col x, 2 (4:1); In Eph xv, 4 (4:31); xvi, 3 (4:32); xxii, 2 (6:9); In il Sal P et A ii, 5; In Ioh lxxvii, 4; In Mat xxiii, 2; xxv, 2; In Rom v, 1 (3:1); In 1 Tim vi, 2 (2:4)

7:3 In 1 Cor xii, 2; In Eph xviii, 1 (5:13); In Heb xxiv, 1; In il Sal P et A ii, 6; In Mat xxiii, 1; xxiii, 2

7:4 De mut nom ii, 4

7:5 In Mat xxiii, 2

7:6 Ad Dem de comp i, 6; De diab tent iii, 4; Ex in ps cxl, 4; In 2 Cor viii, 2; In Gen xvi, 2; In Heb xx, 3; In Ioh i, 5; In Mat i, 15; xi, 9

7:6 cont xxiii, 3; xxiii, 4; xxxviii, 1
7:7 In Acta liii, 5; In Heb xxii, 6; In Rom Argumentum, 1; In 1 Tim i, 2 (1:4)
7:8 Ex in ps ix, 6; In Acta xix, 2 (8:32); In Ioh xx, 1
7:9 Ad e q scan vi; Ex in ps cxiv, 1; In Col x, 1 (4:1); In 1 Cor vii, 3; In Eph xix, 3 (5:21); In Mat xxiii, 5; In 1 Tim i, 2 (1:2)
7:10 Ad e q scan vi; Ex in ps cxiv, 1
7:11 Ad e q scan vi; Ad Stag a dae i, 5; Ex in ps cxiv, 1; In Mat xxiii, 5; lxiii, 1; In 1 Tim viii, 1 (2:10)
7:12 Ad Dem de comp i, 6; Ad pop Anti xiii, 7; Ex in ps v, 1; In 2 Cor xvii, 4; In Ioh lxxvii; In Mat i, 12; xxiii, 6
7:13 Ad Stag a dae i, 3; De Laz vii, 1; vii, 2; De uir lxiv; E viii (2x); In Heb xxix, 2; In Mat xxxviii, 3; xlvii, 3
7:14 Ad pop Anti vi, 7; Ad Stag a dae ii, 4; Adu op i, 8; De Laz iii, 6; E viii; Ex in ps cxix, 2 F in epis cath James 1:2; In 2 Cor xiii, 4; In Heb xxix, 2; xxix, 4; xxxiii, 9; In Phil xv, 5 (4:23); In 1 Thess ix, 5 (5:11); In 1 Tim xvii, 2 (6:12)
7:15 Ex in ps v, 4; In Mat xxiii, 8
7:16 Ex in ps iv, 7; cxliii, 4; In Mat xxiii, 8 (2x); xlii, 1; xlvi, 3
7:17 In Mat xxiii, 8; xlii, 1
7:18 In Mat xxiii, 8; xlii, 1; In Rom xiii, 6 (8:7)
7:19 In Mat xxiii, 8
7:20 In 1 Cor xxiv, 8; In Mat xxiii, 9
7:21 Adu op i, 6; In Acta xxix, 4 (13;41); In Ioh xxxi, 1; lxiii, 3; In 2 Tim vi, 3 (2:26); S Gen ii, 2
7:22 Adu op i, 6; In Acta v, 2 (2:20); In 1 Cor viii, 2; ix, 1; xxxii, 3; In d P Nolo 2; In Gen i, 1; In Heb xxiv, 7; In Ioh lxxii, 3; In Mat xxiv, 1; xxxii, 11; lxxviii, 4; In princ Act ii, 3; In 2 Tim ii, 3 (1:21); vi, 3 (2:26)
7:23 Adu op i, 6; In Acta xix, 5 (9:9); In 1 Cor viii, 2; In d P Nolo 2; In Heb xxiv, 8; In il Hab iii, 6; In Mat xxiv, 1; xxxii, 11; lxxviii 2; lxxviii, 4; In princ Act ii, 3; In 2 Tim ii 3 (1:12); iii, 2 (1:18); vi, 3 (2:26)
7:24 Ad pop Anti iv, 4; Adu op i, 6; Cat ill x, 17; Ex in ps cxi, 2; In Eph i, 1 (1:3); In Gen ii, 5; In Heb xi, 3; In Mat xxxiv, 3; Q nemo 12

| | |
|---|---|
| 7:25 | Ad pop Anti iv, 4; Adu op i, 6; Ex in ps cxi, 2; cxi, 4; In Eph i, 1 (1:3); In Mat xxiv, 3 |
| 7:26 | Ad pop Anti iv, 4; xvi, 2; De mut nom iv, 6; De prof eua 2; In Gen ii, 5; vi, 1; In Mat xxiv, 4 |
| 7:27 | Ad pop Anti iv, 4; xvi, 2; De mut nom iv, 6; De prof eua 2; In Gen viml |
| 7:28 | De Chris prec 5; Ex in ps xliv, 3; In il Fil 5; In Ioh xlii, 1; In Mat xvii, 1 (2x) |
| 7:29 | De Chris prec 5; Ex in ps xliv, 3; In Ioh xii, 1; xlii, 1; In Mat xvii, 1 (2x); xxvi, 2 |
| 8:1 | In Mat xxv, 1 |
| 8:2 | De Chris prec 5; In Col v, 3 (2:5); In Mat xxvi, 2; lvii, 3 |
| 8:3 | Con Iud et gen 3; De Chris prec 3; Ex in ps xlvi, 3; In Ioh iii, 4; xxiv, 2 |
| 8:4 | In Acta ix, 4 (3:26); In Ioh xxxvii, 1; In Mat xxv, 3; xxvi, 2; xxvi, 4; xxix, 2; In 1 Thess x, 1 (5:13) |
| 8:5 | In Ioh xxxv |
| 8:6 | Con Anom xi, 2; In Mat xxix, 1 |
| 8:7 | Con Anom xi, 2; De Chris diuin 2; In 1 or xxvii, 3; In Ioh lxii, 2; In Mat lii, 3 |
| 8:8 | Con Anom xi, 2; De Chris diuin 2; 3; In Ioh lxii, 3; In Mat iii, 8; xxvi, 1; xxvi, 2; xxvii, 1; lii, 3; In para 7; In quat Laz A 2 |
| 8:9 | Con Anom xi, 2; In Mat xxvi, 4; In para 7 |
| 8:10 | Con Anom xi, 2; Ex in ps xliii, 4; In Mat xxvi, 2 (2x) |
| 8:11 | De uir lxxxii; In Is vii, 1; In Mat xvi, 6; xxvi, 2; xxvi, 5; xxi, 4; lxiv, 2; In Rom xiv, 3 (8:17) |
| 8:12 | Ex in ps vi, 4; In Mat xxvi, 2; xl, 3; lxiv, 2; In Rom xiv, 3 (8:17) |
| 8:13 | In Mat xxvi, 2; In quat Laz A 2 |
| 8:15 | In Mat xxvii, 1 (2x) |
| 8:16-18 | In Mat xxvii, 2 |
| 8:19 | In Mat xxvii, 4 |
| 8:20 | De fut uit 5; De prod Iud i, 4; In Acta i, 3 (1:2); lv, 2; In Heb xviii, 4; xxviii, 1; In il Pater s p 4; In Mat ix, 6; xxii, 5; xlvi, 3; lxiv, 4; lxiv, 5 |
| 8:21 | In Mat xiv, 3; xxvii, 6; lxviii, 5 |
| 8:22 | Ex in ps cxiii, 6; In Mat xiv, 3; lxviii, 5; lxx, 2 (2x); In Rom xi, 5 (6:18) |
| 8:25 | In Mat xxviii, 1 |
| 8:26 | In Mat xxviii, 1; lviii, 2 |
| 8:27 | In Mat xxviii, 1; xxviii, 2; l, 2 |
| 8:28 | Adu Iud 8, 8, 6; De diab tent i, 6 |

8:29 Adu Iud 8, 8, 6; Ex in ps xlvi, 6; cix, 4; In Acta xli, 3; In Ioh xlv, 3; In Rom xxv, 6 (14:13); xxxi, 5 (16:16)
8:30 Ad Stag a dae ii, 9; Adu Iud 8, 8, 6
8:31 Adu Iud 1, 7, 5; 8, 8, 6; De diab tent ii, 1
8:32-33 Adu Iud 8, 8, 6
8:34 Adu Iud 8, 8, 6; In Mat xxviii, 4
9:1 In para 4
9:2 De Chris prec 3; In Ioh xiv, 3; xxiv, 2; xxxvii, 1; xxxviii, 1; xliii, 2; lxiv, 2; In Is vii, 5; In Mat xxxii, 1; In para 4
9:3 In Eph viii, 4 (4:2); In Ioh lxiv, 1; In Is vii, 5; In Mat xxix, 2; xxxvi, 2; In para 6
9:4 In Eph viii, 4; In Is vii, 5; In Mat xxix, 2 (2x); xxxvii, 1; In para 6
9:5 In 1 Cor xl, 2; In Eph viii, 4 (4:2); In Mat xxix, 2; lxxviii, 2; In para 6
9:6 De fut uit 5; In Eph viii, 4 (4:2) (2x); In il Fil 5; In Ioh xiv, 3; xxiv, 2; xxix, 2; xlix, 2; lxvii, 4; In para 7 (2x)
9:8 In Mat xxix, 2
9:9 Ex in ps xliv, 2; cx, 4; In Eut ii, 17
9:10 In 1 Cor xxxiv, 10
9:11 In Mat xxx, 3
9:12 De reg 5; In Mat xxx, 5; In para 5; In Rom xxvii, 3 (15:7); Non esse desp 3
9:13 Ad Stag a dae i, 5; De elee 5; De incomp dei v 7; F in epis cath James 1:27; In Ioh xxi, 1; In Mat xxx, 3 (2x); lxxx, 1
9:14 In Ioh xviii, 3; xxix, 3; In Mat xxx, 4 (2x); xxxvi, 2
9:15 In Mat xxx, 4 (2x); xxx, 5; xliii, 3
9:16 Ad pop Anti xvi, 9; In 1 Cor xxxiii, 7
9:17 Ad pop Anti xvi, 9; In 1 Cor xxxiii, 7
9:18 In Mat xxxi, 3; l, 6; lii, 2; In quat Laz A 2
9:19 In quat Laz A 2
9:20 Ex in ps xliv, 10; In il Is Ego 3; In quat Laz A 2
9:21 In il Is Ego 3; In Mat xxxi, 2
9:22 In il Is Ego 3; In Mat xxxi, 2 (2x); lvii, 3
9:23-24 In Mat xxxi, 3
9:28 In Mat xiv, 4
9:30 In 1 Cor xxxii, 9; In Mat xxxii, 1
9:31 In Mat xxxii, 1
9:32 Ex in ps xliv, 6; In Mat xxxii, 2; lvii, 2
9:33 Ex in ps xliv, 3; In Ioh lxxvii; In Mat xxxii, 2

9:34 E i, 2; cxxv; In Mat xxxii, 2; xli, 1
9:35 In Mat xxxii, 3
9:36 In Mat xxxii, 4
9:37 In il Messis 1; 2; In Mat xxxii, 4; xlvii, 1
9:38 In Acta iv, 1 (2:2)
10:1 In Mat xxxii, 4; lvii, 4
10:2 In Mat xxxii, 5
10:3 De diab tent i, 1; De proph obscur ii, 9; In Eph vii, 4 (3:19); In Mat xxxii, 5
10:4 In Mat xxxii, 5
10:5 Ex in ps cxvii, 1; H in il App 16; In Acta ii, 2 (1:8); xviii, 2 (8:2); xxii, 3 (10:23); In Eph ii, 1 (1:11); In Ioh ix, 1; xxxi, 2; xxxi, 4; lxvi, 2 (2x); lxxx, 1; In Mat xxxii, 5 (2x) lii, 1; lv, 2
10:6 In il Sal P et A ii, 2; In Mat xxxii, 5; lxix, 1; In Rom xix, 3 (11:11)
10:7 In il Sal P et A ii, 2; In Mat xxxii, 5
10:8 De san pent i, 2; H dicta in t s Anas 4; In Gen xxxv, 6; In il Sal P et A ii, 2 (2x); In Mat xxxii, 6
10:9 De prod Iud i, 3; ii, 3; Ex in ps xlvi, 3; In Gen liv, 5; In Heb xviii, 4; In il Sal P et Ai, 4; ii, 1; ii, 2 (2x); In Mat xxii, 5; xxxii, 7; xlvi, 4; In Phil ix, 4 (2:30); ix, 5 (2:30)
10:10 In Acta liv, 2; In 1 Cor xxi, 4; In Gen xxxv, 6; In Heb xviii, 4; In il Sal P et A ii, 1; ii, 2; In Mat xxii, 5; xxiii, 2; xxx, 3; xxxii, 7 (2x); xxxiv, 1; In Phil ix, 4 (2:30); ix, 5 (2:30)
10:11 De Laz vi, 3; In Col iii, 3 (1:20); In Hel 7; In il Uid elig 14; In Mat xxxii, 8; In Rom xxxii, 2 (16:23)
10:12 IN il Uid elig 14; In Mat xxxii, 8; In Rom xxx, 4 (16;5)
10:13 In Col iii, 3 (1:20); iii, 4 (1:20); In il Uid elig 14; In Mat xxxii, 8; In Rom xxx, 4 (16;5)
10:14 In Acta xxx, 1 (13:51); In il Uid elig 14; In Mat xxxii, 8
10:15 In il Uid elig 14; In Is iii, 10; In Mat xxxii 8; xxxvi, 3; In Rom xxxi, 4 (16:16)
10:16 Ad pop Anti iv, 10; xii, 6; Ex in ps cix, 3 (2x); F Ier 1:8; H dicta in t s Anas 3; In Col xi, 1 (4:6); In 1 Cor xxxvi, 1; In Eph xix, 1 (5:17); In Heb xxx, 2; In il Uidi dom iv, 2; In Ioh xvii, 4; xxxix, 4; lix, 3; In Mat xxxiv 1; lv, 2
10:17 In Ioh lxxviii, 1; In Mat xxxiii, 4; In 2 Tim

| | |
|---|---|
| 10:17 cont | ix, 2 (4:4) |
| 10:18 | Ad e q scan xiv; In Acta i, 1 (1:2); In Heb xxv, 1; IN Ioh lxxviii, 1; In Mat xxxiii, 4; lv, 2 |
| 10:19 | In Col x, 3 (4:4); In Eph xxiv, 1 (6:20); In Mat xxxii, 7; xxxiii, 4; xxxiv, 1 |
| 10:20 | In Mat xxxiii, 4 |
| 10:21 | De ss B et P 5; In Mat xxxiii, 4 (2x); In Phil x, 4 (3:7) |
| 10:22 | Ad e q scan ix; In il Don non est 5; In Mat xxxiii, 4; xxxiv, 1; xlvi, 1 |
| 10:23 | De ss B et P 5; In Gen lii, 2 |
| 10:24 | In Heb xxviii, 4; In Mat xxiv, 1 |
| 10:25 | In Heb xxviii, 4; In Mat xxxiii, 8; xxxiv, 1; lxi, 5 |
| 10:26 | In Acta xx, 1 (9:14); In Mat xxxiv, 1 (2x) |
| 10:27 | In Acta x, 2 (4:10); In 1 Cor vii, 2; In il Sal P et A ii, 3; In Ioh xv, 2; In Mat xxiii, 3; xxxiv, 2; In Tit i, 2 (1:5) |
| 10:28 | Ad pop Anti vi, 9; Ad Theo i, 15; De res d n I C 4; In Gen xxvii, 5; xxxii, 5; In Ioh xlv, 2; xlv, 3; In Mat xxxiv, 2; In Rom ii, 6 (1:16); xi, 5 (6:18) |
| 10:29 | In Mat ix, 4; xxxiv, 2 |
| 10:30 | In Mat xxviii, 4; xxxiv, 2 |
| 10:31 | In Mat xxxiv, 3 |
| 10:32 | In Eph i, 1 (1:3); In Mat xxxiv, 3 |
| 10:33 | Ex in ps v, 1; In Eph i, 1 (1:3); In Mat vi, 9; xxxiv, 3; In 2 Tim v, 1 (2:14) |
| 10:34 | Ad pop Anti xix, 14; Adu Iud 5, 3, 10; Ex in ps xliv, 5; In Acta xix, 5 (9:9); xxx, 1 (14:4); In 1 Cor vii, 16: In Ioh lvii, 2 |
| 10:35 | Adu Iud 5, 2, 8; 5, 3, 10; De pet mat 4; In Mat xxxv, 2 |
| 10:36 | In Heb xxv, 1; In Mat xxxv, 2; lix, 1 |
| 10:37 | De uir lxxviii; Ex in ps xliv, 4; In Eph xix, 1 (5:17); In Mat xxxv, 3; xxxviii, 3; xlviii, 5; In Phil ix, 2 (2:30); In Rom x, 5 (6:4) |
| 10:38 | Ad pop Anti v, 14; De pet mat 5; Ex in ps xliv 4; In Acta xx, 3 (9:25); In 1 Cor vii, 16; In Eph vi, 3 (3:7); In Heb xxv, 1; In Ioh xxxiv, 1; lxxv, 3; In Mat xxxv, 3 (2x); xxxviii, 3; Om ; Tim x. 1 (3:4) |
| 10:39 | De pet mat 5; In Acta xxvii, 2 (12:17); In Mat xxxv, 3; lxiv, 2 (2x) |
| 10:40 | De per mat 5; F in e-is cath 1 Peter 4:9; In Acta xliii, 3; In Gen xliii, 7; In il Prop 2; In Ioh xxxix, 2; In Mat xxv, 4; In 1 Tim xiv, |

| | |
|---|---|
| 10:40 cont | 2 (5:10); In 2 Tim ii, 2 (1:12) |
| 10:41 | De Anna ii, 4; In Acta xlv, 3; In Gen xlii, 6; lxv, 4; In Mat xxxv, 4; In Phil i, 3 (1:7); In Rom xxi, 4 (12:13); In s Luc 1; In 2 Tim ii, 2 (1:12) |
| 10:42 | De pet mat 6; De paen iii, 2; vii, 6; E clii; In Gen xxvii, 3; xxxiv, 2; lv, 4; In Heb xxxi, 8; In il Uid elig 12; In kal 5; Qual duc 7 |
| 11:2 | In Eph viii, 9 (4:2); In Mat xxxvi, 1; xlix, 1 |
| 11:3 | In Eph viii, 9 (4:2); In Mat xxxvi, 1 |
| 11:4 | In Mat xxvii, 5 |
| 11:6 | In Ioh xxx, 2; In Mat xxxvi, 2 |
| 11:7 | In Mat xxvii, 5; xxxviii, 1 |
| 11:8 | In Mat x, 4; xxxvii, 1; xxxviii, 1 |
| 11:9 | In Mat xxxvi, 3; xxxvii, 2; xxxviii, 1 |
| 11:10 | In Mat xxxviii, 2; xxxviii, 1 |
| 11:11 | In Acta i, 5 (1:5); In Ioh xvi, 3; In Mat xxxvii, 2; xxxviii, 1 |
| 11:12 | De mut nom ii, 1; In Eut ii, 6; In Gen xliii, 3; In Ioh liv, 4; In Mat xxiii, 7; xxxvii, 4; xxxviii, 1; lxix, 4; In 2 Tim x, 4 (4:22) |
| 11:13 | Adu Iud 5, 9, 6; In 1 Cor xxxii, 2; In Mat xxxvii, 4 |
| 11:14 | In Mat lvii, 1; L Diod 3 |
| 11:15 | F Iob 13:17; In Mat xxxvii, 4 |
| 11:16-17 | In Mat xxxvii, 5 (2x) |
| 11:18 | IN Mat xiv, 2; xxxvii, 5; S Gen vii, 4 |
| 11:19 | In Ioh xvi, 1; In Mat xiv, 2; xxx, 2; xxxvii, 3; xxxvii, 5 |
| 11:20 | In Mat xxxvii, 6; xxxviii, 1 |
| 11:21 | In Gen xxv, 2; In Hel 8; In Is i, 3; In Mat xxxvii, 6 (2x); xxxviii, 1; lxxv, 5 |
| 11:22 | In Gen xxv, 2; In Hel 8; In Mat xxxvii, 6; xxxviii, 1; lxxv, 5 |
| 11:23 | In Ioh xxxv; In Mat xxxvii, 6; xxxviii, 1; xlviii, 1 |
| 11:24 | Ex in ps cxlvii, 2; In Mat xxxvii, 6; xxxviii, 1; In Rom xxxi, 5 (16:16) |
| 11:25 | Ex in ps cxxxviii, 1; In Acta xx, 4 (9:25) |
| 11:27 | De incomp dei v, 4; In Ioh xv, 3; lxx, 1; In Mat xxviii, 1; xxxviii, 2; liv, 2 |
| 11:28 | Ad Theo ii, 2; Adu op iii, 14; Cat ill i, 26; De incomp dei v, 7; De paen v, 3; In 2 Cor vi, 2; In il Uidi dom i, 1; In Ioh iv, 4; In Mat xxxviii, 3; lxix, 1; In 1 Thess vi, 4 (4:13); S Gen ix, 6 |
| 11:29 | As Dem de comp i, 5; Adu Iud 1, 11, 4; Cat ill i, 29; i, 30; De bap Chris 1; De consub 4; |

| | |
|---|---|
| 11:29 cont | De cruce et lat i, 5; ii, 5; De fut uit 6; De paen iv, 4; In Acta i, 3 (1:2); vi, 3 (2:36); In Gen ix, 6; xxxiv, 1; In Ioh xlviii, 3; lxx, 1; In Mat iii, 9; xxxviii, 3; xlvi, 4; lxiv, 5; In Phil vi, 1 (2:8); vi, 3 (2:8); xii, 3 (3:17) In 2 Thess i, 2 (Introduction) |
| 11:30 | Adu Iud 1, 11, 4; De Laz iii, 6; De uir lxiv; Ex in ps cxi, 1; In 1 Cor xiv, 7; In Mat xxiii, 7; xxxviii, 3 |
| 12 (p) | In 1 Cor xliii, 5 |
| 12:1 | De Chris diuin 4; In Ioh xxxi, 3 |
| 12:2 | In Mat xxx, 3; xxxix, 1 |
| 12:3 | De Chris diuin 4; In il Pater m 4; In Mat xxxix, 1; xl, 1 (2x); xli, 2 |
| 12:4 | In il Pater m 4; In Mat xxxix, 1; xl, 1 |
| 12:5 | In il Pater m 4; In Ioh xlix, 3; In Mat xxxix, 2; xli, 2 |
| 12:6 | In Mat xxix, 2 |
| 12:7 | In Ioh xiii, 4; In Mat xxxix, 2; xli, 2; lxxx, 1 |
| 12:10 | In Mat xxxix, 1 |
| 12:11 | In Mat xvi, 2 |
| 12:12 | In Mat lxii, 2 |
| 12:13 | In Mat xl, 1 |
| 12:14 | In Mat xxxix, 1; xl, 2 |
| 12:15 | In Mat xl, 2 (2x) |
| 12:16-18 | In Mat xl, 2 |
| 12:19-20 | In Ioh xxiv, 2; In Mat xl, 2 |
| 12:21 | In Mat xl, 2 |
| 12:22 | In Mat xl, 3 |
| 12:23 | In Mat xxxii, 4; xl, 3 |
| 12:24 | In Heb xxviii, 5; In Ioh xix, 2; lviii, 1; In Mat xxxii, 4; xl, 3; xlv, 1; In Rom xxvi, 3 (14:23) |
| 12:25 | Adu Iud 3, 1, 2; In 1 Cor xxxi, 7; In Mat i, 8 In Phil iv, 3 (1:23) |
| 12:27 | In Acta v, 1 (2:17); In Ioh li, 2; In Mat xli, 2; lxiv, 2; S Gen ix, 5 |
| 12:28 | In Acta i, 3 (1:2); In Mat xli, 2 |
| 12:29 | In Acta ii, 4 (1:11); In 1 Cor xxxix, 12; In Ioh lxvii, 3; In Mat xli, 3 |
| 12:30 | In Mat xli, 4 |
| 12:31 | In Mat xli, 4; xli, 5 |
| 12:32 | In Mat xli, 5 |
| 12:34 | In Acta xxxii, 3 (15:11); In 2 Cor vi, 3; In Mat xlii, 1 |
| 12:35 | In Mat xlii, 1 |

| | |
|---|---|
| 12:36 | Cat ill iv, 23; De dec mil 4; Ex in ps xlix, 10; cxl, 5; cxl, 6; In 1 Cor vii, 16; In Mat xlii, 1; lxxxvi, 4; In pata 8; In Phil ix, 5 (2:30); In 2 Tim ii, 3 (1:12) |
| 12:37 | Adu op i, 6; Cat ill ix, 33; De dec mil 4; De proph obscur ii, 10; In Mat xlii, 1; li, 5 |
| 12:38 | In 1 Cor xxxiv, 10 |
| 12:39 | H dicta p imp 3; In il Pater s p 2; In Ioh lxxii, 3; In Mat lxv, 1; lxxix, 2; lxxxviii, 1; In Rom i, 2 (1:4) |
| 12:40 | F Ier 25:11; H dicta p imp 3; In 1 Cor xxxviii 4 |
| 12:41 | De diab tent iii, 3; Ex in ps cxlvii, 2; In Gen xxv, 1; In Mat vi, 4; lxiv, 2; lxxix, 2; In Rom vi, 3 (2:27); xxxi, 5 (16:16) |
| 12:42 | Ex in ps cxlvii, 2; In 1 Cor xvi, 5; In Mat vi, 4; xxxvii, 3; xliii, 2; lxxix, 2 |
| 12:43-44 | Adu Iud 1, 6, 6; In Mat xliii, 4 |
| 12:45 | Adu Iud 1, 6, 6; F Prou 5:4; In Acta i, 6 (1:5); In Mat xliii, 4 |
| 12:47 | In Mat xxvii, 5 |
| 12:48 | In Ioh xxi, 2; lxxxv, 2; In Mat xxvii, 5 |
| 12:50 | In il Prop 2 |
| 13 (p) | De uir lxxviii |
| 13:1 | In Mat xliv, 3 |
| 13:2 | In Mat xliv, 3; xlviii, 2 |
| 13:3 | De Laz vi, 2; In Heb iii, 1; In Mat xlviii, 2 |
| 13:4-5 | In Gen iv, 1; In Ioh i, 6; In Mat xliv, 4; xlviii, 2 |
| 13:6 | In Gen iv, 1; In Heb x, 2; In Mat xliv, 4; xlviii, 2 |
| 13:7 | In Gen iv, 1; In Ioh i, 6; In Mat xliv, 4; xlviii, 2 |
| 13:8 | In Mat xxxix, 3; xliv, 4; xlviii, 2 |
| 13:9 | In Mat xliv, 4; xlviii, 4 |
| 13:10 | In il Hoc scit 2 |
| 13:11-12 | In Mat xlv, 1 |
| 13:13 | Ex in ps cxlii, 6; In 2 Cor viii, 2; In il Hoc scit 2; In Mat xlv, 1; In Rom xxvi, 2 (14:23) |
| 13:14 | In Mat xlv, 2 |
| 13:15 | In Ioh lv, 2; In Mat xxxvii, 3; xlv, 2 |
| 13:16 | In il Hoc scit 1; 2 (2x); In Mat xlv, 2; xlviii, 4 |
| 13:17 | Ex in ps cxvii, 6; In 1 Cor xxi, 2; In diem nat 1; In Heb xxvi, 1; In Mat xlv, 2; In Rom i, 2 (1:2) |
| 13:18 | In Mat xlv, 2 |

13:19-
20 In Mat xliv, 5
13:22 In Gen lix, 2; In Heb x, 2; In Ioh xxiv, 3; In Mat xx, 4; In Rom viii, 7 (4:21)
13:24 Ex in ps xlviii, 2; In d P Op 1; In Ioh xxi, 1
13:25 In d P Op 1
13:29 In Rom xiii, 6 (8:7)
13:30 Ex in ps cix, 4; In Acta xliii, 3; In Mat xlvi, 1; xlvi, 2
13:31 In Mat xlvi, 2
13:32 De diab tent iii, 2; In Mat xlvi, 2
13:33 De diab tent iii, 2; In il Si esur 2; In Mat xlvi, 2
13:36 In Ioh xlvi, 2; In Mat xlvii, 1
13:37-
40 In Mat xlvii, 1
13:41-
42 In Acta xliii, 3; In Heb xiii, 6; In Mat xlvii, 1
13:43 Cat ill iii, 2; iv, 3; vii, 3; Ex in ps xlviii, 6; In Gen xiv, 1; In Mat xlvii, 1; lvi, 7
13:44 In Ioh xv, 1; In Mat xlvii, 2
13:45-
46 In Mat xlvii, 2
13:47 Adu op i, 6; In Acta iii, 2 (1:26); In Mat xlvii, 3
13:48 In Mat xlvii, 3
13:50 In Mat xliv, 2; xlvii, 3
13:51 In Mat xlvii, 2; xlvii, 4 (2x)
13:52 In il Hab ii, 2; In 1 Tim xiii, 1 (4:16)
13:54 In Mat xlviii, 1 (2x)
13:55 In Heb xxviii, 5; In Ioh xvi, 1; In Mat xliv, 1; xlviii, 1 (2x)
13:56 In Eph vii, 4 (3:19); In Mat xliv, 1; xlviii,1
13:57 In Gen xxxii, 4; In Mat xlviii, 1
13:58 In Gen xxxii, 4; In Mat xlviii, 1 (2x)
14 (p) Adu Iud 8, 8, 1; De laud a Paul i; In Ioh xliii, 1; In Tit v, 4 (3:6)
14:1 In Mat xlviii, 2
14:2 In 2 Cor xxviii, 4; In Mat xxiv, 4; liv, 2
14:4 Ad e q scan xix; xxii; Cat ill x, 24; x, 25; x, 26; x, 27; E ad e p d (2x)
14:8 Cat ill x, 24; x, 25; x, 26; x, 27; In 2 Cor xxviii, 4; In Mat liii, 4
14:12 In 2 Cor xxiii, 8; In Mat xxx, 4; liii, 4
14:13 Ex in ps xlix, 9; In Ioh xvii, 1
14:14 F Ier Introduction (2x); In Mat xlix, 1
14:15 In Mat xlix, 1
14:16 In Mat xlix, 1; liii, 1

14:17 In Mat xlix, 1
14:21 In Acta xxi, 3 (9:35)
14:22 In Mat xlix, 3
14:25-27 In Mat l, 1
14:28 In Ioh xliii, 1; In Mat l, 2
14:29 In 2 Cor xxiii, 8; In Mat l, 2; lviii, 2
14:30 In Mat l, 2
14:31 In il Hab i, 4; In Mat l, 2
14:32 In Mat l, 2
14:33 In Mat l, 2; liv, 2
14:34-36 In Mat l, 2
15:3-6 8 In Mat l, 2
15:9 In Ioh lix, 2; In Mat li, 2
15:11 Ex in ps xlix, 9; cxl, 4; In 1 Cor xx, 1; In 2 Cor xxviii, 2; In Heb xxxiii, 6; In Ioh xxxi, 4; In Mat li, 3 (2x); lviii, 2; lxii, 2
15:12 Con e q sub 3; In Mat xlv, 1; li, 4
15:13 Con e q sub 3; In Is iii, 3; In Mat xlv, 1; li, 4
15:14 Con e q sub 3; Ex in ps viii, 5; In Acta xlvi, 3; In Mat li, 4
15:15 In Mat li, 4 (2x); lxii, 2
15:16 De pet mat 4; In Acta ii, 2 (1:8); iv, 3 (2:13); In Gal i, 1 (1:3); In il Pater m 3; In Mat xxviii, 1; li, 4; liii, 4
15:17 Ad pop Anti iii, 16; In Mat li, 4; liii, 4
15:18 Ad pop Anti iii, 16; In Mat li, 4
15:19 In Heb xii, 7; In Mat li, 4; In 1 Thess iv, 3 (3:10)
15:20 In Mat li, 3; li, 4 (2x)
15:21 In Mat xxii, 7
15:22 De prof eua 12; Ex in ps iv, 3; In 2 Cor ii, 5; In Gen xxxviii, 3; xliv, 3; In Mat xxii, 7; In para 5
15:23 De prof eua 12; In Gen xxxviii, 3; xliv, 3; In Mat xxii, 7; lii, 2
15:24 De prof eua 12; Ex in ps cxvii, 1; F Ier 31:33 In Eph ii, 1 (1:11); In Gen xxxviii, 3; xliv, 3; In Ioh ix, 1; xxxi, 2; lxvi, 2; lxxx, 1; In Mat xxii, 7; lii, 2; In Rom xix, 2 (11:11)
15:25 In Gen xxxviii, 3; xliv, 3; In Mat xxii, 7; lii, 2
15:26 Adu Iud 1, 11, 1; De prof eua 12; Ex in ps xliii, 2; cxvii, 1; In Gen xxxviii, 3; xlix, 3; In Heb xx-ii, 9; In Ioh lxvi, 2; In Mat xxii, 7; liii, 3 (2x); In Rom xix, 2 (11:11); Non esse desp 7

15:27 De prof eua 12; Ex in ps xlviii, 2; In Eph xxiv 3 (6:22); In Gen xxxviii, 3; xliv, 3; In Heb xxvii, 9; In Mat xxii, 7; xxii, 8; lii, 3; In Phil x, 1 (3:3)

15:28 De prof eua 12 (2x); Ex in ps vii, 4; In Gen xxxiv, 2; xxxviii, 3; xliv, 3; In Mat xxii, 7; xxvi, 2; lii, 3

15:29-31 In Mat lii, 4

15:32 De cruce et lat ii, 2; In Ioh xviii, 2; In para 3

15:33 In Mat liii, 1

15:34 F Iob 1:8; In Mat lii, 2

15:35-36 In Mat liii, 2

15:37 In Ioh xlii, 3; In Mat liii, 2

15:38-39 In Mat liii, 2

16:1-3 In Mat liii, 3

16:4 In Ioh xxiii, 2; In Mat liii, 3; lvi, 4

16:5 In Mat liii, 4

16:6 In il Pater m 3; In Ioh xxxi, 3; xxxviii, 3; In Mat xlix, 1; liii, 4; lvii, 4

16:7 In Mat liii, 4; lvii, 4

16:8 In Mat liii, 1; lvii, 4

16:9 In il Pater m 3; In Ioh xlii, 5; In Mat xxx, 3; xlix, 3; liii, 1; lvii, 4

16:10 Ex in ps cxiv, 1; In Mat l, 6; liii, 1; lvii,4

16:11 De pet mat 4; In Mat liii, 4; lvii, 4

16:12 In Mat lvii, 4

16:13 In il In fac 5

16:14 In Mat xlviii, 2; liv, 1; lvii, 2

16:15 In Ioh xlvii, 3; In Mat liv, 1

16:16 De pet mat 4; In Gal ii, 4 (2:12); In il In fac 5; In Ioh xxi, 1; In Mat liv, 2

16:17 De inani gloria 49; De paen iii, 4; In Gal i, 1 (1:3); In Ioh xix, 2; xlv, 3; In Mat liv,2; liv, 3

16:18 Adu Iud 5, 2, 8; Con Iud et gen 12; 15; De mtu nom iv, 3; Ex in ps xliv, 10; cxlvii, 3; In 1 Cor vii, 19; In Eut ii, 1; In Heb xxi, 5; In Ioh xix, 2; In Mat liv, 3 (2x); In princ Act ii, 1 (2x); ii, 6; S ante iret 1

16:19 In Acta ii, 1 (1:6); xxxvi, 3 (16:39); In il Uidi dom iv, 4; v, 1; In Mat liv, 3; lxv, 3

16:20 In Mat xlix, 1; liv, 4

16:21 In il In fac 5; In Mat liv, 5; lvii, 2

16:22 Ad e q scan xvii; De consub 6; De pet mat 4;

16:22 cont In Gal ii, 4 (2:12); In il Pater s p 2; In Ioh xxiii, 3; xxxi, 1; xlvii, 4; lxx, 2; lxxiii, 1; In Mat xxx, 4; liv, 5; lv, 1; lvi, 4; lxv, 1; lxxi; lxxxii, 3

16:23 Ad e q scan xvii; De consub 6; De pet mat 4; In Acta iv, 3 (2:13); xxxix, 4; In Gal i, 1 (1:3); In il Pater s p 2; In Mat liv, 6; lv, 1 lxxi

16:24 De laud s Paul vi; In Heb v, 7; In Ioh lx-ii, 1; In Mat lxiii, 2; In Phil xiii, 1 (3:21)

16:25 In Col viii, 5 (3:15); In Mat xxxviii, 3; lv, 3; lvi, 1

16:26 Ad Theo ii, 2; De b Phil 4; Ex in ps xlviii, 5; In Gen xxxi, 7; liv, 5; lv, 3; lix, 7

16:27 De diab tent iii, 3; De Laz iii, 6; De paen iv 3; In Acta ii, 1 (1:6); In Mat lvi, 1

17 (p) De fut uit 6

17:1 In Ioh lxxii, 1; In Mat lvi, 2

17:2 Ad Theo i, 11; In Eut ii, 10; In Mat lvi, 2

17:3 In Mat lvi, 2

17:4 Ad Theo i, 11; De Chris prec 5; In Gal ii, 4 (2:12); In il In fac 5

17:5 In Mat lvi, 5

17:6-8 In Mat lvi, 6

17:9 Ex in ps xlix, 2; In Acta ii, 1 (1:6); In Mat lvi, 6

17:10 In Ioh xvi, 2

17:11 In Mat lxii, 1; In 2 Thess iv, 2 (2:12)

17:12 In Mat lvii, 1; lvii, 2

17:13 In Mat lvii, 1

17:14 In Mat lvii, 3; In para 5

17:15 In Mat lvii, 3

17:16 In il Uidi dom v, 3; In Mat lvii, 3

17:17 Ex in ps cxix, 3

17:19 In il Hab i, 4 (2x); ii, 1; In Mat lvii, 4

17:20 De paen v, 1; Ex in ps cxlv, 4; In 1 Cor xxix, 5; In Eph xxiv, 1 (6:17); In Gen xxx, 5; In Ioh lxiii, 3; In Mat lvii, 4

17:21 In Mat lvii, 4

17:22 In Mat lvii, 2

17:23 In Mat xxx, 4; lvii, 2 (2x)

17:24 In Mat lviii, 1; lxx, 1

17:25-26 In Mat lviii, 2; lxx, 1

17:27 Con e q sub 3; Ex in ps xlix, 9; In Ioh lix, 3; lxiv, 1; In Mat li, 4; lvii, 2; lxx, 1

18 (p) De D et S i, 1; In Philem i, 2 (v3); Q nemo 10

18:1 In Ioh xxiii, 3; lxxi, 1; In Mat lviii, 3

18:6 Adu Iud 3, 1, 4; Adu op iii, 2; De Laz ii, 5; De sac vi, 1; De uir xxi; E ii, 10; In Acta xlvi, 3; In Mat lviii, 4; In Tit i, 3 (1:5)

18:7 De prod Uid ii, 5; In Mat lix, 3; In 1 Tim xii 1 (4:3)

18:8 In Ioh lvii, 2; In Mat lix, 4

18:9 In Mat lix, 4

18:10 In Col iii, 3 (1:20); In il Uidi dom vi, 2; In Ioh xv, 2; In Mat lix, 4; In Rom xxx, 4 (16:5)

18:11 In Mat lix, 4

18:12 Ad pop Anti xiii, 12; Adu Iud 8, 9, 4; Cob 1 et t 3; De Laz vi, 2; In Gal ii, 7 (2:20); In Mat lix, 4

18:13 Ad pop Anti xiii, 12; Adu Iud 8, 9, 4; In Mat lix, 4

18:14 Ad Stag a dae i, 5; Adu Iud 3, 1, 4; 8, 9, 4; De Laz ii, 5; In Acta i, 3 (1:2); In Col iii, 3 (1:20); In il Hab i, 1; In Ioh xlv, 3; In Mat lix, 4

18:15 De dec mil 3; De proph obscur ii, 10; Ex in ps xlix, 7; xlix, 10; cxl, 8; In 1 Cor xliv, 5; I Heb iv, 8; In il In fac 3; In il Uidi dom v, 3; In Mat xxiii, 1; In 1 Tim xv, 2 (5:20); Pec frat 4

18:16 In Acta ii, 3 (1:11); xiv, 1 (6:7); xxxiii, 1 (15:15); In Heb iv, 8; In il Uidi dom v, 3; In Mat xxiii, 1; lx, 1

18:17 In Heb iv, 8; In il Uidi dom v, 3; In Mat xxiii, 1 (2x); lx, 1

18:18 De sac iii, 5; Ex in ps cxlv, 3; In Heb iv, 8; In Mat lx, 2; In princ Act iii, 4; In 2 Tim x, 4 (4:22) (2x)

18:19 In Mat xl, 2; In 1 Tim ii, 1 (1:7)

18:20 Adu Iud 3, 3, 5; De Anna v, 1; De ss B et P 5; Ex in Ps cxxxii; In Acta xxvi, 4 (12:17); xxxvii, 3 (17:150; In Heb xix, 3; In il Uidi dom vi, 2; In mar Aeg 2; In Mat xl, 2; In pronc Act ii, 4; In Rom viii, 7 (4:21); s ante iret 2; S Gen vi, 1

18:21 De dec mil 3; Ex in ps xlix, 7

18:22 In Acta xx, 4 (9:25)

18:23 De dec mil 1; 2; De prod Iud i, 1; De uir xxxii; In Mat lxi, 1

18:24 Ad pop Anti xx, 17; De dec mil 2; 5; De fato et pr iv; In 2 Cor ii, 5; xxx, 4; In Mat lxi, 1; Pec frat 11

18:25 De dec mil 2; 5; In Mat lxi, 1

18:26 De dec mil 2; 6; De paen vii, 3; In Mat v, 7; lxi, 3

| | |
|---|---|
| 18:27 | De dec mil 2; In 2 Cor ii, 5; In Gen xxvii, 6; In Mat v, 7; lxi, 3 |
| 18:28 | Ad pop Anti xx, 17; De dec mil 2; 6; In Gen xxvii, 6; In Mat v, 7; lxi, 1; lxi, 4 |
| 18:29 | De dec mil 2; 7; In Gen xxvii, 6; In Mat v, 7; lxi, 4 |
| 18:30-31 | De dec mil 2; 7; In Gen xxvii, 6; In Ioh xxxix 4; IN Mat v, 7 |
| 18:32 | Ad pop Anti iii, 2; Adu Iud 3, 5, 4; De dec mil 2; 7; In Col viii, 3 (3:15); In Eph xxii, 2 (6:9); In Gen xxvii, 7; In Ioh xxxix, 4; In Mat v, 7; xxiii, 2; lxi, 4 |
| 18:33 | De dec mil 2; In Gen xxvii, 7; In Ioh xxxix, 4; In Mat v, 7 |
| 18:34 | De dec mil 2; In Gen xxvii, 7 |
| 18:35 | De dec mil 2; 7; In Gen xxvii, 7 |
| 19 (p) | De uir lxxxiii |
| 19:2 | In Mat lxii, 1 |
| 19:3 | In Ioh lxi, 1; In Mat lxii, 1 |
| 19:4 | De lib rep 2; In Eph xx, 1 (5:24); In Mat xiv, 2; lxii, 1; In Rom xiii, 4 (7:25); xxiii, 1 (13:1) |
| 19:5 | De n iter 2; In Mat lxii, 1; In Rom xxiii, 1 (13:1); S anti iret 1 |
| 19:6 | Cat ill i, 13; In Mat lxii, 1; S anti iret 1 |
| 19:7 | De lib rep 2; In Mat lxii, 2; In Rom xii 3 (7:3) |
| 19:8 | De lib rep 2; In Mat xvii, 4 |
| 19:9 | In 1 Cor xix, 4 |
| 19:10 | Con e q sub 5; De dec mil 3; De uir xiii (2x); xxxii; xli; In Mat xxiii, 4; lxii, 2 |
| 19:11 | In Mat lxii, 2 |
| 19:12 | Ad Stag a dae ii, 12; Con e q sub 5; De fut uit 4; De uir ii; xiii (2x); xvii; xxxvi; xlix; E ii, 7; Ex in ps cxiii, 5; cxxvii, 3; F Iob 31:1; In Acta xxxii, 3 (15:11); In il Fil 2; In Ioh xxxvi, 2; lxviii, 2; lxxiv, 3; In Mat lxii, 3; lxv, 1; lxxviii, 1; In 1 Thess v, 1 (4:3); In Tit i, 2 (1:5) |
| 19:13 | Ex in ps xlix, 5; In Mat lxii, 4 |
| 19:14-15 | In Mat lxii, 4 |
| 19:16 | Ad pop Anti ii, 14; In il Hoc scit 4; I il Sal P et A ii, 2 |
| 19:17 | In Mat xxvii, 5; lxiii, 1 |
| 19:20 | In Acta xxv, 3 (11:30); In il Sal P et A ii, 2; In Mat lxiii, 1 |
| 19:21 | Ad pop Anti ii, 14; De fut uit 4; De paen vi, 3; Ex in ps xli, 3; In Acta xlv, 2; In 1 Cor |

19:21 cont xxxii, 8; xxiv, 10; In 2 Cor xiii, 4; In Heb xviii, 5 (2x); xxxiii, 9; In il Hoc scit 4; In il Sal P et A ii, 2 (3x); In Ioh xxxix, 4; In Mat xl, 4; lxiii, 1; lxiv, 1; lxv, 1; lxxxvi, 4; In Phil i, 5 (1:7); x, 4 (3:7); In Tit i, 2 (1:5); vi, 2 (3:15)

19:22 In Mat lxiii, 2; In Phil x, 4 (3:7)

19:23 De prod Iud i, 1; Ex in ps ix, 8; In Heb xviii 5; In il Hoc scit 4; In Mat lxiii, 2; In Phil ix, 5 (2:30); x, 4 (3:7); In 1 Thess xi, 4 (5:28)

19:24 In 2 Cor xiii, 4; In Heb xxxiii, 9; In Mat lxiii, 2; IN Phil x, 4 (3:7); In 1 Thess xi, 4 (5:28); S cum pres 3

19:25 In il Hoc scit 4; In Mat xxiii, 4; lxi, 1

19:26 In Mat lxiii, 2

19:27 In 1 Cor x, 5; In il Hoc scit 4; In Mat xlvi, 4; lxiii, 3; In princ Act ii, 5

19:28 De crice et lat i, 2; ii, 2; De uir lxxxii; In Acta ii, 1 (1:6); In Eph iv, 2 (2:7); viii, 1 (4:2); In il Hoc scit 4; In Ioh lxxxii, 2; In Mat xxvi, 6; lxiii, 3; lxiv, 1; S Gen ix, 3

19:29 De fut uit 4; De ss B et P 5; In 1 Cor vii, 19 In Gen xl, 2; In Heb xxv, 4; In il Hab ii, 10; In Mat xv, 5; lxiii, 3; lxiv, 1; lvx, 1; lxxiv 5; xc, 4; In Phil i, 5 (1:7); In princ Act ii, 5; In Rom vii, 8 (3:31); S Gen ix, 3

19:30 In Gen xviii, 5; In Mat xxvi, 6; lxiv, 2

20:1 In Mat lxiv, 2

20:2 In Acta v, 3 (2:20)

20:6 Ex in ps cxx, 1; In il Dom non est 4

20:14 In Ioh ix, 2

20:16 Adu op i, 8; In 1 Cor xxxviii, 6

20:17 F in epis cath 1 Peter 5:3

20:18 In Heb viii, 3; In 2 Thess iv, 4 (3:2)

20:19 In Heb viii, 3

20:20 In Mat lvi, 2; In Rom x, 9

20:21 In Eph viii, 1 (4:2); In Ioh lxvi, 2; In Mat lxv, 2; In Rom x, 9

20:22 In Mat lvi, 2; lxv, 2 (2x)

20:23 De pet mat 1 (2x); In 1 Cor xxxii, 10; In Eph iv, 2 (2:7); In Mat liv, 3; lxv, 2

20:24 In Acta iii, 4 (1:26)

20:25 De Chris prec 2; In Mat lxv, 4 (2x)

20:26 De Chris prec 2; Ex in ps xliv, 6; In 1 Cor xii, 2; In Heb xxv, 4; In Mat lxv, 4

20:27 In 1 Cor xii, 2; In Mat lxiv, 5; lxv, 4

20:28 De Chris prec 2; De consub 4; Ex in ps xliv, 6; In Mat lxiv, 5; lxv, 4

| | |
|---|---|
| 21:1 | In Mat lxvi, 1 |
| 21:2 | In Ioh lxvi, 1; In Mat lxvi, 1 |
| 21:3 | In Mat lxvi, 1; lxxxi, 1 |
| 21:4 | In Mat lxvi, 1 |
| 21:5 | In Mat xvi, 3; lxvi, 1 |
| 21:6-7 | In Mat xvi, 3 |
| 21:8 | In Ioh lxvi, 1; In Mat xvi, 3 |
| 21:9 | Con Iud et gen 3; Ex in ps xiii, 2; cxlv, 2; In Mat xvi, 3 |
| 21:10 | In Ioh lxvi, 1; In Mat xvi, 3; lxvi, 3 |
| 21:11-12 | In Mat xvi, 3 |
| 21:13 | Adu Iud 6, 7, 5; De Anna iii, 4; F Ier 7:11; In Mat xvi, 3 |
| 21:14 | In Mat xvi, 3; lxvii, 1 |
| 21:15 | Ex in ps viii, 2; In Mat xvi, 3 |
| 21:16 | Ex in ps viii, 2; In Mat vii, 2; xvi, 3; lxvii, 1 |
| 21:18 | In Ioh xxxi, 3; In Mat lxvii, 1 |
| 21:19 | De Laz i, 5; In Mat lxvii, 1 |
| 21:21 | In Mat lxvii, 2 |
| 21:22 | In Mat lxvii, 2; In 1 Tim viii, 1 (2:10) |
| 21:23 | In Mat lxx, 1 |
| 21:25-26 | In Mat xi, 1; lxvii, 2 |
| 21:27-30 | In Mat lxvii, 2 |
| 21:31 | De paen vii, 5; In Acta xv, 5 (7:5); In Mat x, 3; lx, 2; lxvii, 2 |
| 21:32 | In Mat lxxv, 5 |
| 21:37 | In Acta xxxi, 3 (14:20) |
| 21:38 | F Prou 1:13; In Rom xvii, 1 (10:3); xix, 2 (11:1) |
| 21:40 | In Heb iii, 5; In Ioh liii, 2 |
| 21:41 | In Acta v, 3 (2:20); In Ioh liii, 2; In Mat lxxiv, 2; In Rom xiv, 3 (8:17) |
| 21:42 | Ex in ps cxvii, 1; cxvii, 5; F in epis cath 1 Peter 2:8 |
| 21:43 | In Heb iii, 4 |
| 21:44 | In Acta x, 2; In Heb iii, 4 |
| 21:45-46 | In Mat lxviii, 2 |
| 22 (p) | De Laz iv, 1; De uir lxxxii; lxxxiv; In Ioh x, 3 |
| 22:2 | Adu op i, 6; Ex in ps xliv, 10 |
| 22:9 | In Mat l, 3; In Rom xix, 2 (11:11); xxx, 1 (15:27) |
| 22:11 | Adu Iud 3, 5, 4; In d P Nolo 2 |
| 22:12 | Adu Iud 3, 5, 4; In Eph iii, 5 (1:22); In d N |

22:12 cont Nolo 2; In il Uidi dom vi, 1
22:13 Adu Iud 3, 5, 4; De sac vi, 4; Ex in ps cxlii, 3; In 2 Cor x, 7; In Eph ix, 2 (4:3); In d P Nolo 2; In Ioh xlv, 2; In Mat lvi, 7; lxix, 2; In Rom xxv, 4 (14:13); In 1 Tim vii, 2 (2:7); In 2 Tim iii, 2 (1:18)
22:16 In Mat lxx, 1
22:17 De elee 2; In Ioh lxi, 1; In Mat lxxxvi, 1
22:20 In Mat lxx, 2
22:21 De elee2; In Mat lxx, 2
22:22 In Mat lxx, 2
22:23 In Ioh lxi, 1; lxiii, 3; In Mat lxvii, 2
22:24 In Mat lxx, 2
22:25-28 In Gen xviii, 4; In Mat lxx, 2
22:29 In 1 Cor xvii, 4; In Gen xviii, 4; In Heb viii 9; In Mat lxx, 2
22:30 De uir lxxviii; In Acta xxxii, 3 (15:11); In Eph xxiii, 3 (6:14); In Gen xviii, 4; xxii, 2
22:31 In Mat lxx, 2
22:32 In Eph xviii, 2 (5:14); In Mat lxx, 2; In Rom xi, 5 (6:18); In 1 Tim xiii, 3 (5:5)
22:33 In Mat lxx, 2
22:36 In Mat xxvii, 4
22:37-38 In Acta xliv, 4; In Is iii, 7; In Mat lxxi, 1
22:39 In Acta xliv, 4; In Gal v, 4 (5:14); In Is iii, 7; In Mat lxxi, 1; lxxvi, 4
22:40 In Gen lv, 3; In Ioh lxxvii, 1; In Mat xliii, 2; lxxi, 1; In 2 Tim vii, 3 (3:7)
22:42 De incomp dei v, 3; Ex in ps cxlv, 2; In Mat lxxi, 1; lxxii, 3
22:43 De incomp dei v, 3; Ex in ps cix, 2; cix, 7; cxlv, 2; In Acta vi, 2 (2:34); In Ioh viii, 1; In Mat xxvi, 9; lxxi, 1; lxxxiv, 3
22:45 Ex in ps cix, 7; In Mat lxxi, 1; lxxxiv, 3
22:46 In Mat lxxi, 1; lxxxiv, 3
23:1 In Mat xxiii, 2
23:2 Ad e q scan xx; De Anna ii, 4; In Acta ix, 4 (3:26); In Gal i, 7 (1:9); In Heb xxxiv, 1; In il Sal P et A ii, 6; In Ioh lxxxvi, 4; In 1 Thess x, 1 (5:13); In 2 Tim ii, 2 (1:12)
23:3 Ad e q scan xx; De Anna ii, 4; In Heb xxxiv, 1; In il Sal P et A ii, 6; In Ioh lxxxvi, 4; In 1 Thess x, 1 (5:3); In 2 Tim ii, 2 (1:12)
23:4 In Mat xxiii, 1; lxxii, 1
23:5 In Col iii, 4 (1:20); In Mat lxxi, 2
23:8 In Gen xxxv, 1; In Ioh lxxi, 1; In Mat lxxii, 3; In princ Act i, 3; In 1 Tim ii, 1 (1:7)

23:9 In Ioh lxxi, 1; In Mat lxxii, 3
23:10 In Ioh lxxviii, 3; In Is i, 1
23:11 In Mat lxxii, 3
23:12 F in epis cath L Peter 5:3; In 1 Cor xl, 6; In Heb xxv, 4; In Mat lxxii, 3
23:13 In Mat lxxiii, 1
23:14 In Rom xxxii, 1 (16:18)
23:15 In Mat lxxiii, 1; In 1 Thess ix, 3 (5:5); x, 1 (5:13);
23:16 In Mat xvii, 5
23:23 De laud s Paul vi; In Mat xxiii, 1; lxiii, 1
23:24 In Mat xxiii, 1; lxiii, 2
23:25-26 In Mat lxxiii, 1; lxxxi, 4
23:27 In Acta xlviii, 3; In Mat lxxiii, 1; lxxiii, 2
23:31 De proph obscur i, 3
23:32 Adu Iud 5, 9, 5; 5, 9, 6; De proph obscur i, 3; In Mat lxviii, 1; lxxiv, 1
23:33-34 In Mat lxxiv, 1 (2x)
23:35 Ex in ps cxlvii, 2; In Mat lxxiv, 1; lxxv, 5
23:36 In Mat lxxiv, 1
23:37 Ad pop Anti xvii, 13; Ad Theo i, 13; De paen viii, 14; De proph obscur i, 3; E iii, 1; Ex in ps xli, 4; xliv, 6; F Ier 25:3; In Eph iii, 2 (1:22); In il Dom non est 5; In Mat lxxiv, 3
23:38 E iii, 1; Ex in ps viii, 5; xliv, 6; cxvii, 6; In Ioh li, 2; liii, 2; lxv, 1; In Mat lxxiv, 3
23:39 In 2 Cor ix, 4; In Ioh lxvi, 2; In Mat lxxiv, 3
24 (p) Adu Iud ix, 4; In Ioh lxvi, 2; In Mat lxxiv, 3
24:2 Adu Iud 5, 3, 13; In Acta ii, 1 (1:6)
24:3 In Acta ii, 3 (1:11); In il Hoc scit 4; In Mat x, 1; lxxv, 1
24:4-5 In Mat lxxv, 1
24:6 In il Hoc scit 6 (2x); In Mat lxxv, 1; lxxvii, 1
24:7 In Acta xi, 2 (4:32); In il Hoc scit 6; In Mat lxxv, 2
24:9 In Mat lxxv, 2 (2x)
24:10 In Mat lxxv, 2
24:11 In Mat lxxv, 2; lxxvi, 2
24:12 Ad Dem de comp i, 3; F Ier 9:4; In Eph vii, 3 (3:19); ix, 3 (4:3); In Ioh lxxii, 5; In Mat xvi, 11; lxxv, 2; In Rom v, 1 (1:31); In 1 Tim ii, 1 (1:7)
24:13 In Mat lxxv, 2
24:14 In Acta i, 1 (1:2); In 1 Cor vi, 6; In Heb xxi, 5; In Mat xxv, 3; lxxv, 2; In 2 Tim i, 1

24:14 cont (Introduction)
24:15 Adu Iud 5, 10, 6; In Is ii, 7; In Mat lxxv, 2
24:19 Ex in ps viii, 5; In Mat lxxvi, 1
24:20 In Mat lxxvi, 1
24:21 Adu op i, 4; Con Iud et gen 8; In Acta v, 3 (2:20); In Heb xxi, 5; In Mat xliii, 4; lxxvi, 1; In Rom xxv, 5 (14:13) (2x)
24:22 In Acta v, 2 (2:20); In Mat lxxvi, 1
24:23 In Mat lxxvi, 2; In 1 Thess ix, 1 (5:2)
24:24 Ad e q scan xii; In Mat x, 1; lxxvi, 2 (2x); In 2 Thess iii, 2 (2:4); In 2 Tim ix, 2 (4:5)
24:25 In Mat lxxvi, 2
24:26 De cruce et lat i, 4; ii, 4; Ex in ps xlix, 2; In Mat lxxvi, 2
24:27 De cruce et lat i, 4; ii, 4; Ex in ps xlix, 2; cxxiv, 3; In Mat liii, 3; lxxvi, 2; lxxvi, 3; In 2 Thess i, 1 (Introduction)
24:28 De coem et de cru 1; 3; In 1 Cor xxiv, 7; In Mat lxxvi, 2
24:29 Ad Stel de comp ii, 4; Ad Theo i, 12; Cat ill iii, 2; De cruce et lat i, 4 (2x); ii, 4 (2x); E ii, 3; Ex in ps xlvi, 2; In Mat liii, 3; lxxvi, 2; lxxvi, 3; In Rom xiv, 10 (8:27); In 1 Thess viii, 1 (4:17)
24:30 Ad e q scan xvii; De cruce et lat i, 4; ii, 4; In Mat lxxvi, 3 (2x)
24:31 Ex in ps xlvi, 2; In Mat lxxvi, 4; In 1 Thess viii, 1 (4:17)
24:34 Ex in ps cx, 6; In Mat lxxvii, 1
24:35 Con Iud et gen 15; De s h Bab 1; De s h Phoc 1; In il Uidi dom iv, 2; In Mat liv, 3; S anti iret 1; 2
24:36 In Acta ii, 1 (1:6); In Mat lxxvii, 1
24:37 In Ioh xxxiv, 3
24:38 In Mat lxxvii, 2; In 1 Tim xv, 3 (5:20)
24:39 In Mat lxxvii, 2
24:40-41 In ascen d n I C 5; In Mat lxxvii, 2; In 1 Thess viii, 2 (4:18)
24:42 In Eph xxiii, 3 (6:14); In Mat lxxvii, 2; In 1 Thess ix, 2 (5:2)
24:43 In Eph xxiii, 3 (6:14); In Mat lxxvii, 2
24:44 In Mat lxxvii, 2
24:45 De sac ii, 4; In Mat lxxvii, 3
24:46 In Mat lxxvii, 3
24:47 De sac ii, 1; In Mat lxxvii, 3
24:48-49 In Mat lxxvii, 4

| | |
|---|---|
| 24:50 | In Mat lxxvii, 4 (2x) |
| 24:51 | De sac iv, 1; iv, 2; In Acta xix, 5 (9:9); In Mat lxxvii, 4 |
| 25 (p) | De diab tent iii, 3; De Laz iii, 10; iv, 1; De uir lxxvii; lxxxiv, E ii, 4; Ex in ps vi, 4; xlviii, 4; In Eph iv, 3 (2:10); In Hel 1; In il Uid elig 6; 15; In Ioh x, 3; lx, 4; In Is iii, 6 |
| 25:1 | Ex in ps vii, 12; In Acta xx, 4 (9:25); In 2 Cor xxiii, 8; In Gal vi, 3 (6:18); In il Sal P et A ii, 2 |
| 25:2 | De paen iii, 2; In il Sal P et A iii, 2; In Mat lxxix, 2 |
| 25:3 | De paen iii, 2; In Eph xxiv, 5 (6:24); In il Sal P et A ii, 2 |
| 25:4-5 | In il Sal P et A ii, 2 |
| 25:6 | Cat ill xi, 2; In il Sal P et A ii, 2; In 1 Thess viii, 1 (4:17); In 2 Thess iii, 1 (1:11) |
| 25:7 | Adu Iud 3, 5, 4; Ex in ps xliv, 12; In il Sal P et A ii, 2 |
| 25:8 | Adu Iud 3, 5, 4; De pet mat 2; De paen iii, 2 (2x); iv, 3; In Eph xxiv, 5 (6:25); In Heb xxviii, 16; In il Sal P et A ii, 2 |
| 25:9 | Adu Iud 3, 5, 4; De pet mat 2; De paen iii, 2; Ex in ps xlviii, 10; In 2 Cor ix, 4; In il Sal P et A ii, 2; In Ioh lxxxiv, 3; In Rom xviii, 6 (11:6) |
| 25:10 | Ad pop Anti vi, 15; Adu Iud 3, 5, 4; De paen iii, 3; In d P Nolo 2; In il Sal P et A ii, 2 |
| 25:11 | Adu Iud 3, 5, 4; De paen iii, 3; In d P Nolo 2; In il Sal P et A ii, 2 |
| 25:12 | Adu Iud 3, 5, 4; De pet mat 2; De paen iii,3; In 1 Cor xxx, 9; In Heb xxviii, 16; xxxi, 7; In d P Nolo 2; In il Hab i, 6; In il Sal P et A ii, 2; In Mat xxiii, 9; lxxviii, 2; In para 3; In Rom xiii, 8 (8:11); In 2 Tim vi, 3 (2:26) |
| 25:13 | Adu Iud 3, 5, 4; Adu op iii, 14; In Gen 1, 2; In Mat lxxviii, 2 |
| 25:14 | In Gen xli, 1; S Gen vii, 1 |
| 25:15 | Adu Iud 8, 9, 10; De Chris prec 1; De fato et pr vi; In Col i, 6 (1:7); In Gen xli, 1 |
| 25:17 | In princ Act iv, 1 |
| 25:19-20 | In Gen xli, 1 |
| 25:21 | Ad pop Anti xii, 16; Ad Stag a dae ii, 10; Adu Iud 8, 9, 10; De Chris prec 3; F Iob 13:5; In Acta xliii, 3; In 1 Cor xliii, 6; In Gen xli, 1; S Gen vii, 1 |

25:22 De Chris prec 3; In Gen xli, 1
25:23 In Gen xxiv, 3; In Mat lvi, 7; lxxviii, 2; S anti iret 5; S Gen vii, 1
25:24 Adu Iud 4, 7, 8; De diab tent iii, 2; De paen vi, 3; De sac vi, 10; Ex in ps vii, 12; F Iob 3:11; In Gen xli, 2; In il Uidi dom ii, 1; In Mat lxxviii, 2
25:25 Adu Iud 4, 7, 8; In Acta xx, 4 (9:25); In Gen xli, 2; In Mat lxxviii, 2
25:26 Ad pop Anti xii, 16; Adu Iud 4, 7, 8; De s h Phoc 2; In Col i, 6 (1:7); In Gen xxxii, 1; xli, 2; In Heb xxxi, 7; In Mat lvi, 7; In 2 Tim iii, 2 (1:18); S anti iret 5
25:27 Ad pop Anti xii, 16; Adu Iud 4, 7, 8; 8, 9, 8; Adu op iii, 21; De Laz i, 3; De paen vii, 3; In Gen xxxii, 1; In il Si esur 1; In Mat lxxviii, 2; In princ Act iv, 2; In Rom xxxi, 1 (16;5)
25:28 Adu Iud 4, 7, 8; In Mat lxxviii, 2
25:29 Adu Iud 4, 7, 8; Cat ill ii, 8; In Mat lxxviii 2
25:30 Adu Iud 4, 7, 8; De sac iv, 1; In Mat xii, 4; lxxviii, 2
25:31 De pet mat 1; De paen vii, 7; In Acta ii, 4 (1:11); In Heb xxxi, 7; In Ioh xxviii, 1
25:32 In Heb xxxi, 7; In Mat xlvii, 3
25:33 De diab tent iii, 3; De uir i; In Heb xxxi, 7
25:34 Ad dem de comp i, 8; Ad Theo i, 9; De pet mat 2; Ex in ps xlvi, 3; In Acta xliii, 3; xlv, 3; In 1 Cor xxx, 9; xlii, 7; In Eph i, 1 (1:4); xvi, 1 (4:32); In Gen iii, 4; v, 2; xiv, 2; xvii, 6; xxxiv, 5; xli, 7; l, 2; lxv, 5; In Heb xviii, 6; xxxi, 8; In il Hab i, 6; In Mat lvi, 7; lxxxix, 3; In Phil Introduction, 3; vi, 3 (2:8); In princ Act ii, 3; In 1 Tim xiii, 3 (5:5); S Gen v, 3
25:35 Ad pop Anti vi, 15; Adu Iud 3, 5, 4; De diab tent iii, 3; Ex in ps xli, 3; In Acta xxv, 4 (11:30); xlv, 3; In Col i, 6 (1:7); In Gen xxxiv, 2; xli, 7; l, 2; In Heb xviii, 6; In Hel 9; In il Uid elig 10; In Ioh lxxxv, 5; In Mat iv, 20; lvi, 7; In Phil i, 5 (1:7); vi, 3 (2:8); In princ Act ii, 3; In 1 Tim xiii, 3 (5:5); S Gen v, 3; vii, 5; viii, 2
25:36 Adu Iud 3, 5, 4; Ex in ps xli, 3; In Gen xxxiv, 2; xxxv, 8; xli, 7; In Heb xviii, 6; In princ Act ii, 3; S Gen v, 3
25:37 In il Uid elig 10
25:40 De paen iii, 1; iii, 2; vii, 7; In Acta xlv,

| | |
|---|---|
| 25:40 cont | 3; In Col xii, 6 (4:18); In Gen xli, 7; lv, 3; lxv, 4; In Rom xxx, 4 (16:5); In 1 Tim xiv, 2 (5:10); In 2 Tim iii, 2 (1:18) |
| 25:41 | De paen vii, 7; De uir iv; xxiv; Ex in ps xlvi, 3; cix, 4; cxliv, 3; In 1 Cor xvi, 5; In d P Nolo 2; In Eph iv, 3 (2:10); xxiv, 5 (6:24); In Gen xvii, 6; l, 2; In Heb xxxi, 8; In il Sal P et A ii, 2; In Is i, 8; In Mat lvi, 7; lxxxi, 4; lxxxv, 4; In Rom xxi, 5 (12:13); xxv, 4 (14:13); xxv, 6 (14:13); In 1 Thess viii, 2 (4:18) |
| 25:42 | Ex in ps iv, 8; In 1 Cor x, 6; In Eph iv, 3 (2:10); In Gen l, 2; In Hen xxxi, 7; In Ioh lxxiv, 3; In Mat xxiii, 9; l, 4; lxxxi, 4; In para 3 |
| 25:44 | Adu Iud 3, 5, 4; In Eph xxiv, 5 (6:24) |
| 25:45 | Adu Iud 3, 1, 5; 3, 5, 4; De Laz ii, 5; In Heb i, 4; In Ioh lx, 6; lxxvii, 4; In Mat xxxv, 5; l, 4; lxxix, 1; lxxxviii |
| 25:46 | De uir lxxxiv; In 1 Cor ix, 1; In 2 Cor xxix, 6; In Ioh xxviii, 1; In Rom xxv, 5 (14:13); In 1 Thess viii, 2 (4:18) |
| 26 (p) | De laud s Paul vi |
| 26:1-2 | In Mat lxxix, 2 |
| 26:3 | In Mat xxix, 3; lxxxv, 2 |
| 26:4-5 | In Mat xxix, 3 |
| 26:6 | De paen vii, 2 |
| 26:7 | In Ioh lxii, 1 |
| 26:8 | In Acta iii, 4 (1:26); In Mat lxxx, 1 |
| 26:9-10 | Adu Iud 5, 2, 2; In Mat lxxx, 1 |
| 26:11 | In Mat l, 6; lxxx, 1 |
| 26:12 | In Mat lxxx, 1 |
| 26:13 | Adu Iud 5, 2, 2; Ex in ps cxlvii, 4; In Mat lxxx, 1 |
| 26:14 | De prod Iud i, 2; i, 4; ii, 2; In Mat lxxx, 2 |
| 26:15 | De cruce et lat i, 2; ii, 2; De prod Iud i, 2; i, 3; ii, 2; In Mat lxxx, 2; lxxx, 3; lxxxi, 3 |
| 26:16 | De cruce et lat ii, 2; De prod Iud ii, 3; In Mat lxxx, 3 |
| 26:17 | De cruce et lat i, 2; ii, 2; De prod Iud i, 4; ii, 4 |
| 26:18 | In Mat lxxxii, 5 |
| 26:20 | Con Iud et gen 4; In Mat lxxxi, 1 |
| 26:21 | De consub 5; De Laz i, 5; In il In fac 6; In Mat lxxxi, 1; In Phil vi, 5 (2:8) |
| 26:22-23 | In Mat lxxxi, 1 |

26:24 In Acta iii, 3 (1:26); In Mat lxxxi, 1
26:25 De consub 5; In Mat lxxxi, 1 (2x)
26:26 De prod Iud i, 5; ii, 5; ii, 6
26:27 De prod Iud ii, 5
26:28 De prod Iud i, 5; ii, 5; In Heb xvi, 4
26:29-30 In Mat lxxxii, 2
26:31 De consub 5 (2x); In Mat lxxxii, 2; In 1 Tim i, 1 (1:2)
26:32 De consub 5; In Mat lxxxii, 2
26:33 De consub 5; In Mat lxxxii, 2; lxxxii, 3
26:34 De consub 5; In Mat lxxxii, 3; lxxxv, 2
26:35 De paen iii, 4; In Ioh lxxxviii, 1; In Mat lvi 4
26:36 In Mat lxxxiii, 1
26:38 In Heb viii, 3; In il Pater s p 4; In Mat lxxviii, 4; lxxxiv, 1
26:39 Cat ill x, 9; De consub 5; 6 (3x); In Heb viii 3; In il Pater s p 1 (2x); 3 (2x); In Mat xxxi 5; lxxxiii, 1; lxxxiv, 1
26:40 In il Pater s p 4; In Mat lxxxiii, 1
26:41 De uir ii; E xvii; In 1 Cor xviii, 6; In Heb v, 7; In il Pater s p 4 (2x); In Mat xiii, 1; lxxxiii, 1; In Rom xxx, 2 (15:31); In s Luc 2
26:42-43,45 In Mat lxxxiii, 1
26:46-48 In Mat lxxxiii, 2
26:49 De mut nom iii, 1
26:50 In Mat lxxxiii, 2
26:52 In Acta xv, 4 (7:5) (2x); In Ioh lxxxiii, 2
26:53 In Ioh liii, 2; lxxv, 4; In Mat lxxxiv, 1
26:54 In Mat lxxxiv, 1
26:55 In Mat lxxxiv, 2; In princ Act ii, 4; In Rom xxi, 5 (12:13)
26:56-58,60 In Mat lxxxiv, 2
26:61 De proph obscur i, 4; In Mat lxxxiv, 2
26:62 In Mat lxxxiv, 2
26:63 In Col vi, 3 (2:15); In Ioh lxxxiv, 2; In Mat lxxxiv, 2 (2x)
26:64 De consub 3; In Col vi, 3 (2:15); In Mat lxxxiv, 2
26:65 Con Iud et gen 8; E i, 4; In Mat lxxxiv, 2
26:66 In Mat lxxxiv, 3
26:68 E i, 4; In Heb xxviii, 5
26:69 Adu Iud 8, 3, 4; De paen iii, 4; v, 2; In Acta v, 1 (2:20); In Mat lxxxiv, 3
26:70 Adu Iud 8, 3, 4; De paen v, 2; In Acta v, 1

| | |
|---|---|
| 26:70 cont | (2:20); x, 3 (4:22); In Ioh lxv, 2; In Mat lxxxv, 1 |
| 26:71-72 | Adu Iud 8, 3, 4; In Acta v, 1 (2:20); In Mat lxxxv, 1 |
| 26:73-74 | Adu Iud 8, 3, 4; In Mat lxxxv, 1 |
| 26:75 | Adu Iud 8, 3, 4; De paen v, 2; In Heb xxxi, 4; In Mat lxxxv, 1 |
| 27:1 | In Mat lxxxv, 2 |
| 27:2 | In Eph viii, 9 (4:2); In Mat lxxxv, 2 |
| 27:3 | De prod Iud ii, 3; ii, 5; In Mat lxxxv, 2 |
| 27:4 | De Laz vi, 9; De paen i, 3; De prod Iud i, 3; E vii, 2; In Mat lxxxv, 2 |
| 27:5 | Ex in ps vii, 13; In Mat lxxxv, 2; lxxxv, 3 |
| 27:6-10 | In Mat lxxxv, 3 |
| 27:13 | Adu Iud 6, 5, 2 |
| 27:15 | In Acta ix, 2 (3:26) |
| 27:19 | In Mat lxxxvi, 1 (2x) |
| 27:20 | In Mat lxxxvi, 1 |
| 27:22 | In Mat lxxxvi, 2 (2x) |
| 27:23 | In Mat lxxxvi, 2 |
| 27:24 | De elee 2; F Iob 9:31; In Mat lxxxvi, 2 |
| 27:25 | Adu Iud 1, 5, 1; 6, 1, 7; H dicta in t s Anas 5; In Mat lxxxvi, 2; lxxxvii, 1; In princ Act iv, 8; iv, 9 |
| 27:26 | In Mat lxxxvi, 2 |
| 27:30 | In Acta viii, 3 (3:12) |
| 27:31 | In Mat lxvii, 3; lxxxvii, 1 |
| 27:32 | In Mat lxvii, 3; In para 3 |
| 27:40 | Ad e q scan xiv; De cruce et lat i, 5; ii, 5 (2x); E i, 4 (2x); In Acta xv, 1 (6:12); xxiii, 3 (10:43); In Col vi, 3 (2:15); In Heb xxviii, 5; In Ioh lx, 2; In Mat lxxxvii, 2; lxxxviii; In Rom xxvii, 2 (15:3) |
| 27:41 | In 1 Cor iv, 3 |
| 27:42 | De cruce et lat i, 5; ii, 5; E i, 4; In Acta ix, 1 (3:18); xiv, 3 (6:7); In 1 Cor iv, 3; In Ioh lx, 2; In Mat lxxxvii, 2; lxxxviii (2x) In Rom xxvii, 2 (15:3) |
| 27:43 | In Acta ix, 1 (3:18); xvi, 1 (7:7); In Mat lxxxvii, 2 |
| 27:44 | In para 3 |
| 27:45 | Ex in ps cxlii, 5 |
| 27:46, 48,50 | In Mat lxxxviii |
| 27:51 | Adu Iud 6, 5, 3 |
| 27:52-53 | In Eut ii, 13; In Mat lxxxviii |
| 27:55-58,61 | In Mat lxxxviii |

| | |
|---|---|
| 27:63 | Cat ill x, 13; De mtu nom iii, 5; In Eph vii, 4 (3:19); In Heb xxviii, 5; In Mat xliii, 2 |
| 27:64 | Cat ill x, 13; De s Bab c Iul 17; In Mat lxxxv 2; xc, 1 |
| 27:65-66 | Cat ill x, 13 |
| 28 (p) | E cxxv |
| 28:1 | In Mat lxxxix, 2 |
| 28:2 | In Acta ii, 3 (1:11); In Mat 1, 6; lxxxix, 2 |
| 28:3,5 | In Mat lxxxix, 2 |
| 28:6 | In Acta ii, 4 (1:11); In Mat lxxxix, 2 |
| 28:7-8 | In Mat lxxxix, 2 |
| 28:9-10 | In Mat lxxxix, 3 |
| 28:13 | E i, 4 |
| 28:15-17 | In Mat xc, 2 |
| 28:18 | H in il App 16; In 1 Cor xxxix, 11; In Ioh lxxx, 1; In Mat xc, 2 (2x) |
| 28:19 | Cat ill i, 23; De san pent ii, 2 (2x); Ex in ps cix, 3; cxlvii, 4; In Acta i, 3 (1:2); In Eph iv, 3 (2:10); xx, 2 (5:27); H in il App 21; In Heb v, 3; In Ioh lxvi, 2; lxxx, 1; In Is ii, 3; In Mat lxix, 1; xc, 2; In 2 Thess v, 4 (3:18) |
| 28:20 | De san pent i, 1; Ex in ps xliv, 2; xliv, 4; In Acta i, 3 (1:2); In 1 Cor vi, 6; In Eph ix, 2 (4:3); In il Messis 3; 4; 5; In Ioh lxxv, 1; lxxxi, 2; In Mat xv, 2; xc, 2; In Phil xiv, 1 (4:7); In 2 Thess v, 3 (3:18); v, 4 (3:18); S anti iret 2 |

## Mark

| | |
|---|---|
| 1:2 | In Ioh vi |
| 1:10 | In Acta iv, 1 (2:3) |
| 1:17 | In Ioh xxiv, 2 |
| 1:24 | De Laz ii, 2; De uir viii |
| 1:30 | In il Uidi dom iv, 3 |
| 1:34 | In Mat xxvii, 2 |
| 1:41 | In Ioh lxiv, 2 |
| 2:4 | In Mat xxix, 1 |
| 2:5 | De paen vii, 1; Ex in ps cxlv, 4; In Heb v, 3 |
| 2:7 | Ex in ps cxlv, 4; In para 6 |
| 2:10 | In il Fil 6; In Ioh lxxviii, 3 |
| 2:14 | In Mat xxx, 1 |
| 2:18-19 | In Mat xxx, 4 |

9:23 In Mat lvii, 3 (3x)
9:24 Ex in ps xlvi, 3; In Mat lvii, 3
9:25 In Ioh iii, 4; xxiv, 2; lxiv, 2; In Mat lvii,3
9:30 In Mat xli, 4
9:32 In Mat xlvii, 1; lviii, 1; lxv, 1
9:34 In Mat lviii, 3
9:38 In Mat xxiv, 2
9:40 In Mat xli, 4
9:43 Ex in ps cxxxvi, 1; In Rom xxv, 4 (14:13)
9:44 In 2 Cor xxix, 6; In Ioh lxiii, 3; In Rom xi, 5 (6:18); xxv, 5 (14:13); In 1 Thess v, 2 (4:8); viii, 2 (4:18)
9:45 In il Prop 5
10:10 In Mat lxii, 2
10:11 In 1 Cor xix, 4
10:14 In Acta iii, 4 (1:26)
10:17-20 In Mat lxiii, 1
10:21 In Acta iii, 4 (1:26); vii, 4 (2:47); In Mat lxiii, 1
10:23 In Mat lxiii, 2
10:24 In Phil ix, 5 (2:30)
10:25 De dec mil 3
10:26 De dec mil 3; In Mat lxi, 1
10:27 De dec mil 3
10:30 In Mat xi, 7; xlvi, 4
10:31 In Gen xviii, 5
10:32 In Mat lxv, 1
10:33-34 In il In fac 5
10:35-37 In Mat lxv, 2
10:38 De ss B et P 6
10:39 In Ioh xxv, 2
10:40 In Ioh lxvii, 1; In Rom xxxi, 4 (16:16)
10:43 In 1 Cor xii, 2
11:13 In Mat lxvii, 1
11:25 De D et S iii, 3; In Heb ix, 8; In il Si esur 6; In 1 Tim viii, 1 (2:10)
12:15 In Mat lxx, 1
12:19-24 In Gen xviii, 4
12:25 In Gen xviii, 4; xxii, 2
12:30 In Acta xliv, 4; In Gen lv, 3 (2x)
12:31 In Gen lv, 3
12:34 In Mat lxxi, 1
12:36 In Ioh viii, 1
12:41 In Col i, 6 (1:7)
12:42 De bap Chris 1; De dec mil 4; De diab tent

| | |
|---|---|
| 12:42 cont | ii, 6; De pet mat 2; In Heb xxxi, 8 |
| 12:43 | In 2 Cor xvii, 2; In Mat lii, 5 |
| 12:44 | In Heb xxviii, 9 |
| 13:3 | In Mat lxxv, 1 |
| 13:7 | In Acta ii, 3 (1:11) |
| 13:16 | F Prou 30:1 |
| 13:22 | In Acta xviii, 3 (8:24) |
| 13:32 | In Acta ii, 1 (1:6); In Mat lxxvii, 1 |
| 14;4 | In Acta iii, 4 (1:26) |
| 14:6, 8-9 | Adu Iud 5, 2, 2 |
| 14:37 | In Mat lxxxiii, 1 |
| 14:38 | Ex in ps cxlii, 6 |
| 14:56-59 | In Mat lxxxiv, 2 |
| 14:65 | In Mat lxxxv, 1 |
| 14:66-67 | Adu Iud 8, 3, 4 |
| 14:68 | Adu Iud 8, 3, 4; De paen iii, 4; In Mat lxxxv, 1 |
| 14:69-71 | Adu Iud 8, 3, 4 |
| 14:72 | Adu Iud 8, 3, 4; In Mat lxxxv, 1; lxxxv, 2 |
| 15:6 | In Acta ix, 2 (3:26) |
| 15:28 | In Acta liii, 1 |
| 15:31 | In para 3 |
| 15:39 | In Mat lxxxviii |
| 15:41 | In Acta iii, 2 (1:26); In Tit vi, 2 (3:15) |
| 15:44 | In Mat lxxxviii |
| 16:5 | Ex in ps xi, 3 |
| 16:9 | In 1 Cor xxxviii, 5 |
| 16:15 | Ex in ps xlvi, 3 |
| 16:18 | In Rom xv, 1 (8:28) |

Luke

| | |
|---|---|
| 1:1 | In Acta xix, 5 (9:9) |
| 1:2 | In Acta i, 2 (1:2); In diem nat 2; In Heb iii 7; In Ioh vi, 2 |
| 1:3 | De mut nom i, 4; In Acta i, 2 (1:2) |
| 1:4 | In Acta i, 3 (1:2); In Mat i, 7 |
| 1:5 | In diem nat 5 |
| 1:6 | De bap Chris 3; In Mat iv, 7 |
| 1:7 | In diem nat 2 |
| 1:8-12 | In diem nat 5 |
| 1:13 | De incomp dei ii, 2; De mut nom ii, 3; In diem nat 5 |

| | |
|---|---|
| 1:17 | In 2 Thess iv, 2 (2:12) |
| 1:18, 20 | De incomp dei ii, 2 |
| 1:21-22,25 | In diem nat 5 |
| 1:26 | In diem nat 3 |
| 1:27 | In diem nat 3; In Mat ii, 7; iv, 9 |
| 1:30 | In Acta ii, 4 (1:11); In diem nat 5 |
| 1:31 | In diem nat 5; In Gen xlix, 2; Pec frat 7 |
| 1:34 | Ex in ps cix, 3; In Gen xlix, 2; In Mat iv, 8; Pec frat 7 |
| 1:35 | Cat ill xi, 17; In diem nat 5; In Gen xlix, 2 (2x); Pec frat 7 |
| 1:36 | De bap Chris 3; In diem nat 5; In Gen xlix, 3; In Ioh xvii, 2; Pec frat 8 |
| 1:37 | Ex in ps cxvii, 4; In diem nat 5 |
| 1:66 | In Ioh xvi, 1 |
| 1:76 | In Mat xiv, 2 |
| 1:79 | Ex in ps cxlii, 3 |
| 2 (p) | In il Uidi dom iv, 6 |
| 2:4 | In diem nat 2; 3 |
| 2:5-6 | In diem nat 2 |
| 2:7 | Ex in ps xliv, 2; In diem nat 2 |
| 2:9 | Ex in ps xlix, 3 |
| 2:10 | Ex in ps viii, 7; In 1 Tim ii, 2 (1:11) |
| 2:13 | Ex in ps viii, 1 |
| 2:14 | Adu Iud 1, 1, 2; De incomp dei i, 6; In ascen d n I C 4; In Col ix, 2 (3:17); In Ioh xv, 1; xxi, 1; In Mat xxv, 4; xxxv, 1; lxviii, 3 |
| 2:25 | In Acta xxxiii, 1 (15:15) |
| 2:26 | In Heb xxiii, 1 |
| 2:34 | In 2 Cor v, 2 |
| 2:39 | In Mat ix, 5 |
| 2:46 | In Ioh xxi, 2 |
| 2:48 | In Acta iii, 2 |
| 3:2-3 | In Mat x, 2 |
| 3:5-6 | In Mat x, 3 |
| 3:7 | De Laz ii, 1; Ex in ps xliv, 11 |
| 3:8 | Cat ill xii, 22; De Laz ii, 1; vi, 6 |
| 3:9 | Ex in ps vii, 11 |
| 3:10 | In Mat xxiv, 4 |
| 3:14 | In Mat xxi, 6; xxiv, 4 |
| 3:16 | Cat ill xi, 13; De mut nom iii, 5; In Acta i, 5 (1:5); H in il App 6; In Ioh lxxv, 1; In Mat iii, 8 |
| 3:17 | H in il App 6 |

| | |
|---|---|
| 6:36 | Ier 2:13; In Heb xxxii, 7; In Ioh lxxxii, 2; |
| cont | In Mat xxxv, 6; xxxix, 3; xlix, 4; lii, 6; In 2 Tim vi, 3 (2:26) |
| 6:37 | In Ioh iv, 4; In Mat lix, 6 |
| 7 (p) | De b Phil 4; Ex in ps cxxvii, 2; In para 4 |
| 7:2 | In Mat xxvi, 1; xxvi, 3 (2x) |
| 7:4 | In Mat xxvi, 4 |
| 7:5 | In Mat xxvi, 3 (2x) |
| 7:6 | In Mat xxvi, 3 |
| 7:7,9 | In para 4 |
| 7:14 | In quat Laz A 2 |
| 7:18 | In Mat xxxvi, 1 |
| 7:21 | In Mat xxxvi, 2 |
| 7:29-30 | De bap Chris 4; In Mat xxxvii, 5 |
| 7:33 | Ex in ps xliv, 8 |
| 7:34 | E i, 3; cxxv; Ex in ps xliv, 8 |
| 7:37 | Ex in ps cx, 4; In Ioh lxii, 1 |
| 7:38 | Ex in ps cxl, 2; In Mat xxx, 1 |
| 7:39 | E i, 3; In Acta xv, 5 (7:5); In para 5 |
| 7:43 | Ad Stel de comp ii, 6 |
| 7:44-46 | Ad Theo i, 15 |
| 7:47 | Ad Theo i, 15; De paen vii, 2 (2x); In Acta xx, 3 (9:25); xxx, 3 (15:15); In Mat lxxxii, 4 |
| 7:48 | Ad Theo i, 15 |
| 8:3 | In Ioh lxxii, 3 |
| 8:5 | In Acta iv, 1 (2:2); In il Pater s p 1 |
| 8:6-7 | In il Pater s p 1 |
| 8:8 | In Acta xxvii, 3 (13:3); In il Pater s p 1; In 2 Tim v, 4 (2:19) |
| 8:9 | F Ier Introduction |
| 8:10 | In Rom i, 3 (1:5) |
| 8:11 | In Acta iv, 1 (2:2) |
| 8:18 | In Mat xlv, 1 |
| 8:22 | In Mat xxviii, 1 |
| 8:26-29 | Adu Iud 8, 8, 6 |
| 8:30 | Adu Iud 8, 8, 6; In Mat xlvi, 4 |
| 8:31 | Adu Iud 8, 8, 6; In Mat xxviii, 2 |
| 8:32 | Adu Iud 8, 8, 6; In Mat xix, 10 |
| 8:33-36 | Adu Iud 8, 8, 6 |
| 8:39 | In Mat xxxii, 1 |
| 8:44 | In Rom viii, 6-8 (4:21) |
| 8:48 | In Mat xxxi, 2; In Rom viii, 6-8 (4:21) |
| 8:49 | In Mat xxxi, 1; xxxi, 2 |

8:50 In Mat xxxi, 2
8:51 In Ioh lxxii, 1; In Mat xxx, 1
9:2 In Mat xxiv, 4
9:3 In il Sal P et A ii, 1
9:4 In il Sal P et A i, 3
9:5 De Laz iii, 6
9:8-9 In Mat xlviii, 3
9:12 In Mat xlv, 1
9:26 In Gen xxiii, 3; In Rom xxvi, 3 (14:22)
9:28 In Mat lvi, 2
9:31 In Mat lvi, 3
9:32-33 In Mat lvi, 4
9:45 In Mat liv, 5; lvii, 2; lviii, 1
9:48 In Acta xlv, 3
9:49 In Mat xxiv, 2; xli, 4
9:50 In Mat xli, 4
9:54 In Mat lvi, 3
9:55 In 1 Cor xxxiii, 5; In Ioh li, 2; In Mat xxix, 3; lvi, 3; In Rom xxi, 4 (12:13)
9:58 De paen ix, 1; Ex in ps xliv, 2; In Ioh xviii, 3; xix, 3; In Rom xxviv, 4 (13:14)
9:62 In Mat xxvii, 6
10:2 In Acta iv, 1 (2:2); In Mat xlvii, 1
10:4 Ex in ps xlvi, 3
10:5 In Rom i, 3 (1:7)
10:7 Ex in ps xliv, 1; In Gen xxxv, 6; In Mat xxxii 7; xxxii, 8; xlvi, 4; In 2 Thess v, 1 (3:8); v, 1 (3:11); In 1 Tim xv, 1 (5:18)
10:8 In Col iii, 4 (1:20); In Mat xlvi, 4
10:12 De Laz iii, 6
10:13 De paen i, 2; Ex in ps cxiii, 2; In Eph ix, 4 (4:3); In Gen xxv, 2; Q reg 2
10:14 In Gen xxv, 2
10:15 In Ioh xxiii, 1
10:17-18 In princ Act ii, 5
10:19 Cat ill iii, 9; De s Bab c Iul 2; Ex in ps vii 3; viii, 7; In Acta i, 5 (1:4); In Col vi, 4 (2:15) (2x); In Eph xxii, 4 (6:13); In Gen xvii, 7; xlii, 2; xlvi, 4; In Ioh lix, 3; In Mat lxv, 6; In Phil vi, 4 (2:8); In princ Act ii, 5; S Gen v, 2
10:20 De san pent i, 5; De uir xxxvi; Ex in ps cxiii 5; In Acta xxxi, 1 (14:18); xli, 3; In Heb xviii, 6; In Ioh lxxii, 5; In Mat xxiv, 1; xxxii, 11; In Phil xiii, 3 (4:3); In princ Act ii, 5
10:21 In Mat xxxviii, 1
10:22 De incomp dei v, 3; In Gal i, 9 (1:16); In Ioh

| | |
|---|---|
| 10:22 cont | lx, 1; In Mat xxxviii, 1; liv, 2 |
| 10:24 | In Ioh viii, 1; In Mat xxvii, 4 |
| 10:25 | In Acta ii, 2 (1:8) |
| 10:30 | Adu Iud 8, 3, 8; In Heb x, 8; In Ioh xxxi, 2 |
| 10:31-33 | Adu Iud 8, 3, 8 |
| 10:34-35 | Adu Iud 8, 3, 8; In Heb x, 8 |
| 10:36-37 | Ex in ps cxliii, 3 |
| 10:41 | In Ioh xliv |
| 10:42 | In Ioh xliv, lxii, 3 |
| 11:1 | De Chris prec 2; In il Pater s p 4 |
| 11:2 | Ex in ps cxix, 2; In il Pater s p 4 |
| 11:4 | Ex in ps cxlix, 1 |
| 11:5 | De paen iii, 4; Ex in ps xliii, 5; In Acta xxxvi, 2 (16:39); In Eph xxiv, 3 (6:22); In Mat xix, 5; Non esse desp 7 |
| 11:6-7 | In Eph xxiv, 3 (6:22) (2x); In Mat xxii, 7; Non esse desp 7 |
| 11:8 | Ex in ps xliii, 5 (2x); In Eph xxiv, 3 (6:22) (2x); In Gen xliv, 4; In Heb xxvii, 9; In Mat xxii, 7; Non esse desp 7 |
| 11:9 | Ex in ps xliii, 5 |
| 11:11-12 | De D et S ii, 4 |
| 11:13 | De D et S ii, 4; In Acta xxxvi, 3 (16:39) |
| 11:15 | In Heb iii, 7; In Ioh lxxxiv, 3 |
| 11:17 | In Mat i, 8 |
| 11:19 | In Rom xix, 1 (11:8) |
| 11:20 | In Mat xli, 2 |
| 11:24 | Ad pop Anti xviii, 13; Adu Iud 1, 6, 7 |
| 11:25 | Adu Iud 1, 6, 7 |
| 11:26 | Ad pop Anti xviii, 13; Adu Iud 1, 6, 7 |
| 11:27 | De Mac iii, 1; In Ioh xxi, 3; In Mat xliv, 2 |
| 11:28 | In Mat xliv, 2 |
| 11:31 | In Is i, 2 |
| 11:32 | Ad pop Anti xx, 22; De s Dros 3; In Is i, 2 |
| 11:33 | In Mat xliii, 7 |
| 11:41 | In Heb ix, 8; In Ioh lxix, 3; lxxxi, 3; In Mat l, 6; lii, 5; In Phil i, 5 (1:7); In Rom xxx, 4 (16:5) |
| 11:47-48 | In Mat lxxiv, 1 |
| 12:3 | In il Sal P et A ii, 3; In Mat lv, 7 |
| 12:7 | Ad Stag a dae i, 5; Ex in ps cxxxviii, 4 |
| 12:8 | In Ioh xvii, 1 |

| | |
|---|---|
| 12:11-12 | In Acta x, 1 (4:8) |
| 12:18 | De Laz ii, 2; Ex in ps cxiii, 4 |
| 12:20 | De Laz ii, 2; In Eut ii, 5; In Gen xlviii, 1; In Mat xxviii, 3 |
| 12:31 | Ex in ps v, 1; cxxvii, 3 |
| 12:32 | In Mat lxxvii, 6 |
| 12:33 | AD pop Anti xvi, 14 |
| 12;34 | De Anna iii, 4 |
| 12:35 | In Eph xxiii, 2 (6:14) |
| 12:42 | De mut nom ii, 1; In Heb iii, 8 |
| 12:43 | In Gen xxxvii, 5 |
| 12:44 | De mut nom ii, 1 |
| 12:46 | De sac iv, 1 |
| 12:47 | Ex in ps vi, 2; In Gen vi, 1; In Ioh lxxxiv, 3; In Mat xxvi, 4; lxxv, 5; In Rom vi, 6 (3:8) xxxi, 5 (16:16) |
| 12:48 | De paen v, 2; Ex in ps vi, 2 |
| 12:49 | De paen vi, 1; Ex in ps xliv, 5; In Ioh xxxiv, 1; xlv-3; In Mat xxxv, 2 |
| 12:50 | Cat ill x, 9; In Ioh xxv, 2 |
| 12;51 | In Acta xix, 5 (9:9) |
| 13:1 | Ex in ps vii, 12 |
| 13:2 | Ad Stag a dae i, 8; De Laz iii, 8 |
| 13:3 | Ad Stag a dae i, 8 |
| 13:4 | De diab tent i, 7; Ex in ps vii, 12; In 2 Cor ix, 4; In Mat lxxxv, 3; In Rom xxv, 5 (14:13) |
| 13:5 | In Mat lxxxv, 3; In Rom xxv, 5 (14:13) |
| 13:7 | In 2 Cor ix, 4 |
| 13:15 | In il Pater m 4 |
| 13:16 | Ex in ps cxv, 5 |
| 13:23 | In Mat lix, 6 |
| 13:26 | In para 3 |
| 13:27 | Adu Iud 6, 7, 4 |
| 13:30 | In Gen xviii, 5 |
| 13:32 | In Rom xxxii, 4 (16;24) |
| 13:33 | De ss mar a 1 |
| 13:34 | De paen iv, 2; In Heb iii, 4; In Ioh lxviii, 2; In Mat lxxv, 5 |
| 13:35 | De mut nom iii, 6; In Heb iii, 4 |
| 14:11 | In 1 Cor i, 5; In Gen xxxiii, 4 |
| 14:12 | In Col i, 3 (1:7); In Phil i, 5 (1:7); In 1 Thess xi, 5 (5:28) |
| 14:13 | In 1 Thess xi, 5 (5:28) |
| 14:14 | In Acta xli, 5; In 1 Thess xi, 5 (5:28) |
| 14:16 | In Gal ii, 7 (2:20) |
| 14:17 | F Iob 1:8 |
| 14:18-20 | De mut nom iv, 1 |
| 14:26 | De uir xlv; lxxiii; In Acta xix, 5 (9:9); In |

| | |
|---|---|
| 14:26 cont | Eph xx, 1 (5:24); In Mat xxxv, 3; xxxviii, 3 |
| 14:27 | De uir lxxiii; In Heb xxv, 1; In Mat xxxv, 3; xxxviii, 3 |
| 14:28-29 | De sac iv, 2 |
| 14:30 | In il Uidi dom v, 1 |
| 14:33 | Ex in ps xliv, 4; In Heb xxv, 1; In Ioh lxxiv, 3; In Mat xxxviii, 3; In Phil vi, 6 (2:8); In Tit v, 2 (2:14) |
| 15:4 | Adu Iud 8, 9, 4; De paen i, 4; In Eut ii, 5 |
| 15:5 | Adu Iud 9, 8, 4 |
| 15:6 | Adu Iud 8, 9, 4; De paen i, 4 |
| 15:7 | Cat ill i, 2; H in san pascha 3; In ascen d n I C 4; In Eph viii, 5 (4:2); In Mat lix, 5; In Phil iv, 1 (1:26) |
| 15:10 | De res d n I C 3 |
| 15:13-17 | In Mat v, 7 |
| 15:18 | De paen i, 4; In Mat v, 7; In Phil xi, 5 (3:12) |
| 15:19-20 | In Mat v, 7 |
| 15:29-30 | Ad Theo i, 7 |
| 15:31 | De paen i, 4 |
| 16 (p) | Ad e q scan xxiv; Ad Stag a dae i, 6; De fato et pr iv; De Laz vii, 3; De uir lxxxii; E iv, 3; cxxv; Ex in ps vi, 4; xlviii, 4; cxxvii, 2; In 2 Cor ix, 4 |
| 16:6 | In Rom xviii, 6 (11:6) |
| 16:8 | Ex in ps cxi, 4 |
| 16:9 | Adu Iud 7, 6, 6; De Laz iii, 10; Ex in ps xlviii, 4; In 2 Cor x, 1; In Gen iii, 6; xxxv, 8; In Heb i, 4; vi, 11; In il Hab iii, 10; In Mat v, 8; In Phil i, 2 (1:5); In 1 Tim xi, 1 (3:16) |
| 16:11 | In Heb iii, 9; In 1 Tim v, 1 (1:19) |
| 16:13 | In Rom xiii, 3-4 (7:23) |
| 16:15 | In Ioh xvi, 4 |
| 16:16 | In 2 Tim iii, 2 (1:18) |
| 16:17 | De s h Bab 2 |
| 16:18 | In 1 Cor xix, 4 |
| 16:19 | Adu Iud 7, 6, 4; 8, 6, 4; De Laz i, 6; vi, 4; Ex in ps vii, 12; In Acta xlviii, 3; In 2 Cor ix, 3; In Gal vi, 3 (6:10); In 1 Tim xii, 3 (4:10); Non esse ad grat 3 |
| 16:20 | Adu Iud 7, 6, 4; 8, 6, 5; De Laz i, 6; De mut nom iv, 5; In Rom xi, 6 (6:18); Q nemo 10 |

16:21 Adu Iud 7, 6, 4; 8, 6, 5; De Laz i, 6; In 1 Cor x, 6; In Rom xi, 6 (6:18)

16:22 Adu Iud 7, 6, 4; 8, 6, 5; De Laz ii, 1; ii, 2; vii, 4 (2x) ; Ex in ps cxv, 5; In Mat xiii, 5

16:23 Adu Iud 7, 6, 4; De Laz vii, 4; E ii, 10; Ex in ps xi, 2; In Eph xxiv, 5 (6:24)

16:24 Ad pop Anti i, 24; Adu Iud 7, 6, 4; De Laz ii, 4; ii, 6; iii, 4; iv, 1; vi, 6; vi, 8 (2x); vii, 4; E cxxv; Ex in ps xlviii, 10; cxlv, 2; In 2 Cor x, 7; In il Ne tim i, 6; In Mat ix, 8; xx, 6; lxxiv, 5; In Phil ii, 4 (1:19); Non esse ad grat 3

16:25 Ad pop Anti vi, 10; Ad Stag a dae i, 3; Adu Iud 7, 6, 4; De dec mil 5; De Laz ii, 6; iii, 1; iii, 4; vi, 8; vii, 4; Ex in ps vi, 2; xlviii, 10; cxli, 1; In 1 Cor xx, 12; In Heb v, 6; In il Hab iii, 7; In Ioh xliii, 2; lxxvii, 4; In Mat lxxiv, 5; In Phil xiii, 4 (4:3); Non esse ad grat 3 (2x)

16:26 Ad Theo i, 9; Adu Iud 7, 6, 4; De Laz iii, 4; iii, 9; vii, 4; In 2 Cor x, 4; In Gen xxxvii, 3; In Heb xxxi, 8; In Ioh lxxxiv, 3; In Mat lxxiv, 5; lxxviii, 1; lxxxi, 4; In Phil xiii, 4 (4:3); In Rom xviii, 6 (11:6)

16:27 Adu Iud 7, 6, 4; In Mat xxviii, 3; Non esse ad grat 3

16:28 Adu Iud 7, 6, 4; Ex in ps cxlv, 2; In Mat xxviii, 3; In Rom xviii, 6-7 (11:6); Non esse ad grat 3

16:29 Adu Iud 7, 6, 4; Adu op iii, 3; Ex in ps cxlv, 2

16:30 Adu Iud 7, 6, 4

16:31 Adu Iud 7, 6, 4; In Gal i, 7 (1:9)

17:1 In Mat lix, 1

17:5 Ex in ps cxv, 2; In 1 Cor xxix, 5

17:7-8 In Philem ii, 4 (v16)

17:10 Ad Stel de comp ii, 4; De mut nom iv, 6; De Paen i, 2; De uir ii; Ex in ps xlix, 5; In Col ii, 3 (1:12); In 2 Cor xxiv, 1; In Gen iv, 8; xxi, 3; xxxi, 2; In Heb ii, 2; In il Uidi dom iii, 1; iv, 4; In il Ut sus 6; In Mat iii, 8; In Philem ii, 3 (v16); In Rom vii, 7 (3:31) In 1 Tim xvii, 1 (6:7); Non esse ad grat 4

17:12 Ad e q scan xxiv

17:18 In Mat xxv, 3

17:22 In 1 Cor xxi, 2

17:26-27 In Heb xxiii, 1

17:34 In Mat lxxvii, 2; In 1 Thess viii, 2 (4:18)

| | |
|---|---|
| 17:35 | In 1 Thess viii, 2 (4:18) |
| 17:37 | De bap Chris 4 |
| 18 (p) | Ex in ps iv, 4; cxxii, 1; cxxx, 1; In Gen v, 5; xxxi, 2; In il Dom non est 4; In kal 6; In Mat xxi, 7 |
| 18:1 | De incomp dei v, 7; In Eph xxiv, 3 (6:22) (2x) In Mat xix, 5; lvii, 5 |
| 18:2 | De Laz iii, 4; De mut nom iv, 2; In Eph xxiv, 3 (6:22) (2x); In Gen xxx, 6; In Mat lvii, 5 |
| 18:3 | De Anna ii, 2; De diab tent ii, 6; De mut nom iv, 2; In Eph xxiv, 3 (6:22) (2x); In Mat lvii 5 |
| 18:4-5 | De Anna ii, 2; De Laz iii, 4; De mut nom iii, 4; In Eph xxiv, 3 (6:22) (2x); In Mat lvii, 5 |
| 18:6 | In Eph xxiv, 3 (6;22) (2x); In Hen xxvii, 9 |
| 18:7 | In Eph xxiv, 3 (6:22) (2x) |
| 18:10 | Ad Stag a dae i, 9; Adu Iud 3, 3, 5; De paen ii, 4; Ex in ps vii, 3; xlix, 10; In d P Op 3; In il Sal P et A ii, 5 |
| 18:11 | Ad Stel de comp ii, 4; Adu Iud 3, 3, 5; De incomp dei v, 7; De Laz vi, 9; De proph obscur ii, 9; In d P Op 3; In Heb xxi, 7; xxvii, 10; In il Sal P et A ii, 5; In il Uidi dom iv, 4; In Mat xix, 1; In Rom x, 6 (6:4); xvi, 6-7 (9: 15); In 2 Tim ii, 3 (1:12); Non esse ad grat 4 |
| 18:12 | Ad pop Anti iii, 8; Adu Iud 3, 3, 5; De laud s Paul v; In il Sal P et A ii, 5; In il Uidi dom iv, 4; In Mat xix, 1; xxx, 4; In Philem ii, 3 (v16) |
| 18:13 | Ad Stel de comp ii, 4; Adu Iud 3, 3, 5; De diab tent ii, 6; De mut nom iv, 4; De proph obscur ii, 9; Ex in ps cxl, 2; In Acta xv, 5 (7:5); In 1 Cor viii, 8; In d P Op 3; In il Uidi dom iv, 4; vi, 3; In Philem i, 3 (v3); In Rom xxv, 6 (14:13); Non esse desp 1 |
| 18:14 | Adu Iud 3, 3, 5; Ex inps vii, 4; cxl, 2; cxlii 3; In 1 Cor viii, 8; In d P Op 3; In Gen xxxiii, 4; In il Sal P et A ii, 5; In Mat xv, 3; In Rom xxv, 6 (14:13) |
| 18:18 | In Mat xxvii, 5 |
| 18:19 | In Acta v, 3 (2:30); In Mat xxvii, 5 |
| 18:26 | In Is Introduction |
| 18:27 | In Mat lxxiv, 5 |
| 18:30 | In Mat xi, 7 |
| 18:31 | In Mat lxv, 1 |
| 18:34 | In Ioh lxvi, 2; In Mat liv, 5; lxv, 1 |
| 19:5 | In Mat xxx, 2 |
| 19:8 | De b Phil 4; De Laz ii, 3; In Eut ii, 17; In |

| | |
|---|---|
| 19:8 cont | Ioh lxxiii, 3; In Mat xxx, 2; lii, 6; lxxxiii, 4; In 1 Thess x, 4 (5:18) |
| 19:9 | In Ioh lxxxviii, 3; In Mat xxx, 2 |
| 19:10 | In Mat lix, 4 |
| 19:11 | F Prou 20:9; In Mat lxv, 2 |
| 19:19 | Ex in ps cxxiii, 2 |
| 19:21 | De paen vi, 3 |
| 19:22 | Ex in ps cxlv, 4; In Eph viii, 4 (4:2) |
| 19:23 | De paen vii, 3; De s h Bab 1 |
| 19:27 | Adu Iud 1, 11, 6; Con Iud et gen 4; In Acta v, 3 (2:30); In Heb iii, 4; In Rom xxv, 5 (14:13) |
| 19:40 | In Mat xiii, 9 |
| 19:41 | Q reg 2 |
| 19:46 | De Anna iii, 4; In Ioh xxiii, 2 |
| 20:5 | In Mat xi, 1 |
| 20:13 | In Acta xxix, 1 (13:17); In Mat lxxvii, 3 |
| 20:17 | Ex in ps cxvii, 5; In Mat lxviii, 2 |
| 20:18 | In Mat lxviii, 2 |
| 20:25 | De elee 2 |
| 20:28-34 | In Gen xviii, 4 |
| 20:35 | E ii, 6; In Gen xviii, 4; xxii, 2 |
| 20:36 | Ad Theo i, 14; In Gen xviii, 4; In Mat lxx, 2 |
| 20:42 | In Ioh viii, 1 |
| 21 (p) | Ex in ps cxxvii, 2; In Hel 1; In Phil xv, 3 (4:15) |
| 21:1 | In Acta xx, 4 (9:25) |
| 21:2 | De Mac ii, 1; De ss mar A 4; E xiv, 5; Ex in ps cxlv, 2; In Gen lv, 4; In Heb i, 4; In il Uid elig 12; Q nemo 6; Qual duc 7; S Gen i, 4 |
| 21:3 | De elee 3; De Mac ii, 1; E xiv, 5; In Gen xxxiv, 2; xlii, 7; In il Uid elig 12; In Mat lii, 5; Qual duc 7 |
| 21:4 | De elee 3; De Mac ii, 1; In Gen xlii, 7; In il Uid elig 12; In Mat lii, 5; Qual duc 7 |
| 21:6 | In Mat lxxv, 1; In Rom xxv, 5 (14:13) |
| 21:7 | In Mat lxxv, 1 |
| 21:13 | In Acta xlvii, 3 |
| 21:15 | In Mat xxxiii, 4 |
| 21:23 | Ex in ps viii, 5 |
| 21:24 | Adu Iud 5, 1, 6; In Acta ii, 1 (1:6); In Rom xxv, 5 (14:13) |
| 21:25-26 | In Rom xxv, 5 (14:13) |
| 21:27 | In Acta ii, 1 (1:6) |
| 22:3 | In Mat lxxxii, 1 |
| 22:4 | In Mat lxxx, 3 |
| 22:7 | In Mat lxxxi, 1 |
| 22:15 | De consub 6; De res d n I C 3; H in san pascha 3; In il Pater s p 2; In Mat lxxxi, 3; lxxxii, |

| | |
|---|---|
| 22:15 cont | 1 |
| 22:19 | In Heb xvii, 6 |
| 22:24 | In Mat lxxxii, 3 |
| 22:27 | De Chris prec 2 |
| 22:30 | In Mat xlvii, 5 |
| 22:31 | De b Phil 2; Ex in ps cxxiii, 1; cxxix, 2; cxxxix, 3; cxliv, 4; In Heb xxxi, 4; In il Dom non est 5; In Mat lxxxii, 3; In para 2; In Phil iv, 5 (1:30); Q freg con 5 |
| 22:32 | De b Phil 2; Ex in ps cxxix, 2; cxliv, 4; In Acta iii, 3 (1:26); In Heb xxxi, 4; In il Dom non est 5; In Ioh lxxiii, 1; In Mat lxxxii, 3; In para 2; In Phil iv, 5 (1:30) |
| 22;33 | In Rom v, 7 (2:16) |
| 22;35 | In 1 Cor iii, 8; In il Sal P et A ii, 2 (2x); In Mat xxxii, 7; lxxxiv, 1; In Phil ix, 6 (2:30) |
| 22:36 | In il Sal P et A ii, 2 (2x); ii, 3; In Mat lxxxiv, 1 |
| 22:37-38 | In il Sal P et A ii, 3; In Mat lxxxiv, 1 |
| 22:42 | In Mat lxxviii, 4 |
| 22:44 | Ex in ps cix, 8 |
| 22:45 | In Ioh lxxii, 4 |
| 22:46 | Ex in ps cxix, 2 |
| 22:48 | De Laz i, 5; In Mat lxxxiii, 2; lxxxviii; In Rom xxi, 4 (12:13) |
| 22:49 | In Mat lxxxiv, 1 |
| 22:54-60 | Adu Iud 8, 3, 4 |
| 22:61 | Adu Iud 8, 3, 4; De paen iii, 4; In Mat lxxxv, 1 |
| 22:62 | Adu Iud 8, 3, 4 |
| 22:64 | In Mat lxxxv, 1 |
| 22:69 | In Acta ii, 1 (1:6) |
| 22:70 | In 1 Tim xviii, 1 (6:16) |
| 23 (p) | De laud s Paul iv; Ex in ps cxxvii, 2 |
| 23:21 | Adu Iud 1, 5, 1; Ex in ps viii, 5 |
| 23:24 | Ex in ps cviii, 2; In Mat xv, 5; lvii, 2 |
| 23:28 | In Col xii, 3 (4:18) |
| 23:34 | Ad pop Anti xxi, 8; De cruce et lat i, 5 (4x); ii, 5 (4x); De fut iut 5; Ex in ps xliv, 6; In 1 Cor vii, 5; In Eph vii, 4 (3:19); In Eut i, 3; In il Ne tim i, 4; In il Pater s p 4; In Mat xviii, 5; lx, 3; lxxix, 3; In princ Act iv, 9; In Rom xxi, 4 (12:13) |
| 23:35 | In Acta ix, 1 (3:18) |
| 23:40 | De cruce et lat i, 2; i, 3; ii, 3; De paen |

| | |
|---|---|
| 23:40 cont | viii, 2; Ex in ps cx, 4; In Mat xxiii, 2; lxxxvii, 2; In para 3; In Phil vii, 3 (2:11); In Tit v, 3 (3:1) |
| 23:41 | De cruce et lat i, 2; i, 3 (2x); ii, 3; De paen viii, 2; F Iob 1:8; In Mat xxiii, 2 |
| 23:42 | Ad e q scan xiv; De Anna iv, 6; De cruce et lat i, 2; i, 3; ii, 2; S Gen vii, 4 |
| 23:43 | De Anna iv, 6; De cruce et lat i, 2; ii, 2; De diab tent i, 3; De paen viii, 2; De proph obscur ii, 4; In 2 Cor xxvi, 2; In Eut ii, 17 In Gen lv, 4; In Ioh xxiv, 2; In quat Laz A 2; S Gen vii, 1; vii, 4; vii, 5 |
| 23:46 | Cat ill xi, 19 |
| 23:47-48 | In Mat lxxxviii |
| 23:49 | In Ioh l, 3 |
| 23:55 | In Acta iii, 1 (1:14) |
| 24:6 | In Acta ii, 4 (1:11) |
| 24:36-38 | In princ Act iv, 6 |
| 24:39 | De consub 6; De cruce et lat i, 4; ii, 4; In Ioh xxxi, 1; lxvi, 3 |
| 24:41 | In princ Act iv, 6 |

John

| | |
|---|---|
| 1:1 | De incomp dei v, 2; De paen v, 2; Ex in ps xliv, 8; In Gal i, 2 (1:3); i, 3 (1:3); In Gen iii, 2; In Heb ii, 2; In Ioh i, 7; In Is vii, 5; In Mat xvi, 2 |
| 1:2 | De paen v, 2; Q nemo 14 |
| 1:3 | De paen v, 3; Ex in ps viii, 9; cxxxviii, 2; In 2 Cor xi, 4; In Gen ii, 3; In Heb ii, 2; In il Fil 3; 6 (2x); In Ioh xxxviii, 4; lxxx, 2; In Mat xvi, 2; xxii, 2; liv, 2; lxxvii, 1; S Gen i, 2 |
| 1:4 | Ex in ps cxxxviii, 2; In Heb ii, 2; In Ioh v, 1; v, 3; lxxx, 2 |
| 1:5 | Cat ill xii, 10; De paen v, 3; Ex in ps xlvi, 2; F Ier 10:11; In Ioh v, 3 |
| 1:6 | De paen v, 3; In Ioh v, 1 |
| 1:7 | In Ioh v, 1 |
| 1:8 | In Eut ii, 6; In Ioh v, 2 |
| 1:9 | In Eut ii, 6; In Gen iii, 2; In Ioh v, 3; lxxx, 2; In Mat xiv, 1 |
| 1:10 | De mut nom iii, 1; Ex in ps xlvi, 3; In Ioh v, 2; viii, 1; ix, 2; In Mat xvi, 2; xvi, 8 |
| 1:11 | De s Bab c Iul 2 (2x); In Heb xxvi, 4; In Ioh xxx, 2; lxxx, 2; lxxxiii, 4; In Mat xvi,8 |

1:12 Adu Iud 1, 11, 2; De paen v, 3; F Ier 3:19; In Col vi, 4 (2;15); In Ioh v, 2; x, 2; In Mat ix, 7; In princ Act iii, 5
1:13 De mut nom ii, 4; Ex in ps cxlvii, 4; In Col v, 4 (2:5); vi, 4 (2:15); In 1 Cor v, 4; In Ioh x, 3; xxvi, 1; lxviii, 1; In Mat ii, 3; In princ Act iii, 5; In Rom xvi, 4 (9:9)
1:14 In Ioh iv, 1; v, 1; In Mat iv, 6; In Phil vii 2 (2:11) (2x)
1:15 H in il App 12; In Heb i, 3
1:16 Ex in ps xliv, 2; xliv, 3; xliv, 9; In Col iii, 3 (1:20); In Ioh lxxv, 1; In 2 Tim ii, 4 (1:12)
1:17 Adu Iud 7, 2, 8; Ex in ps cxvil In Hen iii, 6; In Ioh xiv, 1; xiv, 3
1:18 Adu op iii, 16; Ad e q scan iii; De incomp dei in, 3 (3x); v, 1; In il Fil 6; In Ioh lxxiv, 1; In Is vi, 1; In 1 Tim vii, 1 (2:6)
1:19 In Is vii, 5
1:20 In Ioh xvi, 2
1:21 In Ioh xvi, 2; In Mat lvii, 1 (2x)
1:22-23 In Ioh xvi, 2
1:24 In Ioh xvi, 2; In Mat xi, 1
1:25 In Ioh xvi, 2; In Is vii, 5; In Mat xi, 1
1:26 De bap Chris 2; In Ioh xvi, 2
1:27 In Ioh xvi, 2; In Mat iii, 8; xxxvi, 1; lxvii 2; In 2 Tim ii, 4 (1:12)
1:29 De consub 5; De incomp dei ii, 2; De proph obscur i, 3; In 1 Cor xxxviii, 3; In Ioh xlvi 2; In Is vii, 7; In Mat xi, 6; xxvii, 2; xxxvi, 1; xxxvi, 3; lxvii, 2; S Gen vii, 3
1:30 In Eph vii, 1 (3:11); In Heb i, 3; In Ioh xvii, 1
1:31 De bap Chris 3; In Ioh xvii, 2; In Mat x, 2
1:32 Con Iud et gen 2; In Acta iv, 1 (2:3); In Ioh xvii, 2
1:33 De bap Chris 3; 4; Ex in ps xliv, 2; In Acta vi, 1 (2:22); In Ioh xiii, 2; xvii, 2 (2x); xl, 2; In Mat x, 2; xi, 6; xxxvi, 1
1:34 F in epis cath 1 John 3:8; In Acta i, 2 (1:2) In Ioh xvii, 2; In Mat xi, 6 (2x); lxvii, 2
1:38 In Ioh xviii, 3
1:39 In Ioh xviii, 2; xviii, 3
1:40 In Acta iii, 3 (1:26); In Ioh xviii, 3
1:42 De inani gloria 49; De mut nom iii, 3; In Ioh xix, 1; In Mat xiv, 3; liv, 3
1:44 In Mat xxxvii, 6
1:45 In diem nat 2; In Ioh xx, 1

| | |
|---|---|
| 1:46 | In Ioh xvi, 1; xx, 1; xxxv; li, 2; In Mat ix, 6 |
| 1:47 | In diem nat 2; In Ioh xx, 1 |
| 1:48 | In Ioh xx, 2 |
| 1:49 | In Ioh xx, 3; In Mat liv, 2 |
| 1:50 | In Ioh xlvii, 2; In Mat liv, 2 |
| 1:51 | In ascen d n I C 4; In Ioh xxi, 1; xxviii, 2 |
| 2 (p) | Ex in ps cx, 2 |
| 2:1-2 | In Ioh xxi, 1; In Mat xliv, 3 |
| 2:3 | In il Uidi dom iv, 3; In Ioh xxi, 1; In Mat xliv, 3 |
| 2:4 | In Ioh xxi, 2; lxxxv, 2 |
| 2:5 | Ex in ps cxvii, 3; In Ioh xxii, 1 |
| 2:6-7 | In Ioh xxii, 1 |
| 2:8 | In Ioh xxii, 1; In Mat xliv, 3 |
| 2:9 | H in peon Nin; In Ioh xxii, 1 |
| 2:10 | H in poen Nin; In il Uidi dom ii, 3; In Ioh xxii, 1; In Mat xliv, 3 |
| 2:11 | In Ioh xxi, 1; In Mat xliv, 3 |
| 2:12-13 | In Ioh xxiii, 1 |
| 2:15 | De paen v, 2 |
| 2:16 | Adu Iud 6, 7, 5; In il Pater m 2; In Ioh xxiii, 2; In Mat lxxxviii |
| 2:17 | In Ioh xxiii, 2 |
| 2:18 | De proph obscur ii, 1; In il Pater m 2; In Ioh xxiii, 2; In Mat lxvii, 1; lxvii, 2 |
| 2:19 | De proph obscur i, 4; ii, 1; Ex in ps xliv, 9; In Acta ii, 4 (1:11); In 1 Cor xvii, 2; xli, 3; In 2 Cor xxix, 3; In Gal i, 3 (1:3); In Heb viii, 3; In il Pater m 2; In il Pater s p 1; In il Sal p P et A ii, 3; In Ioh xxiii 3; xlvi, 2; lxvi, 2; lxxii, 3; In Mat xliii, 3; lxv, 1; lxvii, 2; lxxxiv, 2; In Rom i, 2 (1:4) |
| 2:20 | Ex in ps cxxvi, 1; In il Pater m 2; In Mat lxxxiv, 2 |
| 2:21 | In 1 Cor xli, 3 |
| 2:22 | De proph obscur ii, 1 (2x); In il Sal P et A ii, 3; In Ioh xxiii, 2 |
| 2:23 | In Rom xxx, 3-4 (16:5) |
| 2:24 | In Ioh xxiv, 1 |
| 2:25 | In Ioh xxiv, 1; In para 6 |
| 3:1 | In Ioh xxiv, 1 |
| 3:2 | De consub 3; In Acta vi, 2 (2:31); xxiii, 3 (10:43); In Ioh xxiv, 1; lxi, 2 |
| 3:3 | F Iob 1:21; In Ioh xxiv, 2 |
| 3:4 | De Laz vi, 1; De paen i, 2; v, 2; v, 4; Ex in ps vii, 12; Q nemo 14; S Gen vii, 5 |
| 3:5 | In 1 Cor xl, 1; In Rom xxv, 6 (14:13); Qual |

| | |
|---|---|
| 3:5 cont | duc 3; S Gen vii, 5 |
| 3:6 | H in poen Nin |
| 3:7 | H in poen Nin; In Gen i, 3; In Ioh xxvi, 1 |
| 3:8 | H in poen Nin; In 1 Cor xxix, 6 |
| 3:9 | In Ioh xxvi, 2 |
| 3:10 | In Gen xxiv, 8; xxvii, 6; In Ioh xxvi, 2; Q nemo 14 |
| 3:11 | In Acta i, 2 (1:2); In Ioh xxvi, 2; xxx, 1; xxx, 2; xlv, 2 |
| 3:12 | De proph obscur i, 2 |
| 3:13 | In Ioh xlvii, 2; In Mat liv, 1 |
| 3:14 | Ex in ps ix, 4; In Ioh xxvii, 1 |
| 3:16 | Ad e q scan xvii; Adu Iud 3, 4, 8 (2x); De reg 14; De sac ii, 1; In Gal ii, 7 (2:20); In Gen xxvii, 1; In il Pater s p 2; In Ioh xxvii, 2 |
| 3:17 | In Acta xli, 2; In Ioh xxviii, 1; liii, 1 |
| 3:18 | In Ioh xxviii, 1; xxxix, 3; liii, 1; S Gen vii, 5 |
| 3:19 | In Ioh xxviii, 2 (2x) |
| 3:20 | Ex in ps iv, 7; In 1 Cor viii, 4; In Eph xiii, 1 (4:19); xviii, 1 (5:14); In Heb vi, 4; In Ioh v, 4; xxviii, 2; lii, 2; In Mat lxxi, 1; In 1 Tim ii, 1 (1:7) |
| 3:23 | In Ioh xxix, 1 |
| 3:24 | In Ioh xvii, 1; xxix, 1 |
| 3:25 | E i, 3; In Ioh xxix, 1; In Mat xxxvi, 2 |
| 3:26 | E i, 3; In Ioh xviii, 3; xxix, 2 |
| 3:27 | In Ioh xxix, 2; xxxi, 1 (2x); lxx, 1; In Mat xxxvi, 2 |
| 3:28 | In Ioh xxix, 2 |
| 3:29 | Ex in ps v, 2; xliv, 10; In Ioh xviii, 2; xxix 2; In Mat iii, 8; xxx, 4 |
| 3:30 | In Ioh xxix, 3; In Mat xxxvi, 1; lxix, 1 |
| 3:31 | In Ioh xxx, 1 |
| 3:32 | In Ioh xxx, 1; xxxix, 4; xlv, 2 |
| 3:33 | In Ioh xxx, 2; xliv, lxxx, 1 |
| 3:34 | Ex in ps xliv, 9; In Heb iii, 2; In Ioh xxx, 2 |
| 3:36 | In Ioh xxix, 3 |
| 4 (p) | In dicta in t s Anas 1 |
| 4:1 | In Ioh xxxi, 1; In Mat xlix, 1; lxvi, 1 |
| 4:2 | In Ioh xxxi, 1; In Mat xlix, 1 |
| 4:3 | E iii, 5; In Ioh xxxi, 1; In Mat xlix, 1 |
| 4:4-5 | In Ioh xxxi, 2 |
| 4:6 | De Laz vi, 2; In Ioh xxxi, 2; xxxi, 3 |
| 4:7 | In Ioh xxxi, 3 |
| 4:8 | In Ioh xxxi, 3; xxxi, 4 |
| 4:9 | In Ioh xxxi, 4 |

4:10 Ad e q scan vi; De fato et pr iv; De incomp dei iii, 6; In Ioh xxxi, 4; xlv, 1
4:11 Ad e q scan vi; De fato et pr iv; De incomp dei iii, 6; In Ioh xxxi, 4
4:12 In Ioh xxxi, 4; lv, 1
4:13 In princ Act iii, 3
4:14 In Acta iv, 2 (2:13); xxii, 3 (10:23); in Gen xliv, 1; In il Uidi dom iii, 5; In Ioh li, 1; In princ Act iii, 1
4:15-17 In Ioh xxxii, 1
4:18 In Ioh xix, 2; xxxii, 1; In Mat lii, 3
4:19 In Ioh xxxii, 1
4:20 H dicta in t s Anas 1; In Ioh xxxii, 2
4:21 Adu Iud 5, 12, 10
4:22 In Acta xvii, 1 (7:50); In Mat lxiii, 1; In Rom xxx, 1 (15:27)
4:23 In Ioh xxxiii, 1; xxxiii, 2; In Rom i, 1 (1:2)
4:24 Adu Iud 5, 12, 10; De incomp dei v, 5; In 2 Cor vii, 5; In Heb xi, 5; In Ioh iv, 3; xv, 3; xxxiii, 2; In Rom ii, 2 (1:9); In 1 Tim vii, 1 (2:6); In Tit iii, 2 (1:14)
4:25 In Ioh xxxiii, 2; In Mat lvii, 1
4:26 In Ioh xxxiii, 2; lxi, 1
4:27 In Gal i, 1 (1:3); In Ioh xxxiii, 2
4:31 In Ioh xxxiv, 1; In Mat lxvii, 2
4:32-33 In Ioh xxxiv, 1
4:34 In Ioh xx, 3; xxxiv, 1
4:35 In Acta iv, 1 (2:2); In Ioh xxxiv, 1; In Mat xlvii, 1
4:36 In Ioh xxxiv, 2
4:37 In Ioh xxxiv, 2; In Mat xlvii, 1
4:38 De san pent i, 2; In Ioh xxxiv, 2; In Mat xxxii, 4; lxvii, 1; In s Igna 3
4:39 In Acta xviii, 4 (8:25); In Ioh xxxiv, 2
4:44-45 In Ioh xxxv
4:46 In Ioh xxii; xxxv, 3
4:47 In Ioh xxxv, 3
4:48 In Acta xl, 2; In Ioh xxxv, 3
4:49 In Ioh xxxv; In Mat xxvi, 4; lii, 2
4:51-52 In Ioh xxxv, 3
5 (p) Ad Stag a dae iii, 12
5:1 Adu Iud 8, 6, 4; In Mat xxix, 1 (2x)
5:2 Adu Iud 8, 6, 4; In Ioh xxxvi, 1; De res d n I C 4
5:3 Adu Iud 8, 6, 4; In Ioh xxxvi, 1
5:4 Adu Iud 8, 6, 4; H in san pascha 5

5:5 Adu Iud 8, 6, 4; De Chris diuin 2; De diab tent i, 8; In para 1
5:6 Adu Iud 8, 6, 4; De Chris diuin 2; In Mat xxix, 1; lxvii, 4
5:7 Adu Iud 8, 6, 4; De Chris diuin 2 (3x); 3; In Mat lxvii, 4 (2x); In para 3; 4 (2x)
5:8 Adu Iud 8, 6, 4; De Chris diuin 3; In Ioh xxxvii, 1; lxiv, 2; In Mat lxvii, 4
5:9 Adu Iud 8, 6, 4; In Mat xl, 1
5:10 De Chris diuin 3 (2x); In Ioh xxxvii, 2; In Mat xl, 1
5:11 De Chris diuin 3 (2x); 4; In Ioh xxxvii, 2
5:12 De Chris diuin 1; 3; In Ioh xxxvii, 2
5:13 De Chris diuin 3 (2x); In para 4
5:14 De Chris diuin 4; De diab tent i, 8; De Laz iii, 5; De paen vii, 6; Ex in ps iii, 1; cxxi, 2; In Acta i, 6 (1:5); In Is iii, 1; In Mat xxxii, 9; xliii, 5; lxii, 4; In para 3; In Rom xxv, 1 (14:13)
5:15 In Ioh xxxviii, 2; In Mat xxxii, 9
5:16 De Chris diuin 4; In Gal v, 3 (5:11); In il Pater m 3; In Ioh xxxviii, 2; In para 6
5:17 De Chris diuin 1; 4 (2x); De consub 2; In Acta ii, 1 (1:6); In 1 Cor xxxix, 6; In Gen x, 7; In il Fil 1; In il Pater ml; 3; In Ioh iii, 4; xxxvi, 2; xxxviii, 2; xxxix, 1; lxxiv, 2; In Mat xvi, 2; xxxix, 1 (2x) In para 6
5:18 Adu Iud 1, 1, 6; In Acta ii, 1 (1:6); In il Fil 1; In Ioh xxxviii, 3; lviii, 2; lxv, 1; In Rom xv, 1 (8:28)
5:19 Ex in ps viii, 8; xliv, 4; In Acta ii, 1 (1:6) In 1 Cor xvii, 2; In Gal i, 2 (1:3); In il Fil 1 (2x); 6 (2x); In Ioh xxxviii, 3; xlix, 2; lxiv, 1; In Rom xv, 3 (8:34)
5:20 In Acta ii, 1 (1:6); In Ioh xxxviii, 4
5:21 Cat ill i, 22; De consub 2; 3; Ex in ps xliv, 4; In Acta ii, 1 (1:8); In 1 Cor xxix, 6; xxxix, 10; In Heb xiii, 6; In il Fil 6; In Ioh iii, 4; v, 2; xxxviii, 4; xlv, 3; xlix, 2; lxiv, 1; lxviii, 2; lxix, 2; lxxx, 1; In Rom xv, 3 (8:34)
5:22 De pet mat 3 (2x); Da sac iii, 5; In Heb ii, 2; xiii, 6; In il Fil 4; In Ioh lii, 2
5:23 Con Anom xi, 3; De consub 2; De incomp dei iii, 2; Ex in ps viii, 9; cix, 4; In Heb xxxiii, 7; In Ioh iii, 5; iv, 2; lxiv, 1
5:24 In Ioh xxxix, 2; S Gen vii, 5
5:25 In Ioh xxxix, 2
5:26 In Ioh v, 3 (2x); xxxix, 1; xxxix, 2;

| | |
|---|---|
| 5:26 cont | lxxxiii, 4; In Rom xv, 3 (8:34) |
| 5:27 | In Gal i, 2 (1:3); In Ioh xxxix, 3; lxiv, 3 |
| 5:28 | In Ioh xxxix, 3 |
| 5:29 | In Ioh xxxix, 3; xlv, 2; In Rom xiii, 8-9 (8:11) |
| 5:30 | In il Pater s p 3; In Ioh iii, 4; xxx, 1; xxxix, 3; lxiv, 1; lxviii, 2 |
| 5:31 | De consub 4; In Ioh lxxxiii, 3; In Mat lxiii, 1 |
| 5:32 | In Ioh vi |
| 5:33 | In Ioh xl, 1 |
| 5:34 | In Acta xxxiv, 2 (16:24); In Ioh vi (4x); xviii, 2; xl, 2; xlv, 3 |
| 5:35 | In Ioh xl, 2 |
| 5:36 | In Ioh xviii, 2; xl, 2 |
| 5:37 | In Ioh xl, 3; lxxiv, 1 |
| 5:38 | In Ioh xl, 3 |
| 5:39 | De Laz vi, 8; De mut nom iv, 3; In Eph vi, 2 (3:5); In Gen xxiv, 1; xxxvii, 1; xlv, 1; In Ioh xv, 1; xxx, 2; xlv, 2; li, 1; lix, 2; In 1 Tim i, 2 (1:4) |
| 5:41 | In Ioh xli, 1; xlii, 3; xlv, 3; In Tit ii, 4 (1:11) |
| 5:42 | In Ioh xli, 1 |
| 5:43 | Ad e q scan xii; In il Uidi dom ii, 3; In Ioh xli, 1; xlv, 2; In 2 Thess i, 1 (Introduction) iv, 1 (2:10); In 1 Tim vii, 1 (2:6) |
| 5:44 | Ex in ps iv, 7; In 2 Cor xii, 3; In Gen xxiv, 8; In Ioh iii, 5; viii, 1; xxviii, 2; xxxviii, 5; xli, 2; xlv, 2; lvii, 2; lxix, 1; lxxx, 2; In para 2; In Rom xvii, 3 (10:13); In 1 Tim iii, 2 (1:14) |
| 5:45 | In Acta xlviii, 3; In Ioh vi, 1; xli, 2; xlviii, 2; In Rom viii, 9 (4:21) |
| 5:46 | Con Anom xi, 2; De Chris diuin 1; In Eph vi, 2 (3:5); x, 1 (4:4); In Gen viii, 2; In Ioh xli, 2; lviii, 3; In Mat xi, 1; S Gen ii, 1 |
| 5:47 | In Ioh xli, 2 |
| 6:1-2 | In Ioh xlii, 1 |
| 6:3 | In il Pater m 3; In Ioh xlii, 1 |
| 6:4-7 | In Ioh xlii, 1 |
| 6:8 | In Ioh xlii, 2 |
| 6:9 | In Ioh xlii, 2; In Mat xlix, 1; liii, 2 |
| 6:12 | In Ioh xlii, 3 |
| 6:15 | In Ioh xlii, 3; In Mat xlix, 3; liii, 2; lxxxvi, 1 |
| 6:16 | De Chris diuin 3 |
| 6:17 | In Mat liii, 2 |
| 6:19-20 | In Ioh xliii, 1 |

6:21 In Ioh xliii, 1; In Mat 1, 2
6:22-25 In Ioh xliii, 1
6:26 In Ioh xlv, 1; In Mat xlix, 4
6:27 In Ioh lxviii, 2
6:28 In Ioh lvi, 2
6:30 De Chris diuin 1; In Ioh lxi, 1; lxi, 2; lxiv, 1; In Rom xxxii, 1 (16:18)
6:31 De Chris diuin 1; Ex in ps xlvi, 2; In 1 Cor xxxiv, 10; In Ioh xlv, 1
6:32-34 In Ioh xlv, 1
6:35 In Ioh xxxii, 1; xlv, 1
6:36 In Ioh xlv, 1; xlvii, 2
6:37 In Ioh xlv, 2; lxxxi, 2
6:38 In Ioh xlv, 3; In s Igna 3
6:39 In Ioh xlv, 3; lxxxi, 2
6:40 In Ioh xxxviii, 4; xlv, 2; xlv, 3; lv, 1
6:43 In Heb xxviii, 5
6:44 De mut nom iii, 6; Ex in ps cix, 4; cxv, 2; In Ioh v, 3; xlv, 2; xlvi, 1; lxvii, 3; lxx, 1; lxxxvi
6:45 De Laz iii, 3; In Ioh xlvi, 1; li, 1; lxxiv, 1; In Mat i, 1; In Phil xii, 3 (3:17); In 2 Tim ii, 4 (1:12)
6:46 Ad e q scan iii; De incomp dei v, 1; v, 3; v, 4; In 1 Cor xxxiv, 4; In il Fil 6; In Ioh xv, 2; xlvi, 1; l, 2
6:49-51 In Ioh xlvi, 2
6:52 De consub 3; In Ioh xlvi, 2
6:53 In 1 Cor xl, 1
6:55-56 In Ioh xlvii, 1
6:57-58 Cat ill xii, 4; In Ioh xlvii, 1
6:59 In Ioh xlvii, 1
6:60 In Acta lv, 3; In Ioh xlvi, 2 (2x); lxiv, 1; In Mat lxxxii, 1
6:61 De consub 3; In Ioh xlvi, 2; In Mat lxxxii, 1
6:62 In Acta ii, 3 (1:11); In Ioh xlvi, 2; In Mat liv, 1
6:63 In Acta i, 3 (1:2); In Ioh xlvi, 2; lxxviii, 3
6:64 In Ioh xlvi, 2; lxv, 2; lxxxi, 1
6:65 In Ioh xlvi, 2; lxxi, 1; lxxxi, 1
6:66 In Ioh xlvi, 2; liv, 1; In Mat lxxxii, 1
6:67 De consub 3; De paen iii, 4; In Acta xlvi, 3; In Col vii, 5 (3:4); In Heb xxviii, 5; In Ioh xlvii, 3; In Rom v, 7 (2:16)

| | |
|---|---|
| 6:68 | Ex in ps xliv, 3; In Ioh xlvii, 3; In Mat lxv, 4 |
| 6:69 | Ex in ps xliv, 3; cxl, 6; In Ioh xlvii, 3; In Mat lxv, 4 |
| 6:70 | Ex in ps xliv, 3; In Ioh xlvii, 3 |
| 6:71 | De Laz i, 4; In Ioh lxxi, 1 |
| 7:3 | In Ioh xlviii, 1 |
| 7:4 | In Ioh xlviii, 1; In Mat xxvii, 5; xliv, 1 |
| 7:5 | E i, 3; In 1 Cor xxi, 3; In Ioh xxii, 1; xlviii, 1; In Mat xliv, 1 |
| 7:6 | In Ioh xlviii, 2; In Mat xxvii, 5 |
| 7:7 | In Acta iii, 2 (1:26); In Eph xxii, 3 (6:12); In Ioh xlviii, 2; lxvi, 2; lxviii, 2; lxxvii; In Rom xiii, 7 (8:9) |
| 7:11 | Ad pop Anti vii, 6; In Ioh xlix, 1 |
| 7:12 | E i, 3; Ex in ps xliv, 6; cxvii, 5; F in epis cath 1 Peter 2:8; In Eph vii, 4 (3:19); In Heb xxviii, 5; In Ioh xlix, 1; lvii, 2; In Mat lxviii, 2; lxx, 1 |
| 7:13-17 | In Ioh xlix, 1 |
| 7:18 | In Ioh xlv, 3; xlix, 2 |
| 7:19 | In Ioh xxxii, 2; xlix, 2; lix, 2; lxv, 1 |
| 7:20 | In Acta xxxix, 4; In Eph iii, 3 (1:22); In Ioh xlix, 2; lx, 3; In Mat xxxvii, 5 |
| 7:21 | In Ioh xlix, 3 |
| 7:22 | In Ioh xlix, 3; In Rom vi, 4 (2:29) |
| 7:23 | In il Pater m 4; In Ioh xlix, 3; In Mat xvi, 2; xl, 1 |
| 7:24 | In Ioh xlix, 3 |
| 7:25-26 | In Ioh xlviii, 1; In Mat lxviii, 2 |
| 7:27 | In Ioh li, 2 |
| 7:28 | In Acta vi, 1 (2:22); In 1 Cor vii, 5; In il Pater s p 3; In Ioh l, 1; lxiv, 1 |
| 7:29 | In Ioh l, 2 |
| 7:30 | In Ioh xxii, 1; l, 2 |
| 7:31 | In Ioh l, 2; lxi, 2; lxvi, 1 |
| 7:32 | In Ioh l, 2 |
| 7:33 | In Ioh l, 2; lxviii, 1; lxxv, 4; In Mat lxv, 1 |
| 7:34 | In Ioh l, 2; liii, 2; In Mat lxv, 1 |
| 7:35 | In Ioh l, 3 |
| 7:36 | De san pent i, 3 |
| 7:37 | De paen vii, 7; De san pent i, 3; In Gen iii, 1; In Mat lxix, 1 |
| 7:38 | De paen vii, 7; De san pent i, 3; In Gen iii, 1; In Ioh xxxii, 1; In princ Act iii, 1; In Rom xxxii, 3 (16:24) |
| 7:39 | Ad e q scan xvii; De san pent i, 3; In il Pater s p 2;In Ioh li, 1; In Mat xxxii, 4; In |

| | |
|---|---|
| 7:39 cont | Rom xi, 3 (6:14) |
| 7:40 | In Ioh li, 2 |
| 7:41 | In Ioh l, 2; li, 2 |
| 7:42 | In diem nat 2; In Heb xxviii, 5; In Ioh li, 2; In Mat ii, 6 |
| 7:43-44 | In Ioh li, 2 |
| 7:46 | Ex in ps xliv, 3; In Acta xiii, 3 (5:33) |
| 7:47 | In Ioh lii, 1; In Mat xxvii, 5 |
| 7:48 | In Ioh lii, 1; lix, 3; lxvi, 1 |
| 7:49 | In Ioh xxxi, 5; lii, 1; lxvi, 1 |
| 7:50 | In Ioh lii, 1 |
| 7:51 | In Ioh xxiv, 1; lii, 1 |
| 7:52 | In diem nat 2; In Heb xxviii, 5; In Ioh ii, 1; xxxv, 1; xlvii, 1; li, 2; lii, 1; lii, 2; In Mat ix, 6 |
| 8:12 | In Eut ii, 6; In Heb ii, 2; In Ioh v, 3; xxviii, 2; lii, 2; lxiv, 1 |
| 8:13 | In Ioh xl, 1; lii, 2; lx, 1; In Mat xiv, 2; xxxvi, 2 |
| 8:14 | In Ioh xl, 1 (2x); lii, 2; lxxvii, 3 |
| 8:15-16 | In Ioh lii, 2 |
| 8:17 | In Ioh l, 2; lii, 2 |
| 8:18 | In Heb xvi, 1; In Ioh lii, 3 |
| 8:19 | Adu Iud 1, 3, 2; In 1 Cor vii, 5; In Ioh lii, 3 |
| 8:20 | In Ioh xxii, 1 |
| 8:21 | In Ioh liii, 1; liii, 2 |
| 8:22 | In Ioh liii, 1 |
| 8:23 | In Ioh liii, 1; In Rom viii, 7 (4:21) |
| 8:24-27 | In Ioh liii, 1 |
| 8:28 | De consbu 4; In Ioh xlix, 2; liii, 1; lv, 1; lxxii, 3; In Mat lxxxviii, 1; In Rom i, 2 (1:4) |
| 8:29 | In Ioh liii, 1; lxix, 2 |
| 8:30-31 | In Ioh liii, 2 |
| 8:33 | In Gal iii, 2 (3:6); In Ioh liv, 1; lix, 1; In Mat xi, 3; lii, 3 |
| 8:34 | De res d n I C 3 (2x); In il Uidi dom v, 2; In Ioh liv, 1; In 1 Tim xvii, 1 (6:7) |
| 8:35 | In Eph vi, 1 (2:22); In Heb xxv, 8; In Ioh liv, 1 |
| 8:36 | In Ioh liv, 2 |
| 8:37 | F Ier 7:2; In Ioh liv, 2; lv, 1 |
| 8:38 | In Ioh liv, 2 |

| | |
|---|---|
| 8:39 | Ex in ps cviii, 4; In Gen xxxi, 4; In Ioh liv, 2; In Mat xliv, 2; In Rom xix, 4 (11:17) |
| 8:40 | In Ioh xlix, 2; liv, 2 |
| 8:41 | In Ioh liv, 2; lix, 1; In Mat lii, 3 |
| 8:42 | In Heb viii, 2; In Ioh liv, 3 |
| 8:43 | In Ioh liv, 3 |
| 8:44 | Adu Iud 8, 8, 4; De Laz ii, 1; De uir iii; Ex in ps cviii, 2; F in epis cath 1 Peter 1:21; 3:10; In Acta xxxix, 4; In ascen d n I C 3; In Gal v, 5 (5:17); In Ioh liv, 3; In Mat xvii, 5; S Gen vii, 2 |
| 8:45 | In Ioh liv, 3 |
| 8:46 | In 1 Cor xxxviii, 3; In 2 Cor xi, 3; In Ioh liv, 3; lviii, 1; lviii, 2; In Is vii, 6; In Mat xvi, 3 |
| 8:48 | E i, 3; Ex in ps cxvii, 5; F in epis cath 1 Peter 2:8; In Acta iv, 3 (2:13); In Heb xxviii, 5; In Ioh xxxi, 2; xxxv, 1; lx, 3; lxxxiv, 3; In Mat xvii, 1 (2x); xxxvii, 5; lxviii, 2; lxx, 1; In Tom xv, 1 (8:28) |
| 8:49 | Cat ill i, 31; De incomp dei i, 7; In Mat lxxviii, 2 (2x) |
| 8:50 | In Ioh lv, 1 |
| 8:51 | De consub 3; In Ioh xlvi, 1; lv, 1; lxiv, 1 |
| 8:52 | De consub 3; In Ioh xxxix, 2; lv, 1; In Mat xxxvii, 5 |
| 8:53 | In Ioh lv, 1 |
| 8:54 | In Ioh lv, 1; lix, 1 |
| 8:55 | In Ioh lv, 2 |
| 8:56 | De bap Chris 3; De consub 3; In 2 Cor iii, 7; In Eph x, 1 (4:4); In Gen xlvii, 3; In il Pater s p 3; In Ioh viii, 1; xxi, 3; lv, 2; In Rom i, 2 (1:2) |
| 8:57 | De consub 3; In Ioh lv, 2 |
| 8:58 | De Chris prec 5; De consub 3; In Ioh xlix, 2; lv, 2; In Mat xvi, 2 |
| 8:59 | De consbu 3; In Acta i, 1 (1:2); In Ioh lv, 2 |
| 9 (p) | In d P Op 1 |
| 9:3 | In Ioh lvi, 1 |
| 9:4 | In Heb xxiv, 2; In Ioh lvi, 2 |
| 9:5 | In Ioh lvi, 2 |
| 9:6 | De Chris prec 4; In 1 Cor iv, 5; In Ioh xii, 2; xxxviii, 2; In Mat xxxix, 1 |
| 9:7 | De Chris prec 4; In Ioh xii, 2 |
| 9:8 | De Chris diuin 3; In il Hoc scit 2; In Ioh lvii, 1; In princ Act i, 5 |
| 9:9 | In Ioh lvii, 1; In princ Act i, 5 |
| 9:10-11 | In Ioh lvii, 1 |
| 9:12-13 | In Ioh lvii, 2 |

9:14 In Ioh lvii, 2; In Mat xxxix, 1
9:15 In Ioh lvii, 2
9:16 In Ioh xxxix, 2; xl, 3; lvii, 2; lviii, 3; In Mat xxix, 2; xlv, 1; lvi, 3; lxviii, 2; lxx, 1
9:17 In Ioh lviii, 2
9:18 In il Hoc scit 2
9:19 In Ioh lviii, 1
9:20-21 In Ioh lviii, 2
9:22 Ex in ps iv, 7; In il Hoc scit 4; In il In fac 4; In Ioh lviii, 2; lxxvii, 3; In 1 Tim iii, 2 (1:14)
9:24-27 In Ioh lviii, 2
9:28 In Ioh lviii, 3
9:29 In Ioh xx, 2; xl, 1; xlix, 3; l, 1; lviii, 3
9:30-31 In Ioh lviii, 3
9:32 In Ioh lvi, 1; lviii, 3; lxxvii, 1; In Mat lii, 3
9:33 In Ioh lviii, 2
9:34 In Ioh lviii, 3; In Rom vi, 1 (2:19)
9:37 In Ioh xl, 1; lix, 1
9:38 In Ioh lviii, 2; lix, 1
9:39 De Chris prec 4; De diab tent ii, 4; In 1 Cor xxvii, 3; In d P Op 1; In Ioh lvi, 1; lviii, 3; lix, 1; lxi, 1
9:40-41 In Ioh lix, 1
10:1-4 In Ioh lix, 2
10:5-6 In Ioh lix, 3
10:7 In Eut ii, 6
10:8-9 In Ioh lix, 3
10:10 In Ioh lix, 3 (2x); lx, 1
10:11 Ad pop Anti iii, 1; De cruce et lat i, 1; i, 4; ii, 1; ii, 3; De uir iii; Ex in ps cxiii, 2; In Eph vi, 3 (3:7); In il Pater s p 2; In Ioh lix, 3; In Rom xxix, 4 (15:24); In s Igna 1; In 1 Tim x, 1 (3:4); xv, 2 (5:18); S ante iret 3
10:12 In il Pater s p 2; In Ioh lix, 3
10:13 In Ioh xxx, 1
10:15 De incomp dei v, 4; Ex in ps xliv, 4; In il Fil 7; In il Pater s p 1; In Ioh iii, 4; xv, 2 (2x)

10:16 Ex in ps xlvi, 4; cxvii, 5; In Ioh lx, 2; lxv, 1
10:17 Ex in ps xlvi, 4; In il Pater s p 2; In Ioh lx, 2; In Mat xl, 1
10:18 De consbu 6; In 1 Cor xvii, 2; In Gal i, 3 (1:3); In Gen lxvii, 2; In Heb viii, 3; xxviii, 4; In il Fil 4; 5; In il Pater s p 1; 2; In Ioh xxxviii, 4; lx, 2; lxiii, 2; lxxii, 3; lxxxv, 3; In Mat lxxxviii; In quat Laz A 1
10:19 In Ioh lx, 3
10:20 In Eph vii, 4 (3:19); In Ioh lxix, 1; In Mat xxxvii, 5
10:24 In Heb xxviii, 5; In Ioh xxxiii, 2
10:25 In Ioh lxi, 1
10:26-27 In Ioh lxi, 2
10:28 In Ioh xlv, 2; lxi, 2; lxxviii, 3; In Phil vi, 3 (2:8)
10:29 In Ioh lxi, 2; S Gen ix, 4
10:30 De consub 2; 4; 6; In il Fil 7; In Ioh iii, 4; lxi, 2; lxiv, 1
10:31 In Ioh lxi, 2 (2x)
10:32 In Ioh lxi, 2
10:33 Ad e q scan xii; Ex in ps xlix, 3; In Ioh lxi, 2; lxiv, 1; In Mat xxix, 1; lvi, 3
10:34 In Ioh lxi, 2
10:35 In Acta v, 2 (2:20); In Ioh lxi, 2
10:36 In Eph vii, 4 (3:19); In Ioh xl, 1; lxi, 2
10:37 Ex in ps cix, 7; cxxxviii, 1; In Ioh xxxii, 1; lxi, 3; lxiv, 1; lxxiv, 2; In Mat xxix, 1
10:38 Ex in ps cxxxviii, 1; In Ioh xxxii, 1; xl, 3; lxi, 2; In Mat xxix, 1
10:39 In Ioh lxi, 3
10:40 In Ioh lxi, 3; In Mat lxvi, 1
10:41 In Ioh xviii, 2; lxi, 3; In Mat xxxvii, 5; xlvi, 3; lxvi, 1; In 2 Thess iv, 2 (2:12)
10:42 In Ioh lxi, 3; In Mat lxvi, 1; In 2 Thess iv, 2 (2:12)
11 (p) In Eut ii, 13; In quat Laz A 1 (2x)
11:3 In 2 Cor xxix, 2; In Ioh lxii, 1; In quat Laz A 1
11:4 In Acta xv, 3 (7:15); In 2 Cor xxix, 2; In Ioh lxii, 1
11:5 Ad pop Anti v, 6; In Heb iv, 3; In Ioh lxii, 1
11:6 In Ioh lxii, 1; In Mat xxxi, 2
11:7-9 In Ioh lxii, 1
11:11 De coem et de cru 1; H in san pascha 1; In Eph xxiii, 3 (6:14); In Gen xxix, 7; In Ioh lxii, 1; In Mat xxxi, 3; In quat Laz A 2

| | |
|---|---|
| 13:5 | De Chris prec 2; In il Pater s p 4; In Ioh lxx 2; In quat Laz A 1 |
| 13:6 | De hris prec 2; In Ioh lxx, 2 |
| 13:7 | De Chris prec 2; In Ioh lxx, 2; In Mat xii, 1 |
| 13:8 | De Chris prec 2; In Ioh lxx, 2; lxxiii, 1; In Mat xii, 1; liv, 6 |
| 13:9 | De Chris prec 2 In Ioh lxx, 2 |
| 13:10-11 | In Ioh lxx, 2 |
| 13:12 | In Phil vii, 2 (2:11) |
| 13:13 | in Ioh lxxi, 1 |
| 13:14 | In Ioh lx, 6; xxi, 1; In Phil vi, 3 (2:8); In 1 Tim xiv, 2 (5:10) |
| 13:15 | In Ioh lxxi, 1; In Mat lxiv, 5 |
| 13:16 | In Heb Argumentum, 3 (2x); In Ioh lxxi, 2; lxxxiv, 3 |
| 13:17 | In Ioh lxxi, 2 |
| 13:18 | De Laz i, 4; In Ioh lxxi, 1; lxxi, 2 |
| 13:19 | In 1 Cor xxxii, 3 |
| 13:21 | De prod Iud i, 1; ii, 1 (2x); In Ioh lxxii 1 |
| 13:22 | In Ioh lxxii, 1; In Mat lxxxi, 1 |
| 13:24 | In Acta viii, 1 (3:1); In Heb xvi, 1; In Ioh lxx, 2 |
| 13:26 | In Ioh lxxii, 1; In Mat lxxxi, 1 |
| 13:27 | In Acta liv, 3; In Ioh lxxii, 1; In Mat lxxxi, 3; lxxxii, 1 |
| 13:28 | In Ioh lxxii, 1 |
| 13:31 | In Ioh lxxii, 3; lxxvii, 4 |
| 13:32 | In Ioh lxxii, 3; lxxvii, 4 |
| 13:33 | In Ioh lxxvii, 4 |
| 13:34 | H in il App 24; In Heb iii, 10; In Ioh lxxii, 4; lxxxii, 2; In Rom vii, 7 (3:31) |
| 13:35 | De incomp dei i, 1; De sac ii, 5; De san pent ii, 3; In Acta i, 1 (1:2); In 1 Cor xxxii, 10; xxxii, 14; In Heb xxxi, 1; In Ioh lxxii, 4; In Mat xxxii, 11; In Phil iv, 3 (1:27); In princ Act ii, 3; ii, 6; In s Rom 1; S Gen ix, 2 |
| 13:36 | In Acta ii, 3 (1:11); In Ioh lxx, 2; lxxviii, 1; lxxxii, 2; In Rom v, 7 (2:16) |
| 13:37 | In Ioh lxx, 2; lxxiii, 1; lxxxviii, 1; In Mat lvi, 4 |
| 13:38 | In Ioh lxxiii, 1 |
| 14:1 | In Ioh lxix, 1; lxxiii, 1 |
| 14:2 | Ad Theo i, 9; Ex in ps cix, 7; cxi, 3; In 2 Cor x, 1; In Heb Argumentum, 3; xxv, 8; In Ioh liv, 2; lxxiii, 1 |

14:3 Ex in ps xli, 4; In Ioh lxxiii, 1; lxxxvi, 2
14:4 In Ioh lxxiii, 2
14:5 In Ioh lxxiii, 2; lxxviii, 1
14:6 Ex in ps cix, 4; cxv, 2; F Prou 4:10; 10:9; 18:6; In Eph vi, 1 (2:22); In Eut ii, 6 (2x); In Ioh v, 3; viii, 1; lxxiii, 2 (2x); lxxx, 1; lxxxv; In Mat xxxviii, 2
14:7 In Ioh lxxiii, 2; lxxiv, 1
14:8 In Ioh xlii, 1; lxxviii, 1
14:9 De consbu 2; 4; In Ioh iii, 5; lxiv, 1
14:10 In Acta xxvii, 2 (12:3); In il Pater s p 3 (2x); In Ioh xxxv, 3; lxiv, 1; lxxiv, 2; lxxviii, 2; In quat Laz A 2
14:11 In Ioh iii, 4; xxxv, 3; lxxiv, 2
14:12 De s Bab c Iul 1 (2x); 2; Ex in ps xi, 3; In Acta i, 1 (1:2); xii, 1 (5:15); xii, 3 (5:16); xii, 3 (5:16); xli, 1; In Ioh lxiii, 3; lxxiv, 2; In Mat xxxiv, 2; In Phil v, 2 (2:4); In princ Act iv, 7; In 2 Tim x, 4 (4:22)
14:13 In Ioh lxxiv, 2
14:14 In Eph vi, 1 (2:22); In Ioh lxxiv, 2; lxxvi, 2
14:15 De san pent i, 1; In Acta i, 5 (1:5); In Heb xxiv, 9; In Ioh lxxv, 3; lxxvi, 2; In Mat lxxi, 1
14:16 De san pent i, 1; In Acta i, 4 (1:4); i, 5 (1:5); In Ioh lxxxvi, 2
14:17 De san pent i, 1; In Heb xxiv, 7; In Ioh lxxv, 3
14:18 In Ioh lxxv, 1
14:19-20 In Ioh lxxv, 2
14:21 Ex in ps vii, 8; In 1 Cor viii, 7; In Ioh lxxv, 3
14:22 In Ioh lxxv, 3
14:23 Cat ill iv, 4; Ex in ps v, 1; vii, 8; In Eph i, 1 (1:3); vii, 2 (3:19); In Heb xvi, 7; xxvii, 7; In Ioh xlv, 3; lxxv, 3; lxxxii, 2; In 2 Tim ix, 3 (4:8)
14:24-25 In Ioh lxxv, 3
14:26 De pet mat 4; F Ier 31:33; In Heb xiv, 5; In Ioh xxiii, 3; lxxv, 3; lxxviii, 2; In Mat i, 1
14:27 Con Iud et gen 2; De prod Iud ii, 6; Ex in ps cxlvii, 4; F in epis cath 2 Peter 1:2; F Ier 6:14; In Col iii, 3 (1:20); (2x); In 2 Cor ii, 10; In Eph vi, 1 (2:22); In Heb xxxi,

14:27 cont 1; In Ioh lxxv, 3; lxxxvi, In Mat xxxii, 9; In Phil xiv, 2 (4:7)

14:28 In Heb viii, 2; viii, 3; In Ioh lxxv, 3; lxxxi, 2

14:29 De ss B et P 5; In 1 Cor xxxii, 3; In Ioh lxxv, 4; In 1 Thess iii, 3 (3:4)

14:30 In 1 Cor xxxviii, 3; In 2 Cor xi, 3; In Heb iv, 3; xxviii, 4; In Ioh lxvi, 3; lxxv, 4; In Is vii, 6; In Mat xvi, 3

14:31 In Ioh lxiv, 1; lxxv, 4

15:1 F Ier 2:21; In Eph vi, 2 (2:22); In Gen lxvii, 2; In Ioh xix, 3; In Mat xi, 7

15:2 In Ioh lxxvi, 1

15:3 In Ioh lxxvi, 1; lxxxii, 1

15:4 In Ioh lxxvi, 1

15:5 Cat ill xii, 14; De mut nom iii, 4; F Ier 2:21; In Eut ii, 11; In Ioh lxxvi, 1; In Rom xxiv, 2 (13:14)

15:6-7 In Ioh lxxvi, 2

15:8 In Ioh lxxvi, 2; In Rom xv, 5-6 (8:39)

15:9 In Ioh lxxvi, 2; lxxx, 2

15:10 In Ioh lxxvi, 2

15:13 Adu Iud 4, 5, 7; De s mar B 2; De sac ii, 6; In 1 Cor xxxii, 8; In Mat lx, 3; In Rom xxx, (16:5); In s Iul 1; In 1 Tim xvi, 2 (6:2)

15:14 Ex in ps viii, 7; H in il App 21; In Heb xxiii, 7; xxiv, 9; In Ioh xxiv, 1; lxxvii; In Mat xxxiv, 1; In Rom xxiv, 2 (13:14); In 1 Tim xvi, 2 (6:2)

15:15 Cat ill xii, 14; Ex in ps viii, 7; In Ioh i, 3; ii, 8; xxiv, 1; xxx, 1; lxxvii; lxxix, 4; In Mat xxxiv, 1; In 2 Tim vii, 5 (3:14)

15:16 De laud s Paul iv; De mut nom iv, 4; Ex in ps cxliii, 2; H in il App 11; In Gal i, 5 (1:6); In Heb xxviii, 4; In Ioh lxxvii; In Phil iv, 5 (1:30); In Tit i, 1 (1:5)

15:17 In il Pater m 2; In Ioh lxxvii, 1

15:18 In Ioh lxxvii, 1

15:19 In Ioh i, 4; liii, 1; lxxvii; lxxxii, 1; In Rom xiii, 7 (8:9)

15:20 In Ioh lxxvii; In Phil vi, 1 (2:8)

15:21 De proph obscur ii, 2; In Ioh lxxvii, 1

15:22 Ad e q scan xv; Cat ill vi, 5; x, 29; De sac iv, 1; E iii, 1; F Ier 12:10; In Acta i, 6 (1:5); v, 4 (2:20); In d P Op 2; In Gen xxxii, 1; In Heb x, 2; In il Si esur

15:22 cont 4; In Ioh ii, 11; xxviii, 2; lxxvii; lxxxiv, 3; In Mat xxxvi, 3; In Rom xii, 5 (7:8)
15:23 De sac iv, 1; Ex in ps viii, 2; In Ioh lxxvii, 1
15:24 De sac iv, 1; In Ioh lxxvii, 1
15:25 De sac iv, 1; Ex in ps vii, 2; In Ioh xxviii, 2; lxxvii, 1
15:26 In Heb xvi, 1; In Ioh lxxvii, 3
15:27 In Acta i, 2 (1:2); In Ioh lxxvii, 3
16:1 In Ioh lxxvii, 3
16:2 Ad e q scan xiv; In Acta xix, 3 (9:2); In Ioh lxxvii, 3
16:3 In Ioh lxxvii, 3
16:4 In 1 Cor xxxii, 3; In Ioh lxxvii, 3
16:5 E iii, 4; In Acta ii, 3 (1:9); In ascen d n I C 5; In 1 Cor v, 7; In Ioh v, 3; In Mat xxxiii, 1
16:6 E iii, 4; In ascen d n I C 5; In 1 Cor v, 7; In Ioh lxxii, 4; In Mat xxxiii, 1
16:7 De san pent i, 3 (2x); ii, 1; In Acta i, 4 (1:4); i, 5 (1:6); ii, 3 (1:9); In Ioh lxxv, 4; lxxviii, 1; lxxviii, 2; lxxviii, 3; lxxxvi, 1
16:8-10 In Ioh lxxviii, 1
16:11 In 1 Cor xxxviii, 3; In Ioh lxxviii, 1
16:12 De pet mat 4; In Acta i, 2 (1:2); In 1 Cor v, 7; In Ioh lxxvii, 1; lxxviii, 2 (2x); In Mat xxx, 5; liv, 4; In Rom i, 2 (1:5)
16:13 In Ioh lxxviii, 2 (3x)
16:14 In Ioh lxxviii, 2
16:15 In 1 Cor xxxix, 16; In 2 Cor xxix, 3; In Ioh lxxviii, 2
16:17 In Ioh lxxix, 2
16:20 Ad e q scan i, 6; Ex in ps vii, 8; In Eph xvii, 2 (5:4); In Heb xxix, 4; In Ioh lxxix, 1; In Phil xv, 5 (4:23)
16:21 De uir xii; In Gen xvii, 7; In Ioh lxxix, 1
16:22 Ad pop Anti xvi, 14; Ex in ps vi, 5; In Ioh lxxix, 1; lxxxvi, 1
16:23 F in epis cath James 1:2; In ioh lxxix, 1
16:24 In Ioh lxxix, 1
16:25-26 In Ioh lxxix, 2
16:27 In Eph vi, 1 (2:22)
16:28 In Eph xx, 5 (5:33); In Heb iii, 1; In Ioh lxxix, 2

16:29 In Ioh lxxix, 2
16:30 In Ioh lxxix, 2; lxxx, 1
16:32 In Ioh lxxix, 2
16:33 Ad e q scan xiv; Ad Stag a dae i, 3; ii, 4; De Laz iii, 6; Ex in ps vii, 8; In Acta xix, 5 (9:9); xxv, 2 (11:28); In 2 Cor xxvi, 4; In Eph i, 1 (1:3); vi, 1 (2:22); In Gen xxxii, 9; lxiii, 4; In Heb vii, 6; xxi, 5; xxv, 1; xxviii, 5; xxix, 4; In Ioh lxxix, 2; lxxxvi, 1; In Mat x, 8; xxxi, 4; In Phil xv, 5 (4:23); In Rom iii, 4 (1:24); In 1 Thess iii, 4 (3:4); In 2 Tim vii, 3 (3:12)
17:1 Ad e q scan xvii; De consub 6; In Eph viii 2 (4:2); In Gal i, 9 (1:160; In il Pater s p 2; In Ioh xxii, 1; In 1 Thess i, 2 (1: 6)
17:2 In Ioh lxxx, 1; In 1 Thess i, 2 (1:6)
17:3 F in epis cath James 2:19; In Gal iii, 5 (3:20); In Ioh iv, 2; xxxi, 1; lxxx, 2; In Rom i, 1 (1:2); In 1 Thess i, 2 (1:6); In 1 Tim vii, 1 (2:6)
17:4 Ex in ps cix, 4; In Gal i, 9 (1:16); In Ioh xxi, 2; lxxx, 2; In 1 Thess i, 2 (1:6)
17:5 De cruce et lat ii, 1; In Acta iii, 1 (1:14); In Ioh lxxx, 2; In 1 Thess i, 2 (1:6)
17:6 In Ioh lxx, 1; lxxxii, 11
17:7, 9 In Ioh lxxxi, 1
17:10 Ex in ps xliv, 9; cix, 3; In 2 Cor xxix, 3; In Eph i, 4 (1:10); In Gal i, 5 (1:6); In Ioh xlix, 2; lxxxi, 2; In Mat xvi, 7; In Rom ii, 2 (1:9)
17:11 In Gal i, 4 (1:4); In Heb xix, 3; In il Pater s p 3; In Ioh lxxviii, 3; lxxxi, 2; In Phil iv, 3 (1:27)
17:12 In Ioh lxxxi, 2; lxxxiii, 1
17:13 In Ioh lxxxi, 2
17:14 In Ioh lxxxiii, 4
17:15 In Gal i, 4 (1:4); In Ioh lxxxii, 1
17:16 In Eph xxii, 3 (6:12); In Ioh lxxxii, 1
17:17 In Ioh lxxxii, 1
17:19 In 1 Cor xxxviii, 3; In Heb xvii, 4; In Ioh lxxxii, 1
17:20 In Heb xvi, 1; In Ioh lxxxii, 1
17:21 In Acta xxxiii, 3 (15:33); In Heb iii, 10; In Ioh xxxix, 4; lxxxii, 2; In Rom xxvii, 3 (15:7)
17:22-23 In Ioh lxxxii, 2; In Mat xxxii, 11

17:24 In Eph i, 1 (1:4); In Heb xvi, 1; xvii, 9; In Ioh xii, 3; l, 3; lxxxii, 2; In 1 Tim ii, 2 (1:11); iii, 4 (1:14)
17:25 In Ioh viii, 2; lxxxii, 3
17:26 In Ioh lxxxii, 3
18:1 Ad pop Anti xi, 2
18:2 In Ioh lxxxiii, 1
18:3 De prod Iud i, 3; In Ioh lxxxiii, 1
18:4 De Laz i, 5; De mut nom iii, 5; De prod Iud i, 3; Ex in ps xlvi, 2; In Ioh liii, 2; lxxxiii, 1; In Mat lxxxiii, 2
18:5 In Ioh lxxxiii, 1; lxxxiv, 1
18:6 De mut nom iii, 5; In il Pater s p 3; In Ioh xlviii, 1; liii, 2; lxxv, 4; In Rom xxi, 5 (12:13)
18:7 In Ioh lxxxiii, 1
18:8 In 2 Cor iii, 7; In Ioh lix, 3; lxxxiii, 1
18:9 In Ioh lix, 3; lxxxiii, 1
18:10 In Mat lxxxiv, 1
18:11 In Ioh lxxxiii, 2; In Mat lxxxiv, 1
18:12-13 In Ioh lxxxiii, 2
18:14 De prod Iud ii, 3; In Ioh lxxxiii, 2
18:15 In Ioh lxxxiii, 2; In Mat lxv, 4; lxxxiv, 2
18:16 Adu Iud 8, 3, 4
18:17 Adu Iud 8, 3, 4; In Ioh lxxxiii, 2; Q freg con 5
18:18 Adu Iud 8, 3, 4
18:19 In Ioh lxxxiii, 2
18:20 In Ioh xxix, 1; lxxxiii, 3
18:21 In Ioh lxxxiii, 3
18:22 Ex in ps xliv, 6; In Acta xxix, 4; In Ioh lxxxiii, 2
18:23 Cat ill i, 31; De fut uit 5; De incomp dei i, 7 (2x); De s h Phoc 2; Ex in ps xliv, 6; In 2 Cor iii, 7; In Heb xxviii, 5; In Ioh lxx, 1; lxxxiii, 3; In Is iii, 7; In Mat lxxviii, 2; In 1 Tim xvii, 1 (6:7)
18:24 In Eph viii, 9 (4:2)
18:25 In Ioh lxxxiii, 3
18:28 In Mat lxxxiv, 2
18:29 In Ioh lxxxiii, 3
18:30 In Ioh lxxxiii, 4; In Mat lxxxiv, 3
18:31 In Acta xxix, 2; In Ioh lxxxiii, 4; In Mat lxxxiv, 3; lxxxvi, 2
18:32 In il Pater s p 4; In Ioh lxxxiii, 4
18:33-34 In Ioh lxxxiii, 4
18:35 In Ioh lxxxiii, 4; In Rom xxvii, 3 (15:7)
18:36 De pet mat 3; In Acta xxvii, 2 (13:3); In 1

| | |
|---|---|
| 18:36 cont | Cor vii, 17; In Ioh xlii, 3; lxxxiii, 4; In Mat lxxxvi, 1 |
| 18:37 | Ex in ps xlvi, 3; cix, 5; In il Fil 5; In Ioh iii, 3; lxxxiii, 4; In 1 Tim xviii, 1 (6:16) |
| 18:38-40 | In Ioh lxxxiv, 1 |
| 19:4-5 | In Ioh lxxxiv, 1 |
| 19:6 | In Col vi, 3 (2:15); In Ioh lxxxiv, 1 |
| 19:7 | In Ioh lxxxiv, 2 |
| 19:9 | In 1 Cor vii, 5 |
| 19:10 | In Ioh lxxxiv, 2 |
| 19:11 | In Ioh lxxxiv, 2; In Mat lxxxvi, 1 |
| 19:12 | Con Iud et gen 8; E i, 4; Ex in ps xlix, 3; In Acta xxxiv, 1 (16:23); In Cor v, 10; In Ioh lxxxiv, 2 (2x) |
| 19:14 | In Acta xxxiv, 1 (16;23); In Ioh lxxxiv, 2 |
| 19:15 | Adu Iud 1, 11, 4; In Acta ix, 2 (3:26); xvii, 1 (7:35) (2x); In Ioh lxvi, 2; lxxxiv, 2; In Phil v, 3 (2:4) |
| 19:18 | De elee 2 |
| 19:19 | In Ioh lxxxv, 1; In para 3 |
| 19:21 | In Mat xxxv, 2; lxxxiv, 3 |
| 19:22 | In Mat lxxxvii, 2 |
| 19:23 | In Ioh xxxv, 2 |
| 19:24 | In Gal i, 11 (1:18); In Ioh xxxv, 2 |
| 19:25 | In Ioh lxxxv, 2 |
| 19:26 | In Acta iii, 1 (1:14); In Ioh lxxxv, 3 |
| 19:27 | In Ioh lxxxv, 3; In Mat v, 5 |
| 19:28 | In Ioh lxxxv, 3 |
| 19:30 | In Ioh lxxxv, 3; In Mat lxxxvii, 1 |
| 19:31 | In Ioh lxxxv, 3 |
| 19:33 | Cat ill iii, 16 |
| 19:34 | Cat ill iii, 16; In Mat lxxxviii; Qual duc 3 |
| 19:35-36 | In Ioh lxxxv, 3 |
| 19:37 | In 1 Cor xxxviii, 3; In Heb xxxi, 7; In Ioh lxxxv, 3 |
| 19:38 | In Ioh lxxxv, 3 |
| 19:39 | In Ioh xxiv, 1 |
| 20:1-2 | In Ioh lxxxv, 4 |
| 20:3 | In Acta viii, 1 (3:1) |
| 20:6 | In Mat lxv, 4 |
| 20:9 | De pet mat 4; E i, 4; F Ier 25:11; In il Sal P et A ii, 3 |
| 20:13-16 | In Ioh lxxxvi, 1 |
| 20:17 | F Ier 25:11; In Ioh lxxxvi, 1 |

| | |
|---|---|
| 20:18-20 | In Ioh lxxxvi, 2 |
| 20:21 | In Ioh lxxv, 2; lxxxvi, 2 |
| 20:22 | F Ier 1:9; In Acta i, 5 (1:4); In 2 Cor vi, 2; In Ioh li, 2; lxxv, 1; lxxxvi, 2 |
| 20:23 | De sac iii, 5; In 2 Cor vi, 2; In Heb xiv, 3; In Ioh lxxxvi, 2; In princ Act iii, 5 |
| 20:24 | In princ Act iv, 6 |
| 20:26 | In Ioh lxxxvii, 1 |
| 20:27 | De cruce et lat i, 4; ii, 4; In Ioh lxvi, 3; lxxxvii, 1 |
| 20:28 | In Ioh lxxxvii, 1 |
| 20:29 | Ex in ps cx, 4; In Acta xl, 2; In Col xii, 3 (4:18); In 1 Cor vi, 5; In il Hoc scit 2; In Ioh xxiv, 1; lxxxvii, 1 |
| 20:30 | In Ioh lxxxvii, 1 |
| 20:31 | In Ioh lxxxvii, 2 |
| 21:1-2 | In Ioh lxxxvii, 2 |
| 21:4 | In Ioh xlviii, 1 |
| 21:5 | In Acta i, 3 (1:2); In Ioh lxxxvii, 2 |
| 21:7 | In Gal ii, 4 (2:12); In Mat x, 4; l, 2 |
| 21:12 | In Ioh lxxxvii, 2 |
| 21:14 | In 1 Cor xxxviii, 5; In Ioh lxxxvii, 2 |
| 21:15 | De sac ii, 1; ii, 2; In Acta xviii, 5 (8:25); In 1 Cor xxxii, 11; In Ioh xxxiii, 3; lxxii, 1; In Mat lxxvii, 6; In Rom Argumentum, 2; xxix, 4 (15:24); xxxi, 4 (16:16) |
| 21:16 | De b Phil 2; De sac ii, 1; ii, 2; In 1 Cor xxxii, 10; In Mat xlvi, 3; lxxi, 1; lxxvii, 3; lxxvii, 6; In Rom xxiii, 3 (13:9); xxiii, 4 (13:10); xxix, 4 (15:24) |
| 21:17 | De sac ii, 1; ii, 2; In Ioh lxxxviii, 1; In Mat lxxi, 1; lxxvii, 6; In princ Act ii, 4 (2x); ii, 6; In Rom x, 5 (6:4) |
| 21:18 | De laud s Paul vi; In 2 Cor x, 3; In Ioh lxxxviii, 1; In princ Act ii, 6 |
| 21:19-20 | In Ioh lxxxviii, 1 |
| 21:21 | In Acta viii, 1 (3:1); In Ioh lxxxviii, 1; In Mat lxxxii, 3 |
| 21:22-24 | In Ioh lxxxviii, 2 |
| 21:25 | De mut nom i, 4; In Ioh lxxxvii, 2; lxxxviii, 2 |

<u>Acts</u>

| | |
|---|---|
| 1:1 | De mut nom i, 3; i, 4; In Acta i, 2 (1:2); In |

| | |
|---|---|
| 1:1 cont | princ Act iv, 5 |
| 1:2 | In Acta i, 3 (1:2); In princ Act iv, 5 |
| 1:3 | In 1 Cor xvii, 2; In princ Act iv, 5 |
| 1:4 | In Ioh lxxxvii, 2; In princ Act iv, 5 (2x) |
| 1:5 | In princ Act iv, 5 |
| 1:6 | In princ Act iv, 5; In 1 Thess ix, 1 (5:2) |
| 1:7 | In Mat lxxvii, 1; lxxxii, 3; In 1 Thess ix, 1 (5:2) |
| 1:8 | In Eph ii, 2 (1:14); In Ioh lxxxvi; In Mat lxix, 1 |
| 1:9 | De fut uit 6; In Mat lvi, 5; In 1 Thess viii, 1 (4:18) |
| 1:10 | Ex in ps xlvi, 4; In ascen d n I C 4 |
| 1:11 | In ascen d n I C 4; 5; In 2 cor xi, 3; In Heb iii, 4; In 1 Tim xi, 1 (3:16) |
| 1:14 | In Acta xiii, 2 (5:33) |
| 1:15 | Con Anom xi, 4; In 2 Cor xviii, 3; In Rom argumentum, 2 |
| 1:17 | F Ier 12:13 |
| 1:18 | Ex in ps vii, 13; F Prou 1:10; In Rom xxv, 6 (14:13) |
| 1:20 | Ex in ps cviii, 2 |
| 1:21 | In Acta xiv, 3 (6:7) |
| 1:24 | In Acta xi, 1 (4:24) |
| 1:26 | F Ier 12:13 |
| 2:1 | De Elleaz 4; De san pent i, 5; In Acta i, 4 (1:4); In princ Act iv, 5 |
| 2:2 | De Eleaz 4; De san pent i, 5; In Mat xii, 3 |
| 2:3 | De bap Chris 3; De Eleaz 4; De san pent i, 5; In princ Act iv, 5 |
| 2:4 | Con Iud et gen 5; De Eleaz 4 |
| 2:5 | De san pent i, 1; In Heb xvii, 1 |
| 2:9-10 | In Heb xvii, 1 |
| 2:13 | De san pent i, 5; In Acta viii, 2; In 1 Cor xxxvi, 3; In Mat i, 3 |
| 2:14 | In Acta ix, 1 (3:12); In Gal ii, 4 (2:12) |
| 2:17 | In 1 Cor xxvi, 4 |
| 2:22 | In Acta ix, 2 (3:26); ix, 3 (3:26) |
| 2:23 | In Acta ix, 1 (3:17) |
| 2:24 | In Acta ix, 3 (3:26); In il In fac 4; 7 |
| 2:26 | In Acta ix, 1 (3:15) |
| 2:29 | In Mat xxvi, 9; xxxix, 1; lxxi |
| 2:32 | In Acta i, 2 (1:2) |
| 2:34 | In il In fac 4; In Mat vii, 2 |
| 2:35 | In Acta ix, 2 (3:24); In il In fac 4 |
| 2:36 | In Gal ii, 4 (2:12); In Heb i, 2; iii, 1; In Ioh iii, 3 |

4:20 In Acta viii, 1 (3:1); xiii, 2 (5:33); In il In fac 6; In Mat xxiv, 4; xxxiii, 3
4:29 Ex in ps cxl, 2 (2x); In Ioh lxxix, 1
4:30 Ex in ps cxl, 2
4:31 In Ioh lxxix, 1
4:32 Ex in ps xlvi, 5; In 1 Cor vi, 8; xv, 14; xxi, 11; xxiv, 4; In d P Op 2; In Eph xx, 4 (5:33); In Gen xxxiii, 3; In Heb xix, 3; In Ioh lxxv, 5; In Mat xxi, 1; xxxii, 9; In Phil iv, 3 (1:27); In 1 Thess ii, 4 (2:8); In Tit vi, 3 (3:15)
4:33 In Phil xv, 4 (4:19)
4:34 Ex in ps xlvi, 3; In d P Op 2
4:35 In 1 Cor vi, 8; In 1 Thess ii, 4 (2:8); In Tit vi, 3 (3:15)
5 (p) De laud s Paul vi; De uir xxiv; Ex in ps iv, 7; vi, 2; In Is iii, 10; In Mat xvii, 5
5:1 Ex in ps vii, 12
5:3-4 In princ Act iii, 5
5:5 In Gal i, 3 (1:3)
5:8 In Heb xviii, 6; In princ Act iii, 5 (2x)
5:11 In Eph viii, 1 (4:2)
5:13 Ex in ps xlvi, 3; In Acta xli, 2; In princ Act iii, 5
5:15 Ad pop Anti iv, 6; De s Mel 2; Ex in ps xi, 3; cix, 6; H dicta p r m 1; In Acta xxi, 2 (9: 35); In 2 Cor vii, 6; In Eut ii, 14; In quat Laz A 2; In Rom viii, 6 (4:21); xiv, 6 (8:23)
5:19 In Gen xxviii, 5
5:20 In Heb iii, 4
5:28 H dicta in t s Anas 5; In Acta iv, 3 (2:13); x, 2 (4:22); xlii, 1; In Col vi, 3 (2:15); In Mat xxiv, 4; xxxiii, 3; In princ Act iv, 8
5:29 In Col xi, 1 (4:6); In Gen xxviii, 5
5:32 In Ioh lxxxviii, 2
5:34-35 Adu Iud 5, 3, 4; 5, 3, 5
5:36 Adu Iud 5, 3, 4; 5, 3, 5; In Acta xlvi, 3; In Ioh lix, 3; In Mat x, 5; xlviii, 6; lxx, 1
5:37 Adu Iud 5, 3, 4; 5, 3, 5; In Mat x, 5; xlviii, 6; lxx, 1
5:38 Adu Iud 5, 3, 4; 5, 3, 5; In diem nat 1
5:39 Adu Iud 5, 3, 4; 5, 3, 5; In Acta xvi, 1 (7: 22); In diem nat 1; In Ioh xxix, 2
5:40 Adu Iud 5, 3, 4; 5, 3, 5; De uir lxiv; In Rom xxii, 1 (12:14)
5:41 Ad pop Anti xviii, 7; Adu Iud 5, 3, 4; 5, 3, 5; Con Iud et gen 13; 14; De glor in trib 3; De Laz iii, 6; De s Bab 11; E vii, 4; Ex in

| | |
|---|---|
| 8:10 | In Mat xlvi, 4; In 1 Thess iv, 1 (3:8) |
| 8:19 | In Acta xxxiv, 2 (16:24) |
| 8:20 | In Acta iii, 5 (1:26); In Rom xii, 6 (7:13) |
| 8:22 | Cat ill v, 21; In princ Act i, 5; In 1 Tim vii, 2 (2:7) |
| 8:23 | In princ Act i, 5 |
| 8:25 | Ex in ps viii, 7 |
| 8:26 | Ex in ps xi, 3; In Gen xxxv, 1 |
| 8:27 | Ex in ps xliii, 5; In Acta i, 7 (1:5); In Gen xxxv, 1; In il Pater s p 1; In il Sal P et A i, 1 |
| 8:28 | In Gen xxxv, 1; In Mat i, 13 |
| 8:30 | De Laz iii, 3; De mut nom iv, 3; In Gen xxxv, 2; In il Fil 2 |
| 8:31 | De Laz iii, 3; In Gen xxxv, 2 |
| 8:34 | In il Fil 2; In il Messis 5 |
| 8:36 | In il Messis 5 |
| 8:39-40 | In princ Act iii, 5 |
| 9:1 | Ad e q scan xx; Adu Iud 2, 2, 2; De mut nom i, 5; i, 6; ii, 2 (2x); iii, 3; iii, 4 |
| 9:2 | Ad e q scan xx; Adu Iud 2, 2, 2 |
| 9:3 | De mut nom iii, 4; In Gal i, 2 (1:3) |
| 9:4 | De mut nom i, 3; ii, 2; iii, 1; iii, 2 (2x); iv, 4; In Eut ii, 17; In Gal i, 2 (1:3); In Mat xxix, 3; lxxxviii |
| 9:5 | De mut nom iii, 4 (2x); S ante iret 1 |
| 9:7 | In Acta xlvii, 2 |
| 9:8, 11 | De mut nom ii, 2 |
| 9:15 | De mut nom i, 5; In Eph vi, 2 (3:2); In Gal i, 9 (1:16); In Gen xxxi, 2; In il Ut sus 5; In phil ix, 5 (2:30); In Rom xviii, 6 (11:6); xxx, 3 (16:5); In 1 Tim iii, 1 (1:14); Non esse ad grat 4 |
| 9:17 | De mut nom ii, 2 |
| 9:20 | In Mat lxxi, 1 |
| 9:22 | Cat ill v, 19; De mut nom ii, 2; De sac iv, 7; In princ Act i, 5 |
| 9:23 | Cat ill v, 19 |
| 9:24 | Cat ill iv, 10; v, 19; De mut nom ii, 2 |
| 9:25 | Cat ill v, 19; In Mat liii, 2 |
| 9:26 | In 1 Cor xxii, 6 |
| 9:29 | De mut nom ii, 2; De sac iv, 7 |
| 9:31-33 | De mut nom ii, 2 |
| 9:34 | In Eut ii, 11 |
| 9:36 | Adu Iud 7, 6, 6; Ex in ps xlviii, 5; In il Prop 3; In 1 Thess i, 4 (1:7) |

9:37–38 Adu Iud 7, 6, 6

9:39 Adu Iud 7, 6, 6; In Gen xxx, 3; In Ioh lxxxv, 6

9:40 Adu Iud 7, 6, 6; In Eph iii, 1 (1:22); In Gen xxx, 3; lv, 4; In Mat lxxviii, 2; In princ Act iii, 5

9:41 Adu Iud 7, 6, 6; In Gen xxx, 3

9:43 E cxxv

10:1–2 Cat ill vii, 27; vii, 28

10:3 Cat ill vii, 27; vii, 28; Ex in ps xi, 3; In 1 Thess i, 4 (1:7)

10:4 Cat ill vii, 27; vii, 28; De paen iii, 1; vii, 6; Ex in ps iv, 4; vii, 4; xliii, 5; In Acta xxxvi, 3 (16: 39); In 2 Cor xx, 3; In Heb xi, 7; In il Ne tim ii, 4; In Mat l, 6; lxxvii, 6

10:10 Ex in ps cxv, 3

10:14 In Mat li, 3

10:15 In Mat lii, 1; lxxxii, 3

10:20 In Mat lii, 1

10:34 Cat ill ix, 41; In 1 Cor viii, 4; In Gen xxii, 5; lx, 3; In il Dom non est 5

10:35 In 1 Cor viii, 4; In Gen lx, 3

10:40 In princ Act iv, 7

10:41 In Acta i, 2 (1:2); i, 4 (1:2); In ioh xvii, 3; lxxvii, 3; lxxxvii, 1; In Mat lxxxii, 2; In princ Act iv, 7

10:44 In Ioh lxxvii, 3

10:45 In Ioh ix, 2

10:47 In Eph vi, 2 (3:5); In Ioh xxv, 2

11:3 In Ioh ix, 2; In Mat xxxii, 5

11:21 In Ioh lxxiv, 2

11:24 In Acta xv, 2 (7:5); xxi, 1 (9:27)

11:26 Ad pop Anti iii, 3; xvii, 10; In Mat vii, 7

11:28 Ad pop Anti xvii, 10

11:29 Ad pop Anti xvii, 10; De elee 2; In Heb xxviii, 1

11:30 De elee 6; In Acta xxi, 1 (9:27)

12:2 Ad e q scan xiv

12:5 De incomp dei iii, 6; De proph obscur ii, 5; De reg 21; In 2 Cor ii, 5; In Eph xxiv, 1 (6: 20); In Heb xix, 3; In 1 Thess i, 3 (1:7); In 2 Thess iv, 3 (3:2)

12:6 In Eph vii, 2 (4:2)

12:7 Ex in ps xi, 3; In Eph viii, 5 (4:2)

12:8 In Eph viii, 5 (4:2); In il Sal P et A ii, 1; In Phil ix, 5 (2:30)

12:9–10 In Eph viii, 5 (4:2)

16 (p) cont motu; E cxxv; In Gal ii, 2 (2:5); v, 3 (5:11)
16:1 In princ Act iv, 4; In 2 Tim i, 2 (1:5); S Gen ix, 5
16:2 In princ Act iv, 4; In 1 Tim Argumentum, 1
16:3 De sac i, 8; In Mat li, 3; In princ Act iv, 4; In Rom xvi, 1 (9:3); xxvi, 2 (14:21); In 1 Tim Argumentum, 1 i, 2 (1:5)
16:4 In Mat v, 6
16:7 In 1 Thess iii, 3 (2:18)
16:14 Ex in ps cxv, 2; In 1 Cor xv, 14; In Rom i, 3 (1:5)
16:15 E cxxv; Ex in ps cxiii, 5; In Mat lxxiii, 3
16:16 In Eph x, 1 (4:4)
16:17 Adu Iud 6, 6, 8; 6, 6, 9; De Laz ii, 2; De uir viii; In Acta xli, 3; In 1 Cor xxix, 3; In Eph x, 1 (4:4); In il In fac 2; In Tit iii, 2 (1:14)
16:18 Adu Iud 6, 6, 9; In Eph xxii, 4 (6:13); In Eut ii, 11; In Mat xiii, 3
16:19-22 In il Dil deum 2
16:23 In Eph viii, 2 (4:2); In il Dil deum 2
16:24 Ad pop Anti i, 16; In il Dil deum 3
16:25 Ex in ps xli, 2; cxlv, 3; cxlv, 4; In Eph viii, 2 (4:2); In Gen xxx, 6; In il Dil deum 3
16:26 In il Dil deum 3
16:27 In il Dil deum 3; In kal 5 .
16:28 In il Dil deum 3
16:29 Ex in ps cxlv, 3; In Acta i, 7 (1:5); In Eph viii, 3 (4:2); viii, 5 (4:2); In il Dil deum 3
16:30 Ex in ps cxlv, 4; In Eph viii, 5 (4:2); viii, 9 (4:2); In Eut ii, 14; In il Dil deum 3; 4
16:31 In Eph viii, 5 (4:2); In il Dil deum 4
16:32 In Eph viii, 5 (4:2)
16:33 In Eph viii, 5 (4:2); In il Dil Deum 4; S ante iret 4; S cum iret 1
16:34 In il Dil deum 4
16:37 In Acta xlvii, 1
17 (p) De proph obscur 3
17:5 In Rom xxxii, 2 (16:21); In 1 Thess i, 1 (1:3); i, 2 (1:6)
17:6 In Mat xxxiii, 5; In 1 Thess i, 1 (1:3); i, 2 (1:6)
17:7 In Mat xxxiii, 5; lxxxvi, 1; In 1 Thess i, 2 (1:6)
17:8-9 In 1 Thess i, 2 (1:6)
17:16 S Gen ii, 2

| | |
|---|---|
| 20:22 | In Eph viii, 7 (4:2); In Rom xxxii, 4 (16:24) |
| 20:24 | In Heb iv, 6 |
| 20:25 | In Phil xv, 1 (4:14); In s Eust 4 |
| 20:26 | In Eph xi, 2 (4:12); xi, 6 (4:16); In il Hoc scit 5; In 2 Tim iv, 4 (2:10); Non esse ad grat 2 |
| 20:27 | Adu Iud 1, 8, 2; Non esse ad grat 2 |
| 20:28 | De san pent i, 4; In Gal i, 2 (1:3); In il Hoc scit 5 (2x); In Rom i, 2 (1;5); In s Eust 4 |
| 20:29 | Ad e q scan xiv; In Acta liii, 4; In il Hoc scit 5; In s Eust 4; In 2 Tim ix, 2 (4:4) |
| 20:30 | Ad e q scan xiv; In Mat lix, 1; In s Eust 4 |
| 20:31 | De ss mar A 3; De sac iv, 8; E iii, 9; Ex in ps vi, 4; In Col xii, 2 (4:18); xii, 3 (4:18); In Eph xvii, 2 (5:4); In Gal iv, 3 (4:20); In il Hoc scit 5; In Mat vi, 8; In 1 Thess iv, 4 (3:13); In 2 Tim viii, 3 (3;14) |
| 20:32 | In 2 Tim ii, 1 (1:12) |
| 20:34 | Cat ill viii, 3; De laud s Paul i; iii; In 1 Cor xx, 12; xl, 6; In il Sal P et A i, 5; ii, 1; In Ioh xliv, 1; In Mat viii, 6; In Phil xv, 1 (4:14); In 1 Tim xi, 2 (3:16); In 2 Tim x, 1 (4:13) |
| 20:35 | In il Sal P et A i, 5; In Ioh xliv, 1; In Phil xv, 1 (4:14); In 1 Thess vi, 1 (4:12); viii, 1 (4:17); In 2 Thess v, 1 (3:11) |
| 20:37 | Ex in ps cxl, 6 |
| 21 (p) | In Mat lxxxvi, 2 |
| 21:8 | In Acta xiv, 3 (6:7) |
| 21:9 | In 1 Cor xxvi, 4; In il Uidi dom iv, 3 |
| 21:11 | In Mat x, 4 |
| 21:13 | In Eph viii, 7 (4:2); In Rom xxxii, 3 (16:24); In 1 Thess iv, 4 (3:13) |
| 21:17 | In Gal i, 11 (1:18) |
| 21:18 | In Gal i, 11 (1:18); In Mat v, 6 |
| 21:20 | De cruce et lat i, 5; ii, 5; De proph obscur i, 4; In Gal i, 11 (1:18); ii, 1 (2:2); In Heb Argumentum, 1 (2x); In il In fac 3; 12; In Mat v, 6; lxxxvi, 2; In princ Act iv, 4 |
| 21:21 | In Heb Argumentum, 1 (2x); vii, 4; xxxiv, 4; In il In fac 3; 12; In princ Act iv, 4 |
| 21:22-23 | In il In fac 3; In princ Act iv, 4 |
| 21:24 | In Eph iv, 3 (3:1); In il In fac 3; In princ Act iv, 4; In Rom xvi, 1 (9:3) |
| 21:25 | In Eph iv, 3 (3:7) |
| 21:26 | De sac i, 8; In Eph vi, 3 (3:7); In Rom xxvi, 2 (14:2) |
| 21:28 | In Heb vii, 4 |
| 21:29 | In Gal v, 3 (5:11) |

<u>Romans</u>

1:21
cont ps cxlii, 3; In il Hab i, 3
1:22 Ad pop Anti x, 6; Ex in ps xlviii, 5; In Acta ii, 5 (1:11); In Is v, 7
1:25 De diab tent ii, 3; In Eph xviii, 3 (5:14); In Gen vi, 4; In Ioh iv, 3; In Mat lv, 8
1:26 E vii, 3
1:27 E vii, 3; Ex in ps vii, 12; ix, 7; cxxiv, 2; In Is v, 5
1:28 In Col viii, 5 (3:15); In Eph xiii, 1 (4:17); In Ioh lxviii, 2; In Mat xxxviii, 1
1:32 Ad pop Anti xii, 13; Adu Iud 1, 4, 10; De D et S ii, 1; Ex in ps xlix, 7; cxlvii, 3; In Ioh xlii, 3; In Rom xxv, 4 (14:13); In 2 Tim i, 4 (1:7)
2:1 De D et S ii, 1
2:3 Ad pop Anti xii, 15; De Laz iii, 5; Ex in ps cxlvii, 3
2:4 Ad pop Anti xii, 15; De Laz iii, 5; Ex in ps ix, 6; cxlvii, 3; In Eph iv, 4 (2:10) (2x); In Gen xxv, 2; In Ioh xxxviii, 2
2:5 Ad pop Anti xii, 15; De Laz iii, 5; Ex in ps cxlvii, 3; In 1 Cor xxiv, 10; In Gen xxv, 2; In Ioh xxxviii, 2; In 2 Tim iii, 3 (1:18)
2:6 Ad pop Anti xii, 15; Ad Theo i, 9; Ex in ps cxlvii, 3; In Gen xliii, 2; In Ioh xxviii, 1
2:7 Ex in ps cxlvii, 3; In Ioh lxxvii, 1
2:8 Ex in ps xlix, 3; cxlvii, 3; In Mat xxxvi, 3
2:9 Ad pop Anti xii, 14; Ex in ps xlix, 3; cxlvii, 3; In Mat xxxvi, 3
2:10 Ad pop Anti xii, 13
2:11 In Acta xxiii, 1 (10:35); In Col x, 2 (4:1)
2:12 Ad pop Anti xii, 13; De paen vi, 5; Ex in ps vi, 2 (2x); vii, 5; xlix, 3; In Gen xviii, 1; xix, 6; In Ioh ix, 2; In Mat xxxvi, 3 (2x); lxxv, 5 (2x); In Rom xi, 5 (6:18); xxxi, 5 (16:16)
2:13 Ex in ps xlix, 6; In Gen i, 1; xlvii, 14; In il Si esur 4; In Mat lxvii, 2; In Phil v, 3 (2:4)
2:14 Ex in ps vii, 4; xlix, 6; cx, 6; cxlvii, 3; F Ier 3:12; In Acta xxiii, 2 (10:43)
2:15 De paen vi, 5
2:16 Ad pop Anti xii, 13; In Is ii, 4
2:17 In Ioh lii, 4; In Is i, 5; In Mat xxiv, 1; S Gen viii, 1
2:18 In Is i, 5; In Mat xxiv, 1
2:19-
20 In il Si esur 4; In Is ii, 5; In 2 Tim viii, 4

| | |
|---|---|
| 2:19-20 cont | (3:14) |
| 2:21 | Ex in ps xlix, 6; In Gen viii, 5; In Ioh lii, 4; In Is i, 5; i, 8; In Mat xvi, 5; In Rom v, 5 (2:13) |
| 2:22 | Ex in ps xlix, 6 |
| 2:23 | Ex in ps xlix, 6; In Ioh lii, 4 |
| 2:24 | Cat ill vi, 10; In Acta xxiii, 3 (10:43); xlvi 3; In il Messis 2; In Ioh ix, 2; In 1 Thess vi 1 (4:12); S cum pres 2 |
| 2:25 | In Gal ii, 3 (2:9); In Is i, 5 |
| 2:27 | In Rom xii, 3 (7:5) |
| 2:28 | F Ier 4:4; In Phil x, 2 (3:2) |
| 2:29 | De laud s Paul vi; F Ier 4:4; In Col vi, 2 (2:10); In Gen v, 6; xxxi, 2; In Phil x, 2 (3:2); In Tit ii, 4 (1:11) |
| 3:1 | In Rom xiii, 5 (4:2); S Gen viii, 2 |
| 3:3-4 | In Gal ii, 7 (4:2); In Ioh lii, 1; In Rom xviii, 5 (11:6) |
| 3:6 | Ex in ps xlix, 3 |
| 3:8 | In Heb xiii, 9; In 1 Tim iv, 1 (1:16) |
| 3:9 | In Rom viii, 5 (4:2) |
| 3:12 | In Ioh ix, 2 |
| 3:16 | In Rom x, 1 (5:14) |
| 3:19 | In Ioh ix, 2 |
| 3:20 | In Gal ii, 7 (2:20); In 1 Tim ii, 2 (1:9) |
| 3:21 | Adu Iud 7, 3, 2 |
| 3:22 | In Ioh ix, 2; In Rom xvii, 3 (10:13) |
| 3:23 | Adu Iud 2, 1, 7; Ex in ps cx, 6; In Ioh ix, 2 (2x); xxviii, 1; xxxv, 1; liv, 1; In Mat xxx, 3; In Rom xvi, 4 (9:10) (2x); In s Iul 1; In 1 Tim iv, 1 (1:16) |
| 3:24 | In Ioh ix, 2; xxxv, 1; liv, 1 |
| 3:27 | In Rom viii, 5 (4:2) |
| 3:29-30 | In Rom xvii, 3 (10:43) |
| 3:31 | In Heb ix, 4; In Mat xvi, 3 |
| 4:2 | In Phil v, 2 (2:4); In Rom xvi, 10 (9:31); In 1 Tim iii, 2 (1:14) |
| 4:3 | Cat ill viii, 7; In 2 Cor iii, 6; In Gal iii, 2 (3:6); In Gen xxvii, 3; xxxvi, 5; xxxix, 5; lxiii, 4 |
| 4:5 | De dec mil 5; In il Hab i, 5 |
| 4:10 | In Rom vi, 2 (2:25) |
| 4:11 | In Gen xxvii, 3; xxxix, 5 |
| 4:14 | In Ioh li, 2 |
| 4:15 | Ex in ps cx, 6; In Eph v, 2 (2:15); In Ioh li, 2; In Rom xii, 5 (7:7) |
| 4:16 | In Ioh li, 2 |
| 4:17 | Ex in ps cxli, 1; cxlviii, 2; In Ioh iv, 2; |

| | |
|---|---|
| 4:17 cont | xlii, 2 |
| 4:18 | Ad e q scan x; H dicta p imp 3; In Rom xvii, 2 (10:9) |
| 4:19 | Ad e q scan x (2x); De incomp dei ii, 5; In il Hoc scit 2 (2x); In Rom xvii, 2 (10:9); Non esse desp 4 |
| 4:20 | Ad e q scan x; De incomp dei ii, 5; Ex in ps cxv, 2; In il Hoc scit 2; In Rom xvii, 2 (10:9); Non esse desp 4 |
| 4:21 | Ex in ps cxv, 2; In Col iv, 4 (2:24); In Rom xxvii, 2 (10:9); Non esse desp 4 |
| 4:22 | H dicta p imp 3; Non esse desp 4 |
| 4:23 | Non esse desp 4 |
| 4:24 | H dicta p imp 3; Non esse desp 4 |
| 5:1 | De glor in trib 3 |
| 5:2 | De glor in trib 3 (2x); Ex in ps xli, 6 |
| 5:3 | Ad e q scan xxi; Ad pop Anti i, 23; iv, 4; xvi, 9; xvi, 12; xviii, 10; De Anna v, 3; De glor in trib 1 (2x); 4; E xviii; cii; cvii; ccvii; Ex in ps iv, 4; xli, 6; cxli,1; F Iob 1:20; In dicta in t s Anas 4; In Acta xlii, 4; In 2 Cor i, 3; In Mat xvi, 14; In princ Act ii, 1; Q nemo 5 |
| 5:4 | Ad e q scan xxi; Ad pop Anti i, 23; iv, 4; De glor in trib 4; De res mort 4; 5; E xvii; cvii (2x); ccvii; Ex in ps iv, 4; H dicta in t s Anas 4; In Acta xxxiv, 2 (16:24); In 2 Cor ix, 1; In Mat lxxix, 5; In princ Act ii, 1 |
| 5:5 | Ad pop Anti 1:23; De glor in trib 4; De res mort 4; 5; Ex in ps iv, 4; cxvii, 2; cxlv, 1; H dicta in t s Anas 4; In Ioh xxxvi, 2; In Mat xvi, 13; In Phil iii, 1 (1:20); In 1 Tim xii, 3 (4:10); S Gen ix, 4 |
| 5:7 | In Col ii, 3 (1:12); In Eph xx, 2 (5:26); In Ioh xxvii, 2 |
| 5:8 | Ad e q scan xvii; Adu Iud 3, 4, 8; In Eph xx, 2 (5:26); In il Dom non est 5 |
| 5:9 | Adu Iud 3, 4, 8 |
| 5:10 | Ad e q scan xvii; De ss B et P 6; In Heb xxxii 7; Rom xvi, 5 (9:10); In 2 Thess ii, 1 (1:2) |
| 5:11 | Ex in ps xliii, 6; cx, 1; In Eph i, 2 (1:5); S Gen viii, 2 |
| 5:12 | H in il App 17; In Ioh lxvii, 2 |
| 5:14 | In Heb iv, 2; In 1 Tim ix, 1 (2:15) |
| 5:15 | In Heb iv, 3; S Gen vii, 3 |
| 5:16 | In Rom xx, 1 (15;14) |
| 5:20 | In ascen d n I C 3; In d P Op 1; In Heb i, 1; xvii, 3; In Ioh lvi, 2; In Rom vi, 5 (3:8); |

| | |
|---|---|
| 5:20 cont | xii, 5 (7:7); In 1 Tim iv, 1 (1:16); S Gen vii 3 |
| 5:21 | In 1 Cor ix, 6 |
| 6:1 | In Heb ix, 7; In Rom vi, 5 (3:8) |
| 6:2 | In Heb ix, 7; In Rom vi, 5 (3:8); In Phil iii, 2 (1:21); In Philem iii, 2 (v25) |
| 6:3 | Adu Iud 2, 2, 1; Cat ill x, 8 |
| 6:4 | Adu Iud 2, 2, 1; Cat ill ix, 12; x, 11; In Acta i, 7 (1:5); In Col viii, 1 (3:7); In 1 Cor xl, 2; In Heb ix, 6; In Ioh xxv, 2; In Mat x, 2; In Phil xi, 2 (3:10); In Rom xxiv, 2 (13:14); In 2 Tim v, 1 (2:14) |
| 6:5 | Cat ill x, 10; In Heb ix, 6; In Ioh xxv, 2; In Phil xi, 2 (3:10); In Rom xxi, 5 (7:7); xxiv, 2 (13:14); In 2 Tim v, 1 (2:14) |
| 6:6 | Cat ill vii, 22; ix, 12; x, 8; In Gal ii, 7 (2:20); In Heb ix, 6; In Ioh xxi, 2; In Rom xi, 5 (6:18); In 2 Tim v, 1 (2:14) |
| 6:7 | Adu op iii, 14; De Laz ii, 2; Ex in ps cx, 1; In 1 Cor xi, 5; xxxix, 12; In Mat xxvii, 7; In 1 Tim x, 1 (3:4) |
| 6:8 | Cat ill x, 11 |
| 6:9 | De incomp dei ii, 6; Ex in ps xliv, 4; xlviii, 5; H dicta p imp 3; In Acta lii, 2; In 2 Cor vi, 3; In Heb ix, 6; In Is vii, 7 |
| 6:10 | In 2 Cor vi, 3; In Is vii, 7 |
| 6:14 | Cat ill xi, 29; In Rom xii, 5 (7:7) |
| 6:15 | In Philem iii, 2 (v25) |
| 6:16 | In 2 Cor ii, 8 |
| 6:17 | In Mat xxxviii, 1; In Rom i, 1 (1:2) |
| 6:18 | In Rom i, 1 (1:2) |
| 6:19 | Ex in ps cxi, 1 (2x); In 1 Cor xxiv, 1; In Mat lxviii, 4; In 1 Tim v, 1 (1:19) |
| 6:21 | Ex in ps cxlii, 4; In Eph xviii, 1 (5:8); In Mat xvi, 14; In Phil xiii, 1 (3:21) |
| 7:8 | In Rom x, 4 (6:1) |
| 7:11 | In 1 Cor xli, 6 |
| 7:14 | In 2 Cor vi, 2 |
| 7:15 | In Ioh xl, 2 |
| 7:19 | In Mat xvi, 9 |
| 7:22 | Ex in ps cx, 6 |
| 7:23 | De uir lxxxiv; In Eph xii, 2 (4:22); In Gal v, 5 (5:17) |
| 7:24 | De uir lxxxiv; In Phil iii, 2 (1:21) |
| 8:1 | In Mat xvi, 6 |
| 8:2 | In Gal ii, 7 (2:19); In Ioh xiv, 1; In Mat xvi, 6 |
| 8:3 | De uir lxxxiv; Ex in ps cxxiii, 2; In Gal iii, 3 (3:12); In Heb xiii, 4; xiv, 6; In Ioh lxx, |

| | |
|---|---|
| 8:3 cont | 1; In Mat xvi, 3; In Phil vii, 2 (2:11) (2x) |
| 8:4 | Ex in ps cxxiii, 2; In Mat xvi, 3 |
| 8:6 | In Eph v, 3 (2:16); In Mat xxiii, 8 |
| 8:7 | Ad Theo i, 13; In Gal i, 4 (1:4); In Heb xviii 4; In Mat xxiii, 8; In 1 Tim iii, 4 (1:14) |
| 8:8 | In 1 Cor xlii, 2; In Gal v, 5 (5:17); In Gen xxiv, 2 |
| 8:9 | In 1 Cor xlii, 2; In Gal v, 5 (5:17); In Gen xxii, 3; In 1 Tim xiii, 4 (5:5) |
| 8:10 | In Ioh lxxviii, 3; In Rom xxiv, 2 (13:14) |
| 8:11 | In Ioh lxxviii, 3 |
| 8:13 | In Philem ii, 4 (v16) |
| 8:15 | In Heb iv, 7; In Ioh xiv, 2; lxxviii, 3 |
| 8:16 | De incomp dei v, 5 |
| 8:17 | Ex in ps xlviii, 7; In il Hab iii, 7; In Ioh lxxx, 3; In 2 Tim x, 4 (4:22) |
| 8:18 | Ad pop Anti i, 24; De glor in trib 2; E cxviii ccvii; ccxi; Ex in ps cxlii, 4; In Eph xxiv, 2 (6:22); In Gen xxv, 7; In Heb xxviii, 7; In Mat xxxviii, 3; In 1 Tim iv, 3 (1:17) |
| 8:20 | In diem nat 6 |
| 8:21 | Ad e q scan vii; Ad pop Anti x, 10; Ad Theo i, 11; De glor in trib 2; In diem nat 6; In Gen xxii, 5; In Rom xviii, 6 (11:6) |
| 8:22 | Ad pop Anti v, 5; De glor in trib 2 |
| 8:23 | Ad pop Anti v, 5; De laud s Paul vi; Ex in ps cxiv, 2; cxix, 2; In Mat xix, 7 |
| 8:24 | Ad Theo i, 2; H hab p p Gothus 2; In 1 Cor xxiv, 5; In 2 Cor ix, 2; In Gen xxxvi, 5; In Heb v, 5; In Mat xxxiv, 3; In para 6; In 2 Tim i, 1 (1:2) |
| 8:25 | In Heb v, 5 |
| 8:26 | De D et S ii, 4; Ex in ps xli, 3; cxlii, 6; In Gen xxx, 5; In Heb xxxii, 4; xxxiii, 8 |
| 8:27 | Ex in ps vii, 10; cxxxviii, 1; In 1 Cor vii, 7; xi, 5; In para 8; In Rom xiii, 6 (8:7) |
| 8:28 | Ad pop Anti xvii, 1; Ex in ps cxv, 2; In Acta xxv, 1 (11:19); In Eph ii, 1 (1:11); In Gen lxvii, 5; In il Dil deum 1 (3x) |
| 8:29 | Cat ill xii, 14; F Ier 1:5; In Acta xxx, 2 (14:15); In Col ii, 2 (1:11); In Eph ii, 1 (1:11); In Tit i, 1 (1:5) |
| 8:31 | Ex in ps cxvii, 2; F Prou 20:9; In Acta xv, 3 (7:15); In Rom x, 6 (6:4) |
| 8:32 | Ad e q scan xvii; De sac ii, 1; In Col vi, 2 (2:10); In Eph i, 1 (1:3); In Eut ii, 16; In Gal ii, 7 (2:20); In Gen xxxiv, 5; xxxiv, 6; xlvii, 3; In Heb iv, 3; In Ioh lx, 1; In Mat |

| | |
|---|---|
| 8:32 cont | xxiii, 5; 1, 3; lix, 5; In Rom x, 5 (6:4) |
| 8:33 | In Gen xliv, 5; In Ioh liv, 2 |
| 8:34 | In Col iv, 2 (1:24); In Gen xliv, 5; In Heb xiii, 6; In Ioh liv, 2; In Mat xviii, 5; In Rom xxiv, 2 (13:14) |
| 8:35 | Ad Dem de comp i, 8; De laud s Paul vi; De res mort 4; In Eph vi, 3 (3:7); xxii, 4 (6:13); In Gen lv, 2; In Heb xvi, 8; In Ioh lxxxvii, 3; In Mat xxxviii, 3; In i Thess iv, 4 (3:13) |
| 8:36 | De mut nom i, 5; De res mort 4; Ex in ps xliii, 8; H dicta in t s Anas 3; In Acta xxvi, 2 (12:17) |
| 8:37 | Ad Dem de comp i, 7; De res mort 4; Ex in ps xlvii, 10; In Heb xxviii, 7 |
| 8:38 | Ad Dem de comp i, 8; Adu Iud 1, 7, 9; De laud s Paul 1; In Eph viii, 3 (4:2); xxii, 4 (6:13) In Heb xvi, 8; In Mat iv, 17; in Rom xxxii, 3 (16:24) |
| 8:39 | Ad Dem de comp i, 8; Adu Iud 1, 7, 9; De Anna v, 2; De laud s Paul 1; In 1 Cor xxii, 6; In Eph viii, 3 (4:2); In Heb xvi, 8; In Rom xxxii 3 (16;24) |
| 9:1 | Ad Dem comp i, 8 |
| 9:2 | Ad pop Anti xviii, 8; De cruce et lat i, 5; De laud s Paul ii; De paen i, 1; Q reg 2 |
| 9:3 | Ad Stag a dae iii, 11; De cruce et lat i, 5; ii, 5 (2x); De incomp dei iii, 2; De laud s Paul i; 11; vi; De paen i, 1; De s Bab c Iul 10; De sac iii, 7; iv, 6; Ex in ps xlviii, 5; In Acta vi, 3 (2:36); xxxvii, 1; In Col i, 3 (1:7); xii, 3 (4:18); In 1 Cor xxv, 4; xxxiii, 2; xxxiii, 5; In Eph vii, 4 (3:19); In Gal i, 10 (1:17); In Gen xxix, 2; In Heb Argumentum, 2; In il In fac 10; In Mat xvii, 3; In Phil iv 1 (1:26); In Rom xxxi, 3 (16:16); xxxii, 3 (16:24) (2x); Q reg 2 |
| 9:4 | Ex in ps cxxxiv, 6; F Ier 3:19; In Ioh xiv, 1 (2x); In Rom xiv, 2 (8:14); Q reg 2 |
| 9:5 | De incomp dei v, 2; In 1 Cor xx, 6; In Ioh iv, 3; xxxiii, 1; In Mat iv, 6; In Rom xix, 7 (11:35) |
| 9:6 | Ex in ps xlvi, 4; F Ier 31:34; In Mat vii, 2; ix, 7 |
| 9:7 | Ex in ps xlvi, 4; cxi, 2; In Mat ix, 7 |
| 9:8 | Ex in ps xlvi, 4; cxv, 4; In Mat ix, 7 |
| 9:10 | In Rom xvi, 6 (9:15) |
| 9:11-12 | Ex in ps cxxxviii, 1 |
| 9:13 | De paen vii, 1; Ex in ps cxxxviii, 1; In 2 Tim |

9:13
cont vii, 1 (3:7)
9:14 In 1 Cor xxxi, 7; In Rom xvi, 6 (9:15)
9:15 Ex in ps cxxxvii, 2; cxliii, 1; In 2 Cor ii, 5; In Heb xii, 5
9:16 In Heb xii, 5 (2x); In il Dom non est 2; 5
9:17 Ex in ps cxxxiv, 4; F Ier 50:2
9:18 De incomp dei 11, 5
9:19 De incomp dei ii, 5; In Heb xii, 5
9:20 Ad e q scan ii; Ad Stag a dae i, 7; De incomp dei ii, 4; ii, 5 (2x); Ex in ps vii, 8; cxxxix, 4; cxl, 4; In 1 Cor xxix, 6; In Heb viii, 4; In Mat lxxxi, 2; In Rom ii, 4 (1:13)
9:21 De incomp dei ii, 5
9:25 H in il App 16
9:27 F Ier 31:34; In Rom xviii, 4 (11:5)
9:28 In Eph i, 4 (1:10); In Mat xi, 4
9:29 Ad pop Anti xvii, 13; In Is i, 4; In Rom xviii 4 (11:5)
9:30 In IOh ix, 1 (2x); lix, 1; In Mat x, 2; In Rom xviii, 3 (10:21)
9:31 In Ioh lix, 1; In Rom xviii, 3 (10:21)
9:32 In Ioh ix, 1; In Mat x, 2
10:1 De laud s Paul iii; Ex in ps xlviii, 5; In Acta xxxvii, 1; In 1 Cor xxxiii, 5; In Eph vii 4 (3:19); In il In fac 10; In Rom xvi, 3 (9:6)
10:2 De laud s Paul iii; In Acta xx, 4 (9:25); In Eph vii, 4 (3:19); In Mat vi, 9; In 1 Tim iii, 1 (1:14)
10:3 Ex in ps v, 4; In Gal iii, 5 (3:22); In ioh ix, 1; In Mat x, 2; xxxviii, 1; In Rom vii, 1 (3:19); xvi, 6 (9:15)
10:4 In Mat xvi, 3; In Phil xi, 1 (3:19); In 1 Tim ii, 1 (1:7)
10:5 In Tit i, 1 (1:5)
10:6-7 In Eph v, 2 (2:15); In Ioh xlvii, 3
10:8 In Eph v, 2 (2:15)
10:9 In Eph v, 2 (2:15); In Rom xvi, 9 (9:28)
10:10 Cat ill i, 19; In il Hab i, 2; i, 5; In Rom xxvi, 3 (14:22)
10:12 Cat ill xi, 26; De coem et de cru 2; De dec mil 5 (2x); Ex in ps xliii, 2; cxxxiv, 1; In Ioh ix, 2; In Mat xix, 6; In 2 Tim x, 5 (4:22)
10:13 In Acta v, 1 (2:20); In 1 Cor i, 4
10:14 In Eph iv, 2 (2:8); In Mat xliv, 6
10:15 Ex in ps v, 2; In Gal i, 5 (5:17); In Mat xxxii, 9; In Rom i, 2 (1:2)
10:17 Ex in ps xlviii, 2; In Gal v, 5 (5:17); In 2

| | |
|---|---|
| 10:17 cont | Tim iv, 1 (2:7) |
| 10:18 | In Acta v, 4 (2:20); In Heb xiv, 6; In Mat xxv 3; lxxv, 2; In princ Act iii, 1 |
| 10:20 | De proph obscur i, 6; In Ioh ix, 1; In Is Introduction; vi, 5 |
| 11 (p) | In Eph vi, 1 (2:12) |
| 11:1 | F Ier 31:34; In 1 Cor vii, 5 |
| 11:2 | F Ier 14:19; In 1 Cor vii, 5; In Ioh lx, 1; In Rom xix, 6 (11:25) |
| 11:4 | In Heb xxiii, 1; In Mat xxi, 5 |
| 11:6 | Adu Iud 2, 2, 1 |
| 11:7 | In Ioh ix, 1 |
| 11:8 | In Mat xxxv, 2 |
| 11:11 | Ex in ps cxxxiv, 3; In 1 Cor vii, 5; In Rom xix, 6 (11:25) |
| 11:13 | In Acta xxxvii, 2; In 1 Cor xxix, 4; In Heb Argumentum, 1; In Rom xxix, 1 (15:14) |
| 11:14 | In 1 Cor xxxiii, 5; In Heb Argumentum, 1 |
| 11:16 | Adu Iud 1, 11, 1 |
| 11:17 | Adu Iud 1, 11, 1; In Mat xxv, 6 |
| 11:20 | De laud s Paul iii |
| 11:21 | De laud s Paul iii; In Rom xxix, 1 (15:14) |
| 11:22 | In il Uidi dom v, 3 |
| 11:23 | Adu Iud 7, 2, 6 |
| 11:24 | In Eph vii, 4 (3:19) |
| 11:25 | In Col vi, 2 (2:10); In Mat lxvi, 2; In 1 Tim iii, 2 (1:14) |
| 11:26 | De laud s Paul iii; Ex in ps cviii, 2; F Ier 14:19; In Ioh v, 3; In Mat lxvi, 2 |
| 11:28 | In Mat ix, 7 |
| 11:29 | De dec mil 7; De laud s Paul iii; In Acta i, 6 (1:5) |
| 11:31 | Delaud s Paul iii |
| 11:33 | Ad e q scan ii; Adu Iud 1, 1, 1; Con Anom xi, 2; De diab tent i, 8; De incomp dei i, 5; Ex in ps xli, 4; xlvi, 3; In Eph iv, 2 (2:7); In Eut ii, 9; In Gen iv, 5; In Ioh xxvi, 1; In Mat lxi, 2 |
| 11:34 | Ad e q scan ii; Con Anom xi, 2 (2x); De mut nom iii, 1; De incomp dei v, 3 |
| 11:35 | Ad e q scan ii |
| 11:36 | Ad e q scan ii; Ex in ps viii, 9 |
| 12:1 | Ex in ps xlix, 5; cl, 1; In 2 Cor xxx, 3; In Heb xi, 5; In Ioh lxxiv, 3; lxxxii, 1 |
| 12:2 | Ex in ps vi, 5; In Phil xii, 4 (3:17) |
| 12:3 | In 1 Cor xxix, 1; In Rom xxii, 1 (12:6) |
| 12:4 | In 1 Cor xxix, 1 |
| 12:5 | In Heb vi, 4 |
| 12:6 | De uir xxxvi |

12:8 De elee 4; In 1 Cor xxix, 1
12:10 De D et S iii, 6; In Acta xl, 4; In Gen xxxiii 4
12:12 De Anna ii, 2; De paen i, 2; In Mat xix, 5
12:14 Ad pop Anti vi, 7; In 2 Cor v, 5
12:15 Ad pop Anti xvii, 15; Ad Stag a dae i, 1; De Anna iii, 1; Ex in ps cxl, 5; cxli, 3; In Col xi, 3 (4:11); In 1 Cor xxxiii, 4; In Ioh xxxvii, 3; In Rom vii, 4 (3:31); xix, 8 (11: 35); In s Rom 1; In 2 Tim i, 4 (1:7)
12:16 Ad pop Anti xvii, 15; De mut nom iii, 1; In Gal i, 9 (1:17); In Is v, 7; In Phil vii, 5 (2:11); In Rom xxix, 1 (15:14); In 2 Tim i, 4 (1:7)
12:17 De Anna ii, 6; De sac vi, 9; In Ioh lvii, 3
12:18 De incomp dei i, 7; Ex in ps vii, 5; In Heb xxx, 2; In Phil ii, 1 (1:9); In Rom xxi, 3 (12:10); In 2 Thess v, 3 (3:16)
12:19 Ex in ps ix, 3; In Gen lii, 2; In Ioh li, 3
12:20 De uir xlix; Ex in ps cxxvii, 3; In Acta l, 4 In 1 Cor xliv, 7; In Heb xxv, 4; In il Si esur 1; 5; In Phil iv, 4 (1:30)
12:21 Adu op iii, 14; In 1 Cor xvii, 1; In il Si esur 6
13:1 Ad pop Anti vi, 2; In 2 Cor xv, 4; In Ioh lx, 4
13:2 De D et S i, 6; In Eph xx, 1 (5:24); S Gen iv 3
13:3 In 1 Cor ix, 1; In Phil ii, 5 (1:19); In 1 Tim ii, 2 (1:9); S Gen iv, 2 (2x)
13:4 Ex in ps vii, 11; cxlviii, 4; In 2 Cor xv, 4; In Mat xvi, 13; S Gen iv, 2 (2x)
13:5 In 1 Tim vi, 1 (2:4)
13:7 In Col xi, 1 (4:6); In Eph xix, 1 (5:17); In Mat lxx, 2
13:8 E xxii; In Gen xxxiii, 1; In il Dil deum 1; In Phil ii, 1 (1:9)
13:9 De laud s Paul iii
13:10 De sac ii, 5; De san pent ii, 3; In Eph ix, 4 (4:3); In Heb xix, 4; In Ioh lxxvii, 1; In princ Act ii, 3; In 2 Tim vii, 3 (3:7)
13:11 De uir lxxiii; In 2 Cor xii, 1; In Heb i, 2; xix, 3; xxi, 3
13:12 In Hel 1; In Ioh lvi, 3; In Mat x, 6
13:13 In Ioh v, 4; In Rom iii, 3 (1:17)
13:14 In Acta xxvii, 3 (13:3); In Col x, 5 (4:4); In 1Cor xiii, 7; In Gen x, 3; In Heb vii, 11; xiii, 11; xxix, 7; In Ioh i, 2; In Phil ix, 5 (2:30); In Rom xiv, 1 (8:13)

| | |
|---|---|
| 14:1 | In 2 Cor xxix, 2; In Rom Argumentum, 2; In 1 Thess x, 2 (5:14); In Tit iii, 2 (1:14) |
| 14:2 | In 2 Cor xxix, 2; In Rom Argumentum, 2 |
| 14:4 | De uir lxxviii; Ex in ps cxxxiv, 1; In Mat xxiii, 1; In Rom xxix, 1 (15:14) |
| 14:6 | In Gen x, 2 |
| 14:7 | Ex in ps xi, 2 |
| 14:8 | In Philem ii, 4 (v16) |
| 14:9 | In Acta xxxviii, 4; In Mat lxx, 2 |
| 14:10 | Ad Theo ii, 5; De uir lxxviii; Cat ill ix, 15; In Acta xxxviii, 4; In 1 Cor xi, 3; xx, 1; In Gen xlii, 3; In Heb xxiii, 9; In Mat xxiii, 1; In Rom xiii, 8 (8:11); xxix, 1 (15:14); In 2 Tim ii, 3 (1:12); In Tit v, 3 (2:1); S Gen vii 4 |
| 14:15 | Ad pop Anti xii, 13; De prof eua 5 |
| 14:20 | Cat ill ix, 15; Q reg 5 |
| 14:21 | Con e q sub 4; In 1 Cor xiii, 6 |
| 15:1 | Adu op iii, 2 |
| 15:2 | In Mat lxxvii, 5 |
| 15:3 | De b Phil 2; Ex in ps cxiii, 2; In 1 Cor xxiv, 6; In Ioh xv, 3; In Mat lxxvii, 5; In Rom xxviii, 1 (15:8) |
| 15:4 | In Heb viii, 9; In Ioh xxx, 2; xxxvii, 1; In Rom xxviii, 3 (15:13); In 1 Tim xiii, 1 (4:16) |
| 15:8 | In 1 Cor viii, 5 |
| 15:9 | In Eph v, 2 (2:15); In Mat lxix, 2; In Rom i, 3 (1:5) |
| 15:12 | In Mat vii, 2; x, 3 |
| 15:13 | Ex in ps cxiii, 5 |
| 15:14 | De mut nom i, 2; Ex in ps cxlii, 4; In Gen iv, 6; In Ioh ii, 11; In Rom Argumentum, 2 |
| 15:15 | In Gen xxxii, 1; In Rom Argumentum, 2; x, 4 (6:1) |
| 15:16 | In Rom Argumentum, 2 |
| 15:18 | In Eph vi, 3 (3:7) |
| 15:19 | De Eleaz 5; In 1 Cor vi, 8; xiii, 6; In Rom xviii, 5 (11:6); In 2 Tim ix, 2 (4:7) |
| 15:20 | In Acta xxviii, 2 (13:15) |
| 15:21 | In 1 Cor vii, 6 |
| 15:22 | In Acta lv, 2; In 1 Thess iii, 3 (2:18) |
| 15:23 | De Eleaz 5; In Acta lv, 2; In 1 Thess iii, 3 (2:18) |
| 15:23 | De Eleaz 5; In Acta lv, 2; In 1 Thess iii, 3 (2:18) |
| 15:25 | De laud s Paul iv; In Acta lv, 3; In 1 Cor xliii, 1; In Gal ii, 4 (2:10) (2x); ii, 6 (2:15); In Heb Argumentum, 2; In Rom Argumentum, 1 |
| 15:26 | In Gal ii, 6 (2:15); In Phil iv, 3 (1:30) |

| | |
|---|---|
| 15:27 | In Gal ii, 6 (2;15); In Phil i, 2 (1:5) |
| 15:29 | In Acta lv, 3 |
| 15:30 | De proph obscur ii, 4; In 2 Cor xxx, 3 (2x) |
| 15:31 | De proph obscur ii, 4 |
| 15:32 | In Acta lv, 3 |
| 16 (p) | In Ioh lxi, 4 |
| 16:1 | De laud s Paul iii; De prof eua 6; De stud p 4; H Dicta p r m 3; In Phil xiii, 3 (4:3) |
| 16:2 | De laud s Paul iii; De prof eua 6; In 2 Cor xxi, 1; In Rom xxxi, 3 (16:16) |
| 16:3 | De prof eua 6; De stud p 4; In Acta xl, 2; In il Sal P et A i, 1 (2x); ii, 1; ii, 4 |
| 16:4 | De prof eua 6; Ex in ps xlvi, 3; In 2 Cor xii 4; In il Sal P et A ii, 4; In Mat liii, 7 |
| 16:7 | In 1 Cor xliv, 3 |
| 16:12 | In il Sal P et A i, 3 |
| 16:18 | In Mat xxiii, 8 |
| 16:19 | In Rom xxix, 1 (15:15) |
| 16:20 | Ex in ps cxiii, 5; In 2 Cor v, 5; In Eph x, 1 (4:4); xxii, 4 (6:13); xxii, 5 (6:13); S Gen v, 3 |
| 16:22 | In Gal vi, 3 (6:12) |
| 16:25 | In Gal i, 6 (1:7) |

## 1 Corinthians

| | |
|---|---|
| 1:1 | De mut nom i, 6;lv, 1; iv, 3; In 1 Thess i, 1 (1:2) |
| 1:4 | De mut nom iv, 5; De paen vii, 3; In 2 Cor ii, 6; In Eph iii, 1 (1:20); In Heb ii, 8 |
| 1:5 | De laud s Paul iv; De mut nom iv, 5; De paen vii, 3; In 1 Cor ii, 3; In Heb ii, 8 |
| 1:6 | In 1 Cor ii, 3; In Heb ii, 8 |
| 1:7 | De laud s Paul iv; In 1 Cor ii, 4; In Heb ii, 8 |
| 1:8 | In 1 Cor ii, 7 |
| 1:9 | Ex in ps viii, 7; viii, 9; In 1 Cor ii, 8; In 2 Cor xxx, 3; In Ioh v, 3; xlv, 3; In Mat lix 3 |
| 1:10 | Adu Iud 3, 2, 3; in d P Nolo 1; In 1 Thess iv, 3 (3:10) |
| 1:11 | In 1 Cor iii, 3 |
| 1:12 | Adu Iud 3, 2, 4; De mut nom iv, 6; In 1 Cor iii, 4 |
| 1:13 | Adu Iud 3, 2, 4; In 2 Cor iii, 1 |
| 1:14 | Adu op ii, 2; In Acta xxxix, 2; In 1 Cor iii, 6; In 2 Cor iii, 1 |
| 1:15-16 | In 1 Cor iii, 6 |

1:17 De Eleaz 4; De mut nom iv, 5; In Acta xxxvii, 2; In 1 Cor iii, 6; In 2 Cor iii, 1; xxiii, 3; In Heb Argumentum, 2
1:18 De diab tent ii, 3; De Eleaz 4; In 1 Cor v, 2; In 2 Cor xxix, 3
1:19 De mut nom iv, 5
1:20 De Eleaz 4 (4x); In 1 Cor iv, 4
1:21 Ex in ps xlix, 2; In 1 Cor iv, 4
1:22 De Eleaz 4; De laud s Paul iv; In 1 Cor iv, 5; In il Pater s p 2
1:23 Ad e q scan xv; De diab tent ii, 3; De Eleaz 4; De laud s Paul iv; Ex in ps xlix, 9; In Acta xxxvii, 2; In 1 Cor iv, 5; In 2 Cor xxix 3
1:24 Ad e q scan xv; De Eleaz 4; In 1 Cor iv, 5; In 2 Cor xxix, 3; In Ioh v, 1
1:25 Cat ill viii, 5; De Eleaz 4; In 1 Cor iv, 6; In 2 Cor xxix, 3; In Eph xxx, 1 (1:20); In Rom iii, 3 (1:23)
1:26 De laud s Paul iv
1:27 De laud s Paul iv; De mut nom iv, 5; In Ioh xx, 1
1:28 De laud s Paul iv
1:29 In 1 Cor v, 3
1:30 In 1 Cor v, 4; xx, 5; In Mat i, 4
2:1 De Laz iii, 3; De mut nom iv, 5; In 2 Cor xxiii, 3
2:2 De uir xlix
2:3 De laud s Paul iv; De sac iii, 7; In 1 Cor iii, 5; vi, 2; xxiv, 1; In 1 Thess ii, 2 (2:2)
2:4 De Laz iii, 3; In Acta xi, 3 (4:33); In Cor vi 3
2:5 In 1 Cor vi, 3; In 2 Cor iii, 1
2:6 De Laz iii, 3
2:7 Ad e q scan iii
2:8 Ad e q scan iii; F Ier 14:14; In 1 Cor vii, 5
2:9 Ad e q scan iii; Ad pop Anti ii, 3; v, 5; Ad Theo i, 13; Cat ill viii, 11; ix, 2; De incomp dei i, 5; De paen iii, 4; De s Bar 2; E xcvi; Ex in ps iv, 10; v, 1; xli, 4; cxix, 3; cxxvii 3; F Ier 14:14; F Prou 19:8; In 1 Cor vii, 6; In 2 Cor i, 4; ii, 7; iii, 4; In Eut ii, 2; In Gen xvii, 10; xxvii, 2; xxxvi, 5; In Heb ii, 1; vi, 11; xxiii, 6; xxviii, 8; In il Hab i, 9; ii, 7; In il Ne tim i, 4; ii, 4; In Is vii, 4; In Mat xi, 7; liv, 9; In 1 Tim ii, 2 (1:11); xv, 4 (5:20); S Gen i, 4; vii, 5
2:10 Ad e q scan iii; De san pent ii, 2 (2x); Ex in ps cxlii, 6; cxliii, 2; In Acta ii, 2 (1:8); In 1 Cor vii, 7; In Eph iii, 1 (1:22); In Heb

| | |
|---|---|
| 2:10 cont | ii, 2; In Ioh i, 3; In Mat lxxvii, 1 |
| 2:11 | Ad e q scan iii; De incomp dei v, 1; v, 3; De proph obscur ii, 9; De sac iii, 14; De san pent ii, 2; Ex in ps xliv, 3; In Acta xxxiv, 1 (16:23); In 1 Cor xxxiv, 4; In Heb ii, 2; xvii 8; In Ioh xxiii, 1; lxxviii, 2; In Mat xl, 2 |
| 2:12 | In Heb ii, 2 |
| 2:13 | F Prou 1:6 |
| 2:14 | Ad Stel de comp ii, 2; De uir xiv; F Prou 1: 6; In Acta xxxix, 2; In 1 Cor vii, 9; In 2 Cor xxix, 3; In Eph iii, 1 (1:22); v, 4 (2:16); In Heb xxxiv, 7; In Ioh xxiv, 3; In Mat xxiii, 3; liv, 7; In Rom xiii, 8 (8:9) |
| 2:15 | Ad pop Anti x, 4 |
| 2:16 | In 1 Cor vii, 7; In 2 Cor viii, 2 |
| 3:1 | De incomp dei v, 4; Ex in ps iv, 7; xliii, 5; xliv, 8; In Acta lv, 3; In 1 Cor Argumentum, 2; Argumentum, 3; ii, 4; In Ioh xxx, 2; In Is vi, 6 |
| 3:2 | De uir xlix; Ex in ps iv, 7; xliii, 5; In 1 Cor Argumentum, 2; In Eph vi, 2 (3:4); ix, 1 (4:3); In Heb viii, 6; In Ioh xxv, 3; xxx, 2 |
| 3:3 | De mut nom iv, 6; Ex in ps xliii, 5; In 1 Cor viii, 5; In Eph ix, 3 (4:3); In Heb viii, 5; In Is vi, 6; In Ioh xlviii, 3; liv, 3 |
| 3:4 | In 1 Cor viii, 5 |
| 3:5 | In 1 Cor viii, 5; In Mat lxxii, 3 |
| 3:6 | Ad pop Anti iii, 7; De mut nom iv, 5; In 1 Cor v, 4; viii, 5; In Eph xi, 2 (4:12); xi, 5 (4: 16); In Is iii, 3; In Rom xi, 5 (6:18); In 1 Tim x, 2 (3:6) |
| 3:7 | In 1 Cor viii, 6; In 2 Cor xv, 5; xxvii, 4; In Eph xi, 2 (4:12); In Mat xxi, 3; In Rom xi, 5 (6:18) |
| 3:8 | De pet mat 3; E iii, 8; iii, 9; clxxxii; In 1 Cor viii, 6; In Eph xi, 2 (4:12); In Ioh xiii 1; In Rom xi, 5 (6:18) |
| 3:9 | In Cor viii, 6 x, 4; In 2 Cor xii, 1; In Phil iv, 1 (1:26) |
| 3:10 | In Col iii, 2 (1:18); In 1 Cor viii, 6; ix, 5; In Eph vi, 2 (2:22); In Heb ix, 2; In princ Act ii, 2 |
| 3:11 | In 1 Cor viii, 7; In Eph vi, 1 (2:22); vi, 2 (2:22); In Eut ii, 6; In il Pater m 2 |
| 3:12 | De pet mat 5; Ex in ps xliv, 12; xlviii, 10; H in il App 7; In 1 Cor ix, 5; In Eut ii, 15; In Heb ix, 2; In 1 Tim xvii, 1 (6:7) |
| 3:13 | Con Iud et gen 8; De paen vi, 3; Ex in ps |

| | |
|---|---|
| 3:13 cont | cxlii, 4; H in il App 7; In 1 Cor xxx, 9; In Phil vi, 6 (2:8) |
| 3:14 | De proph obscur ii, 5 |
| 3:15 | H in il App 7 |
| 3:16 | Ad Theo i, 1; Cat ill xi, 34; In 1 Cor ix, 7; In diem nat 6; In Rom xiii, 8 (8:9) |
| 3:17 | Ad Theo i, 1; In 1 Cor ix, 7; In diem nat 7; In il Uidi dom iii, 3 |
| 3:18 | De laud s Paul iv; De mut nom iv, 5; In 1 Cor ix, 8; xxvi, 7; In Eph xv, 2 (4:31); In Is v, 7; In Mat xxxviii, 1 |
| 3:19 | De mut nom iv, 5 (2x); De prof eua 10 |
| 3:20 | In 1 Cor x, 3 |
| 3:21 | In 1 Cor x, 4; In Tit i, 1 (1:5) |
| 3:22 | In 1 Cor viii, 2; x, 4; xxvi, 2; In Heb iii, 4; In Ioh xix, 3; lxxv, 2; lxxxvi, 4 |
| 4:1 | De reg 17; In 1 Cor x, 5 |
| 4:2 | In 1 Cor x, 5 |
| 4:3 | In 1 Cor Argumentum, 3; In Gal i, 7 (1:10); In Phil v, 3 (2:4); In 2 Tim ii, 3 (1:12) |
| 4:4 | Ad Stel de comp ii, 5; De incomp dei v, 6; De Laz vi, 9; Ex in ps vi, 1; xlix, 7; cxxix, 2; In 1 Cor xxxix, 5; In Eph xxii, 5 (6:13); In Mat vi, 9; In Phil v, 3 (2:4); In Philem ii, 3 (v16) |
| 4:5 | Ad Stag a dae i, 9; De Anna v, 3; De dec mil 5; De proph obscur ii, 9; In Ioh xxxiv, 2; In Mat xxiii, 1 (2x) |
| 4:6 | De mut nom iv, 6; H hab p p ?othus 5; In 1 Cor Argumentum, 3; In Phil iii, 2 (1:20); In Rom xxxi, 3 (16:16); Pec frat 4 |
| 4:7 | Ad e q scan iii; Cat ill ix, 11; De mut nom iv, 6; In 1 Cor x, 5; xii, 3; In 2 Cor v, 3; In Eph ix, 2 (4:3); In Heb xxiii, 9; In 1 Tim xvii, 1 (6:7); In 2 Tim vi, 1 (2:21) |
| 4:8 | In 1 Cor Argumentum, 2; xii, 4; In 2 Cor xxiii 2; In s Rom 1 |
| 4:9 | Cat ill iii, 8; In 1 Cor xii, 5 |
| 4:10 | De incomp dei ii, 2; In 1 Cor xii., 6; xvi, 11; In 2 Cor xxiii, 2; In Heb xxviii, 6 |
| 4:11 | Ad Dem de comp i, 7; Ad pop Anti i, 22; De laud s Paul iv; De stud p 4; In 1 Cor vi, 8; xii, 2; xxi, 3; xxi, 7; In Heb xxviii, 5; In il Sal P et A ii, 1; In Mat xc, 4; In para 8; In s Luc 2 |
| 4:12 | Ad Dem de comp i, 7; Cat ill viii, 3; De laud s Paul vi; In Acta xlviii, 2; In Heb xxviii, 3; In il Sal P et A ii, 1; In 1 Tim vi, 2 (2: 4); x, 3 (3:7) |
| 4:13 | Ad Dem de comp i, 7; In Acta viii, 3 (3:12); |

| | |
|---|---|
| 4:13 cont | In Heb xxviii, 7; In 1 Tim vi, 2 (2:4) |
| 4:14 | In 1 Cor xiii, 3 |
| 4:15 | De mut nom iv, 5; De paen i, 1; In 1 Cor xiii, 4; In 2 Cor iv, 3; In 1 Thess i, 1 (1:2) |
| 4:16 | De b Phil 2; In 1 Cor xiii, 5; In princ Act iv, 4; In Rom xxxii, 4 (16:24) |
| 4:17 | Ad pop Anti i, 8; xvi, 11; In 1 Cor xxxvii, 2; xliv, 1; In 2 Cor i, 2; In Rom xxx, 1 (15; 27); In 1 Tim Argumentum, 1 |
| 4:18 | Adu Iud 3, 2, 2; In 1 Cor ii, 7; xiv, 1; xiv, 1; xxviii, 3; In 2 Cor xxi, 1; In Rom xxxi, 3 (16:16) |
| 4:19 | In Col i, 1 (1:2); In 1 Cor xiv, 2; xliii, 3; In 2 Cor i, 1; xxi, 1 |
| 4:20 | In 1 Cor xiv, 1 |
| 4:21 | Ex in ps xiv 1, 3; cix, 3; In 1 Cor ii, 7; xiv, 4; In 2 Cor xxi, 1; In Gal i, 1 (1:3); In 1 Tim v, 2 (1:20) |
| 5 (p) | De res mort 2 |
| 5:1 | Adu Iud 3, 2, 2; 8, 3, 6; De Laz vi, 4; De paen i, 2; E ii, 2 (2x); In 1 Cor xxxvi, 7; In Eph xvii, 1 (5:4) |
| 5:2 | Ad Stag a dae iii, 14; Adu Iud 8, 3, 6; De mut nom iv, 6; De paen i, 2 (3x); De res mort 6 (3x); E ii, 2; Ex in ps ix, 10; In 1 Cor Argumentum, 2; In 2 Cor xv, 2; In Ioh lvii, 3; In Rom v, 1 (1:30); xxxii, 4 (16:24) |
| 5:3 | Adu Iud 8, 3, 6; De res mort 6; In Col i, 1 (1:2); In 1 Cor xv, 3; In 2 Cor iv, 5; In Rom xxxii, 3 (16;24) |
| 5:4 | Adu Iud 8, 3, 6; De res mort 6 (3x); In Rom xxxii, 3 (16:24); In 1 Tim v, 2 (1:20) |
| 5:5 | Ad Stag a dae i, 3; Ad Theo i, 8; Adu Iud 8, 3, 6; De dec mil 5; De diab tent ii, 4 (2x); De incomp dei v, 5; De laud s Paul vi; De Laz iii, 5; De mut nom iii, 1; E iv, 3; Ex in ps cxli, 1; In 2 Cor xv, 3; In Heb v, 6; In il Hab iii, 7; In Ioh xxxviii, 1; In Mat ix, 2; In princ Act iii, 5; In Rom xiii, 6 (8:7); In 1 Tim v, 2 (1:20) |
| 5:6 | De paen i, 2; Ex in ps xi, 1; In 1 Cor xv, 5; In 2 Cor iv, 5 (2x); xv, 3; In Heb xxxi, 1; In Mat xli, 5 |
| 5:7 | Adu Iud 3, 4, 3; In 1 Cor xv, 5; In Eph xxiii, 2 (6:14) |
| 5:8 | Adu Iud 3, 3, 9; De cruce et lat i, 1; ii, 1; De san pent 1 (2x); H in mar 1; In kal 2; In Mat xxxix, 3 |

5:11 E ii, 2; In Heb xxv, 7; In Mat xxx, 2; In 2 Thess v, 3 (3:18); In 1 Tim vii, 1 (2:4); In Tit i, 2 (1:5)
5:12 Adu op ii, 2; De fato et pr ii; In Col xi, 2 (4:11); In 1 Cor xvi, 2; xxv, 2; In 2 Cor xxix, 3; In Mat lx, 1
5:13 In Ioh lvii, 3; In Mat iv, 14
6:1 Ad pop Anti xvi, 1; Adu Iud 3, 2, 2; In 1 Cor xvi, 4; In Phil v, 3 (2:4)
6:2 De s Dros 3; In 1 Cor xi, 2
6:3 De laud s Paul v; De s Dros 3; In 1 Cor xi, 3 xvi, 5; In Mat lxxix, 2; In Rom xvii, 5 (10: 13); xxxi, 5 (16:16); xxxii, 4 (16:24)
6:4 In 1 Cor xvi, 6
6:5 De uir lxviii; In Cor x, 4; xvi, 6
6:6 In 1 Cor x, 4; xvi, 6
6:7 Ex in ps vii, 14; cxxxix, 2; In 1 Cor xvi, 7; xxvi, 1; In 2 Cor xxiii, 8; In Gen xxxii, 2; In Heb xx, 7; xxv, 5; In Ioh xvi, 1; xli, 2; In Mat xvi, 9; In 1 Thess x, 3 (5:18)
6:8 In 1 Cor xvi, 7; xxvi, 1; In Gen xxxiii, 2
6:9 Ad Dem de comp i, 2; Cat ill v, 11; ix, 17; De Eleaz 5; De res d n I C 2; De san pent i, 3; ii, 1; In 1 Cor ix, 1; xvi, 8; xxxvii, 3; In Eph iv, 1 (2:3); In Heb xxx, 3; In Mat xvi 11; lvii, 6; In Tit v, 4 (3:6)
6:10 Ad Dem de comp i, 2; Cat ill v, 11; ix, 17; De Eleaz 5; De res d n I C 2; De san pent i, 3; ii, 1; H in mar 1; In 1 Cor xvi, 8; xxxvii 3; In Heb xxx, 3; In Ioh lxv, 3; In Mat xvi, 11; lvii, 6; In 1 Tim vi, 2 (2:4); In Tit v, 4 (3:6)
6:11 Cat ill ix, 17; De Eleaz 5; De san pent i, 3 (2x); ii, 1 (2x); Ex in ps xli, 3; In 1 Cor xvi, 9; In 2 Cor xxx, 3; In Gen i, 2; In Ioh lxxviii, 3; In Mat x, 2
6:12 In Acta v, 4 (2:20)
6:13 In 1 Cor xxiii, 2; In Phil ix, 5 (2:30)
6:14 Ex in ps xliv, 9; In 1 Cor xvii, 2
6:15 De uir xxv; Ex in ps xliii, 9; In Ioh lxiii, 3; In Mat xlviii, 8; In Rom vi, 6 (3:8)
6:16 De Anna iii, 4; In 2 Cor xv, 3; xxix, 1
6:17 In 1 Cor xviii, 1; In Eph xx, 4 (5:32); xx, 5 (5:33)
6:18 Ex in ps xliii, 9; In 1 Cor xviii, 2; In 2 Cor xv, 3; In Rom iv, 3 (1:27)
6:19 Ad Theo i, 1; Cat ill xi, 34; De Anna iii, 4; De diab tent iii, 1; Ex in ps xi, 2; xi, 3; In 1 Cor x, 6; xviii, 3; In Rom xii, 3 (7:3); xiv, 1 (8:13)

6:20 Con e q sub 4; Ex in ps cxii, 1; cxlv, 1; In 1 Cor x, 6; xxvi, 1; In Rom xii, 3 (7:3); In 1 Tim iv, 3 (1:17) (2x)

7:1 De lib rep 1; De uir xii; xxiv; xxix; Ex in ps cxiii, 5; In 1 Cor Argumentum, 3; In il Prop 2; In Rom Argumentum, 2

7:2 De lib rep 1; De uir xix; xxvii; xxviii; xxix; In 1 Cor xix, 2; In 2 Cor xxiii, 8; In il Prop 1; 2; 3; 5 (2x); In Mat vii, 8

7:4 Ad Theo ii, 3; De uir xxviii (2x); xxix (2x); In 1 Cor xxxiii, 3; In Eph xx, 9 (5:33); In il Prop 4 (2x); 5 (2x); In Mat vii, 8

7:5 De uir xix; xxix; xxxiv (2x); xl; lxxv; Ex in ps cxlv, 4; In 1 Cor xix, 3; In 2 Cor xxiii, 8; In Gal ii, 2 (2:4); In Gen xxx, 5; In il Uid elig 4 (2x); In Mat lxxxvi, 4; In 1 Thess v, 3 (4:8); In 1 Tim xiv, 2 (5:10); In Tit v, 2 (2:14)

7:6 De n iter 3; De uir xxxiv; In Gal ii, 2 (2:4); In il Uid elig 4

7:7 De n iter 3; De uir xxxiv; xxxvi (2x); xli; Ex in ps iv, 2; cxiii, 5; In Eph i, 2 (1:5); In Gal ii, 2 (2:4); In Heb xvi, 10; xviii, 2; In il Dom non est 2; In Rom xxi, 1 (12:5); In 1 Tim x, 2 (3:7)

7:8 De uir xxxvi; xxxix; xli; In 1 Cor xix, 3; In il Dom non est 2

7:9 De uir xix; xxxviii; xxxix (2x); In 1 Cor xix, 3; In 2 Cor xxiii, 8

7:10 De uir xii; xxxix; In 1 Cor xix, 4; In Mat lxxxvi, 4

7:11 De uir xl; xli; In 1 Cor xix, 4; In Eph vi, 4 (3:7)

7:12 De dec mil 7; De uir xii; xli; In 1 Cor xix, 4; In 2 Cor xxx, 4; In Gen xxvi, 2

7:13 In Gen xxvi, 2; In il Sal P et A i, 3; In Ioh lxiii, 3; In Is iii, 6; S Gen v, 1

7:14 In 2 Cor xvi, 1; In Heb x, 7; In il Sal P et A i, 3

7:15 In 1 Cor xix, 4; In 2 Cor xvi, 1; In Eph xx, 5 (5:33); In il Sal P et A i, 3; In Mat lxiv, 2; In Rom xxii, 2 (12:18)

7:16 De uir xlvii; In 1 Cor xix, 4; In 2 Cor xvi, 1; In Gen xvii, 9; xxvi, 2; In il Sal P et A i, 3; In Ioh lxi, 4; lxix, 3; In Rom xxxi, 1 (16:6); Non esse desp 7; S Gen v, 1

7:17 In 1 Cor xix, 5; In Rom xxx, 1 (15:27)

7:19 In Rom ii, 6 (1:16)

7:21 In Philem Argumentum; S Gen v, 1

7:22 F in epis cath 1 Peter 1:21; S Gen v, 1

7:23 Cat ill xii, 50; Con e q sub 10; De uir xli; Ex in ps xlviii, 5; In 1 Cor xvii, 1; xix, 5; In Heb xxv, 8; In Mat liv, 7; In Rom xii, 3 (7:3); xiv, 1 (8:13)

7:25 Adu op iii, 14; De Chris prec 3; De paen vi, 3; De uir ii; xxxiv; xli; lxxv; In 1 Cor xix, 7; In 2 Cor xxiii, 8; In Mat lxxviii, 1

7:26 De lib rep 4; De uir xlii; In Eph xxi, 2 (6:4) In Mat xv, 5

7:27 De uir xlvii; In 1 Cor xix, 7

7:28 Ad Theo ii, 5; De lib rep 4; De uir xxxix; xlvii; lxxv (2x); Ex in ps xliv, 12; cxxvii, 3; In 1 Cor xix, 7; xxxvi, 3; In Ioh lxxx, 3; In Mat xv, 5; In 2 Tim vii, 4 (3:7)

7:29 De uir lxxii; lxxiii; In Heb ii, 2; vii, 11; ix, 3; In Mat vii, 8; In Rom xxiv, 1 (13:11); In 1 Tim x, 1 (3:4)

7:30 De uir lxxv; In Mat lxxiv, 4

7:31 De uir lxxiii; Ex in ps cix, 6; In Gen xliii, 1; xxxv, 7; xliv, 6; In Heb ii, 2; vii, 11; In Mat vii, 8; lxx, 2; lxxiv, 4 (2x); In Rom xiv, 6 (8:23); xx, 2 (12:2)

7:32 De uir xxxiv; lxxiii; In 1 Cor xxxvi, 3; In Mat xv, 5; xxii, 5; Q reg 9

7:33 De uir xiv; xxxiv; lxxv (2x); In 1 Tim x, 3 (3:4)

7:34 Con e q sub 6; De paen iv, 3 (2x); De uir lxxv; E ii, 4; In il Uid elig 15; In Ioh xiv, 2; In Mat lxxviii, 2; In 1 Tim xv, 1 (5:15); Qual duc 7

7:35 Ad Theo ii, 5; De n iter 3; De uir xi; lxxv; lxxvi (2x); In 1 Cor xix, 7; In 2 Cor xxiii, 8; In il Uid elig 15; In Mat lxxviii, 2; In 1 Tim xiv, 2 (5:10); xv, 1 (5:15); Q reg 6

7:36 De lib rep 4; De uir lxxviii; In 1 Cor xix, 7

7:37 De uir lxxviii

7:38 De ss B et P 3; De uir lxxviii

7:39 De lib rep 1; 3 (2x); 4; De n iter 1; De uir xxix; In il Uid elig 5

7:40 Ad uid iun 2; Adu Iud 8, 8, 2; De lib rep 1; 3; 4; De n iter 1 (2x); 6; De uir xii; In Gal ii, 1 (2:2); In il Uid elig 5; In 1 Thess viii, 1 (4:17); In 2 Tim vii, 4 (3:7)

8:1 De laud s Paul v; In Mat lxiv, 5

8:2 Ad e q scan ii; De incomp dei ii, 6; De laud s Paul v; In 1 Cor xx, 3; In Mat lxiv, 5; In 1 Thess vii, 3 (4:15)

8:3 Ex in ps cxliii, 2; In 1 Cor xx, 3; In Mat lxiv, 5

8:4 De incomp dei v, 3; In 1 Cor xx, 4
8:5 De incomp dei v, 3; Ex in ps xlix, 1 (2x); In 1 Cor xx, 5
8:6 De incomp dei v, 1; De s h Phoc 3; In Gal iii, 5 (3:20); In Gen xiv, 2; In Heb iv, 5; In 1 Tim vii, 1 (2:5); In 2 Tim iii, 1 (1:18)
8:7 In 1 Cor xx, 7
8:8 In 1 Cor xx, 9; xxiii, 2
8:9 In Col xii, 2 (4:18); In 1 Cor xx, 10; In princ Act iii, 2
8:10 Adu Iud 1, 5, 7; Cat ill vi, 15; In 1 Cor xx, 10
8:11 Cat ill vi, 20; In 1 Cor xx, 10; In Gen xliii, 4; In Heb xxxi, 1
8:12 De sac vi, 1; In 1 Cor xx, 10; In 2 Cor xvii, 2; In Gen vii, 2; Q reg 5
8:13 Adu op iii, 2; Con e q sub 4; Ex in ps xlix, 9; In Acta xlvi, 3; In 1 Cor xiii, 6; xx, 11; In 2 Cor xvii, 2; In Gen vii, 2
9:1 In Col xii, 3 (4:18)
9:2 De uir xlii; In 1 Cor Argumentum, 3; xxi, 3; In 2 Cor iv, 3
9:3-5 In 1 Cor xxi, 3
9:6 In 1 Cor xxi, 3; In il In fac 15; In Ioh lxxx, 2
9:7 In 1 Cor xxi, 4; In Gal iii, 4 (3:15); In Mat xxx, 3
9:8 In 1 Cor xxi, 5
9:9 In 1 Cor xx, 5; In 2 Cor xv, 3; In Mat xxx, 3; In 1 Tim iii, 2 (1:14)
9:11 In 1 Cor xxi, 6; In 2 Cor xx, 1; In Gal vi, 6 (6:6); In Phil xv, 2 (4:15)
9:12 Ex in ps xliii, 2; In 1 Cor xxi, 6; In 2 Cor xxiv, 2
9:13 In 1 Cor xliii, 3; In 1 Thess iii, 1 (2:12)
9:14 Ex in ps vii, 4; In Acta xxxvii, 2; In 1 Cor xxii, 1; In Gal vi, 2 (6:6); In Mat xxx, 3; In 1 Thess iii, 1 (2:12)
9:15 Ex in ps vii, 4; In 1 Cor xxii, 2; xxxii, 14; In 2 Cor xvii, 2; xxiii, 5; xxvii, 2; In Heb xxviii, 7; In Phil xv, 1 (4:14); Q reg 4
9:16 De paen vi, 3; Ex in ps vii, 4; In 1 Cor xxii 3; In Eph xi, 1 (4:7); In il Sal P et A i, 5; In Rom ii, 5 (1:14); In 1 Tim i, 1 (1:2); In Tit i, 2 (1:5)
9:17 Ex in ps vii, 4; In Col xii, 2 (4:18); In 1 Cor xxii, 3; In Ioh ix, 1; S cum pres 3
9:18 De laud s Paul 1; De paen vi, 3; Ex in ps vii 4; In 1 Cor xxii, 3; xxxii, 14; In 2 Cor

9:18 cont xxiii, 6; xxvii, 2; In il Sal P et A i, 5; In Ioh xliv, 1

9:19 In 1 Cor xxii, 4; In princ Act iv, 4

9:20 Adu Iud 5, 3, 2; De incomp dei ii, 7; De laud s Paul iii; In 1 Cor xxii, 5; In princ Act ii, 4; iv, 4; In Tit ii, 1 (1:14)

9:21 Ad pop Anti xvi, 9; Adu Iud 5, 3, 2; De incomp dei ii, 7; De laud s Paul iii; In Acta xlvii, 1; In 1 Cor xxii, 5; In princ Act i, 3 iv, 4; In Tit iii, 1 (1:14)

9:22 De laud s Paul iii; In Acta xliii, 2; In 1 Cor xxii, 5; In il In fac 3

9:23 In 1 Cor xxii, 5

9:24 In 1 Cor xxx, 1

9:25 De Laz iii, 9; De uir vii; Ex in ps v, 6; H in san pascha 5; In 1 Cor xxiii, 1

9:26 Ad pop Anti iii, 8; De uir i; In 1 Cor xxiii, 2; In Eph vi, 3 (3:7); In Gal ii, 1 (2:2); In Heb v, 7; vii, 7; In Mat lxxvi, 5

9:27 Ad pop Anti i, 9; Ad Stel de comp ii, 7; Con e q sub 5; De laud s Paul vi (2x); De Laz iii 6; De paen i, 4; Ex in ps xlix, 6; F Iob 31:1 In Acta xliv, 2; In Cor xiii, 7; xxiii, 2; In Eph xxii, 4 (6:13); In Gen xxii, 7; In Heb ix 1; xxxiii, 9; In Phil iv, 1 (1:26); viii, 1 (2:16); xi, 4 (3:10); In Rom xvi, 2 (9:6); xxxii, 3 (16:24); In 1 Tim v, 1 (1:19); xvi, 1 (5:23); Q freg con 2; Q reg 7

10:1 De Eleaz 2; Ex in ps vii, 12; cxlii, 4; In 1 Cor xxiii, 3; In d P Nolo 1; In Mat xxxix, 4

10:2 De Eleaz 2; De paen i, 4; Ex in ps vii, 12; In 1 Cor xxiii, 3; In d P Nolo 1

10:3 De Eleaz 2; Ex in ps vii, 12; Ex in ps cxlii, 4; In 1 Cor xxiii, 3; In d P Nolo 1; In Mat lxiv, 4; In Rom xiv, 2 (8:14)

10:4 Con Anom xi, 1 (2x); De Eleaz 2; Ex in ps vii, 12; cxlii, 4; In 1 Cor xxiii, 3; In d P Nolo 1; In Heb xxvi, 4; In Ioh lvii, 1; In Mat lxiv, 4; In Rom xiv, 2 (8:14).

10:5 Ex in ps vii, 12; cxlii, 4; In 1 Cor xxiii, 3; xxiii, 4; In d P Nolo 1; In Mat lxiv, 4

10:6 Con Anom xi, 1; In 1 Cor xiii, 4; In d P Nolo 1

10:7 In 1 Cor xxiii, 4; In d P Nolo 1; In Mat vi, 9

10:8 Ex in ps xliii, 9; In d P Nolo 1; In 1 Thess viii, 3 (4:18)

10:9 In d P Nolo 1; In 1 Cor xxiii, 4; In 1 Thess viii, 3 (4:18)

10:10 De b Phil 2; Ex in ps cxl, 5; In Heb xxxiii,

| | |
|---|---|
| 10:10 cont | 1; In d P Nolo 1; In 1 Cor xiii, 4; In Phil viii, 2 (2:16) (2x); In 1 Thess viii, 3 (4:18) |
| 10:11 | De Hanna iii, 2; De Laz iii, 3; Ex in ps xliii 4; cxlii, 4; H dicta p imp 3; In Acta xxix, 4; In 1 Cor xxiii, 5; In Heb viii, 9; In Ioh xxx 2; xxxvii, 1; In Mat ii, 10; In Rom xxxi, 1 (16:5) |
| 10:12 | Ad Stel de comp ii, 7; De prod Iud i, 2; ii, 2; In 1 Cor xxxviii, 8; In Eph xxiii, 1 (6:14); In Gen xxix, 1; In Heb x, 1; In Mat xxvi 7; lxvii, 4; In Phil xi, 4 (3:10); In Tit v, 3 (3:1); Q freg con 2 |
| 10:13 | Ad pop Anti vi, 3; Ad Stag a dae i, 6; iii, 14; In Col viii, 6 (3:15); In Gen xxvi, 3; xxxii, 9; In Heb v, 7; xxviii, 7; xxix, 1; In il Dom non est 5; In para 2; In Rom iii, 4 (1:24); xii, 1 (6:19) |
| 10:14 | In 1 Cor xxiv, 2 |
| 10:15 | In 1 Cor xxiv, 2; xxvi, 5 |
| 10:16 | In 1 Cor xxiv, 3; In Rom viii, 8 (4:21) |
| 10:17 | In 1 Cor xxiv, 4; In Rom viii, 8 (4:21) |
| 10:18 | In 1 Cor xxiv, 5; In Rom viii, 8 (4:21) |
| 10:19 | In 1 Cor xxiv, 5; In Eph v, 1 (2:12) |
| 10:20 | In 1 Cor xxiv, 5 |
| 10:21 | Adu Iud 1, 7, 5; 3, 2, 2; In 1 Cor xxiv, 6 |
| 10:22 | In 1 Cor xxiv, 6; S ante iret 1 |
| 10:23 | In 1 Cor xxiv, 6; In Gen vii, 2 |
| 10:24 | Adu Iud 7, 6, 3; Adu op iii, 2; Cat ill v, 14 Con e q sub 4; Ex in ps xliv, 8; In 1 Cor xxiv, 6; xxxiii, 3; In il Uid elig 7; In Ioh lx, 1; In Mat lxxvii, 5 |
| 10:26 | In 1 Cor xxv, 1 |
| 10:27 | In Heb xxv, 7; In Mat xlvi, 4 |
| 10:28-29 | In 1 Cor xxv, 1 |
| 10:30 | In 1 Cor xxv, 2 |
| 10:31 | De Laz i, 6; Cat ill vi, 8 (2x); vi, 11; vi, 12; vi, 17; De s Bab c Iul 12; In Col xii, 6 (4:18); In 1 Cor xxv, 3; In kal 1; 3; 6; In Mat xlviii, 10; In Rom xxiv, 3 (13:14) |
| 10:32 | Cat ill vi, 7; vi, 14; Con e q sub 4; In 1 Cor xxv, 3; xxvi, 1; In Gen vii, 1; In Ioh lvii, 3; In Mat xv, 12; In Rom xxii, 2 (12:18) |
| 10:33 | Con e q sub 3; In 1 Cor xxiv, 6; xxv, 3; In Mat iv, 18; In Phil iv, 1 (1:26) |
| 11:1 | De cruce et lat i, 5; ii, 5; De laud s Paul iii, vii; In 1 Cor xxv, 3; In Ioh lxx, 1; lxxxiii, 5; In Rom xxxii, 4 (16:24) |

11:2 Ex in ps xliv, 10; In Rom xxix, 1 (15:15)
11:3 In 1 Cor xxvi, 1; In Eph xx, 4 (5:31); In Gen xvii, 4; lxvi, 2; Q reg 6
11:4 Adu Iud 3, 2, 2; In 1 Cor xii, 14; xxvi, 4
11:5 Adu Iud 3, 2, 2; In Eph xv, 4 (4:31)
11:6 Ad pop Anti v, 6; In 1 Cor xxvi, 4; In Eph xv 4 (4:31)
11:7 Ad pop Anti iii, 18; In 1 Cor xxvi, 4; xxvi, 5; In Eph xv, 4 (4:31); In Gen viii, 4; In 2 Tim viii, 1 (3:5); S Gen xv, 3
11:8 In 1 Cor xxvi, 5; In Eph xv, 4 (4:31); In Gen xv, 3
11:9 Ad Stag a dae i, 2; In 1 Cor xxvi, 5; In Eph xv, 4 (4:31); In Gen xv, 3; In 1 Tim ix, 1 (2:15)
11:10 In ascen d n I C 1; In 1 Cor xxvi, 5; In Eph xv, 4 (4:31); In Mat lix, 4
11:11 In 1 Cor xxvi, 5; xxvii, 2; In Eph xv, 4 (4:31); In Gen xv, 3
11:12 In 1 Cor xxvi, 5; In Eph xv, 4 (4:31); In Mat xxxii, 8
11:13 In 1 Cor xxvi, 5; In Eph xv, 4 (4:31)
11:14 De inani gloria 16; In 1 Cor xxvi, 5; xxx, 1 In Eph xv, 4 (4:31); In Gal v, 5 (5:17)
11:15 In 1 Cor xxvi, 5; xxx, 1; In Eph xv, 4 (4:31)
11:16 In 1 Cor xxvi, 2; xxvi, 5; xxvii, 3
11:17 In d P Op 3; 4; In il Uidi dom iii, 3
11:18 De paen vi, 5; In 1 Cor xxvii, 2; In d P Op 3
11:19 Ad e q scan xii; xix, De diab tent iii, 1; In Acta xl, 2; xlvi, 3; In 1 Cor xxvii, 3; In d P Op 1 (2x); 2; 4
11:20 In 1 Cor xxvii, 4; In d P Op 4
11:21 Adu Iud 3, 2, 2; In Col vii, 5 (3:4); In 1 Cor xxvii, 4; In d P Op 4; 5
11:22 Adu Iud 3, 2, 2; In 1 Cor xxvii, 4; xxxvi, 9; In d P Op 4 (2x)
11:23 In 1 Cor xxvii, 5; In d P Op 4 (2x)
11:24 H dicta in t s Anas 3; In d P Op 4; In 1 Cor xxvii, 5
11:25 De san pent i, 1; In 1 Cor xxvii, 5
11:26 Adu Iud 3, 4, 2; 3, 4, 3; De reg 14; H dicta in t s Anas 3; In Acta xxi, 4 (9:35); In 1 Cor xxvii, 6; In Eph iii, 4 (1:22); In Mat lxxxii, 1; In 1 Tim v, 3 (1:20)
11:27 De Laz iii, 5; E iv, 3; In 1 Cor xxvii, 6; In Mat vii, 6; In 2 Tim iv, 2 (2:10); Non esse ad grat 1
11:28 In 2 Tim viii, 3 (3:14); Non esse ad grat 1
11:29 In 1 Cor xxviii, 2; In Gen xi, 7; lvii, 7;

| | |
|---|---|
| 11:29 cont | In Ioh xlvi, 4 |
| 11:30 | Ad Stag a dae i, 3; De diab tent i, 8; De Laz iii, 5; De uir xxiv; E ii, 3; iv, 3; Ex in ps cxli, 1; In 1 Cor xxviii, 2; In 1 Cor ix, 4; In Heb v, 6; In il Hab iii, 7; In il Prop iii, 7; In Is iii, 1; In para 6; In Phil ix, 2 (2:27); In 1 Tim v, 3 (1:20) |
| 11:31 | De dec mil 5; De diab tent i, 8; De Laz iii, 5; iv, 7; De ss mar A 3; E iv, 3; Ex in ps iv 8; xlviii, 9; cxli, 1; In 1 Cor xxviii, 2; In 2 Cor xiv, 4; In il Hab iii, 7; In il Sal P et A ii, 6; In Mat xli, 6; xlii, 3; lxiv, 5 |
| 11:32 | Ad Stag a dae i, 3; De dec mil 5; De diab tent i, 8; De Laz iii, 5; De uir xxiv; E iv, 3; Ex in ps iv, 8; cxli, 1; In 1 Cor xv, 4; xvi, 2; xxviii, 2; In il Hab iii, 7; In Ioh xxxviii, 1; In Mat lxiv, 5; In Rom iii, 1 (1:18); v, 6 (2:16) |
| 11:33 | In 1 Cor xxviii, 3; xxxvii, 3; In d P Op 5 |
| 11:34 | In 1 Cor xxviii, 3 |
| 12:2 | In Gen lvii, 6 |
| 12:3 | In Col ix, 2 (3:17); In 1 Cor xxix, 3; In Ioh lxxxvi, 1 |
| 12:4 | In 1 Cor xx, 7; xxix, 4; In Ioh lxxxvi, 1 |
| 12:5 | In 1 Cor xxix, 4 |
| 12:6 | De san pent ii, 1; In 1 Cor xxix, 4; xxx, 3 |
| 12:7 | De san pent i, 4; In 1 Cor xxix, 1; xxix, 4; In Heb iii, 8 (2x); In Ioh lxxviii, 3 |
| 12:8 | De Anna iii, 1; De san pent i, 4; Ex in ps xliv, 3; In Acta xv, 2 (7:5); In 1 Cor xxix, 5; In Rom i, 2 (1:5) |
| 12:9 | De Anna iii, 1; Ex in ps xliv, 3; In 1 Cor xxix, 5 |
| 12:10 | De Anna iii, 1; Ex in ps xliv, 3; In 1 Cor xxix, 5; In 1 Thess xi, 1 (5:22) |
| 12:11 | De Anna iii, 1; De san pent ii, 1 (2x); In 1 Cor xxix, 5; xxix, 6; In 2 Cor xxx, 3; In Ioh lxxv, 1; In Rom i, 2 (1:5); xiv, 7 (8:27); xxi, 1 (12:6) |
| 12:13 | De san pent i, 4; In 1 Cor xxx, 2; In Ioh xv, 3 |
| 12:14 | In 1 Cor xxx, 2 |
| 12:15 | In 1 Cor xxx, 3 |
| 12:16 | In 1 Cor xxx, 3; In Ioh lvi, 2 |
| 12:17 | In 1 Cor xxx, 3 |
| 12:18 | In 1 Cor xxx, 4; In Eph xi, 2 (4:7); xix, 5 (5:21); In Heb iii, 8 |
| 12:19-20 | In 1 Cor xxx, 5 |

| | |
|---|---|
| 12:21 | Ad pop Anti xi, 12; In s Rom 1 |
| 12:22 | In 1 Cor xxxi, 2 |
| 12:23 | De ss mar A 1; In 1 Cor xxxi, 2 |
| 12:24-25 | In 1 Cor xxxi, 3 |
| 12:26 | Cat ill v, 14; De sac iii, 14; In Mat lviii, 7; In s Rom 1 |
| 12:27 | Cat ill xii, 14; E ii, 10; In 1 Cor xviii, 1; xxvi, 1 |
| 12:28 | In 1 Cor xxxii, 2; In Eph ix, 2 (4:12); In Gal i, 2 (1:3); In princ Act iii, 3 |
| 12:29 | Adu Iud 3, 2, 2; In 1 Cor xxxii, 4 |
| 12:30 | In 1 Cor xxxii, 4 |
| 12:31 | De laud s Paul iii; In 1 Cor xxxii, 5; In Heb ii, 2; iii, 10; In Mat xxxii, 11; xlvi, 4; In Rom xxi, 1 (12:6) |
| 13 (p) | In 1 Cor xvii, 1 |
| 13:1 | In 1 Cor xxxii, 6; In Heb iii, 10 |
| 13:2 | In 1 Cor xxxii, 7; In Heb iii, 10; In il Hab i, 4; In Mat xxiv, 2 |
| 13:3 | De incomp dei i, 2; In 1 Cor xxv, 5; In Heb iii, 10; In Ioh xxxvii, 3; In Mat lxxvii, 5; In Rom xxvii, 3 (15:7); In s Rom 1 |
| 13:4 | De san pent ii, 3; In Mat lxxi, 1 |
| 13:5 | Adu op iii, 14; De san pent ii, 3; In Acta xl 2; In 1 Cor xxxiii, 3; In Heb xix, 4; In Ioh lvii, 3; S Gen ix, 2 |
| 13:7 | De mut nom iv, 2; In 1 Cor xxxiii, 4 |
| 13:8 | De incom dei i, 2; E cxxx; In 1 Cor xxxiii, 5; In Mat lx, 3 |
| 13:9 | Ad e q scan ii; De incomp dei i, 3; ii, 5 (2x); De laud s Paul v; Ex in ps cxii, 2; cxliii, 2; In 1 Cor vii, 2; xxxiv, 2; In Eph xi, 3 (4:13); In Mat xxxviii, 2 |
| 13:10 | Ad e q scan ii; In 1 Cor xxxiv, 2; In Mat xvi 6 |
| 13:11 | Ad e q scan ii; De incomp dei i, 3; Ex in ps v, 1; cxii, 2; In 1 Cor xxxiv, 2; In Eph xvii 2 (5:4) |
| 13:12 | Ad e q scan ii; Ad Theo i, 11; De mut nom iv 4; Ex in ps cxii, 2; cxliii, 2; F Iob 35:10; In 1 Cor xxxiv, 2; In 2 Cor v, 2; x, 4; In Eph xi, 3 (4:13); In Heb xxviii, 4; H in il App 11; In Phil iii, 3 (1:24); In Tit i, 1 (1:5) |
| 13:13 | De incomp dei 1, 2; iii, 5; In 1 Cor xxxiv, 5; In 1 Thess ix, 3 (5:8) |
| 14:1 | In 1 Cor xxxvi, 1; In Eph ix, 4 (4:3) |
| 14:2-4 | In 1 Cor xxxv, 1 |

| | |
|---|---|
| 14:5-6 | In 1 Cor xxxv, 2 |
| 14:7-9 | In 1 Cor xxxv, 3 |
| 14:10-11 | In 1 Cor xxxv, 4 |
| 14:12-14 | In 1 Cor xxxv, 5 |
| 14:15 | De incomp dei v, 5; Ex in ps cxlv, 3; In 1 Cor xxxv, 5 |
| 14:16-17 | In 1 Cor xxv, 6 |
| 14:18 | In 1 Cor xxxv, 7; In princ Act iii, 4 |
| 14:19 | In 1 Cor xxxv, 7 |
| 12:20 | Ad pop Anti v, 11; Adu Iud 6, 7, 3; F Prou 1:4; In Ioh lxxx, 1; lxxx, 2; In Mat xxxvi, 3; lxii, 4; lxxix, 5 |
| 14:21 | In 1 Cor xxxvi, 1 |
| 14:22 | De san pent i, 4; In 1 Cor xxxvi, 2; In Mat xii, 3 |
| 14:23 | In 1 Cor xxxvi, 2 |
| 14:24-25 | Ex in ps cix, 3; In 1 Cor xxxvi, 2 |
| 14:26 | In 1 Cor ii, 4 |
| 14:27 | In 1 Cor xxxvi, 4; xxxvi, 5 |
| 14:28 | In 1 Cor xxxvi, 5 |
| 14:29 | In 1 Cor ii, 4; xxxii, 2; xxxvi, 6 |
| 14:30-31 | In 1 Cor xxxvi, 6 |
| 14:32 | In 1 Cor xxxvi, 6; In Rom xiv, 7 (8:26) |
| 14:33 | In 1 Cor xxxvi, 7; xxxvii, 2 |
| 14:34 | De s h Phoc 4; De sac iii, 9; In Mat vii, 7 |
| 14:35 | Adu Iud 2, 3, 4; De s h Phoc 4; In 1 Cor xxxvii, 1; In Eph xx, 6 (5:33); In il Uid elig 9; In Mat vii, 7; In Rom xxxi, 1 (16:6); In 2 Thess v, 5 (3:18); In 1 Tim ix, 1 (2:15) (2x) |
| 14:36 | In 1 Cor xxxvii, 2; In Rom xxx, 1 (15:27) |
| 14:37-39 | In 1 Cor xxxvii, 3 |
| 14:40 | In 1 Cor xxxvii, 4 |
| 15 (p) | In Rom xiii, 8 (8:11) |
| 15:1 | In Acta i, 1 (1:2); In il In fac 7 |
| 15:3 | In 1 Cor xxxviii, 2 |
| 15:4 | In 1 Cor xxxviii, 4 |
| 15:5 | In Acta i, 1 (1:2); In 1 Cor xxxviii, 5 |
| 15:6 | In 1 Cor xxxviii, 5; In Is vi, 6 |
| 15:7 | In 1 Cor xxxviii, 5 |
| 15:8 | De diab tent i, 1; De laud s Paul v; In 1 Cor |

15:8 cont xi, 2; xxxviii, 5; In Eph vii, 1 (3:11); In Gal i, 1 (1:11); In il Ut sus 5; In Is vi, 4; In Mat xxv, 5

15:9 Ad Stel de comp ii, 6; Adu cath 2; De mut nom iii, 4; De paen ii, 4; De proph obscur ii, 8; De uir xxxv; In 1 Cor xxxviii, 6; In Eph vii, 1 (3:11); xi, 4 (4:16); In Gal i, 1 (1:7); In Gen xxxi, 2; In il Ut sus 5; In Ioh i, 1; In Mat iii, 8; xxv, 5; lxxii, 4; In Rom v, 6 (2:16); In 1 Tim iv, 2 (1:17); Non esse ad grat 4; Q freg con 5

15:10 Cat ill iv, 10; De mut nom iv, 4; De pet mat 3; De paen ii, 4; iii, 4; De uir xxxvi; In Acta i, 1 (1:2); In 1 Cor x, 5; xxxii, 14; xxxviii, 7; In 2 Cor xxii, 2; In Eph ix, 2 (4:3); In Gal i, 2 (1:3); In Gen xxv, 7; xxxi, 2; In Phil iv, 4 (1:30); In Rom Argumentum, 1; xvi, 9 (9:24); In 1 Tim iii, 2 (1:14)

15:11 Ex in ps xlvi, 5; In 1 Cor xxxviii, 7; In s Igna 2

15:12-13 In 1 Cor xxxix, 2

15:14 In 1 Cor xxxix, 3; In 2 Tim v, 2 (2:18)

15:15 H in san pascha 1; In 1 Cor xxxix, 4; In Gen xxxvi, 5; In quat Laz A 1

15:16-17 In 1 Cor xxxix, 4

15:18 De coem et de cru 1; H in san pascha 1; In 1 Cor xxxix, 4; In 1 Thess vii, 1 (4:15)

15:19 In 1 Cor xxxix, 4

15:20-21 In 1 Cor xxxix, 5

15:22 De res mort 7; In 1 Cor x, 2; xxxix, 5

15:23 De res mort 7; Ex inps cix, 2; In 1 Cor x, 2; xxxix, 5; In 1 Tim xv, 4 (5:20)

15:24 Ex in ps cix, 2; cix, 4; cxiv, 2; In 1 Cor xxxix, 5; In Ioh xlv, 2; lxx, 1

15:25 De consub 4; Ex in ps cix, 2; In 1 Cor xxxix, 6; In 1 Tim ii, 2 (1:11)

15:26 Ex in ps cxiv, 3; In 1 Cor xxxix, 6; In Mat xxxvi, 3; In Rom xi, 4 (6:16)

15:27 De consub 4; In 1 Cor xxxix, 7; In Ioh lxiv, 1

15:28 F Prou 10:3; In 1 Cor xxxix, 7

15:30 In 1 Cor xl, 3; In Mat xxxiii, 5

15:31 Ad pop Anti vi, 8; Ad Theo i, 14; Adu Iud 8, 8, 3; Con e q sub 5; De laud s Paul 1; v; De mut nom i, 5; De s mar B 1; Ex in ps xliii, 8; cx, 2; In 1 Cor x, 5; xl, 3; In 2 Cor xxv, 1; In Eph vi, 3 (3:7); In Gen xi, 4; xxv, 7;

15:31
cont In Mat xxxiii, 5
15:32 Ad pop Anti i, 20; De mut nom i, 20; De mut nom ii, 5 (1:15); In 1 Cor xl, 3; In Eph xii, 1 (4:17); In Heb xv, 9; In Phil xiii, 1 (3:21)
15:33 De fato et pr ii; De incomp dei ii, 7; Ex in ps xi, 1; In 1 Cor xl, 4; In Gen v, 2; xvi, 3; In Heb xx, 8; In Ioh lvii, 3; lxvi, 3; In Mat ii, 10; vi, 8; In 1 Thess ii, 4 (1:8)
15:34 In 1 Cor xl, 4; In 2 Cor xxix, 6
15:35 Adu Iud 3, 2, 3
15:36 In Mat lxxvii, 1; In 1 Thess vii, 1 (4:14)
15:37 In 1 Cor xli, 3
15:38 Ad pop Anti x, 4; In 1 Cor xli, 3; In Rom xxxii, 2 (16:24)
15:39 In 1 Cor xli, 4
15:40 In 1 Cor x, 2; xli, 4
15:41 Ad Theo i, 19; Adu op iii, 5; De Laz vi, 9; De pet mat 5; Ex in ps cix, 7; In Col vii, 3 (3:4); In 1 Cor xli, 4; In Eut ii, 15; In Mat lv, 5; In Rom xxxi, 4 (16:16) (2x)
15:42 In 1 Cor xli, 4
15:45 In Col iii, 2 (1:18); In 1 Cor xli, 6; In Ioh xxv, 2
15:46 In 1 Cor xli, 6
15:47 De mut nom ii, 4
15:48 In 1 Cor xlii, 1
15:49 In 1 Cor xlii, 2; In Ioh x, 2
15:50 In 1 Cor xlii, 2
15:51 De res mort 7; In 1 Cor vii, 2; xlii, 3; In Phil xi, 3 (3:10); In Rom xix, 6 (11:25)
15:52 De res mort 7; In 1 Cor xlii, 3; In Eph iii, 1 (1:22); In Heb xxxii, 3; In Mat lxxviii, 1; In 1 Thess vii, 1 (4:15)
15:53 In Col viii, 3 (3:15); In 1 Cor xlii, 3; In Eph xxiv, 5 (6:24); In Ioh lxvi, 3; In Rom xiv, 6 (8:20); S Gen vii, 4
15:54 De coem et de cru 2; In 1 Cor xlii, 4
15:55 De coem et de cru 2; Ex in ps xlvi, 2; In 1 Cor xlii, 4
15:56 H in il App 18; In 1 Cor xlii, 4
15:57 In 1 Cor xlii, 4
15:58 In 1 Cor xlii, 5; In Heb xii, 5
16 (p) In il Sal P et A ii, 1
16:1 De elee 1; 2; In Gal ii, 4 (2:10); In Rom xxx, 1 (15:27)
16:2 De elee 1; 3 (2x); 4; De laud s Paul iv; In 1 Cor xliii, 2; In Gal ii, 4 (2:10); In 2 Tim i, 4 (1:7)

16:3 De elee 4; 5; Ex in ps xlix, 9; In 1 Cor xliii 4; In Gal ii, 4 (2:10)
16:4 De elee 4; 5; In 1 Cor xliii, 4; In Heb Argumentum, 2; In Phil iv, 5 (1:30); In Rom Argumentum, 1
16:5 In 1 Cor xliii, 5; In 2 Cor i, 1
16:6 In 1 Cor xliii, 5; In 2 Cor i, 1; iii, 3; In Rom xxix, 3 (15:24)
16:7 In 1 Cor xliii, 5; In 2 Cor iv, 2
16:8 In 1 Cor xliii, 5; In 2 Cor i, 2; ii, 3
16:9 In 1 Cor xliii, 5; In 2 Cor ii, 3
16:10 Ad pop Anti i, 8; In 1 Cor xiv, 1; In 2 Cor i, 2 (2x); In Phil ix, 1 (2:22); In 1 Tim Argumentum, 1
16:11 In 1 Cor xiv, 1; xliv, 1; In 2 Cor i, 2; In 1 Tim Argumentum, 1
16:12 In Acta xl, 2; In 1 Cor xliv, 1; In 2 Cor xxiii, 2
16:13 In 1 Cor xliv, 2; In Eph xxiii, 1 (6:14); In Mat xlvi, 1
16:15 De laud s Paul iii; In 1 Cor ii, 4; xliv, 5; In Phil xiii, 3 (4:3)
16:16 De laud s Paul iii
16:17 In 1 Cor xliv, 3
16:18 De laud s Paul iii; In 1 Cor xliv, 3
16:19 Ad pop Anti i, 20; In 1 Cor xliv, 3; In Rom xxx, 3 (16:5)
16:20 Cat ill xi, 34; In 1 Cor xliv, 4
16:21 In 1 Cor xliv, 4; In Rom xxxii, 4 (16:24)
16:22 Adu Iud 2, 3, 8; In 1 Cor xliv, 4; In Rom xvi 1 (9:3); xxxi, 2 (16:8)
16:23-24 In 1 Cor xliv, 4

2 Corinthians

1:2 In 2 Cor i, 3
1:3 Ad uid iun 1; De incomp dei v, 7; Ex in ps cxiii, 4; In 2 Cor i, 3; In Eph iii, 1 (1:22); xxiii, 2 (6:14); In 2 Tim iii, 2 (1:18)
1:4 Ex in ps cxlii, 4; In 2 Cor i, 3; In Mat liii 5; In para 2
1:5 In 2 Cor iii, 1; xxvi, 3; In para 2
1:6 In 2 Cor ii, 2; iii, 2
1:7 In 2 Cor ii, 1; ii, 2
1:8 Ad pop Anti xiv, 1; Ex in ps cxi, 3; In Acta xlii, 1; In 2 Cor ii, 3; v, 1; In Mat xxviii, 1; In Phil iv, 4 (1:30); Q freg con 5
1:9 Ad pop Anti xiv, 1 (2x); Ex in ps cxi, 3;

| | |
|---|---|
| 1:9 cont | cxvii, 3; In 2 Cor ii, 3; ix, 1; In Phil iii, 1 (1:20); iv, 4 (1:30) |
| 1:10 | De incomp dei iii, 6; De proph obscur ii, 4; Ex in ps cxi, 3; In 2 Cor ii, 4; In Mat xxviii, 1; In Phil iv, 4 (1:30) |
| 1:11 | De incomp dei iii, 6; De proph obscur ii, 4; In Acta xxxvii, 3 (17:15); In 1 Cor xxi, 8; In 2 Cor ii, 4; In Mat xxiii, 5; In 1 Thess i, 3 (1:7); In 2 Thess iv, 3 (3:2) |
| 1:12 | In 2 Cor iv, 4; In Mat cciii, 5 |
| 1:13 | In 2 Cor xxiii, 3; In Phil xv, 1 (4:14) |
| 1:14 | Adu Iud 7, 6, 5; In Phil iv, 2 (1:26) |
| 1:15-16 | In 2 Cor iii, 2 |
| 1:17 | In 1 Cor xliii, 5; In 2 Cor iii, 2; iii, 3; xxiv, 1 |
| 1:18 | In 2 Cor iii, 3; xxiv, 1; xxviii, 2 |
| 1:19-20 | In 2 Cor iii, 4 |
| 1:21 | Cat ill xi, 27; In 2 Cor iii, 4; In Eut ii, 11; ii, 12 |
| 1:22 | Ex in ps xliv, 3; In 2 Cor iii, 4; viii, 2; In Eph ii, 2 (1:14); xxiii, 2 (6:14); In Eut ii, 11; ii, 12; In Heb ix, 5 |
| 1:23 | In 2 Cor xxviii, 2; In Phil ix, 1 (2:21); In 1 Thess iii, 3 (2:18) |
| 1:24 | De sac ii, 3; In 2 Cor iv, 1; In Eph xi, 5 (4:16) |
| 2 (p) | De res mort 2 |
| 2:1 | In 2 Cor iv, 1 |
| 2:2 | Ex in ps xii, 1; In 2 Cor iv, 2; In il Pater m 1; In Mat vi, 10; In Rom xxiii, 5 (13:10) |
| 2:3 | In 2 Cor iv, 2 |
| 2:4 | Ad Stag a dae iii, 11; De laud s Paul iii; In 2 Cor iv, 3; xv, 1; In Eph xvii, 2 (5:4); In Mat lviii, 7; In Phil i, 1 (1:4); xv, 6 (2:23); In Rom xxxii, 3 (16:24); In 1 Thess iv, 4 (3:13) |
| 2:5 | In 2 Cor i, 1; iv, 4; In Rom xix, 6 (11:25) |
| 2:6 | Ad Theo i, 8; In 2 Cor i, 1; iv, 4; In Rom xiii, 6 (11:25); In 2 Thess v, 3 (3:18) |
| 2:7 | Ad Stag a dae ii, 1; iii, 14; De diab tent ii 4; De paen i, 3; De sac iii, 17; In 1 Cor xxxviii, 8; In 2 Cor iv, 4; In Ioh lxxviii, 1; In Mat lxxxvi, 4; In Rom xiii, 6 (8:7); xxxii 4 (16:28); S Gen ix, 2 |
| 2:8 | De diab tent ii, 4; De laud s Paul iii; De paen i, 3; E ii, 2 (2x); In 2 Cor iv, 4; In Rom xiii, 6 (8:7); In s Rom 2; In 2 Thess v, 3 |

| | |
|---|---|
| 2:8 cont | (2:18); Q freg con 5; S Gen ix, 2 |
| 2:9 | Ex in ps xlviii, 5; In 2 Cor iv, 5; In il Ut sus 2; In Rom xiii, 6 (8:7) |
| 2:10 | In 2 Cor iv, 5; In il Ut sus 2; In Mat lxxxvi, 4; In Rom xiii, 6 (8:7) |
| 2:11 | De diab tent ii, 4; De paen i, 3; De sac ii, 3; E ii, 2; In 1 Cor xxxviii, 1; In 2 Cor v, 5; In Eph xxii, 4 (6:13); In il Ut sus 2; In Mat lxxxvi, 4; In Rom x, 6 (6:4); xiii, 6 (8:7); xxxii, 3 (16:24) (2x); In s Rom 2; Q freg con 5 |
| 2:12 | E ii, 11; In 2 Cor xiv, 1; In il Ut sus 2 |
| 2:13 | Ad Stag a dae iii, 11; E ii, 11; In 2 Cor v, 1; xiv, 1; xvi, 4; xviii, 1 |
| 2:14 | De laud s Paul ii; In 2 Cor v, 1; v, 2; In s Iul 2 |
| 2:15 | In 2 Cor v, 2; In Gen xxvii, 2; In 1 Tim ii, 3 (1:11) |
| 2:16 | Ad e q scan xv; In Acta xxx, 2 (14:15); In 2 Cor v, 3; vi, 1; In Eut ii, 14; In Mat xv, 12; In 1 Tim ii, 3 (1:11) |
| 2:17 | In 2 Cor vi, 1; In il Ut sus 2 |
| 3 (p) | De uir lxxv |
| 3:1 | In 2 Cor xxi, 1; xxviii, 2 |
| 3:2 | De b Phil 3; In 2 Cor vi, 1 |
| 3;3 | De Eleaz 4; In 2 Cor vi, 1; vi, 2; In Mat i, 1 |
| 3:4 | In 2 Cor vi, 2 |
| 3:5 | In Acta xxx, 2 (14:15); In 2 Cor vi, 2; In Eut ii, 14 |
| 3:6 | De Eleaz 4; In 2 Cor vi, 2; xiii, 1; In Eut ii, 14; In Rom xi, 3 (6:14); xii, 5 (7:7) |
| 3:7 | In 2 Cor vii, 3 |
| 3:8-9 | In 2 Cor vii, 1 |
| 3:10 | De sac iii, 4; Ex in ps viii, 7; In 1 Cor xxxiv, 3; In 2 Cor vii, 2 |
| 3:11 | In 2 Cor vii, 2; In Ioh xiv, 1 |
| 3:12 | De proph obscur i, 6; In 2 Cor vii, 2 |
| 3:13 | De proph obscur i, 6; Ex in ps viii, 7; In 2 Cor vii, 2; In Heb xxxii, 3 |
| 3:14 | In 2 Cor vii, 3 |
| 3:16 | De diab tent ii, 3; In 2 Cor vii, 4 |
| 3:17 | In 2 Cor vii, 5 |
| 3:18 | Cat ill iii, 25; Ex in ps viii, 7; In 2 Cor vii, 5 (2x); viii, 3; In Heb xxxii, 3; In Ioh lxxxii, 3 |
| 4:2 | In 2 Cor viii, 1; xxiii, 3 |
| 4:3 | In 1 Cor vii, 2; In 2 Cor viii, 2 |
| 4:4 | In 2 Cor viii, 2; viii, 3; In Mat xxxviii, 1 |

4:5 De mut nom ii, 1; In Col ix, 2 (4:11); In 2 Cor viii, 3; In Eph xxii, 1 (6:8); In Phil v, 3 (2:4); vii, 2 (2:11); In 1 Tim xvii, 1 (6:7)
4:6 In 2 Cor viii, 3
4:7 Ad pop Anti x, 7; In 2 Cor viii, 3; xiii, 1; In Eut ii, 11; In 2 Tim x, 3 (4:20)
4:8 De res mort 3 (2x); Ex in ps xlviii, 10
4:9 De res mort 3; In 2 Cor ix, 1
4:10 De laud s Paul i, 1; In 2 Cor ix, 1; xiii, 1; In Phil xi, 2 (3:10); xi, 4 (3:12): In 2 Tim v, 1 (2:14)
4:11 In 2 Cor ix, 1; In Heb xxviii, 7
4:12 In 2 Cor ix, 1
4:13 De res mort 3; Ex in ps cxv, 1; cxv, 2 (2x); In 2 Cor ix, 2; In il Hab i, 1; i, 2; ii, 1 (2x); iii, 1; In Is vii, 4
4:14 De res mort 3 (2x); Ex in ps cxv, 1; In 2 Cor ix, 21; In il Hab i, 4 (2x)
4:15 In 2 Cor ix, 2; xi, 5
4:16 Adu Iud 8, 5, 9; De Laz v, 1; De paen v, 4; De prof eua 4; De res mort 3 (3x); 4 (2x); In 2 Cor ix, 2; In Gen i, 4; x, 2; In Mat lxxix, 5; Q Nemo 4
4:17 Ad Stel de comp i, 5; Ad Theo i, 14; Adu Iud 8, 5, 9; De glor in trib 2 (2x); De laud s Paul ii; vi; De paen vi, 2; De res mort 4; Ex in ps iv, 12; H hab p p Gothus 2; In Acta xliv, 1; In 2 Cor ix, 2; In Gen xxv, 5; In Heb xxviii, 7; In il Hab i, 4; In il Hoc scit 1; In Ioh lxxxvii, 3; In Mat xvi, 14; xxiii, 7; xxxviii, 3; In Rom xiii, 8 (8:9); xiv, 4 (8:18); In s Iul 1
4:18 Ad Stel de comp i, 5; Cat ill viii, 11; De glor in trib 2; De laud s Paul vi; De res mort 4 (2x); E i, 1; Ex in ps iv, 12; cxiv, 3; H hab p p Gothus 2; In Acta lii, 4; In 2 Cor ix, 2; In Gen xxv, 7; xxxv, 8; lxiii, 4; In Heb xvi, 8; xxxiii, 1; In il Hab i, 4; In il Uidi dom iv, 3; In Ioh xlv, 3; lxxxvii, 3; In Mat xxiii, 7; In s Iul 1
5:1 De res mort 2; 5; In il Hab i, 2
5:2 Adu Iud 8, 5, 9; Ex in ps xli, 6; In 2 Cor, 2
5:3 De res mort 7; 8; Ex in ps xliii, 3; In 2 Cor x, 2
5:4 Ad Dem de comp i, 7; De laud s Paul vi; De res mort 7; 8; Ex in ps cx, 2; cxiv, 2; cxix, 2; cxlix, 1; In Acta ix, 3 (3:26); In 2 Cor x, 3; In Eph xvii, 2 (5:4); In Heb xxiv, 5
5:5 De rest mort 8 (2x); In 2 Cor x, 3

5:6 In 2 Cor x, 4
5:7 In 1 Cor vi, 5; In 2 Cor x, 4
5:8-9 In 2 Cor x, 4
5:10 Ad Theo ii, 2; De dec mil 4; In Acta xxxviii, 4; In 1 Cor xxxix, 4; In 2 Cor x, 5; In Gen xliii, 2; In Ioh xxxiv, 3; xxxix, 1; xlv, 3; S Gen vii, 4
5:11 In Acta xlvi, 3
5:12 In 2 Cor vi, 1 (2x); xi, 1; xxxviii, 2; In Gal i, 7 (1:10)
5:13 De laud s Paul v; In 2 Cor xi, 2; xxi, 1
5:14 In 2 Cor xi, 2; xii, 1; In Gen xxxiv, 5
5:15 In 2 Cor xi, 2; In Gen xxxiv, 5; In Rom xii, 3 (7:3); xiv, 1 (8:13)
5:16 In 2 Cor xi, 3
5:17 Cat ill iv, 1; iv, 12 (2x); iv, 16; iv, 22; iv, 26; Ex in ps xliv, 1; cxlix, 1; In 2 Cor xi, 4; In Gal ii, 2 (2:5); In Ioh xxvi, 1
5:18 In Col iii, 2 (1:20); In 2 Cor xi, 4
5:19 Ad Theo i, 13; In 2 Cor xi, 5; In il In fac 9; In Ioh lxxxii, 1; In Mat xvi, 12
5:20 Ad Theo i, 13; De Laz i, 5; Ex in ps xli, 4; In ascen d n I C 2; In Col iv, 2 (1:24); In 2 Cor xi, 5; xvii, 3 (2x); In il In fac 9; In Ioh xx, 3; lxxxvi, 4; In Mat lxxix, 3; In Rom i, 1 (1:2); v, 6 (2:16); xv, 3 (8:34); xxiv, 2 (13:14); In s Iul 5; In 1 Thess v, 1 (4:3)
5:21 In 1 Cor v, 4; xxxviii, 3; In 2 Cor xi, 5
6:2 Ad Theo i, 10; In Heb vii, 6
6:3 In Acta xliii, 2; In 2 Cor xi, 2; In Eph vi, 3 (3:7); In il Hab iii, 6
6:4 De uir xxxvi; H dicta in t s Anas 3; In Acta xliii, 2; In 2 Cor xi, 2; xiii, 1; In Eph vi, 3 (3:7); In Heb xxviii, 5; In il Hab iii, 6
6:5 De uir xxxvi; H dicta in t s Anas 3; In Acta xliii, 2; In 2 Cor xi, 2; xiii, 1; In Eph vi, 3 (3:7); In Heb xxiii, 5; In il Hab iii, 6; In Phil iv, 1 (1:26); In 1 Thess v, 1 (4:3)
6:6 De uir xxxvi; In 2 Cor xi, 2; In Phil iv, 1 (1:26); In 1 Thess v, 1 (4:3); In 1 Tim x, 2 (3:7)
6:7 In 2 Cor xi, 2
6:8 In 2 Cor xii, 3; In Heb xxviii, 5; In Phil xii, 4 (3:17)
6:9 In 2 Cor xii, 4
6:10 Ex in ps cxi, 2; In 1 Cor xv, 13; In 2 Cor xii, 4; xiii, 1; In Heb xviii, 4; xxviii, 5; In 1 Tim xi, 2 (3:16)
6:11 Ad pop Anti ix, 1; In Rom xxxii, 3 (16:24)
6:12 Ad pop Anti ix, 1; De laud s Paul i; In Acta

6:12 cont xliv, 4; In Eph ix, 3 (4:3); S post red ii, 4
6:13 F Prou 7:3; In Acta xliv, 4; In 2 Cor xiii, 1
6:14 Ad pop Anti xi, 14; De Laz vii, 1; In 2 Cor xiii, 1; In Eph xvii, 3 (5:4); In Ioh i, 6
6:15 Ad pop Anti xi, 14; In 2 Cor xiii, 1; In Mat xxxi, 4
6:16 Adu Iud 6, 7, 7; De ss mar A 1; Ex in ps cxxii 1; In 2 Cor xiii, 1; In diem nat 6; In Heb xvi 4
6:17 De uncomp dei ii, 7; In 2 Cir xiii, 1
7:1 In 2 Cor xiii, 1; In Ioh xiv, 2
7:2 In Acta xliv, 4; In Mat xxxii, 10; Qual duc 5
7:3 In 2 Cor xiv, 1
7:5 De res mort 2; In Acta liii, 4; In 2 Cor xiv, 1; In Eph xx, 8 (5:33); In il Hab iii, 3; In Mat lix, 1; lxxv, 2
7:6 Ex in ps cxlvi, 1; In 2 Cor v, 1; xiv, 1
7:7 In 2 Cor xiii, 1
7:8 In 2 Cor xiv, 1; In il Hab i, 1
7:9 In 2 Cor xiv, 1; In il Hab i, 1 (2x); Qual duc 1
7:10 Ad pop Anti v, 13; xviii, 8; De paen vii, 6; De prof eua 5; In 2 Cor xv, 2; In Eph xxiv, 3 (6:22); In il Is Ego 4; In kal 4; In Mat xv, 4; In Phil xv, 6 (4:23); Qual duc 1
7:11 Ex in ps xlvi, 3; In 2 Cor i, 1; xv, 2; In Mat ii, 11
7:12-13 In 2 Cor xv, 2
7:15 In 2 Cor i, 1; xviii, 1
8:1 In 2 Cor xvi, 2; In d P Op 2; In Heb Argumentum, 2; In Rom xxx, 1 (15:27)
8:2 In 2 Cor xvi, 2; In d P Op 2; In Heb Argumentum, 2; In il Uid elig 12
8:3 In 2 Cor xvi, 3; In d P Op 2; In Heb Argumentum, 2
8:4 In 2 Cor xvi, 3; In d P Op 2
8:5 In 2 Cor xvi, 3; In Heb x, 6; In Mat xv, 6
8:6 In 2 Cor v, 1; xvi, 4
8:8 In 2 Cor xvii, 1
8:9 De Chris prec 6; In 2 Cor xvii, 1; In Mat xxii, 6; In Phil vi, 1 (2:8); In Rom xxvii, 2 (15:3); In Tit vi, 1 (3:11)
8:10-11 In 2 Cor xvii, 1
8:12 In Heb xxxii, 8
8:14 In Acta xxiii, 3 (10:43); In Gen xx, 5; In il Hab 19; In Mat xxxv, 4; In Phil ii, 3 (1:19);

| | |
|---|---|
| 8:14 cont | xv, 2 (4:15) |
| 8:15 | In Eph xxiii, 3 (6:14) |
| 8:16 | In 2 Cor v, 1 |
| 8:17 | In 2 Cor xviii, 1 |
| 8:18 | De mut nom i, 4; In Acta i, 1 (1:2); i, 2 (1:2); In 2 Cor xviii, 1; In Ioh xviii, 3; In 2 Tim x, 1 (4:13) |
| 8:19 | In 2 Cor xviii, 1 |
| 8:20 | De sac vi, 9; Ex in ps xlix, 9; In Acta xlvi, 3; In 2 Cor xviii, 1 |
| 8:21 | De sac vi, 9; In Acta xlvi, 3; In 2 Cor xviii, 1; In Eph vi, 3 (3:7) |
| 8:22 | In 2 Cor v, 1; xviii, 2 |
| 8:23 | In 2 Cor v, 1; xviii, 1; xviii, 2 |
| 8:24 | In 2 Cor xviii, 2 |
| 9:2 | In 2 Cor i, 1; In Phil iv, 3 (1:30); In Rom Argumentum, 1; xxx, 1 (15:27) |
| 9:3 | In 2 Cor xix, 1 |
| 9:4 | In 2 Cor xix, 1; xxiv, 1 |
| 9:5 | In 1 Cor xliii, 4; In 2 Cor xix, 2; In Rom xxx, 1 (15:29) |
| 9:6 | Ex in ps cxi, 5; In 2 Cor xix, 2; In Gen xxxiv 3; In il Hab ii, 7; In Mat v, 8; lxvi, 3; In Rom xxi, 1 (12:8) |
| 9:7 | In Acta vii, 3 (2:46); In 2 Cor xix, 2; In d P Op 3; In Phil i, 3 (1:7); In Rom xxi, 1 (12:8); In 1 Tim xiv, 2 (5:10); In Tit vi, 2 (3:15) |
| 9:8 | In 2 Cor xix, 2; xxi, 2; In Mat lv, 7 |
| 9:9 | In 2 Cor xix, 1; xix, 2 |
| 9:10 | In Phil xv, 3 (4:19); S Gen vii, 5; viii, 2 |
| 9:12 | In 2 Cor xx, 2; In Ioh xiii, 4 |
| 9:13 | In 1 Cor xliii, 4; In 2 Cor xx, 2 |
| 9:14 | In 2 Cor xx, 2 |
| 9:15 | Ad e q scan ii; De diab tent i, 3; De incomp dei i, 5; Ex in ps xli, 4; In 2 Cor xx, 2; In Mat xii, 3 |
| 10:1 | In 2 Cor xxx, 1 |
| 10:2 | In 2 Cor xxx, 1; In il Ut sus 3 |
| 10:3 | In 2 Cor xxi, 2 |
| 10:4 | Adu Iud 6, 1, 2; De laud s Paul iv; De pet mat 1; In 2 Cor xxi, 2 |
| 10:5 | Adu Iud 6, 1, 2; De laud s Paul iv; De pet mat 1; De sac iv, 7; Ex in ps cxxv, 1; cxliii, 2; F Prou 6:30; In 1 Cor ix, 6; In 2 Cor xxi, 2; In Eph xxiv, 3 (6:22); In Heb iii, 6; In princ Act i, 3; i, 4; L Diod 4 |
| 10:6 | In 2 Cor xxi, 3; xxiii, 1; xxx, 1; In Mat xl, 2 |

| | |
|---|---|
| 10:7 | In Ioh xvi, 1 |
| 10:8 | In 2 Cor xxii, 1 |
| 10:9 | In 2 Cor xxii, 2; In il Ut sus 3 |
| 10:10 | De sac iv, 6; In 1 Cor xi, 2; xxxv, 11; In 2 Cor i, 1; xxii, 2; xxix, 2; In il Ut sus 3; In 1 Thess ii, 3 (2:6) |
| 10:11 | In 2 Cor xxii, 2; In il Ut sus |
| 10:12-14 | In 2 Cor xxii, 2 |
| 10:15 | In Rom xviii, 5-6 (11:6) |
| 10:17 | Ex in ps cxxx, 1 |
| 11 (p) | De laud s Paul i; In Rom xiii, 8 (8:9) |
| 11:1 | De laud s Paul v; In 2 Cor xi, 2; xxv, 1; In il Ut sus 1; 2; 10 |
| 11:2 | Cat ill i, 1; i, 4; xii, 14; De laud s Paul v; De paen iv, 3 (4x); De prof eua 3; De proph obscur i, 6; De sac iv, 7; De uir i; Ex in ps v, 2; H in il App 26; In Col xii, 1 (4:13); xii, 6 (4:18); In Eut ii, 1 (2x); ii, 13; In Heb xxviii, 16; In il Ut sus 2; In Mat lxix, 1; In Rom xxiv, 2 (13:14); In 1 Tim xv, 1 (5:15); Q reg 5 |
| 11:3 | De prof eua 3; De sac iii, 7; In 2 Cor xiv, 1; xxiii, 1; xxvii, 1; In Eph xxii, 4 (6:13); xxiv, 4 (6:24); In Gal ii, 5 (2:12); In Rom xxv, 2 (14:5); xxxii, 3 (16:24) |
| 11:4 | In 2 Cor xxiii, 1; xxiv, 1 |
| 11:5 | In 2 Cor xxiii, 2 |
| 11:6 | De laud s Paul iv; De sac iv, 6; In 2 Cor i, 1; xxiii, 3; In Rom Argumentum, 2 |
| 11:7 | In 2 Cor xxiii, 4 |
| 11:8 | In 1 Cor xxi, 7; xxv, 3; In 2 Cor xvii, 3; xxiii, 4; In Phil xv, 1 (4:14); In 1 Thess ii, 1 (2:12) (2x) |
| 11:9 | De sac iii, 7; In 1 Cor xxi, 7; In 2 Cor xxiii, 5; In Mat xxv, 4; In 1 Thess iii, 1 (2:12) |
| 11:10 | In Acta xlv, 2; In 2 Cor xxiii, 6; xxvii, 2; In Phil xv, 1 (4:14) |
| 11:11 | In 2 Cor xxiii, 6; xxvii, 2 |
| 11:12 | In Acta xxxix, 1; In 2 Cor i, 1; xxiii, 6; xxiv, 1; xxiv, 2; xxvii, 2; In Phil xv, 1 (4:14) |
| 11:13 | In 2 Cor xxiii, 2; xxvi, 1; In Mat lxxv, 2 |
| 11:14 | In 1 Cor xxvii, 3; In 2 Cor xxiv, 1; In Eph xxii, 4 (6:13) |
| 11:15 | De prod Iud i, 1; ii, 1; In 1 Cor xvi, 5; xxvii, 3; In 2 Cor xxiv, 1; In Eph xxii, 4 (6:13) |

11:16 In 2 Cor xxiv, 1; xxv, 1; In il Utu sus 4
11:17 De laud s Paul v; In 2 Cor xi, 2; xxiv, 1; In 2 Cor xxv, 1; xxvi, 2; In il Ut sus 5; 10
11:18 In 2 Cor xxiv, 2; xxv, 1; In il Ut sus 4
11:19 In 2 Cor xxiv, 2; In il Ut sus 4
11:20 In 1 Cor xxi, 6; In 2 Cor xxiv, 1; xxiv, 2; In s Igna 3; In 1 Thess ii, 3 (2:6)
11:21 De laud s Paul v; In 2 Cor xi, 2; xxiv, 2; In Gen xi, 5; In il Ut sus 4; In s Igna 3
11:22 Ex in ps cxv, 5; In 2 Cor xxv, 1; In Gen xi, 5; In il Ut sus 4
11:23 Ad pop Anti xvi, 9 (2x); Ad Theo i, 14; De glor in trib 4; E ii, 8 (2x); Ex in ps xli, 6; In 2 Cor xxv, 1; In Gal i, 8 (1:10); In Gen xi, 5; lv, 3; In il Hab iii, 6 (2x); In il Ut sus 4 (2x); In Ioh lx, 2; In Phil iv, 1 (1:26)
11:24 Ad Theo i, 14; De cruce et lat i, 5; ii, 5; E iii, 8; Ex in ps xli, 6; In 1 Cor xiii, 6; In 2 Cor xxv, 1; In Eut ii, 11; In Gen xi, 6; In Heb xxviii, 5; In il Hab iii, 6; In Phil iv, 1 (1:26)
11:25 Ad pop Anti xvi, 9; Ad Theo i, 14; De cruce et lat i, 5; ii, 5; E iii, 8; Ex in ps xli, 6; In 1 Cor xiii, 6; In 2 Cor xxv, 1; xxv, 2; In Gen xi, 6; lv, 3; In Heb xxviii, 5; In il Hab iii, 6; In Phil iv, 1 (1:26)
11:26 Ad Theo i, 14; E iii, 8; Ex in ps xli, 6; In 2 Cor xxv, 1; In Gen xi, 6; lv, 3; In Heb xxviii, 5; xxviii, 7; In il Hab iii, 6; In Mat lix, 1; lxxv, 2; In Phil iv, 1 (1:26)
11:27 Ad Theo i, 14; E iii, 8; Ex in ps xli, 6; H idcta in t s Anas 3; In Acta li, 4; In 1 Cor xv, 13; In 2 Cor xxv, 2; In Gen xi, 6; lv, 3; In il Hab iii, 6; In Mat xl, 4; In s Luc 2
11:28 Ad Stag a dae iii, 11; Ad Theo i, 14; E iii, 8; iii, 9; H dicta in t s Anas 3; In 2 Cor xii 5; xxv, 2; In Gen xi, 6; In il Hab iii, 6
11:29 Ad Stag a dae iii, 11; Adu Iud 4, 7, 10; 7, 6, 3; De laud s Paul ii; De s Bab c Iul 10; De sac iii, 7; E iii, 9; In Acta xliii, 2; In 1 Cor xxxii, 14; In 2 Cor xxv, 2; In Eph xvii, 2 (5:4); In Mat lviii, 7; lxxvii, 6; In Phil iv, 1 (1:26); ix, 2 (2:28); In Rom xxix, 4 (15:24); In s Igna 3; In s Rom 1; Q reg 2; Qual duc 1
11:30 Ad pop Anti xvi, 9; De glor in trib 4; E iii, 9; In 1 Cor vi, 2; In 2 Cor xxv, 2
11:31 In 2 Cor xxv, 2; In Gen lx, 4
11:32 H dicta in t s Anas 3; In Acta xx, 3 (9:25); In 1 Cor vi, 2; In 2 Cor xxv, 2; xxvi, 1; In

| | |
|---|---|
| 11:32 cont | Gal i, 11 (1:17) |
| 11:33 | Cat ill v, 19; H dicta in t s Anas 3 |
| 12 (p) | De laud s Paul ii |
| 12:1 | De laud s Paul v |
| 12:2 | Ad pop Anti i, 15; De laud s Paul v (2x); De sac iv, 6; In 2 Cor xxvi, 1; In Eph viii, 1 (4:2); In Heb xxviii, 7; In il Ut sus 6; In princ Act iii, 5 |
| 12:3 | De sac iv, 6; In 2 Cor xxvi, 1; In Mat vi, 9 |
| 12:4 | Ad pop Anti i, 15; De incomp dei v, 4; De mut nom i, 6; De sac iii, 7; iv, 6; In Acta ii, 1 (1:6); In Col x, 3 (4:4); In 2 Cor xii, 4; In Eph viii, 1 (4:2) |
| 12:5 | De laud s Paul v |
| 12:6 | Ad pop Anti i, 17; x, 7; De laud s Paul v; Ex in ps cxxx, 1; In Acta xxx, 1 (14:18); In 2 Cor ix, 1; xxvi, 2; In Hel 6; In 1 Thess iv, 1 (3:8) |
| 12:7 | Ad pop Anti i, 15; Ad Stag a dae i, 3; De laud s Paul vi; E iv, 3; Ex in ps cxv, 2; cxli, 1; In 2 Cor ii, 3; iii, 3; ix, 1; xxvi, 2; In Hel 6; In Mat x, 8; In s Eust 2 (2x); In 1 Thess iv, 1 (3:8); In 2 Tim x, 3 (4:20); Q freg con 5 |
| 12:8 | Ad pop Anti i, 16; Ad Stag a dae i, 3; iii, 11; E iii, 9; iv, 3; Ex in ps vii, 4; cxv, 2; cxli, 1; cxlv, 5; In 2 Cor iii, 3; xxvi, 3; xxix, 2; In Gen xxx, 5; In Heb xxviii, 5; xxxiii, 9; In il Pater s p 4; In Rom ii, 3 (1:11); xiv, 6 (8:26); xv, 1 (8:28); In s Eust 2 (2x) |
| 12:9 | Ad e q scan xxi; Ad pop Anti i, 16; xvi, 9; Ad Stag a dae i, 3; De cruce et lat ii, 2; De glor in trib 4; De Mac i, 2; De prof eua 8; E i, 5; Ex in ps vii, 4; cxiv, 1; cxv, 2; cxli, 1; cxlv, 5; H dicta in t s Anas 5; In Acta x, 4 (4:22); xxxi, 1 (14:20); xxxiv, 2 (16:24); In 1 Cor v, 3; In 2 Cor iii, 3; viii, 3; ix, 1; xxvi, 3; xxix, 2; In Eph viii, 7 (4:2); ix, 1 (4:3); In Gen xxx, 5; In Heb xxviii, 5; xxix, 2; xxxiii, 9; In il Dil deum 2; In il Pater s p 4; In Mat xxxiii, 3; lx, 2; In Phil i, 3 (1:7); In Rom xv, 1 (8:28); xvii, 6 (11:6); In s Eust 2 (2x) |
| 12:10 | Ad pop Anti xvi, 9; De glor in trib 4; De laud s Paul ii; Ex in ps cxiv, 1; cxli, 1; cxliv, 4; F Ier 20:7; In Col x, 3 (4:4); In 1 Cor vi, 2; In 2 Cor xxvi, 3; xxix, 2; In Heb xxviii, |

| | |
|---|---|
| 12:10 cont | 5; xxxiii, 9; In il Dil deum 2; In il Pater s p 4; In Mat xvi, 14; In Rom xv, 1 (8:28) |
| 12:11 | De laud s Paul v; Ex in ps cxxx, 1 (2x); In Acta xliv, 1; In 2 Cor xxi, 1; xxii, 2; In Eph vi, 3 (3:7); In il Ut sus 4; In 1 Tim xvi, 1 (5:23) |
| 12:12 | In 1 Cor ii, 4; xx, 2; In 2 Cor xxii, 2; xxvii 1 |
| 12:13 | In 1 Cor ii, 4; In 2 Cor xxvii, 2; In Eph vi, 3 (3:7); In 1 Thess ii, 3 (2:6) |
| 12:14 | In 2 Cor xxvii, 2 |
| 12:15 | De laud s Paul iii; In 2 Cor iv, 3; xiii, 1; xxii, 3; xxvii, 2; In Mat xxxii, 10; lxvi, 2 |
| 12:16-17 | In 2 Cor xxii, 3 |
| 12:18 | In 2 Cor v, 1; xxii, 3 |
| 12:19 | In 2 Cor vi, 1; xxviii, 2 |
| 12:20 | De laud s Paul iii; De sac ii, 2; In 2 Cor iv, 1; vi, 1; xxii, 3; xxviii, 2; xxx, 1; In Rom xxxii, 3 (16:24); In s Igna 3 |
| 12:21 | Ad pop Anti iii, 13; Ad Stag a dae iii, 11; Ad Theo i, 18; De laud s Paul iii; De Laz v, 3; De paen i, 4; v, 2; vii, 1; E vii, 3; In 1 Cor xi, 4; In 2 Cor iv, 1; iv, 2; xxiii, 1; xxviii 2; xxix, 1; xxx, 1; In Phil viii, 2 (2:16); In s Igna 3; Pec frat 4 |
| 13:2 | Ad Theo i, 18; In Col vii, 5 (3:4); In 2 Cor iv, 1; xxix, 1; xxx, 1 |
| 13:3 | Ad uid iun 2; De incomp dei ii, 5; De Mac i, 1; De paen vii, 1; In 1 Cor ii, 7; In 2 Cor, 7; xxix, 2; xxx, 1; In Gen lx, 3; In il Sal P et A i, 3; In 1 Thess viii, 1 (4:17) |
| 13:4 | De cruce et lat ii, 2; In 2 Cor xxix, 2; xxix 3 |
| 13:5 | In 1 Cor xxviii, 1; In 2 Cor xxix, 4 |
| 13:6 | In 2 Cor xxix, 4 |
| 13:7 | De s Bab c Iul 10; In Acta iii, 5 (1:26); In 2 Cor xxix, 2; xxix, 4; In Rom xvi, 8 (9:24) |
| 13:8 | In 2 Cor xxix, 4 |
| 13:9 | De incomp dei v, 4; In 2 Cor xxix, 4 |
| 13:10 | In Rom xxxii, 3 (16:24); In 1 Thess v, 2 (1:20) |
| 13:11 | De incomp dei v, 2; In 2 Cor xxx, 1 |
| 13:12 | De incomp dei v, 2; Ex in ps cxl, 6; In 2 Cor xxx, 2 |
| 13:13 | In 2 Cor xxx, 2 |
| 13:14 | In 1 Cor xx, 7; In 2 Cor xxx, 4 |

Galatians

| | |
|---|---|
| 1:1 | In Acta xxvii, 1 (13:3); In 2 Cor i, 2 |
| 1:2 | In 2 Cor i, 2 |
| 1:3 | De incomp dei iii, 2; Ex in ps cxxxiv, 6; In 2 Cor i, 2; In Phil x, 2 (3:4) |
| 1:4 | De incomp dei iii, 2; Ex in ps cxxxiv, 6; In Eph iv, 1 (2:3); xxii, 3 (6:13); In Heb viii, 3; In Mat lv, 8 |
| 1:5 | De incomp dei iii, 2; Ex in ps cxxxiv, 6; In Mat lv, 8 |
| 1:6 | In Col ii, 1 (1:11); In Gal iii, 1 (3:1); iv, 3 (4:20); In Heb viii, 6; x, 4; In Is i, 7; In 2 Tim iv, 2-4 (2:9) |
| 1:8 | De prof eau 3; In 1 Cor xxvii, 3; In d P Op 1; In Rom xxxi, 2 (16:8) |
| 1:9 | De prof eua 3; In Rom xxv, 2 (14:5) |
| 1:10 | De mut nom i, 6; E cxxv; In Acta xlvi, 3; In Eph xxii, 1 (6:8) |
| 1:11 | In Gal i, 11 (1:18) |
| 1:12 | In Eph vi, 2 (3:2) |
| 1:13 | Ad Stel de comp ii, 6; De laud s Paul iv; De mut nom i, 6; In Eph xi, 5 (4:16); In Ioh x, 1 In Mat xxx, 1 |
| 1:15 | De laud s Paul iv; F Ier 1:5; In Mat lxiv, 3 |
| 1:16 | De laud s Paul iv; In Acta xxi, 1 (9:27); xxxi 2 (14:18) |
| 1:17 | In Acta xxi, 1 (9:27) |
| 1:18 | In Heb xxviii, 7; In il In fac 7; 8; In Rom xxxii, 4 (16:24) |
| 1:19 | In Ioh xlviii, 2 |
| 1:21 | De mut nom iii, 3 |
| 2:1 | In Acta xxi, 1 (9:27); In il In fac 3; 7; 15 |
| 2:2 | In il In fac 3; In Mat lxxvi, 5 |
| 2:4 | Ad e q scan xiv |
| 2:6 | De res d n I C 3; E cxxv; In 1 Cor xxxix, 1 |
| 2:8 | In Acta xxxvii, 1; In 1 Cor xxix, 4; In Heb Argumentum, 1; In il In fac 9; In Mat lxix, 1 (2x) |
| 2:9 | De elee, 1; F Prou 9:21; In Acta xxv, 2 (11:30) (2x); xxxvii, 1; In 1 Cor xxxix, 1; In Eph x, 2 (4:4); In Heb Argumentum, 2; In Mat lvii, 3 |
| 2:10 | De elee, 1; 2; In Acta xiv, 3 (6:7); xxv, 2 (11:30); xxv, 3 (11:30); In Heb Argumentum, 2 In Phil iv, 5 (1:30) |
| 2:11 | In il In fac 1 (2x); 2 |
| 2:12 | In il In fac 2; 13 |
| 2:13 | In il In fac 2; In Rom xxvi, 2 (14:21) |
| 2:14 | In il In fac 2 |
| 2:15 | In Acta xlvii, 1; In il In fac 18 |

2:16 In il In fac 18
2:17 In Col vii, 1 (2:18); In il In fac 19
2:18 In il In fac 19
2:20 Ad Stel de comp ii, 6; Con e q sub 5; De sac vi, 2; De laud s Paul vi; In Acta lii, 4; In Gen viii, 6; xxxiv, 5 (2x); xxxiv, 6; lx, 3 (2x); In Ioh xxxix, 4; In Phil iii, 2 (1:21) (2x); ix, 5 (2:30); In Rom xxiv, 2 (3:14); xxxii, 3 (16:24)
2:21 Adu Iud 2, 2, 1
3:1 De laud s Paul v; Ex in ps cxl, 8; In Gal i, 1 (1:3); v, 2 (5:1); In il Hoc scit 1; In Tit i, 1 (1:5)
3:3 In 1 Thess vi, 2 (4:13)
3:4 Ad Theo i, 8; De laud s Paul iv; De res mort 2; H dicta in t s Anas 3; In Eph vi, 4 (3:7); In Gal i, 5 (1:6); In Heb viii, 4; x, 4; In Phil iv, 3 (1:3); In Rom xiii, 8 (8:9)
3:5 Ad Theo i, 8; In Gal ii, 7 (2:30)
3:8 Ex in ps cxi, 2
3:13 Ex in ps xliv, 4; In ascen d n I C 2; In 1 Cor xxxviii, 3; In 2 Cor xi, 5; In Gen iii, 4; In il Uidi dom vi, 4; In Ioh xiv, 4; In Phil vii 3 (2:11)
3:18 F Ier 34:12
3:19 In Heb iii, 6
3:23 In Rom x, 3 (5:18)
3:24 Ad pop Anti vii, 4
3:27 Cat ill ii, 11; iv, 4; ix, 12; xi, 7; xii, 13; De paen vii, 7; De res d n I C 3; Ex in ps xliv, 10; H in san pascha 4; In Col x, 5 94:4) (2x); In Ioh i, 2
3:28 Ad Dem de comp i, 3; Cat ill xi, 21; Ex in ps vii, 10; In Acta v, 2 (2:20); In Col vi, 4 (2:15); xii, 5 (4:8); In 1 Cor xii, 12; xl, 6; In d P Nolo 3; In Eph xx, 1 (5:24); In Mat lxxiii, 3; In Philem i, 1 (v3); In Rom xxx, 3 (16:4); In s Igna 1; S post red i, 1
4:4 De prod Iud i, 4; ii, 4; In il Fil 3; In Ioh xxvi, 1; In Is ii, 2; In Mat iv, 6; In Tit v, 3 (3:3)
4:5 De prod Iud i, 4; ii, 4
4:6 De san pent i, 4; In Eph i, 1 (1:2); In Rom xiv, 3 (8:16)
4:9 In Col vi, 1 (2:8)
4:10 Adu Iud 3, 4, 2; In Is ii, 4; In kal 2; In princ Act iv, 3
4:11 Adu Iud 3, 4, 2; In Gal ii, 5 (2:12); In kal 2; In princ Act iv, 3; In Rom xxxii, 3 (16:24)
4:12 Adu Iud 3, 3, 1; De uir xxxv

| | |
|---|---|
| 4:13 | In 1 Cor vi, 2 |
| 4:14 | In 1 Cor vi, 2; In 2 Cor vi, 4; xii, 4; In Mat liii, 7; In Rom xxxi, 3 (16:16) |
| 4:15 | Ex in ps xlvi, 3; cix, 4; In Acta xliv, 4; In 2 Cor xii, 4 (2x); xiii, 1; In il Sal P et A ii, 5; In Mat liii, 7; In Rom xxix, 4 (15:24) |
| 4:17 | In Gal i, 1 (1:3) |
| 4:18 | In Col i, 1 (1:2); In Heb ii, 2 |
| 4:19 | Ad Stag a dae iii, 11; Ad Theo i, 8; De laud s Paul i; iii; De paen i, 1 (3x); Ex in ps cxi 8; In Acta xi, 4 (4:34); In 2 Cor xiii, 1; In Gal i, 1 (1:3); In Heb ix, 8; xxi, 3; xxiii, 9; xxxi, 3; In Phil x, 1 (3:3); In Rom xxxii, 3 (16:24); In 2 Tim i, 1 (1:2) |
| 4:20 | In Gal i, 1 (1:3); In Heb viii, 6 |
| 4:21 | De paen vi, 5; In il Hab ii, 5; In Rom vii, 1 (3:19) |
| 4:22 | De paen vi, 5; In il Hab ii, 5; In Mat xvi, 9; In Rom vii, 1 (3:19) |
| 4:23 | De paen vi, 5 |
| 4:24 | Ad pop Anti vii, 8; In il Hab ii, 5; ii, 6 (2x); Non esse desp 4 |
| 4:25 | Adu Iud 1, 4, 7; Non esse desp 4 |
| 4:26 | Adu Iud 1, 4, 7; Ex in ps cxlvii, 3; In Eph xxiii, 2 (6:14); xxiii, 3 (6:14); In s Luc; Non esse desp 4 (2x) |
| 4:28 | De mut nom ii, 4; Non esse desp 4 |
| 4:31 | Non esse desp 4 |
| 5:2 | Ad Theo i, 8; Adu Iud 2, 1, 4; 2, 1, 5; 2, 2, 1; 2, 2, 2; 3, 3, 9; 8, 5, 5; De mut nom i, 6; iv, 3; De sac i, 8; In 1 Cor xxxvii, 3; In 2 Cor xxi, 1; In d P Op 1; In Gal i, 1 (1:3); ii, 2 (2:5); In Gen xxxix, 5; In Is ii, 4; In Mat ix, 7; In princ Act iv, 5; In Rom xxxi, 3 (16:16) |
| 5:3 | Adu Iud 2, 2, 2; 2, 2, 3; In Col vii, 1 (2:19) |
| 5:4 | Ad Theo i, 8; Adu Iud 2, 2, 1; 2, 3, 9; 6, 7, 4; In 1 Cor xxvii, 3; In Gal i, 1 (1:3); iii, 3 (3:5); In Gen xxxix, 5; In Heb xxxi, 3; In Phil iv, 1 (1:26); In Rom xiii, 6 (8:7); xxxv, 2 (14:6) |
| 5:6 | In Gal ii, 3 (2:9) |
| 5:7 | In Heb viii, 4; x, 4 |
| 5:9 | Adu Iud 3, 1, 5 |
| 5:10 | De D et S ii, 3; In 1 Cor xxxviii, 2; xl, 4; In Gal i, 5 (1:6); In Heb viii, 4; x, 4; In Rom xxix, 1 (15;15) |
| 5:12 | F Prou 11:26; In Mat lxii, 3 |
| 5:15 | Ad pop Anti iii, 12; Adu Iud 3, 1, 6; In Col |

| | |
|---|---|
| 5:15 cont | ii, 1 (1:11); In Heb xxi, 7 |
| 5:17 | Ex in ps xli, 2 |
| 5:18 | In Ioh lxxviii, 3 |
| 5:19-20 | Cat ill i, 32; De sac ii, 2 |
| 5:21 | De sac ii, 2 |
| 5:22 | Cat ill i, 33; iv, 27; De san pent ii, 3; Ex in ps xliv, 9; In Acta i, 8 (1:5); In Gen iv, 8; In il Dom non est 1; In Ioh lxxv, 5; lxxix, 5; In Mat lv, 7; In Rom i, 4 (1:7) |
| 5:23 | Cat ill i, 33; iv, 27; In Ioh lxxv, 5 |
| 5:24 | Cat ill iv, 28; Ex in ps xlvii, 1; xliii, 6; In Gen xvi, 6; xxxiv, 5; In Mat lxx, 2; In Rom xi, 5 (6:18); In 1 Tim x, 1 (3:4) |
| 6 (p) | De laud s Paul 1 |
| 6:1 | Adu op iii, 2; In Gen xliii, 4; In Mat xii, 3; In Rom xxvii, 2 (15:1); Q freg con 6; S Gen ix 1 |
| 6:2 | De mut nom ii, 1; In Col viii, 4 (3:15); In Heb xxx, 7; In Rom viii, 7 (4:21) |
| 6:4 | De prof eua 1; De proph obscur ii, 9; In Mat lxxxii, 3; In 2 Tim ii, 3 (1:12) |
| 6:5 | In 1 Cor xliv, 5 |
| 6:8 | In 1 Cor xlii, 2; In Mat xxiv, 4 |
| 6:9 | De Laz ii, 5; In Eph xxiii, 3 (6:14); In Heb viii, 4 |
| 6:10 | De Laz ii, 5; De paen ix, 1; In Heb x, 7; x, 8 |
| 6:11 | In Rom xxxii, 4 (16:24) |
| 6:13 | In 1 Tim ii, 1 (1:7) |
| 6:14 | Ad e q scan xvii; Ad pop Anti i, 9; xv, 8; Adu Iud 3, 4, 8; Con e q sbu 5; De laud s Paul vi; Ex in ps xliii, 6; cxxx, 1; In Acta lii, 4; In Heb xxiv, 1; In il Pater s p 2; In Mat xliii, 2; liv, 7; In Phil iii, 2 (1:21); xiii, 1 (3:21); In Rom ii, 6 (1:16); xvii, 5 (10:13); In 2 Tim ii, 1 (1:10) |
| 6:15 | In Gal ii, 2 (2:5) |
| 6:16 | Ex in ps cxlv, 4 |
| 6:17 | Ad pop Anti xv, 13; In Acta x, 4 (7:5) (2x); xxxix, 2 (3x); In Eph viii, 2 (4:2); vii, 7 (4:2); In Mat xvi, 14; In Philem i, 1 (v3); In Rom xxxii, 2 (16:24) |

Ephesians

| | |
|---|---|
| 1:1 | Cat ill xi, 10 |
| 1:3 | Ex in ps cxiii, 5; In Rom ii, 1 (1:8) |

1:10 In Col iii, 3 (1:20); In Is ii, 2
1:17-18 In Eph vii, 2 (3:18)
1:19 De mut nom i, 6; In Eph iv, 1 (2:5); vii, 1 (3:11)
1:21 De incomp dei iv, 2; v, 2; Ex in ps xli, 4
1:22 Cat ill xii, 14; Ex in ps xliv, 10
1:23 Cat ill xii, 14; In Col vi, 2 (2:10); In Rom xxiv, 2 (13:14)
2:3 In Ioh lx, 6
2:4 In Col vii, 1 (2:19); In Mat v, 2
2:6 De diab tent i, 2; Ex in ps xi, 3; xliv, 10; In Col vi, 2 (2:10); In Eph Argumentum; ix, 2 (4:3); In Heb iv, 4; In 1 Tim xv, 4 (5:20); S Gen ii, 1
2:7 De diab tent i, 2; i, 3; In Heb iv, 4
2:8 Ex in ps cxv, 2; In Acta xxx, 3 (14:15); In 1 Cor i, 1; In Gal iii, 3 (3:12)
2:10 In 2 Cor vii, 5
2:13 In Heb v, 1
2:14 De prod Iud ii, 6; Ex in ps xliv, 5; cxvii, 5; In Col iii, 2 (1:20); In Mat iii, 4
2:15 Ex in ps cxvii, 5; In 1 Cor xx, 5; In Eph vi, 1 (2:22); In Ioh lx, 2
2:16 De prod Iud ii, 6
2:19 Cat ill x, 15; Ex in ps cxlii, 3; In princ Act ii, 2; In s Luc 3
2:20 Ex in ps cxvii, 5; In princ Act ii, 2
3:1 Ex in ps cxv, 5; In Acta lii, 4; In Philem i, 1 (v3)
3:3-4 In Heb xxxiv, 6
3:5 De incomp dei iv, 2; In Col v, 1 (1:28); In Eph Argumentum
3:6 In Col vi, 2 (2:10); In Heb vi, 4
3:8 De incomp dei iv, 2; In 1 Cor vii, 4; In il In fac 7; In il Ut sus 5; In Mat xxv, 5
3:9 De incomp dei v, 2; In Col v, 1 (1:28) (2x)
3:10 De incomp dei iv, 2; In Col v, 1 (1:28); In 1 Cor vii, 2; In Eph Argumentum; In ioh i, 3; In 1 Tim xi, 1 (3:16)
3:14 In 2 Cor xiii, 1
3:16 In Rom xxiv, 2 (13:14); Non esse desp 8
3:17 Ad pop Anti xix, 5; In Rom xxiv, 2 (13:14)
3:20 Ad pop Anti xxi, 1; De dec mil 6; E i, 2; ccxxxix; Ex in ps cxiii, 5; In Eph xxii, 5 (6:13); In 2 Tim ii, 1 (1:10); Non esse desp 1; 8
3:21 Ex in ps cxiii, 5
4:1 Ad pop Anti xvi, 8

4:3 Ex in ps cxv, 5
4:5 In Col viii, 4 (3:15); In 1 Cor ix, 5
4:8 Ex in ps xlvi, 2
4:9 In ascen d n I C 3
4:10 In Acta ii, 3 (1:11); In ascen d n I C 3
4:11 In 1 Cor viii, 2; In il Hab i, 3
4:12 De s h Bab 2; In 1 Cor viii, 2; In il Hab i, 3
4:13 De uir xvi; Ex in ps v, 1; In d P Op 1; In il Hab i, 3
4:14 In il Hab i, 3
4:17 De Laz v, 3; In 1 Cor xv, 1
4:19 Ex in ps vi, 5; In il Pater m 1
4:20 De laud s Paul vi
4:25 Cat ill v, 14; In Col viii, 4 93:15); In Mat xv, 14
4:26 Ad Dem de comp i, 3; Ad pop Anti xx, 13; Adu op iii, 14; In Acta xxxiii, 4 (16:12); xli, 15; In Ioh iv, 4; In Mat xvi, 12; In 1 Thess iv, 5 (3:13)
4:27 F in epis cath 1 John 3:8
4:28 In Ioh xliv, 1; In Phil vi, 3 (2:8)
4:29 Ad pop Anti xv, 11; Cat ill iv, 25; De inani gloria 28; De prod Iud ii, 2; Ex in ps cxl, 5; In Acta xxxi, 4 (14:20); In Col xii, 6 (4:18); In Gen xv, 5; In Heb i, 4; In il Prop 1 (2x); In Phil x, 5 (3:7)
4:30 Cat ill iv, 25
4:31 Adu op iii, 14; De Laz iii, 6; In Gen liii, 5; In Ioh xxvi, 3
5:1 De laud s Paul iii; In Rom xix, 8 (11:35)
5:2 Ad e q scan xvii; De laud s Paul iii; H in il App 23; In Eph x, 1 (4:4); In il Fil 4; In il Pater s p 2; In Ioh lxix, 2; lxxx, 2
5:4 Ad pop Anti xv, 11; De Laz i, 12; In Col xii, 6 (4:18); In 1 Cor vii, 16; In Heb xv, 8; In Mat vi, 10
5:5 De incomp dei v, 2; In Heb iv, 7; xv, 7
5:6 Ex in ps cxlii, 4
5:8 In Eph xx, 21 (5:26); xxii, 3 (6:.12); In 1 Thess xi, 1 (5:22)
5:12 In Ioh v, 4
5:14 De coem et de cru 1; In Mat lxvii, 4
5:15 In Eph xxiv, 2 (6:22)
5:18 Adu Iud 8, 1, 1; Cat ill v, 6; De res d n I C 1; 2; Ex in ps xli, 1; In Mat 1, 4
5:19 Ex in ps cxlvi, 1
5:21 In Eph xxii, 1 (6:8); In il Prop 4
5:22 In Eph i, 1 (1:2); In il Prop 4
5:23 Con Anom xi, 4; In Eph xx, 5 (5:33); In Gen xiv, 4

5:25 Ad e q scan xvii; Cat ill i, 16-17; xi, 9; De Chris prec 6; In 1 Cor xix, 2; In Rom xxvii, 2 (15:3); Qual duc 2; 3; S Gen iv, 2
5:26 Cat ill i, 16-17; xi, 9; In Ioh lxxxii, 1; Qual duc 2
5:27 Cat ill i, 16; i, 17; i, 18; iv, 32; xi, 10; De paen v, 3; De sac iv, 2; Ex in ps v, 2; In Eph iii, 2 (1:22); Qual duc 2
5:28 Non esse desp 6; Qual duc 3 (2x)
5:29 Qual duc 3
5:30 In Heb vi, 4; In Ioh xlvi, 3; Qual duc 3 (2x)
5:31 Cat ill i, 11; xi, 3; In Eph xx, 3 (5:29); xx, 5 (5:33); xx, 8 (5:33); Qual duc 3
5:32 Cat ill i, 11; i, 13; xi, 3; In Col xii, 5 (4:18); In Gen lvi, 1; In Mat lxix, 1; Qual duc 3 (2x)
5:33 In 1 Cor xix, 2; In il Prop 4; S Gen iv, 2
6:1 In 1 Cor xxvi, 6; In Eph i, 1 (1:2); In Mat xxxv, 3; li, 2
6:2 E ccxxxviii; Ex in ps cxxvii, 3; In 1 Cor xxvi 6; In Mat xv, 5; li, 2
6:3 In 1 Cor xxvi, 6
6:4 Adu op iii, 4; E ccxxxviii; In 1 Cor xxvi, 6; In il Uid elig 9; 11; In princ Act iv, 3; In 1 Tim ix, 2 (3:1)
6:5 In Eph i, 1 (1:2)
6:7 In Tit iv, 3 (2:10)
6:8 In Eph xx, 6 (5:33)
6:9 In Col x, 2 (4:1) (2x); In Mat xliii, 5; In Philem i, 3 (1:3); In 1 Tim xvi, 2 (6:2)
6:10 H dicta in t s Anas 1; 2
6:11 Cat ill i, 1; In Gen iii, 5; In Heb xvi, 7; In s Bar 4
6:12 Ad pop Anti iii, 7; Ad Stag a dae i, 4; De incomp dei iv, 2; De sac ii, 2; De Stud p 2; Deuir xxvii; xlix, E xv; Ex in ps vi, 5; cxliii, 1; H dicta in t s Anas 1; In Acta xxvii, 3 (13:3); xxxi, 3 (14:20); xliv, 2; In 1 Cor xxxix, 6; In Eph iv, 1 (2:3); In Gal v, 5 (5:17); In Gen iii, 5; xliv, 6; In Heb v, 8; In il In fac 8; In Mat vi, 9; xxiii, 7; In Phil viii, 1 (2:16); ix, 3 (2:30); In Rom xxxvi, 4 (16:24); In s Bab c Iul 3; In s Bar 1; 4; In 1 Thess iii, 4 (3:4); In 2 Tim iv, 1 (2:7)
6:13 In Eph xxiii, 1 (6:14)
6:14 Ex in ps v, 2; cxxiii, 2; In Gen iii, 5; In Heb v, 8 (2x); In princ Act iii, 5
6:15 Cat ill xi, 9; Ex in ps v, 2; In Ioh i, 2

6:16 De sac iv, 3
6:17 De sac iv, 3; F Prou 1:13; In Heb v, 8; In princ Act iii, 5
6:18 In Gen iii, 5; xxx, 5; In Heb vii, 11
6:19 In Eph Argumentum; In Gen xxiv, 1; S cum pres 1
6:20 Ex in ps cxv, 5
6:21 In Col xi, 1 (4:8); In 2 Cor ii, 3
6:22 De prof eua 6; In Col xi, 1 (4:8); In 2 Cor ii, 3

Philippians

1:1 Ad pop Anti xvi, 8
1:3-4 In Eph iii, 1 (1:20)
1:7 De paen i, 1; De prof eua 4; E xciii; H dicta in t s Anas 2; In 2 Cor xiii, 1; In Phil xv, 2 (4:14); In Rom Argumentum, 1
1:8 In 1 Tim ii, 3 (1:11)
1:12 Ad e q scan xiv; De laud s Paul iv; De prof eua 4; 5; 7 (2x); H dicta in t s Anas 5; In 2 Cor xii, 5; In Phil Argumentum, 2; ix, 1 (2: 21)
1:13 De laud s Paul iv; De prof eua 4; 7; In Eph viii, 7 (4:2); In Phil Argumentum, 1; ix, 1 (2:21)
1:14 Ad e q scan xiv; xx; Ad pop Anti xvi, 8; Con Iud et gen 13; 14; De laud s Paul iv; vii; De prof eua 4; 7; H dicta in t s Anas 5; In Col x, 3 (4:4); x, 4 (4:4); In 2 Cor xii, 3; In Eph viii, 7 (4:2)
1:15-16 De laud s Paul iv; De prof eua 9
1:17 De laud s Paul iv; De prof eua 9; 10
1:18 De laud s Paul iv; De prof eua 1; 3; 9; 10; In Heb xxviii, 11; In 1 Tim iii, 4 (1:14)
1:19 In 1 Thess i, 3 (1:7)
1:21 In 1 Tim xiv, 4 (5:10); S ante iret 1; S cum iret 1
1:22 In Gal i, 4 (1:4); In il Is Ego 4; In s Eust 2
1:23 Ad uid iun 3; De laud s Paul ii; De ss B et P 3 (2x); E iv, 2; Ex in ps cxiv, 2; cxix, 3; In Acta xx, 3 (9:25); In Col i, 3 (1:7); xii, 3 (4:18); In Eph viii, 2 (4:2); In Gen xlv, 2; In il Is Ego 4; In Is Argumentum; In Mat xxiii 9; xxviii, 3; lxxvii, 6; In Rom xvi, 2 (9:6); In 2 Tim ix, 2 (4:7)
1:24 Ad Dem de comp i, 7; De laud s Paul i; ii; vii; De prof eua 10; E iv, 3; In Acta xx, 3

1:24 cont (9:25); In Col i, 3 (1:7); xii, 3 (4:18); In Eph viii, 2 (4:2); In il Is Ego 4; In Is Argumentum; In Mat lxxvii, 6

1:25 In Phil Argumentum, 1

1:29 Ad pop Anti xvi, 9; De Anna v, 3; De laud s Paul vii; Ex in ps xli, 6; In 1 Cor xxxiii, 7; In Eph vi, 4 (3:7); viii, 2 (4:2); In Phil Argumentum, 1; xiv, 1 (4:7); xv, 2 (4:14)

1:30 In Acta xxxi, 1 (14:18)

2:1 Ad e q scan xvii; De sac vi, 13

2:2 Ad e q scan xviii; In Acta iii, 5 (1:26)

2:3 Ad e q scan xvii; De Chris prec 6; De D et S iii, 6; H in il App 23; In Gen iv, 8; In Phil vi, 3 (2:8)

2:4 In Gen vii, 2; In Mat iv, 18

2:5 Ad e q scan xvii; De Chris prec 6; In il Fil 3; In Eph x, 1 (4:4); xi, 2 (4:10); In Phil vi, 1 (2:8)

2:6 Ad e q scan xvii; De mut nom ii, 1; In 1 Cor xxxix, 7; In Eph x, 1 (4:4); xi, 2 (4:10); In Eut ii, 6; In Gal i, 2 (1:31); In Heb ii, 2; In il Fil 3; 4; In il Pater s p 2; In Ioh iii, 4; iv, 3; vi, 1; xxxviii, 4; lxxx, 2; In Phil vi, 1 (2:8); In princ Act iv, 4

2:7 Ad e q scan xvii; De Chris prec 6; De mut nom ii, 1; In 1 Cor iv, 2; xxxix, 7; In Eph vii, 4 (3:19); viii, 1 (4:2); xi, 2 (4:10); In Gen xxiii, 6; In Heb ii, 2; viii, 3; xxxii, 7; In il Fil 3; 4; In il Pater s p 2; In Ioh xxi, 1; lx, 3; lxix, 2; lxxx, 2; In Mat iv, 6; In Phil vi, 1 (2:8); In princ Act iv, 4; In Rom xxvii, 2 (15:3); In 1 Tim xvii, 1 (2:7)

2:8 Ad e q scan xvii; In 1 Cor xxxix, 7; In 2 Cor xi, 5; In Eph vii, 4 (3:19); xi, 2 (4:10) (2x) In Gen xxxiv, 6; In il Pater s p 2

2:9 In 1 Cor xxxix, 7; In Eph xi, 2 (4:10) (2x); In Heb xxviii, 4

2:10 Cat ill xi, 22; In 1 Cor xxxii, 6; In Heb xxviii, 4; In Mat xxxvi, 3

2:11 In 1 Cor iv, 11; In Mat xxxvi, 3

2:12 In Col i, 1 (1:2); In 1 Cor xiv, 1; xxviii, 3; In Gen iv, 1; viii, 4; S post red ii, 2

2:13 In 1 Tim iii, 2 (1:14)

2:14 In Heb xxxiii, 1

2:15 Adu op iii, 2; In 1 Cor iv, 11; In princ Act i, 5; In 1 Tim x, 3 (3:7)

2:16 De uir i; In princ Act i, 5

2:17 Con Iud et gen 13; 14; De laud s Paul i, 1; De ss B et P 3; E vii, 3; Ex in ps v, 5; cx,

2:17 cont 2; cxiv, 2; In Mat xxxviii, 14; In Phil Argumentum, 1; ix, 1 (2:21)
2:18 Con Iud et gen 13; 14; De laud s Paul i, 1; ii; De ss B et P 3; Ex in ps v, 5; cx, 2; cxiv 2; In Mat xxxviii, 4
2:19 In Phil Argumentum, 1 (2x)
2:20 In Phil Argumentum, 2; ix, 1 (2:21); xv, 4 (4:19); In 1 Thess i, 1 (1:3)
2:21 In 2 Cor ii, 18; In Ioh lx, 1
2:22 Ad pop Anti i, 9; In 1 Cor xliv, 1; In 2 Cor i, 2; In 1 Thess i, 1 (1:3); In 1 Tim Argumentum, 1
2:23 In 1 Thess i, 1 (1:3)
2:24 In Phil Argumentum, 1 (2x)
2:25 Ad pop Anti x, 7; In Phil ix, 1 (2:21); ix, 6 (2:30)
2:26 In Phil Argumentum, 2
2:27 Ad Stag a dae iii, 11; In 2 Cor xxix, 2; In il Sal P et A ii, 5; In Phil iv, 4 (1:30); ix, 6 (2:30); In 2 Tim x, 3 (4:20)
2:29 In Tit i, 3 (1:5)
2:30 De prof eua 6; In il Sal P et A ii, 5; In Mat lvi, 4; In 2 Tim iii, 1 (1:18); In Tit i, 3 (1:5)
3:1 De fato et pr iv; E iv, 1; In Gen iv, 6; In Ioh xviii, 1; xxxii, 3; li, 3
3:2 Adu Iud 1, 11, 2; De incomp dei ii, 6; In Col xii, 2 (4:18); In 1 Cor xxvii, 3; In Mat xix, 1; In Phil Argumentum, 2; In Rom xxv, 2 (14:5)
3:3 Adu Iud 1, 11, 2; In Ioh xiv, 1
3:4 In 1 Cor xxxv, 7
3:5 Adu Iud 3, 3, 2; Ex in ps cxv, 5; In 1 Cor xxxv, 7
3:6 Adu Iud 2, 2, 2; 3, 3, 2; In 1 Cor xxxv, 7; In Ioh xiv, 1; In 1 Tim iv, 1 (1:16)
3:7 Adu Iud 3, 3, 2; 3, 6, 2; De incomp dei ii, 6; De sac i, 8; In 1 Cor xxxv, 7
3:8 De incomp dei ii, 6
3:9 De incomp dei ii, 6; In Rom xvi, 2 (9:6)
3:10 De incomp dei ii, 6; De ss B et P 6; In Heb ix, 6
3:11 In Phil xiii, 4 (4:3)
3:12 De incomp dei i, 1; Ex in ps cxliii, 2; H in il App 11; In Tit i, 1 (1:5)
3:13 De incomp dei ii, 5; ii, 6; De laud s Paul ii; v; Ex in ps cxix, 1; In Mat xvi, 14; In Philem ii, 3 (v16)
3:14 In Eph xvii, 3 (5:4); In Mat xvi, 14
3:15 De incomp dei ii, 6; In Rom xxvi, 3 (14:23)
3:17 De laud s Paul vii; In Acta i, 3 (1:2); xlv, 1

| | |
|---|---|
| 3:17 cont | In Phil xiv, 2 (4:9) |
| 3:19 | De fato et pr vi; In 1 Cor xvii, 1; xxxiv, 10; In Eph xviii, 3 (5:14); In Heb xxv, 5; xxix, 4; In Ioh xlvi, 1; In Mat vi, 10; xxi, 2; In Rom xiii, 3-4 (7:23); xxxii, 1 (16:18); Q reg 8 |
| 3:20 | Ad Theo ii, 5; Cat ill vii, 12; Ex in ps cxlii 3; In 2 Cor iii, 5; xv, 5; In Eph i, 1 (1:3); x, 2 (4:4); xxiii, 2 (6:14) (2x); In Heb xvi, 6; In Phil iii, 2 (1:21); xii, 2 (3:14); In s Luc 3; In 1 Tim x, 3 (3:7) |
| 3:21 | De fut uit 6; Ex in ps cix, 6; cix, 7; In 1 Cor xxxix, 9; xli, 2; In 2 Cor xi, 3; In Rom xiv, 6 (8:23) |
| 4:1 | De incomp dei iv, 5; In Acta xi, 4 (4:34); In Eph xxiii, 1 (6:14) |
| 4:3 | In Rom xxx, 3 (16:5); In 1 Tim Argumentum, 2 |
| 4:4 | Ad pop Anti xviii, 2; xviii, 3; Ad Stag a dae iii, 14; De Laz v, 3; In Acta xv, 4 (7:5); xvi 3 (7:34); In 1 Cor xv, 6; In il Is Ego 5; In Mat vi, 8; xxxvii, 8; In 1 Tim ii, 3 (1:11) |
| 4:5 | De incomp dei i, 7; De uir lxxiii; In Acta ii, 1 (1:6); In 2 Cor xii, 1; In Heb i, 2; xix, 3; In il Hab iii, 15; In Ioh xxxiv, 3; In Mat lxxiv, 4; lxxvii, 4; In Phil Argumentum, 2 (2x) |
| 4:6 | De uir lxxiii; In 1 Cor ii, 1; In Heb i, 2; xix, 3; In il Hab iii, 5; In Ioh xxxiv, 3; In Mat lxxiv, 4; lxxvii, 4 |
| 4:7 | Ad e q scan ii; De diab tent i, 3; De incomp dei i, 5; In 2 Cor xx, 2; In Heb ii, 1 |
| 4:9 | De laud s Paul vii |
| 4:10 | In Phil Argumentum, 2 |
| 4:12 | In Mat xc, 4; In Phil xii, 9 (3:17); Qual duc 1 |
| 4:14 | In 2 Tim iii, 1 (1:18) |
| 4:15 | In 2 Cor xxiii, 5; In Phil Argumentum, 2; i, 3 (1:7) |
| 4:16 | Ex in ps xliii, 2; In 2 Cor xvii, 3; In Phil Argumentum, 2; In 2 Tim iii, 1 (1:18) |
| 4:17 | In 2 Cor xx, 2; In Tit vi, 2 (3:15) |
| 4:18 | In Phil Argumentum, 1; ix, 3 (2:30); ix, 4 (2:30) |
| 4:22 | In Rom Argumentum, 1; xxxii, 2 (16:23) |

Colossians

1 (p) In Philem iii, 1 (v23)
1:1 In Col v, 1 (1:29)
1:3 In Eph iii, 1 (1:20)
1:5 In Col ii, 2 (1:12)
1:6 In Col v, 2 (1:23); In 1 Cor xxxvii, 2; In Mat lxxv, 2; In Rom xxx, 1 (15:27)
1:7 In Col xii, 2 (4:18)
1:8 In Col xii, 1 (4:13)
1:9 In il Ut sus 2
1:12 In Col iv, 1 (1:22)
1:13 De coem et de cru 2; In Col iii, 2 (1:18); iv, 1 (1:32); vi, 2 (2:10)
1:15 In Eph vi, 1 (2:22); In Eut ii, 6; In Ioh xv, 1
1:16 Ex in ps cxxxviii, 2 (2x); cxlii, 5; In Eph xxii, 3 (6:12); In Gen ii, 3; In Ioh v, 2; v, 3; S Gen i, 2
1:17 Ex in ps cxxxviii, 2
1:18 De sac iv, 2; In Col iii, 2 (1:18); In Ioh xlv 3; In 1 Thess vii, 1 (4:14)
1:20 De ss mar B 1; In Col vii, 1 (2:19); In Heb xii, 2; xvii, 2
1:21 In Col vi, 2 (2:10)
1:22 De prod Iud ii, 6
1:23 In Col i, 1 (1:2); xii, 2 (4:18); In Mat lxxv, 2 (2x)
1:24 Ad pop Anti xvi, 9; xviii, 10; Con Iud et gen 13; 14; De Anna v, 3; De gloria in trib 3; De s mar B 1; De s Bab c Iul ii; De sac iv, 2; E vii, 4; cii; ccvii; Ex in ps xli, 6; cxi, 1; In Acta xliv, 1; In 1 Cor xiv, 7; In 2 Cor i, 4; In Eph viii, 2 (4:2); In Gal v, 5 (5:17); In Gen xxxii, 9; In Mat xvi, 14; In Phil xi, 2 (3:10); In Rom xxxii, 2 (16:24); In s Igna 3; Q nemo 5
1:28 De laud s Paul iii
2:1 In Col i, 1 (1:2); In 2 Cor xiii, 1
2:2 In 2 Cor xiii, 1
2:3 In Mat lxxvii, 2
2:4 In Col vii, 1 (2:19)
2:5 In Col i, 1 (1:2); In Ioh xxx, 1
2:8 In Col vii, 1 (2:19); xii, 2 (4:18); In Rom xxv, 2 (14:5)
2:11 Cat ill ix, 12; In Col viii, 1 (3:7); In Gen xxxix, 5
2:12 In Col viii, 1 (3:7); In Gen xxxix, 5; In Mat x, 2
2:14 Cat ill iii, 21; De san pent i, 5; Ex in ps

| | |
|---|---|
| 2:14 cont | xlvi, 5; In Ioh xxxix, 4; In Mat xxxvi, 3 |
| 2:15 | De coem et de cru 3; Ex in ps xlvi, 5; In 1 Cor xxiv, 7; xxxviii, 3 |
| 2:16 | De uir lxxviii; In Ioh xxvii, 2; In Rom xxv, 2 (14:5) |
| 2:18 | In Rom xxv, 2 (14:5) |
| 2:19 | In Ioh v, 2 |
| 2:20 | De uir lxxviii; H in il App 24; In Rom Argumentum, 2 |
| 2:21-22 | De uir lxxviii; In Rom Argumentum, 2 |
| 2:23 | In Acta xxxvii, 3 (17:15); In Rom Argumentum,2 |
| 3:1 | Ad pop Anti xi, 10; Cat ill vii, 12; vii, 20; Ex in ps cxlii, 3; In Eph iii, 3 (1:22); In kal 3 |
| 3:2 | Ad pop Anti xv, 8; Cat ill ii, 28; vii, 13; In il Uidi dom vi, 2 |
| 3:3 | Adu Iud 6, 5, 2; Cat ill vii, 21; vii, 22; Ex in ps cxliii, 3; In Col xi, 2 (4:11); In 2 Cor xv, 5; In Eph i, 1 (1:3); vi, 4 (3:7); In Rom xiv, 4 (8:18); xxiii, 3 (13:8); In 2 Tim iv, 4 (2:10) |
| 3:4 | Adu Iud 6, 5, 3; In 1 Cor vii, 20; In Rom xxiii, 3 (13:8) |
| 3:5 | De Anna iii, 3; De D et S ii, 1; In Col viii, 1 (3:15); In Gen iv, 8; In Heb xx, 5; In Ioh lxv, 3; lxxiv, 3; In Rom vi, 6 (3:8); xi, 5 (6:18); In 1 Tim x, 1 (3:4) |
| 3:6 | In 1 Cor xv, 1; In 1 Thess ix, 3 (5:5) |
| 3:7 | In 1 Cor xv, 1 |
| 3:9 | Ex in ps xi, 1; cxlix, 1; In Rom xi, 1 (6:6) |
| 3:10 | Cat ill ii, 11; In 1 Cor ix, 10 |
| 3:12 | In Rom xiv, 8 (8:27) |
| 3:13 | In Ioh xxxix, 4 |
| 3:14 | Ex in ps cxv, 5 |
| 3:15 | In Gen xxvi, 5; In Mat xxv, 4 |
| 3:16 | De sac iv, 4; In Heb viii, 9; In Ioh xvii, 4 |
| 3:17 | Ex in ps cl, 1; In Mat lv, 7 |
| 3:18 | In Eph xx, 1 (5:24) |
| 4:3 | In Acta lii, 4; In Col i, 1 (1:2) |
| 4:4 | In Col i, 1 (1:2) |
| 4:5 | In Col xi, 2 (4:11); In il Ut sus 2 |
| 4:6 | De sac iv, 8; v, 2; Ex in ps cxl, 4; In Eph vi, 3 (3:7); In il Ut sus 2; In Mat 3; In Rom Argumentum, 1 |
| 4:9 | In Col i, 1 (1:2); xi, 2 (4:11) |
| 4:10 | In Col xi, 2 (4:11); In Rom xxxi, 2 (16:7) |
| 4:14 | E ccxli |

4:16 In Col i, 1 (1:2); In Philem ii, 1 (1:6)
4:17 In Col i, 1 (1:2); In Philem i, 1 (v3); In Rom Argumentum, 1

## 1 Thessalonians

1:2 In Eph iii, 1 (1:20)
1:6 In 2 Cor xvi, 2; In il Hab iii, 5 (2x)
1:8 In 1 Cor xxxvii, 2; In 2 Cor xvi, 2; In il Hab i, 4; In Rom ii, 1 (1:8); In 2 Thess ii, 2 (1:4)
1:9 In 2 Cor xiii, 1; In Phil 1:30
2:1 In Phil iv, 3 (1:30)
2:3, 5 In Eph vi, 3 (3:7)
2:6 In Ioh iii, 6
2:7 In 2 Cor xiii, 1
2:8 In Acta xlix, 4; In 2 Cor xiii, 1
2:9 Ad pop Anti ii, 23; De sac iii, 7; In 2 Cor xii, 2; In il Sal P et A i, 5; In Mat viii, 6
2:14 Ad pop Anti i, 19; Con Iud et gen 13; 14; De laud s Paul iv; De prod Iud ii, 1; H dicta in t s Anas 3; In 2 Cor xvi, 3; In Eph vi, 4 (3:7); In Gal ii, 4 (2:10); In Heb Argumentum, 2; xxii, 3; In il Hab iii, 5; In Mat xv, 8; In Rom xviii, 4 (11:5); In 1 Thess i, 2 (1:4); vi, 2 (4:13)
2:15 Con Iud et gen 13; 14; De laud s Paul iv; De prod Iud i, 1; ii, 1; H dicta in t s Anas 3; In Mat xv, 8; lxix, 1; In Rom xviii, 4 (11:5)
2:16 Adu op i, 6; De laud s Paul vi; De prod Iud ii 1; Ex in ps cxlii, 4; In Acta xxv, 2 (11:30); xxxvii, 2
2:17 E ii, 12 (3x); xciii; In Col i, 3 (1:7); In il Hoc scit 7; In Phil ix, 1 (2:21); In Rom xxxii 3 (16:24); In 2 Tim ix, 2 (4:7)
2:18 Ad pop Anti i, 30; E ii, 12
2:19 In 1 Cor xxxiii, 3; In Gen viii, 1; In Mat lviii, 7; In Phil iv, 2 (1:26); In 2 Tim ii, 2 (1:12)
3:1 E ii, 12; ii, 13; In Acta xlii, 2; In Col xi, 1 (4:8); In 2 Cor ii, 2; In 2 Thess Argumentum
3:3 In 2 Cor ii, 2; In Eph vii, 1 (3:13)
3:4 In 2 Thess iii, 3 (2:5)
3:5 De prof eua 6
3:6 In 1 Thess i, 1 (1:3)
3:8 In Eph viii, 1 (4:2); In Gen vii, 1; In Mat lviii, 7; In s Bar 1; In s Rom 1; In 2 Tim ii, 2 (1:12)
3:10 In Rom xxxii, 3 (16:24); In 2 Thess Argumentum

5:19 In il Hab i, 5; In Ioh 1, 3; In 2 Tim i, 2 (1:6)
5:20 In 1 Cor xxix, 5
5:21 In 1 Cor xxix, 5; In princ Act iv, 2

## 2 Thessalonians

1:6 Ad Stag a dae iii, 14; De laud s Paul vi; In Eph xiii, 1 (4:21); In Heb iii, 6; In il Hab iii, 5; In Rom xiii, 8 (8:9)
1:7 Ad Stag a dae iii, 14; De laud s Paul vi; In Heb iii, 6; In il Hab iii, 5; iii, 10
1:9 Ex in ps cxlii, 4; In 1 Cor ix, 1; In Rom xxxi 5 (16:16)
2:1 In 2 Thess Argumentum
2:2 In 1 Thess xi, 1 (5:22); In 2 Thess Argumentum
2:4 In Ioh xli, 2; In 2 Thess Argumentum
2:7 Ad e q scan xx; De elee 1; In Eph xxii, 4 (6:13); In Rom xxxi, 5 (16:16)
2:8 Ex in ps xliv, 4
2:9-10 In Mat lxxvi, 2
2:11 In Ioh xli, 2
2:12 Ad e qscan xii; In Ioh xli, 2
2:15 In 2 Tim iii, 1 (1:18)
3:1 In Mat xliii, 7
3:6 In Rom xxxii, 1 (16:18)
3:7 In 2 Thess v, 4 (3:18)
3:8 In 2 Cor v, 3
3:10 Ad pop Anti xii, 5; De elee 6; In Heb xi, 8; In il Hab ii, 8; ii, 9; In il Sal P et A i, 5; In Mat xxx, 6; xxxv, 5
3:13 In Acta xxxiii, 4 (16:12); In Heb xi, 8; In il Hab ii, 8; In Mat xxxv, 5; xxxv, 6
3:14 Con 1 et t 4; Ex in ps cxl, 7; In 1 Cor xvi, 2; xxxiii, 6; In il Hab ii, 9; In Mat xxxv, 5
3:15 In il Hab ii, 9; In Mat xxxv, 5
3:17-18 In 2 Thess Argumentum

## 1 Timothy

1:3 In Eph Argumentum; In Tim Argumentum, 3
1:4 In Tit vi, 1 (3:4)
1:5 De laud s Paul iii
1:9 Ad pop Anti vi, 2; vii, 5; Adu op iii, 14; Cat ill iv, 27; F Iob 1:1; In 1 Cor xvi, 9; In il Uid elig 10; In Mat xi, 2; xvi, 6; S Gen iv, 2

1:12 Ad pop Anti xii, 2; Ad Stel de comp ii, 6; De laud s Paul v; De proph obscur ii, 8; Ex in ps cx, 4; In 1 Cor xxxviii, 7; In il Ut sus 5; Q freg con 5

1:13 Ad pop Anti v, 6; xii, 2; Ad Stel de comp ii, 6; De diab tent i, 1; De mut nom i, 6; De proph obscur ii, 8; Ex in ps cx, 4; In Acta xix, 4 (9:4); In 1 Cor xxii, 6; xxxviii, 7; In 2 Cor xxii, 3; In Eph xii, 1 (3:11); In il Ut sus 5; In Ioh x, 1; In Phil iv, 4 (1:30); In Rom xxxi, 2 (16:7); In 2 Tim i, 1 (1:4); Q freg con 5

1:14 In Acta xix, 4 (9:4); De mut nom i, 6

1:15 Ad Stel de comp ii, 6; De diab tent i, 1; De incomp dei v, 6; De mut nom i, 6; iv, 6; De proph obscur ii, 8; In Acta xix, 4 (9:4); In Gal i, 2 (1:17); In il Ut sus 5 (2x); In Ioh x, 1; Non esse ad grat 4

1:16 De mut nom i, 6; Ex in ps cx, 4; In Acta xix, 4 (9:4); In 1 Cor xxii, 6; In Gal i, 1 (1:16); In il Ut sus 5; In Ioh x, 2; Q freg con 5

1:17 De incomp dei iii, 2

1:18 In il Hab i, 10

1:19 In Acta liii, 5; In il Hab i, 10; In Ioh xxxiii, 1

1:20 In princ Act iii, 5; In Rom xxxii, 4 (16:24)

2 (p) De uir lxxv

2:1 In 1 Cor xxxiii, 5; In 2 Cor ii, 6; In Ioh vii 2; In Rom xxiii, 3 (13:6)

2:2 In Rom xxiii, 3 (13:6); In Tit iv, 2 (2:5)

2:4 Ad Stag a dae i, 5; Adu Iud 7, 6, 11; De incomp dei ii, 7; v, 5; In Col v, 2 (2:5); In Gen iii, 4; xxi, 6; xxix, 5; xliv, 2

2:5 De uir vii; F Prou 1:9; In Phil vii, 3 (2:11)

2:8 De cruce et lat i, 1; ii, 1; Ex in ps ix, 6; cxl, 2; In Acta xvii, 3 (7:5); In Gen xxx, 6; xxxii, 3; xxxiv, 4; xlix, 3; In Mat xix, 11; xxiii, 5; li, 5; In princ Act ii, 4

2:9 Cat ill i, 34; xii, 45; De uir l; E ii, 6; In Col vii, 5 (3:4); In 1 Cor xxvi, 6; In Gen xxi 6; xxxvii, 5; xli, 5; In Heb xxviii, 11; xxviii, 13; In il Ne tim i, 5; In Ioh lxi, 4; In Mat xvii, 3; xlix, 5; lxxxix, 4; In Philem i, 1 (1:3); In Rom xxx, 3 (16:5); In 1 Tim xii 3 (4:10)

2:10 Cat ill i, 36

2:11 S Gen iv, 1

2:12 De sac iii, 9; In il Sal P et A i, 3; In Phil ix, 5 (2:30); In Rom xxxi, 1 (16:6); In Tit

2:12 cont iv, 1 (2:5); S Gen iv, 1; v, 1
2:14 De Anna i, 3; De uir xlvi; E iii, 3; Ex in ps vi, 2; In 1 Cor xxvi, 2; In Rom xxv, 3 (14:13); xxxi, 4 (16:16); S Gen iv, 1; v, 1
2:15 Adu op iii, 20; De Anna i, 3; i, 4; De inani gloria 19; De ss B et P 6; In Rom xxxi, 1 (16:6); xxxi, 1 (16:7); In 1 Thess vi, 4 (4:13); In 1 Tim xiv, 1 (5:10)
3:1 De sac iii, 11; In s Igna 2
3:2 In Acta iii, 4 (1:26); In s Igna 2; In 1 Tim Argumentum, 2
3:3 In Acta iii, 4 (1:26); In s Igna 2
3:4 Adu op iii, 4; In Acta iii, 4 (1:26); In 1 Tim Argumentum, 2
3:5 In Acta iii, 4 (1:26); In Rom vi, 6 (3:8); In Tit iv, 5 (2:10)
3:6 H hab p p Gothus 3; In Acta iii, 4 (1:26); In il Uidi dom iii, 3; In Is iii, 3; In Mat xv, 3; lxv, 6; In 2 Thess Argumentum, 1
3:7 De sac ii, 4; In Acta iii, 4 (1:26); In Col xi, 2 (4:11); In 1 Cor xvi, 2; In 1 Tim xv, 3 (5:20)
3:8-9 In Acta iii, 4 (1:26)
3:14 In 2 Tim i, 1 (1:2)
3:15 In 2 Tim x, 1 (4:13)
3:16 De b Phil 3; In Ioh xv, 1; lxxiii, 2
4:1 De uir v; In il Hoc scit 6; In princ Act iii, 4; In 2 Tim vii, 1 (3:7)
4:2 De uir v; In 1 Cor xxvii, 3; In Mat vii, 8; In 2 Tim vii, 1 (3:7)
4:3 De uir v
4:4 In princ Act i, 2
4:7 Ad Stag a dae ii, 4
4:11 In 1 Tim xvii, 1 (6:7)
4:12 In Is iii, 3; In 1 Tim Argumentum, 2; x, 2 (3:6); In 2 Tim vi, 2 (2:24)
4:13 De sac iv, 8; In Acta xix, 5 (9:9); In 1 Cor xxix, 5; In Rom xxi, 1 (16:5)
4:14 In 1 Cor xxix, 5; In Heb xxx, 5; In Phil i, 1 (1:2); In 1 Tim v, 1 (1:19)
4:15 In Heb viii, 9; In 1 Tim xv, 2 (5:18)
4:16 De sac iv, 8; In 1 Tim xv, 2 (5:18)
5:2 De Anna iii, 5; In 1 Tim Argumentum, 2
5:5 Ad uid iun 2; De n iter 3; 6; In Acta xxxvi, 3 (16:39); In Heb xxvii, 9; In Mat xxxi, 6; In 1 Thess vi, 4 (4:13)
5:6 Ad pop Anti v, 6; xv, 11; Ad uit iun 2; Adu op iii, 14; De Laz iii, 6; De n iter 3; De stud p 2; De uir 1; In Acta xxvii, 3 (13:3);

| | |
|---|---|
| 5:6 cont | In 1 Cor xxcii, 7; xxxix, 15; xxxix, 17; In Mat xvii, 3; lxxiv, 4; In Phil ix, 5 (2:30); xii, 4 (3:17); In 2 Tim vii, 4 (3:7) |
| 5:8 | Adu op iii, 2; In princ Act iv, 3; In 1 Tim vii, 1 (2:4) |
| 5:9 | Ad uid iun 2; De Mac i, 3; De uir xxxix; In il Uid elig 1 (2x); 4 |
| 5:10 | Ad uid iun 2; De Anna i, 4; De Mac i, 3; In il Sal P et A i, 3; In il Uid elig 2; 4; 6; 11; 15; In 1 Thess vi, 4 (4;13); In 1 Tim ix, 2 (3:1); In 2 Tim vii, 4 (3:7) |
| 5:11 | Ad uid iun 2 (2x); De fato et pr vi; De n iter 3 (2x); De uir xxxviii; In Heb xviii, 2; In il Dom non est 3; In il Uid elig 3 (2x) |
| 5:12 | De uir xxxviii; In il Dom non est 3 |
| 5:13 | De n iter 3; In Eph xix, 5 (5:21); In Heb xxi, 7; In il Uid elig 3 |
| 5:14 | De n iter 3; 5; In Eph i, 1 (1:5); In Heb xviii, 2 (2x); In il Uid elig 3; In 2 Tim vii 4 (3:7) |
| 5:15 | In 1 Tim xiii, 2 (5:3) |
| 5:16 | De uir xxxvi; In Acta xlv, 4; In il Uid elig 2 |
| 5:17 | De sac iv, 8; Ex in ps xliv, 1; In 1 Cor iii, 6; xxi, 5; xxxii, 2; In Ioh xxii, 1; In 1 Thess x, 1 (5:13) |
| 5:18 | In Ioh lxxxii, 4 |
| 5:20 | In Eph vi, 4 (3:7); In heb iv, 8; In Mat xxiii, 1 |
| 5:22 | Ad pop Anti i, 1; De dec mil 4; De sac iv, 1; In Col viii, 3 (3:15); In Phil i, 1 (1:2); In s Igna 2; In 1 Thess v, 1 (4:3) |
| 5:23 | Ad pop Anti x, 7; Adu Iud 8, 7, 12; De res d n I C 1; E iv, 3; Ex in ps cxxvii, 2; In Acta xx, 4 (9:25); In 2 Cor xxix, 2; In Eph xix, 1 (5:18); In il Is Ego 4; In Mat lvii, 5; In para 8; In Phil ix, 6 (2:30); xii, 3 (3:17); In Rom xxix, 2 (13:14); In 1 Tim i, 2 (1:2); In Tit i, 3 (1:5) |
| 5:24 | De uir xxiii; In 1 Thess viii, 4 (4:18) |
| 6 (p) | De uir xlvii |
| 6:1 | In 1 Cor xix, 5; In Philem, Argumentum |
| 6:2 | In 1 Cor xix, 5; In Gen xxix, 7 |
| 6:3 | In il Sal P et A ii, 1 |
| 6:6 | In 2 Cor vi, 4; In Mat lvi, 9; In Phil ix, 4 (2:30) |
| 6:7 | Ad pop Anti vi, 9; Ad Theo ii, 5; De fato et pr iv; F Iob 1:21; In Phil ix, 4 (2:30); Q nemo 4; S ante iret 1; S cum iret 1 |
| 6:8 | Ad pop Anti xix, 4; Adu op iii, 14; De ss B |

6:8 cont et P 2; In il Sal P et A ii, 4; In 1 Cor xiii, 7; xvii, 1; xxxv, 9; In 2 Cor vi, 4; xv, 4; xxiii, 8; In Gen xviii, 2; xxxvii, 4 (2x); In Heb xxviii, 11; In Phil ix, 4 (2:30) (2x); In Tit v, 2 (2:14)

6:9 In Acta liii, 5; In 1 Cor xiii, 7; xxxvi, 3; In 2 Cor xxiii, 8; In Eph xiii, 4 (4:24); xx, 3 (5:27); In Mat lxxiv, 4; In Phil ix, 4 (2:30); In Tit v, 2 (2:14)

6:10 Adu op iii, 6; De prod Iud i, 3; ii, 3; De uir lxxxi; In Acta xxix, 4 (13:41); In 1 Cor xxiii 8; xl, 4; In 2 Cor xiii, 4; xxiii, 8; In Gen xx, 5; xxxvii, 4; In Heb xxiv, 8; In il Hab i, 10; In Mat xxxii, 6; lxiii, 1; lxiii, 4; lxxi, 1; lxxiv, 4; In Rom xi, 5 (6:18); S ante iret 5

6:12 In 1 Cor xxxi, 7

6:13 In Acta xxx, 2 (14:15); In 2 Tim ix, 1 (4:1)

6:15 De incomp dei iii, 2 (2x); De paen vii, 3

6:16 De incomp dei iii, 2 (2x); iii, 5; In Ioh v, 3; xv, 1; In Mat li, 5

6:17 Ad pop Anti ii, 13; ii, 19

6:18 Ex in ps cxi, 2

## 2 Timothy

1:1 Ex in ps viii, 9

1:3 In 1 Cor viii, 4

1:4 In Acta xxxiii, 4 (16:12); In Col xii, 4 (4:18); In 2 Cor xiii, 1; xiii, 3; In 2 Tim i, 1 (1:2); ix, 2 (4:7)

1:5 Ex in ps cxv, 5; In Acta xxxiii, 4 (16:12); S Gen ix, 5

1:6 In 1 Cor xxix, 4

1:7 In Heb iv, 7

1:10 De incomp dei v, 2; In Heb iv, 6

1:15 Ad e q scan xiv; In Phil i, 2 (1:5)

1:16-17 H dicta in t s Anas 3

1:18 In 2 Tim x, 2 (4:18)

2:4 In 1 Cor xlii, 5; In Gen xi, 7

2:5 Ad pop Anti iii, 8; De Laz iii, 9

2:6 Ad pop Anti iii, 7; In Heb viii, 3

2:9 Ad pop Anti xvi, 8; xvi, 12; De laud s Paul vii; In Acta lii, 4; liii, 1; In Col x, 3 (4:4); In 1 Cor xiii, 6; In s Eust 2

2:10 In 1 Cor xxxiii, 3; In 1 Thess i, 2 (1:4)

2:11 In 2 Cor iii, 7; ix, 1; In 2 Tim x, 4 (4:22)

2:12 Ex in ps xlviii, 7; H dicta in t s Anas 3; In

2:12 cont Col ii, 3 (1:13); vi, 2 (2:10); In 1 Cor ii, 8; In Eph iv, 2 (2:6); In Heb vi, 9; In il Fil 6; In il Hab iii, 7; In Ioh xxxviii, 4; lxxxvii, 3; In Mat lxiv, 2; In Phil xi, 2 (3:10)
2:14 De Anna iv, 3; In Ioh lxiv, 3
2:16 De fato et pr ii; In 1 Cor xxxviii, 1; In 2 Tim viii, 2 (3:9)
2:18 In 1 Cor xxxviii, 1; In 2 Thess Argumentum, 1
2:19 In Ioh lx, 1
2:20 In il Fil 2; In 2 Tim vii, 1 (3:7)
2:21 F Prou 18:9; In il Fil 2
2:22 De Anna iv, 2
2:24 De laud s Paul iii; De laz i, 4; De sac iv, 8; In 1 Cor xxxiii, 5
2:25 De laud s Paul iii; De Laz i, 4; De sac ii, 4; In 1 Cor xxxiii, 5; In Gal vi, 4 (6:17); In Gen viii, 3; viii, 4; In Heb x, 9; In Mat xxix, 3; In Tit vi, 1 (3:11)
2:26 Ad pop Anti i, 6; De laud s Paul iii; In Gal vi, 4 (6:17); In Heb x, 9
3:1 In Acta liii, 4; In il Hoc scit 1; 3; 5; 6 (2x); In princ Act iii, 4 (2x)
3:2 In Acta liii, 4
3:5 In Mat xxiii, 3
3:6 Ex in ps cxxv, 1
3:8 Ad e q scan xx; In Eph xxiv, 5 (6:24)
3:11 In 2 Tim x, 1 (4:14)
3:12 Ad Stag a dae ii, 4; De laz iii, 6; Ex in ps cxix, 1; In Acta xxiv, 3 (11:16); In Gen lxiii, 4; In Heb v, 7; In il Hab iii, 7; In 1 Thess iii, 4 (3:4)
3:14 De sac iv, 8
3:15 De sac iv, 8; Ex in ps cxv, 5; In 1 Tim x, 2 (3:6)
3:16 De Laz iii, 2; De sac iv, 8; Ex in ps cxlii, 5; In Heb viii, 9; In Ioh xl, 4
3:17 De sac iv, 8; In il Hab ii, 7; In Ioh xl, 4; In 1 Thess iv, 3 (3:10)
4:2 Ex in ps cxl, 8; In Gal vi, 4 (6:17); In Gen x, 1; In Ioh xviii, 4; In Mat xxiii, 1; In Phil ii, 3 (1:19); In Tit v, 3 (2:15); Non esse ad grat 1; S Gen ix, 1
4:5 In 1 Cor xxix, 4
4:6 Con Iud et gen 13; De laud s Paul ii; In Col i, 1 (1:2); In Heb Argumentum, 2; In Phil viii, 4 (2:16); In Rom Argumentum, 1; xx, 2 (12:1); In 2 Tim i, 1 (1:2); ix, 1 (3:17)
4:7 De incomp dei ii, 6; De laud s Paul ii; De

| | |
|---|---|
| 4:7 cont | pet mat 3; In Acta xxxviii, 4; In Eph xxii, 5 (6:13); In Eut ii, 17; In il Hab iii, 10; In Mat liii, 7; In Phil xii, 1 (3:14); In s Iul 1; S ante iret 5; S cum iret 2 |
| 4:8 | De laud s Paul ii; De pet mat 3; Ex in ps iv, 10; v, 6; In Eph viii, 2 (4:2); In il Hab iii 10; In s Iul 1; In 1 Thess iii, 5 (3:4) |
| 4:9 | In 2 Tim i, 1 (1:2) (2x) |
| 4:10 | In Acta i, 1 (1:2); In Phil i, 2 (1:5); In Philem iii, 1 (v24) |
| 4:11 | In Acta iii, 1 (1:24); In 1 Tim Argumentum, 2 |
| 4:13 | In il Sal P et A ii, 1; In Phil ix, 5 (2:30); In 2 Tim i, 1 (1:2); vi, 2 (2:23) |
| 4:14 | Ad Stag a dae iii, 11; De laud s Paul vi; H dicta in t s Anas 4 |
| 4:15 | De laud s Paul vi; H dicta in t s Anas 4; In Mat xxiii, 3; In Rom xxxii, 1 (16:18); In 2 Tim iv, 3 (3:2) |
| 4:16 | In Acta lv, 3; In Heb Argumentum, 2; In Phil Argumentum, 1; i, 2 (1:5); iii, 1 (1:20); In 2 Tim i, 1 (1:2); vi, 2 (2:23) |
| 4:17 | In Mat xxxiii, 5; In Phil iv, 4 (1:30) |
| 4:18 | In Eph xi, 6 (4:16); In Phil iv, 4 (1:30) |
| 4:20 | Ad pop Anti x, 7; In Philem iii, 1 (v24) |
| 4:21 | In Phil ix, 5 (2:30) |

## Titus

| | |
|---|---|
| 1:4 | In 2 Cor xiii, 1 |
| 1:5 | In Phil i, 1 (1:2); In 1 Tim x, 2 (3:7) |
| 1:6 | In Eph xxi, 4 (6:4); In Phil i, 1 (1:2) |
| 1:7 | De sac iv, 8; In Acta iii, 4 (1:26); In Phil i, 1 (1:2); In s Igna 2 |
| 1:8 | In Acta iii, 4 (1:26); In s Igna 2 |
| 1:9 | De sac iv, 8; In Acta iii, 4 (1:26); In s Igna 2 |
| 1:11 | In Tit vi, 2 (3:15) |
| 1:12 | F Ier prologue; In Mat vi, 8; In Rom xxxii, 1 (16:18) |
| 1:13 | Adu Iud 2, 3, 7; In 2 Tim vi, 2 (2:24); In Tit iii, 2 (1:14) |
| 1:15 | In Mat xxv, 2 |
| 1:16 | De Anna iii, 5; In Acta xlvii, 3; In Eph xiii, 1 (4:22); In Ioh xxviii, 1; l, 2; lxxxii, 4; In 1 Tim vii, 1 (2:4); xiv, 1 (5:8) |
| 2:3 | In Mat xvii, 3 |
| 2:4 | In Gal ii, 7 (2:20); In Mat xvii, 3 |
| 2:5 | In Mat xvii, 3 |

| | |
|---|---|
| 2:7 | In Eph xxiv, 4 (6:24) |
| 2:8 | In Mat xxix, 3 |
| 2:11 | Adu Iud 5, 12, 9; De bap Chris 2; De pet mat 3; Ex in ps cxvii, 6; H in il App 1; 10; 19; In Mat lvii, 1 |
| 2:12 | Adu Iud 5, 12, 0; De bap Chris 2; Ex in ps cxvii, 6; In Mat lvii, 1 |
| 2:13 | De bap Chris 2; Ex in ps cxvii, 6; In Ioh iv, 3; In Mat lvii, 1; In Phil vi, 2 (2:8) |
| 2:15 | In 1 Tim i, 2 (1:2); In 2 Tim vi, 2 (2:24) |
| 3:3 | Cat ill xi, 5; De san pent i, 3; In Eph xx, 2 (5:26); In Ioh lx, 6 |
| 3:4 | De san pent i, 3; In Tit v, 4 (3:6) |
| 3:5 | Cat ill iii, 17; ix, 12; De san pent i, 3; In 2 Cor xi, 3; In Ioh xxiv, 2; In Rom xvi, 4 (9:9) |
| 3:8 | In Phil iv, 5 (1:30) |
| 3:10 | In Gal v, 3 (5:12); In Mat xxiii, 3; In 1 Tim xvii, 1 (6:7); In 2 Tim vi, 2 (2:24) |
| 3:12 | In Tit i, 1 (1:5) |
| 3:13 | De laud s Pauk iii; In Tit i, 1 (1:5) |
| 3:14 | In Phil iv, 5 (1:30) |

<u>Philemon</u>

| | |
|---|---|
| 1 | Ad pop Anti xvi, 6; In 2 Cor xiii, 1; In Rom xxx, 3 (16:5) |
| 2 | In Col i, 1 (1:2); In Philem Argumentum; In Rom xxx, 3 (16:5) |
| 4 | In Acta xx, 4 (9:25) |
| 7 | Ex in ps xliii, 2; In Philem Argumentum |
| 8 | De mut nom iv, 3; Ex in ps xliii, 2 |
| 9 | De mut nom iv, 3; In Col i, 1 (1:2); In 2 Cor xxxi, 1; In Eph viii, 1 (4:2); In Rom Argumentum, 1; xxxi, 3 (16:16) |
| 10 | Ad Theo i, 18; De Laz vi, 7; In Col i, 1 (1:2); In Eph viii, 5 (4:2); In Philem Argumentum |
| 11 | Ad Theo i, 18; De Laz vi, 7 |
| 12 | Ad Theo i, 19; De Laz vi, 7; In Tit i, 2 (1:5) |
| 13-14 | Ad Theo i, 18; In Col xi, 1 (4:9) |
| 15-17 | Ad Theo i, 18 |
| 18 | Ad Theo i, 18; In Philem Argumentum |
| 19-20 | In Philem Argumentum |

Hebrews

| | |
|---|---|
| 8:11 | In Heb xiv, 6; In Mat i, 1; In Rom xxvi, 4 (14:23) |
| 8:12 | In Heb xiv, 6 |
| 8:13 | Ex in ps xlviii, 10; In 1 Cor xv, 10; In Heb iii, 5; xix, 1; xxxiv, 7; In il Hab ii, 2; In Rom x, 4 (6:4); x, 5 (6:4) |
| 9:1-3 | In diem nat 3 |
| 9:4 | Ad pop Anti xvii, 11; In diem nat 3 |
| 9:5 | In diem nat 3 |
| 9:6-7 | In diem nat 3; In Heb xv, 2 |
| 9:8-9 | In Heb xv, 3 |
| 9:10 | In Heb xiii, 3; xv, 3 |
| 9:11-12 | In Heb xv, 4; xix, 1 |
| 9:13-14 | Adu Iud 7, 4, 2; In Heb xv, 5 |
| 9:17 | In Gal iii, 4 (3:15) |
| 9:19-20 | In Heb xvi, 3 |
| 9:21-22 | In Heb xvi, 4 |
| 9:23 | In Heb xvi, 6 |
| 9:24 | Cat ill x, 2; In diem nat 3; In Heb xv, 4 |
| 9:26 | In Rom x, 2 (6:10) |
| 9:27 | In Heb xvii, 4; In Rom x, 2 (6:10) |
| 9:20 | De cruce et lat i, 1; ii, 1 (2x); In Heb xvii, 4; In Ioh xxxix, 1; In Rom x, 2 (6:10) |
| 10:1 | Adu Iud 7, 3, 2; In Col iv, 3 (1:24); In Heb xvii, 5 |
| 10:2-4 | In Heb xvii, 5 |
| 10:5 | Adu Iud 7, 2, 7; 7, 3, 2; 7, 4, 1; In 2 Cor vii, 3; In Heb xvii, 5; xix, 1 |
| 10:6 | Adu Iud 7, 2, 7; 7, 4, 1; In Heb xvii, 5 |
| 10:7 | Adu Iud 7, 2, 7; (2x); 7, 4, 1; In 2 Cor vii, 3; In Heb xvii, 5 |
| 10:8 | In Heb xvii, 5 |
| 10:9 | Adu Iud 7, 4, 2; In Heb xvii, 5 |
| 10:10 | Adu Iud 7, 4, 2 |
| 10:12 | In Heb xiii, 8; In Rom xv, 3 (8:34) |
| 10:14 | In Heb xviii, 3; xx, 2; In 1 Thess vi, 2 (4:13) |
| 10:15-17 | In Heb xviii, 3 |
| 10:18 | F Ier 31:30; In Heb xviii, 3 |
| 10:19 | Cat ill x, 2 |
| 10:20 | Cat ill x, 2; In Heb xv, 1; xv, 4; xx, 1 |
| 10:22 | In Heb xxi, 2 |
| 10:24 | Ex in ps xi, 1; In Acta xxxviii, 3 (17:15); In Heb xix, 3 |

10:25 Ex in ps cxlix, 1; In Heb xix, 3; xx, 1; xxx, 2; In Ioh xix, 1; lxxviii, 4
10:27 In Eph ii, 3 (1:14); In Mat lxxxii, 6
10:28 De paen vi, 5; Ex in ps vi, 2; vii, 5; In Acta i, 6 (1:5); In Heb xx, 3; In Ioh xxviii, 1; xlvi, 4; In Mat lxxv, 5; In Rom xi, 5 (6:18)
10:29 De paen vi, 5; Ex in ps vi, 2; vii, 5; In Acta i, 6 (1:5); In Eph xviii, 1 (5:8); In Heb xx, 3; In Ioh xxviii, 1; In Mat lxxv, 5; In Rom xi, 5 (6:18); In Rom xii, 5 (7:8)
10:30 In Heb xx, 4
10:31 In 1 Cor ix, 3; In Heb xx, 4; xxi, 4; In il Uidi dom vi, 4
10:32 Cat ill ix, 12; Con Iud et gen 13; 14; De res mort 2; De laud s Paul iv; E vx; E ad e p d (2x); Ex in ps cxlii, 4; H dicta in t s Anas 3; In Heb vii, 3; xxii, 1; xxix, 1; xxix, 3; In il Hab iii, 4; In Mat xv, 9; In Phil iv, 3 (1:30)
10:33 Ad e q scan xix; Con Iud et gen 13; 14; De res mort 2; De laud s Paul iv; E xv; E ad e p d (2x); H dicta in t s Anas 3; In il Hab iii, 4; In Mat xv, 9; In Phil iv, 3 (1:30)
10:34 Ad e q scan xix; Con Iud et gen 13; 14; De elee 2; De res mort 2; De laud s Paul iv; H dicta in t s Anas 3; In Eph vi, 4 (3:7); In Gal ii, 4 (2:9); In Heb Argumentum, 2; xxvi, 3; xxxiii, 2; In il Hab iii, 4; In Iuu et Max 2; In Phil iv, 3 (1:30); In Rom x, 6 (6:4); In 1 Thess vi, 2 (4:13)
10:35-36 In Heb xxi, 3; In il Hab iii, 5
10:37 H dicta in t s Anas 4; In 2 Cor xiii, 1; In Heb Argumentum, 3; xxi, 2; In il Hab iii, 5; In Ioh xlv, 3; In Mat x, 6; lxxiv, 4; lxxvii, 4; In Rom xxiv, 1 (13:11)
10:38 In Heb xxii, 1; In Phil viii, 2 (2:16)
11 (p) In Eph xxiv, 2 (6:22)
11:1 Cat ill ii, 9; In 1 Cor xxxiv, 5; In Gen xxxvi, 5; In Heb xxi, 4; xxii, 1; In il Hab iii, 8; In Ioh lxxxvii, 1
11:2 In Heb xxi, 4
11:3 In il Hoc scit 1
11:4 Adu Iud 8, 8, 2; De paen vii, 5; In Gen xix, 6; xxvii, 3; In Heb xxxii, 2
11:5 H dicta p imp 2; In Heb xxii, 4
11:6 Cat ill ii, 15; De incomp dei v, 5; Ex in ps cxxxviii, 2; cxliii, 2
11:7 In Gen xxv, 5

| | |
|---|---|
| 11:38 cont | In Ioh xvi, 3; In mar Aeg 2; In Mat iv, 20; In princ Act i, 1 |
| 11:39 | In Heb xi, 1; In il Hab iii, 8 |
| 11:40 | In Heb xi, 1; In il Hab iii, 9; In 1 Thess viii, 1 (4:18); S Gen vii, 5 |
| 12:1 | Ad e q scan xix; Adu Iud 8, 8, 3; Ex in ps xlviii, 4; H dicta in t s Anas 4; In Heb xxviii, 3 |
| 12:2 | In Heb xxviii, 4; In Ioh lxxvii, 4; In Mat lxxxv, 1; In Rom xxvii, 2 (15:31); In 1 Tim xviii, 1 (6:16) |
| 12:3 | In Heb xxviii, 6; In 1 Tim xviii, 1 (6:16) |
| 12:4 | In Col viii, 6 (3:15); In 1 Cor xxiv, 1; In Mat xviii, 7; In 1 Thess iii, 4 (3:4); In 2 Thess iii, 1 (1:11); In 2 Tim x, 2 (4:18) |
| 12:6 | Ad pop Anti i, 22; De Laz i, 12; Ex in ps vii, 8; In Mat xiii, 7 |
| 12:7 | Ad Stag a dae iii, 14; De paen iv, 5; Ex in pscx, 3; In Heb xxix, 2 |
| 12:8 | Ad Stag a dae iii, 14; Ex in ps cxvii, 4; In Heb Argumentum, 3; xxix, 3 |
| 12:9 | Ad pop Anti vii, 5; In Heb xxix, 3; In Ioh lxxix, 4 |
| 12:10 | In Heb xxix, 3 |
| 12:12 | In 1 Cor xxxviii, 8; In Heb Argumentum, 3 (2x); vii, 3; In Mat lxvii, 4 |
| 12:13 | De incomp dei iv, 5; In Heb Argumentum, 3 |
| 12:14 | Cat ill vii, 32; De paen vi, 5; In Col viii, 3 (3:15); In 1 Cor ix, 1; In Eph iv, 3 (2:10); In Gen xxxvi, 6; xliv, 6; In Heb xxx, 2; xxxiii, 2; xxxiii, 3; In Ioh xiv, 2; lxiii, 3; In Mat xv, 6; lxiv, 4; In 1 Thess v, 1 (4:3); v, 4 (4:8); In 2 Tim x, 3 (4:21) |
| 12:15 | In Heb xxx, 4 |
| 12:16 | Ad e q scan xiii; De paen vii, 1; H in il App 19; In Heb xxxi, 2; xxxiii, 3; In Phil viii, 2 (2:16); In 2 Tim vii, 1 (3:7) |
| 12:17 | In Heb xxxi, 3 |
| 12:18 | Ex in ps cxlvii, 3; In Mat ii, 1. |
| 12:22 | De b Phil 1; Ex in ps ix, 6; cix, 3; cxlvii, 3; In Mat ii, 1; Non esse ad grat 4 |
| 12:23 | De b Phil 1 (2x); Ex in ps cxlvii, 3; In Mat ii, 1 |
| 12:24 | In Acta liv, 2; In Mat ii, 1 |
| 12:25-27 | In Heb xxxii, 2 |
| 12:28 | In Heb xxxii, 2; xxxiii, 4 |
| 12:29 | De incomp dei v, 5; In Heb xxxii, 1; xxxii, 2; In Rom xvi, 8 (9:20) |
| 13:1 | In Gen xliii, 7; In Heb xxxiii, 1 |

| | |
|---|---|
| 13:2 | De Laz ii, 5; In Gen xli, 3; In Heb xi, 10; xxxiii, 1 |
| 13:3 | Ad pop Anti xvii, 15; In Col xi, 3 (4:11); In Eph ix, 1 (4:3); In Heb xxxiii, 2; In il Uid elig 15; In Rom xix, 8 (11:35); xxii, 2 (12:16) |
| 13:4 | Ad Theo ii, 3; De uir vii; viii; In Col xii, 6 (4:18); In 1 Cor xii, 11; In 2 Cor ix, 3; In Heb xxx, 3; xxxiii, 2; In Mat li, 5; In 1 Tim x, 1 (3:4); In Tit v, 2 (2:14) |
| 13:5 | Ad pop Anti vi, 3; In Heb xxxiii, 2 |
| 13:6 | In Heb xxxiii, 2 |
| 13:7 | In Heb xxxiii, 3; xxxiv, 1 |
| 13:8 | In Heb xxxiii, 3 |
| 13:9 | In Heb viii, 7; xxxiii, 3 |
| 13:10 | In Heb xxxiii, 3; In Rom viii, 8 (4:21) |
| 13:11 | De coem et de cru 1; In Heb xxxiii, 4 |
| 13:12 | In Heb xxxiii, 4 |
| 13:13 | In Heb Argumentum, 3; xxxiii, 4; In Mat lxxxv 1 |
| 13:14-15 | In Heb xxxiii, 4 |
| 13:16 | In Heb xi, 5; xxxiii, 4 |
| 13:17 | Cat ill x, 2; De sac iii, 17; vi, 1; In Acta xliv, 4; In 2 Cor xv, 5; In il Hoc scit 5; In Ioh lxxxvi, 4 (2x); In Phil i, 1 (1:3); vi 3 (2:8); In Rom xxix, 4 (15:24); In 1 Thess x, 1 (5:13); In 2 Tim ii, 2 (1:12); In Tit i 3 (1:5) |
| 13:18-20 | In Heb xxxiv, 4 |
| 13:21 | In Acta xviii, 1 (7:58); In Heb xxxiv, 4 |
| 13:22 | In Heb xxxiv, 5 |
| 13:23 | In Heb Argumentum, 2; xxxiv, 5; In 1 Tim Argumentum, 1 |
| 13:24 | In Heb xxxiv, 5; In Rom Argumentum, 1 |
| 13:25 | In Heb xxxiv, 5 |

## James

| | |
|---|---|
| 1:6-8 | Ex in ps xii, 3 |
| 2:6 | In Acta xlii, 4 |
| 2:10 | In Eph iv, 3 (2:10) |
| 2:13 | In Philem iii, 2 (v25) |
| 2:17 | De paen ix, 1 |
| 2:18 | Ad pop Anti v, 6 |
| 2:20 | In il Hab i, 10 |
| 2:26 | In Gen ii, 5; In Philem ii, 1 (v6) |

| | |
|---|---|
| 4:6 | In Acta xxix, 4 (13:41); In 1 Cor i, 4; In il Uidi dom iii, 4; In Mat lxv, 6 |
| 5:10 | De glor in trib 3 |
| 5:13 | De ss B et P 3; In Heb iv, 7 |
| 5:14 | De sac iii, 6 |
| 5:15 | De sac iii, 6; In Heb ix, 8 |
| 5:16 | In il Uidi dom i, 4 |
| 5:17 | Ad pop Anti i, 21; In Acta xxxvi, 3 (16:39); In Hel 6 |

1 Peter

| | |
|---|---|
| 1:1 | De paen ix, 1 |
| 1:24 | In Gen xxviii, 3; In Ioh xlii, 3 |
| 2:10 | H in il App 16 |
| 2:11 | In 1 Cor x, 5 |
| 2:19-20 | Ad pop Anti vi, 9 |
| 2:21 | In Col vii, 1 (2:19); In 1 Tim xviii, 1 (6:16) |
| 2:22 | Cat ill x, 10; De bap Chris 3; H in il App 18; In 2 Cor xi, 3; In Eph iii, 3 (1:22); In Eut ii, 6; In Gal iii, 3 (3:13); In Heb xxviii, 4; In Ioh xxvii, 2; lxxxii, 1; In 1 Tim xi, 2 (3:16) |
| 3:6 | In 1 Cor xxvi, 6 |
| 3:7 | De s Dros 3 |
| 3:15 | De sac iv, 3; iv, 8; In 1 Cor iii, 8; In Gen iv, 4; In Ioh xvii, 4; In Mat xxxiii, 5 |
| 4:8 | Ad pop Anti xx, 13; In Acta xl, 3 |
| 5:5 | In il Uidi dom iii, 4; In 2 Thess Argumentum, 2 |
| 5:8 | Adu Iud 3, 1, 7; 3, 1, 8; Ad Stag a dae i, 4; Ex in ps vii, 3; cxxxix, 3; In Acta xxxii, 3 (15:11); In Eph xvii, 1 (5:5); In Gen iv, 1; xxiii, 6; In Ioh lix, 3; In Phil vi, 4 (2:8); In 1 Thess iii, 4 (3:4); In s Iul 3 |
| 5:13 | In Mat lxxxv, 1 |

2 Peter

| | |
|---|---|
| 3:10 | In Acta xxiii, 4 (10:43) |
| 3:13 | In Rom xiv, 6 (8:20) |

1 John

| | |
|---|---|
| 1:1 | Ex in ps xliii, 1 |

| | |
|---|---|
| 1:5 | In Ioh v, 3 |
| 2:2 | In Eut ii, 6 |
| 2:9 | In 1 Tim vii, 1 (2:4) |
| 3:5 | In Eut ii, 6 |
| 3:9 | In Eph xiii, 2 (4:22) |
| 3:10 | In 2 Tim vi, 3 (2:26) |
| 5:16 | Ex in ps xlix, 7 |

## Jude

| | |
|---|---|
| 7 | In Rom iv, 3 (1:27) |

## Revelation

| | |
|---|---|
| 1:15 | In Ioh xv, 1 |
| 1:16 | In Phil vi, 2 (2:8) |
| 2:20 | In 1 Cor xxvii, 7 |
| 4:8 | In Mat xix, 7 |
| 7:17 | In Rom xv, 3 (8:34) |
| 15:6 | In Eph xxiii, 2 (6:14) |
| 20 (p) | In Gen xix, 6 |
| 20:9 | In Eph xxiii, 2 (6:14) |
| 22:16 | In Eph vi, 2 (2:22) |